The Depth of the Human Person

The Depth of the Human Person

A Multidisciplinary Approach

Edited by

Michael Welker

WILLIAM B. EERDMANS PUBLISHING COMPANY

GRAND RAPIDS, MICHIGAN / CAMBRIDGE, U.K.

Published 2014 by
Wm. B. Eerdmans Publishing Co.
2140 Oak Industrial Drive N.E., Grand Rapids, Michigan 49505 /
P.O. Box 163, Cambridge CB3 9PU U.K.

Printed in the United States of America

21 20 19 18 17 16 15   8 7 6 5 4 3 2

Library of Congress Cataloging-in-Publication Data

The depth of the human person : a multidisciplinary approach /
edited by Michael Welker.
     pages   cm
  Includes bibliographical references.
  ISBN 978-0-8028-6979-1 (pbk.: alk. paper)
  1. Theological anthropology — Christianity. 2. Philosophical anthropology.
  3. Human beings.   I. Welker, Michael, 1947- editor of compilation.

BT701.3.D47   2014
233´.5 — dc23
                                                    2014005081

www.eerdmans.com

Contents

Acknowledgments

This book documents the results of an interdisciplinary and international dialogue about the depths of the human person. It forges new paths toward a multidisciplinary anthropology. Over several years we brought together theologians, philosophers and ethicists, scientists from the areas of biology, psychology, and physics, and scholars in the fields of Old Testament, New Testament, patristic studies, systematic anthropology, and law. The scholars came from the USA, England, Scotland, Germany, Japan, and India.

The project was made possible by the generosity of the John Templeton Foundation, Philadelphia, which financed the consultations in the framework of its support of the dialogue between science, theology, and religious studies. It was also supported by the hospitality of the Evangelische Kirche im Rheinland, Düsseldorf, which opened the doors of its FFFZ Tagungshaus for several of our meetings.

We are most grateful to Dr. John Templeton Jr., President of the Foundation, to Dr. Paul Wason, Drew Rick-Miller, and Heather Micklewright in Philadelphia. We also thank Präses Dr. Nikolaus Schneider, Vizepräses Petra Bosse-Huber, Vizepräses Christian Drägert, Prof. Dr. Bernd Wander, and the staff of the FFFZ for their kind support. One of our meetings took place in the Internationales Wissenschaftsforum Heidelberg. We are indebted to Dr. Ellen Peerenboom, Gudrun Strehlow, and the team of the IWH. Special thanks go to Dr. Markus Höfner, who turned out to be a perfect organizer of the project over many years.

Finally, we acknowledge our gratitude to our publisher William Eerdmans ("What can I say but that we are drawn into these depths as the most irresisting of basophobes?"), and to Henning Mützlitz, who patiently created a print-ready copy.

MICHAEL WELKER

Introduction

Michael Welker

In dialogues about anthropology, theologians, philosophers, and scientists wrestled with a polarization between "mentalistic" and "physicalistic" approaches for many years.[1] They felt trapped in dualisms and reductionisms on both sides and tried to escape and overcome this situation with "multi-dimensional" approaches that could do justice to the "complexity of human personhood."

I. Introductory Questions

The philosopher **Andreas Kemmerling** ("Why Is Personhood Conceptually Difficult?") is provoking with respect to both the laments about "reductionisms" and the hopes for an alternative. He begins his contribution with an open attack on seemingly reductionistic, in fact wrong and misleading statements such as "You're nothing but a bunch of neurons" (Francis Crick) or ". . . you are your brain" (Michael Gazzaniga, Manfred Spitzer). He calls these remarks "pseudo-scientific stupidities" and quotes John Langshaw Austin: ". . . There is nothing so plain boring as the constant repetition of assertions that are not true, and sometimes not even faintly sensible."

---

1. W. S. Brown, N. Murphy, and H. N. Malony, eds., *Whatever Happened to the Soul? Scientific and Theological Portraits of Human Nature* (Minneapolis: Fortress Press, 1998); M. Jeeves, ed., *From Cells to Souls — and Beyond: Changing Portraits of Human Nature* (Grand Rapids: Eerdmans, 2004); E. K. Soulen and L. Woodhead, eds., *God and Human Dignity* (Grand Rapids: Eerdmans, 2006).

1

On the other hand, he warns against dreams "to regain a complex concept of human personhood," which had been inspired by the antique identification of "person" and *prosopon,* "the mask" as the interface of individual private and public human relations. Kemmerling speaks of a "bewildering conceptual plenitude of person." The concept of a person is "a vexing one," and it is "inexhaustibly rich." With respect to Descartes and Locke, he analyzes two of the most influential philosophical classics, which used the concept for very different purposes. For Descartes, the concept of a person expresses the commonsensical impression of a mind-body union, which clear metaphysical thought cannot validate. For Locke, the concept of the person is a complex idea, based on consciousness and memory, most relevant to support ideas and practices in morals and law.

The theologian **Michael Welker** describes the initial research project and its transformation in the course of the dialogue. He examines the rich anthropology of Paul ("Flesh–Body–Heart–Soul–Spirit: Paul's Anthropology as an Interdisciplinary Bridge-Theory"), which is framed by the dualism of "spirit and flesh," anthropological modes of the dualism of eternity and finitude. Although "flesh" stands for the ultimately futile attempt to sustain one's life by securing nourishment and reproduction and for the sobering fact that life lives at the expense of other life, it should not be demonized as such. The human heart, with its cognitive emotional and voluntative capacities, is of flesh, and our fleshly basis is the core of our natural and historical unique identity. On the other hand, Paul warns the tongues-speaking Corinthians against an enthusiasm for a direct encounter with God in pure spirit. "Better five words spoken with reason than 10,000 words uttered in tongues" (1 Cor. 14:19).

The qualification of the framing dualism opens sensitivities for Paul's appreciation of the body as both fleshly and shaped by mind and spirit, by the polyphony of its members and powers, moving beyond and against the self-preserving tendencies of the flesh. Like almost all of the biblical authors, Paul does not ascribe any special salvific power to "the soul." It just stands for the mind-body unity, for the whole person ("a village of two hundred souls"). Anthropological investigations should rather focus on the heart, the conscience, and the spirit, on their enormous powers and their enormous vulnerabilities to distortion and corruption. Political, legal, and moral interests are, according to Paul, in urgent need of a genuinely theological orientation, if the human spirit is to be led by the Spirit of God and its saving and ennobling powers.

The theologian **Philip Clayton** ("Emergence, the Quest for Unity, and God: Toward a Constructive Christian Theology of the Person") starts with reflections on the complex unity of the human person "from the standpoint of an emergentist interpretation of biological and cultural evolution." He attempts to connect the scientific picture of persons "as complex bio-physical-psycho-social units" with a theologically grounded understanding of a divine spiritual agency. He then challenges Christian theology to come up with an answer to the question: In what way could both sets of results be supplemented by "specifically Christian affirmations about human nature"? These "supplements," however, should be compatible with the interdisciplinary "emergentist interpretation" and with theological and metaphysical perspectives on divine agency.

Clayton proposes eight levels of a "multifaceted human unity," which spans the empirical unity of the existing person, the unity of the mind or the soul, the spiritual unity of body and soul, the unity of the image of God and the corporate unity of the body of Christ, the unity with Christ in the Spirit and — in and through it — with the will and the life of God. One could read this as an interdisciplinary yet theologically oriented proposal, to capture the dynamic unity of the person as an "elevated" and "ascending" existence.

II. Scientific Perspectives

The physicist and theologian **John Polkinghorne** ("Towards an Integrated Anthropology") argues that science and theology should help each other in dealing with the vexing complexity of the human person. They should acknowledge "that the context for hominid evolution was much richer than the physico-biological setting that canonical Darwinian theory supposes." He proposes to work with a model of a mind/body complementarity for which the wave/particle duality of light could become a paradigm example. In his view, a reconceptualization of the soul is required, which could allow us to develop a "dual-aspect, energy/information scientific description" of anthropological complexity. The important role of information in evolutionary processes should become deciphered with respect to the soul as "information-bearing pattern."

With these ideas, John Polkinghorne does not want to argue for an intrinsic immortality of the soul: "As far as naturalistic thinking is concerned, the pattern carried by the body will dissolve with the body's decay. Yet it is a perfectly coherent Christian hope that the faithful God will not allow that pattern to be lost, but will preserve it in the divine memory." Polkinghorne encourages future dialogue and research to use the differentiated and subtle insights into biblical anthropology to penetrate the extremely rich concept of "information" that would be needed to deal with the vexing complexity of the human person.

The psychologist **Malcolm Jeeves** argues that a "holistic model of the human person does most justice to the scientific understanding of ourselves" ("Brains, Minds, Souls, and People: A Scientific Perspective on Complex Human Personhood"). He first describes the fast changes in the "accepted scientific story" in the area of mind-brain research over the last decades. In recent years, studies of the localization of functions within the brain have had to be qualified and corrected with respect to the evidence of the brain's plasticity. The power of top-down effects on the brain has become increasingly evident and important in the study of mind-brain links.[2]

Although our mental capacities and behaviors are "firmly embodied in our physical makeup," there is clear evidence for an irreducible interdependence between the cognitive level and the physical level of human existence. This leads Jeeves to postulate — against Descartes — a "primary ontological reality of 'person,'" a "duality without dualism," as he says. He concludes with remarks on the relation of neuropsychological, evolutionary psychological, and theological claims about the imago Dei. The attempts to identify the imago Dei with the capacity to reason, the capacity for moral behavior and moral agency, and the capacity for personal relatedness have served as boundary markers to distinguish human beings and animals. All these former boundaries are now open fields of research. Jeeves argues for a genuinely theological top-down approach that sets the divine activity "apart from all others in heaven and on earth" and provides anthropological orientation without stressing speciestic arguments.

Warren S. Brown, also a psychologist, pushes the question further: "In what ways are we humans nested within the biological world and to what extent do we transcend biology?" ("The Emergence of Human Distinctiveness"). He discusses several candidates for human neurocognitive distinctiveness: the enhanced size of the frontal lobes of humankind, specific neurons, relatively unique to the human brain ("Von Economo Neurons"), the capacity to use language, etc.[3] He then proposes to step toward a theory of dynamical systems in order to understand what others have called "the holism of difference"

2. Cf. more recently T. Fuchs, *Das Gehirn — ein Beziehungsorgan. Eine phänomenologisch-ökologische Konzeption,* 3rd ed. (Stuttgart: Kohlhammer, 2012).

3. Cf. also M. Tomasello, *The Cultural Origins of Human Cognition* (Cambridge, MA: Harvard University Press, 1999); *Origins of Human Communication* (Cambridge and London: MIT Press, 2008).

(Matthias Jung: "Differenzholismus des Menschlichen"),[4] which divides the realm of humans from the primates and other species.

Brown distinguishes different levels of organization, the development of more complex forms of environmental response and interaction, as well as greater degrees of freedom. These differences of ordered complexity can occur on thermodynamic, psychological, social, or other levels. Brown speaks of a "cultural scaffolding," which shapes the environments in order to improve the interactive processes with them. He warned against cognitivist and computational views that dissociate minds "from embodied life in the world." Like Malcolm Jeeves, he concludes with encouragement that we should take specific shapes of our social, cultural, and religious environments more seriously in order to understand human distinctiveness.

The biologist **Jeffrey Schloss** ("Hierarchical Selection and the Evolutionary Emergence of 'Spirit'") reflects on the tension between what could be called the "evolutionary solidarity" of all creation and the obvious observation of different levels and hierarchies of life. He starts with the critique of "three hallmark postulates of reductionism in twentieth-century biology": the triumph of mechanism over vitalism, the propagation of the gene as "the 'atom' of biology," and the claim that the human mind is primarily concerned with the enhancement of reproductive fitness.

Schloss describes the long battle between mechanism and vitalism and its impacts on the extrusion of "spirit" and "soul" in so-called serious science and educated common sense. He shows how the unification "of Darwinian selection and Mendelian genetics in the synthetic theory of evolution" transforms and yet prolongs this situation of a scientist naturalism, which culminates in the speculative invention of so-called "memes" ("ideational replicators" as twins of the genes).[5] He questions that social and cultural evolution could be "wholly reducible to or constrained by genetic selection." He proposes to consider that there are life-enhancing and ennobling "ideas," which are "not (merely) transmitted, or intuitively innate, or rationally constructed, but discovered." At this level, he sees the need and the potential to rethink the emergence of "spirit."

4. Matthias Jung, *Der bewusste Ausdruck. Anthropologie der Artikulation* (Berlin and New York: De Gruyter, 2009), pp. 54-58.

5. The term "memes" was invented by Richard Dawkins, *The Selfish Gene* (Oxford: Oxford University Press 1976), and has been popularized by Susan Blackmore, *The Meme Machine* (Oxford: Oxford University Press, 2000).

III. Sources of the Traditions

The Old Testament scholar **Andreas Schüle** ("'Soul' and 'Spirit' in the Anthropological Discourse of the Hebrew Bible") draws attention to the fact that "worldviews matter, when it comes to anthropological concepts such as 'body,' 'soul,' or 'spirit.'" However, a simple juxtaposition of an ancient (religious) worldview and a modern (scientific) worldview will not be helpful at all. He describes an important change of worldviews already reflected by the anthropological discourse of the Old Testament. This change is connected with the shift of anthropological concentration from the soul (*nefesh*) to the spirit (*ruach*).

The Persian period brings a shift from belief in a cultic presence of God to belief in God's cosmic presence. A highly differentiated discourse develops the conceptuality of divine and human spirit in order to grasp this presence. Different traditions connect the spirit with different basic functions. At least one of these traditions discourages any speculation about a material and spiritual human existence beyond its life on earth (Ecclesiastes). Over against this, we see at the edge of the Old Testament canon within its Greek transmission the emergence of the idea of a soul in God's hands, possibly an immortal soul (Wisdom of Solomon 2:23). Only the view that the soul can be rescued by God's saving work but not a created immortality is shared by the other biblical traditions.

The contribution of the New Testament scholar **Gerd Theissen** ("*Sarx, Soma,* and the Transformative *Pneuma*: Personal Identity Endangered and Regained in Pauline Anthropology") opens our eyes to the fact that in Paul's letters "often but not always" the body *(soma)* "has a positive connotation in ethical, ecclesiological, and eschatological contexts." However, when Paul contrasts the "internal and external" human being, he can associate the body with the flesh *(sarx)* and connect it with very negative statements. Theissen shows that Paul is not trapped into a static dualistic anthropology, but rather develops a "transformative" anthropology and cosmology. While the flesh "represents the (biotic-based) energy of life that must be repressed . . . the body is the energy that can be sublimated" by the transformative power of the spirit.

Theissen identifies ethical (Rom. 12:1), ecclesial (1 Cor. 12:12ff.; Rom. 12:4ff.), and eschatological (1 Cor. 15:44; Rom. 8:11) transformations of the body. By nature, the body is passive and mortal, but by the power of the spirit it can be given new life and become the bearer of eschatological hope. A similar ambivalence has to be noticed with respect to the human spirit. Paul can identify the human mind and human spirit, he can stress the opposition of the human mind/spirit and the divine spirit, and he can praise the salvific encounter of the human spirit with the Holy Spirit and the Spirit of Christ. With some reflections on "the dissociative soul in ancient Egypt and ancient Greece" and on "the renewal of an integrated concept of personhood in early Christianity," Theissen illuminates the *weltanschauliche* background of Paul's seminal anthropology.

The patristic scholar **Volker Henning Drecoll** ("Augustine's Aporetic Account of *Persona* and the Limits of *Relatio:* A Reconsideration of Substance Ontology and Immutability") analyzes the term "person" in Augustine's work in general and in his brilliant book *De trinitate* in particular. He shows that the term *persona* is a cipher in his Trinitarian theology and that he avoids "the term *relatio* as quasi-ontological term." This casts conventional attempts to make use of Augustine's "psychological doctrine of the Trinity" to explain notions of the person — divine and human — into a negative light.

Drecoll cautiously encourages exploring the relation of love as a candidate to address the puzzling issues in Trinitarian theology and anthropology that caused Augustine and his followers to experiment with the notions of *persona* and *relatio*. Still, this attempt comes with a host of problems. Do the risks of failure and disappointment in human love require us to look for a radical difference between divine and human love? How can we reconcile the notion of a loving God with Augustine's insistence on divine immutability?

Eiichi Katayanagi, a Japanese scholar of religious studies and philosophy, encourages us to take a more positive view of the epistemological potentials in Augustine's work ("Augustine's Investigation into Imago Dei"). He sees Augustine's notion of the imago Dei as connected with this conviction that human beings have the "capacity of openness to eternity." Similar to Drecoll, he is convinced that the relation of love offers a clue to grasp the essence of the human persona. The reflexive character of the will, concentrated on and shaped by love, "reveals both the essential nature of the human mind and God as the source of the mind."

Katayanagi stresses the fascinating attempt in Augustine's work to reconstruct the mind in search of its not-yet-known self. He describes the difference of a hidden unconscious and a conscious knowledge (*se nosse* and *se cognitare*). A deep hidden knowledge is embedded in pre-thematic memory. This knowledge has a Trinitarian structure, which, however, only becomes obvious in the emergence of the temporal knowledge that is found in the *cogitatio*. In this longing and loving outreach into the eternal depth of the imago Dei, the human being finds itself "already touched by God" and constituted as a true person.

The exploration of faith and emotions is further pursued by systematic theologian **Markus Höfner** ("The Affects of the Soul and the Effects of Grace: On Melanchthon's Understanding of Faith and Christian Emotions"). He starts with the observation that, according to biblical witnesses and many theological classics, the believer's relation to God is seen as deeply shaped by emotions. He explores those "internal affections which are not within the individual's power." He also uses key texts of the reformer Melanchthon in order to reconstruct the process of phenomenological and theological clarification.

Höfner draws attention to two developments and moves in Melanchthon's thought, which are not only seminal for his own theology but could also offer systematic inspiration for anthropological research today. One shift could be called: From the meditation of "inner" powers to the observation of "outer" expressions. In this shift, Melanchthon's theologically interested theory of affects starts to use medical thinking and natural philosophy. The second shift overcomes bipolar constellations, for example, the concentration on the dual "affect and reason." Höfner can show that Melanchthon uses reflections on the shaping of affects through rhetoric to observe interdependencies between affects, reason (understanding), and will. Already in Reformation days we thus find pathways toward an "anthropology of articulation."

Origen V. Jathanna, a theologian from India, concludes the third part of the book with reflections on "The Concept of 'Body' in Indian Christian Theological Thought." He observes in the Indian culture as well as across the globe today a strange tension between a cult and glorification of the body and a rejection or denigration of the body. He relates this tension to anthropological dualisms, which concern many contributions to this book. He also unfolds a stunning map of philosophical and theological positions in India, particularly in the twentieth century, on which we can identify different views on body, soul, and other dimensions of the human person. Different anthropological constellations are intertwined with different genuinely theological orientations, especially Christological, eschatological, and ethical perspectives. Theological and anthropological paradigms shape each other.

Jathanna observes the tendency in the contemporary realm of thought to contextualize reflections on the human person. Even the body is no longer considered "in isolation, but in the context of interpersonal, communitarian, gender-relational, societal, economic, structural, and ecological dimensions of the human existence." This opens many opportunities not only for interdisciplinary but also for interreligious dialogues and the common search for insight and truth. Jathanna welcomes this situation but also reminds theologians that the perspective of the new creation in Jesus Christ, the hope of the "resurrectional transformation" and eschatological fulfillment should not be lost.

IV. Contemporary Challenges

The last part of the book begins with the question of whether the theological claim that human beings are created in the "image of God" can offer an equivalent to the concept of the dignity of the human person. The theologian **Bernd Oberdorfer** poses this question ("The Dignity of Human Personhood and the Concept of the 'Image of God'") and objects to quick and simple answers. He explores the talk about the image of God in biblical creation narratives, reflects on the Christological recalibration of the imago Dei in the New Testament, and analyzes three different ways of interpreting it in the history of Christian theology (quality, duty, relation).

The tension between the Christological interpretation of the imago Dei and the insistence on the universal validity of human dignity gives rise to a second set of questions. How do we relate specific religious ideas and symbols to normative concepts in general public life? How do we deal with different and even conflicting theological interpretations of specific religious ideas and symbols? Oberdorfer describes several routes of discourse and debate as future challenges and tasks in the churches, the academy, civil societies, and different secular publics.

Stephan Kirste, professor of law, deals with the topic "Human Dignity and the Concept of Person in Law." He first reconstructs important steps in the history of the concept of "human dignity" and the attempts to interpret it as a legal term. The legal discourse led to a broad consensus that human dignity can only be defined "negatively from possible violations of it." This again led to questions for a threshold to discriminate real violations of human dignity from all sorts of bothering and pestering among human beings.

Kirste shows that these questions have caused legal scholars to look back for philosophical and theological sources. Philosophical work on the concept of "the person" became relevant, and many discourses between law and philosophy have struggled to conceptualize the idea of a "legal person." The final Solomonic formula comes as an impressive self-affirmation of legal thought: "The respect for human dignity" materializes "as the right to be recognized as a legal person."

The theologian **Frank Vogelsang** ("On the Relation of Personhood and Embodiment") describes the perspectives of broad common sense and popular philosophy concerning personhood and dignity. In the constructive parts of his contribution, he focuses on person-to-person interaction and the phenomenon and theories of mutual recognition. Drawing on the "phenomenology of the body," developed by Maurice Merleau-Ponty, he intends to deepen personalistic thought of the past and relate the philosophical to the scientific discourse. Simple imaginations of "the world in our body" and "our body in the world" have to be overcome and refined.

Following Merleau-Ponti, Vogelsang captures partial intransparencies in our relation to our bodily existence that have a deep impact on our most basic social interactions. We need a theory of recognition that can deal with our always partially opaque relation to ourselves and with the intransparency even of the most intimate "other." He claims that "personhood stems from human encounters and mutual recognition." It has to be seen whether this proposal can lead to an explanation and understanding of why personhood is conceptually so difficult.

Maria Antonaccio, a professor of religious ethics, defends the "depths of the human person as moral agent" against the illusion that a description of "the facts of human nature could exhaust" these depths ("Can Ethics Be Fully Naturalized?"). She describes current efforts to "naturalize" ethics and offers a typology of current debates over naturalization. Constructively, she tries to delineate a path between an ethical naturalism, which comes with "the danger of moral mediocrity and moral conventionalism," and an "ethics of heroism or of the superhuman," which can be bred from naturalist and nonnaturalist positions alike.

In a final set of reflections, she assesses criteria for a "naturalized ethics" that tries to avoid descriptive impoverishment by ignoring natural empirical effects of human existence. For the sake of an ethical realism, moral theory cannot escape the dialogue with the natural sciences. The danger on the other side is the normative impoverishment that occurs when principles of obligation become sacrificed with respect to "realistic adaptation" to natural conditions and human reality constituted only by so-called "scientific facts." Both dangers can culminate in a collapse of normative and descriptive attempts in ethical theory. This would also lead to a theoretical impoverishment.

Practical theologian **Isolde Karle** ("Beyond Distinct Gender Identities: The Social Construction of the Human Body") draws attention to the fact that contemporary anthropology emphasizes "the multitude of interdependencies between body, soul, and spirit." Yet with respect to sexual identity, "the body continues to represent a solid and unshakable objective point of reference." Following Pierre Bourdieu's influential book "Male Domination," she argues that the dichotomous gender metaphysics is a product of bourgeois nineteenth-century thought. In various ways, it conditions a dualistic habitus that is correlated with open and hidden forms and practices of male domination and violence.

Karle charges popular counterarguments (mostly based on the topic of motherhood) and twentieth-century theological affirmations of "the system of two genders." She challenges theology to stop seeing the plurality of individuals and the variety of "gender migrants" as a threat to the institution of marriage and broader social order. The orientation toward the powers of new creation, in which there is no longer "male and female" (Gal. 3:28), and a gender system "that continues to oppress and disfigure souls and bodies" should draw us away from a fixation on the "anatomical details of a body" to the "life in the spirit of Christ, the spirit of love, trust, and freedom."

William Schweiker, a theological ethicist ("Moral Inwardness Reconsidered"), wants to develop a "theological and also humanistic vision of the soul." He engages exemplary positions in contemporary psychological and philosophical anthropology (Marc Hauser and Mary Midgley), which show a remarkable neglect for "human vulnerability that characterizes our lives as moral and religious beings." Schweiker draws attention to the rich "cultural resources" that are to be found in the writings of Plato and Paul. He does not argue for a restitution of a Platonic or a so-called biblical worldview, but for a new type of thinking arising at their intersection.

It is a rich notion of a theologically oriented "moral inwardness" that has to deal with the double danger of divinization or profanization of the soul. Schweiker argues that the antique classics provide stronger arguments than the contemporary voices for the freedom of the soul and its "right to have rights," but also for the real danger that "the integrity of the self can be lost, forsaken." Deep visions and strong arguments are needed to counter cultural and religious, political and moral distortions, which threaten the human mind and life with various forms of decadence and degeneration, and also authoritarianism and tyranny.

Günter Thomas, a systematic theologian, concentrates on challenges "connected with intensive experiences of finiteness encounter (particularly) in the later phases of life" ("Human Personhood at the Edges of Life: Medical Anthropology and Theology in Dialogue"). He describes a multiple crisis connected with higher rates of aging and illness that most anthropologies are unable to address for structural reasons. He argues for the development of a theological framework that allows us to move beyond the affirmation of "intellectualism and moral self-determination."

He shows that a Christological and pneumatological framework can host "social narrations" of personhood and human life that can incorporate its vulnerability, endangerment, and self-endangerment, but also its eschatological destinations, which contest that "decay, frailty, and death are . . . the last reality that human beings will face." This does not open a space of sheer illusions, but rather an area of deep individual and trans-individual experience and hope that is not monopolized by theology and religious faith.

I. Person and Personhood: Introductory Questions

Why Is Personhood Conceptually Difficult?

Andreas Kemmerling

The concept of a person is a vexing one.

There is ample evidence for this claim, both in time-honored works and in recent publications. Before I concentrate on some of the old stuff, let me briefly turn to recent examples. The following sample of quotations from a Nobel laureate, a leading neuroscientist, and a German professor of "neurodidactics," may illustrate how deep the confusion about what a person is can go among the educated, even today. Francis Crick stated his *Astonishing Hypothesis* as follows:

> "You" . . . are in fact no more than the behaviour of a vast assembly of nerve cells and their associated molecules. As Lewis Carroll's Alice might have phrased it: "You're nothing but a bunch of neurons." This idea is so alien to the ideas of most people alive today that it can truly be called astonishing.[1]

A few years later, this "idea" seemed not anymore astonishing to Michael Gazzaniga, who prefers to put it this way: Some simple facts make it

> . . . *clear* that you are your brain. The neurons interconnecting in its vast network . . . — that is you.[2]

---

1. F. Crick, *The Astonishing Hypothesis — The Scientific Search for the Soul* (New York: Scribner's/Macmillan, 1994), p. 3.

2. M. Gazzaniga, *The Ethical Brain* (Chicago: Chicago University Press, 2000), p. 31 (italic is mine).

It required the brilliancy of a German professor to take it to a further extreme. He found a way to expand Crick and Gazzaniga's point by enriching it with a homespun piece of congenial ludicrousness. In a German radio broadcast in November 2006, Manfred Spitzer declared:

You don't *have* your brain, you *are* your brain.

Maybe this is a world record. Is it humanly possible to display more fundamental confusion in less than ten syllables? (Well, in fairness to Spitzer, in German, the saying doesn't take less than ten.) One is almost inclined, with respect to someone who says such a thing, to believe at least the first part of his *dictum*.

Note that in these three quotations we are addressed directly, by use of the word "you." As who or what might we consider ourselves so addressed (given that we are, in the same breath, straightforwardly identified with our brains)? Clearly not as human beings. Human beings aren't just brains. Almost all of them have one.[3] And some of them use it, before they make grand claims. Let's assume that this much is known even to those who would make, or agree to, such claims as the ones I quoted. It's unlikely that even they simply confuse a human being with one of his or her organs.

So assuming that we are not addressed, in the statements quoted above, as members of the species *Homo sapiens,* the question remains: As whom or what do Crick, Gazzaniga, and Spitzer presume to address us, when they say "you"? Well, I guess, we are meant to be addressed as *persons.* What the two neuroscientists and the professor of "neurodidactics" want to tell us seems to be this:

You, the *person* you are, are your brain.

A human person nothing but his or her brain? The negative answer is obvious again. You, as person, are you altogether. When considered as a person, you are considered, so to say, as the completeness of what you are. You are not just an assemblage of certain parts, facets, or aspects of yours, however interesting or prominent each of them may be. You're *not* what or how you feel. You are *not* how you came to be what you are. You are *not* what you did or may accomplish. You are not your looks, moods, skills, genes, memories, sentimentalities, failures, hobbies, hopes, or sexual obsessions. You are not

3. The pitiable exceptions include anencephalics, microcephalics, hydrocephalics, and some brainless adult human beings, occasionally mentioned in the literature, for whom there seems to be no scientific label yet.

your intelligence, deftness, body, body/mass index, charm, career, musicality, brain, character, hormonal state, social behavior, or innermost thinking. All the items just mentioned, and indefinitely many more of those, contribute, or may contribute, to you as a person. But they aren't you. Obviously, none of them, taken separately, is you. Arguably, even all of them together, taken collectively in their (impossible) summation, isn't you either. In brief, "You are your brain" is to be taken as seriously as "You are what you eat." It may sound nice as an advertisement jingle, but taken literally, it's just rubbish.

I shall not go into this once more.[4] Instead I shall address, in what follows, a different, an etiological, kind of question: How can it happen that some people get so confused as to identify persons (and for that matter themselves) with their brains? Part of the explanation seems to me to be this: Our very idea, or concept, of a person is utterly baffling. And I shall investigate some of the reasons why this is so.

*   *   *

Given that the concept of a person is a vexing one, what is it that makes it so?

There are various ways in which a concept may perplex us. First, there are concepts that may strike one as inherently unthinkable — or, to put it less sloppily: Concepts such that the items of which they purport to be concepts seem unthinkable. Infinity may serve as an example. (Ask a theologian or a philosopher, if you are keen on more examples of this sort.) Second, there are concepts that are, or seem, analysis-proof in a very peculiar way. They are, or seem to be, innocent, well-functioning nonprimitive concepts that we, as normal speakers, have fully mastered; and, moreover, we are perfectly in the clear about what we consider as their most important ingredients. Nevertheless there is at least one further conceptual ingredient that consistently resists our attempts to make it explicit. Knowledge is an example. It is fairly uncontroversial that knowledge entails truth, belief, and justification, and it

---

4. For arguments against the "thesis of person/brain-identity," cf. my "Ich, mein Gehirn und mein Geist — Echte Unterschiede oder falsche Begriffe?," in *Das Gehirn und sein Geist,* ed. N. Elsner/G. Lüer (Göttingen: Wallstein, 2000), pp. 221-43. — But let me warn you. You'll probably find nothing in this paper that you do not know anyway. Trying to point out the obviously obvious almost inevitably results in dull papers. What excuse is there for a philosopher to engage in this sort of business nevertheless? Well, as J. L. Austin once put it: "Besides, there is nothing so plain boring as the constant repetition of assertions that are not true, and sometimes not even faintly sensible" (*Sense and Sensibilia* [Oxford: Oxford University Press, 1962], p. 5).

is also clear that knowledge is not merely justified true belief — but nobody has been able to pinpoint what else is required for knowledge. The concept of knowledge contains at least one component, that vexing "last bit," which seems inexplicable. Third, there are concepts that are, or at least seem to be, paradoxical, although they appear to be well functioning, some of them even indispensable, concepts. Take the concept of being uninteresting. It lends itself to the comparative and the superlative form. But isn't the most uninteresting event of all times *ipso facto* an interesting one? I, for one, would be anxious to be informed about it. Or take the concept of a belief. One holds each of one's beliefs to be true (this is what believing is, after all), but at the same time, a sane person believes that some of his beliefs are false. Or take truth itself. The so-called Liar-paradox has been known and unsolved since ancient times: "What I hereby say is not true." Or, for that matter, take any of those countless concepts for which a paradox of the *Sorites* type can be construed — like, famously, for the concept of a heap itself.

The conceptual difficulties concerning personhood seem to be of an altogether different kind. *Prima facie,* personhood is nothing inherently unthinkable; there's no problem with a deeply hidden conceptual "last bit" (we'd be happy to get hold only of the uncontroversial first bits); and we have no compelling reason to think that the very concept itself is paradox-ridden.[5]

On the one hand, the word "person," as it is commonly used, seems to be not much more than a singular form of the word "people"; it serves to denote human beings like you and me. In normal conditions, as soon as we have recognized an adult human being, we have recognized a person; we don't need any extra information about special features of this particular human being in order to draw the "further" conclusion that he or she is a person. In the absence of very weighty counterevidence or of compelling reasons to withdraw judgment, the presumption, concerning any human being, that he or she is a person, is not just epistemically admissible or reasonable, it is morally obligatory.[6] The *application* of the concept of a person, in familiar standard cases,

---

5. One may think that the *person* clearly is a vague concept (i.e., allows for borderline cases) and that therefore at least a paradox of the *Sorites* type can be construed. But I am not sure about it. The sad fact is, I think, that *person* is a concept so extremely indeterminate that we cannot even definitely say whether it is vague or not.

6. Note that a presumption is not just an assumption, however plausible. As Whately once put it magisterially: "According to the most correct use of the term, a 'Presumption' in favour of any supposition, means, not (as has been sometimes erroneously imagined) a preponderance of probability in its favour, but, such a *preoccupation* of the ground, as implies that it must stand good till some sufficient reason is adduced against it; in short, that the *Burden of proof* lies

does not appear to involve problems that are harder than those involved in recognizing people: normal members of the human race.

But *the concept itself* is problematic. At least it is difficult to say, in plain words or, for that matter, more refined ones, what a person is — even given the most basic and austere sense of the word "person."

1. *Person* as an Ontological Category Concept

Two attempts at clarification. The first one concerns the question how much psychology comes with the concept of a person. Addressing this question seems necessary in the light of the best recent discussions concerning personhood I am aware of.[7] When I talk in the following, interchangeably, of "the concept of a person," of "*person,*" or of "(the concept of) personhood," I do not have a psychological concept in mind. *Person,* as I shall consider it, is an ontological concept. For it is meant, by me here, to pick out a special category of entities — a category that is worth considering when the question is raised: "What sorts of particulars are part of the ultimate furniture of the world as we know it?" As an answer I'd mention, with no attempt at originality: physical bodies, fields of gravitation, events, abstract particulars (sets, numbers, propositions, and maybe others), and . . . persons.

I don't mean to be making a big claim here. I am not saying that persons are particulars that *do,* in the final analysis, belong to the ultimate furniture of the world as we know it, i.e., particulars that cannot be reduced to (combinations of) more basic particulars. I would simply like to rank them among those entities that should be considered carefully as candidates. (Descartes for example, as we shall see, considered them as candidates, but decided not to assign to them the ontological status of basic entities.) Now — and that's what I'd like to emphasize at this point — the ontological concept of a person should be kept as pure and austere as possible. In particular it should be kept distinct from any psychological notion, however seemingly close, like, e.g., the concept of a personality. A personality, I take it, is something a person *has* (and presumably it is not a particular, but some universal that, at least in principle, different persons may share; but even if

---

on the side of him who would dispute it." (Richard Whately, *Elements of Rhetoric,* 1828, ⁶1841, 120; Whately's italics). For an attempt at an outline of a theory of presumption, see O. Scholz, *Verstehen und Rationalität* (Frankfurt am Main: Klostermann, 1999), part II, pp. 148-59.

7. I am thinking here of authors like, e.g., Bernard Williams, Robert Nozick, Derek Parfit, David Lewis, and Martine Nida-Rümelin.

personalities would have to be accepted as particulars, they'd be particulars different in kind from persons). What I'm trying to draw your attention to is not that *person* and *personality* are distinct concepts (this is banal). Rather it is the less obvious point that the tight and rigid connections between these concepts run only in one direction. Personality conceptually requires personhood; but not vice versa.[8]

The sparse ontological concept of a person I shall consider in the following is psychologically neutral, or noncommittal, in a thoroughgoing way: It does not exclude, for example, the conceptual possibility of one and the same person's changing his or her personality abruptly and completely. Psychological similarity, continuity, or conscious self-accessibility over time is not a *conceptual* ingredient in personal identity. It is, indeed, a *factual* ingredient in the human persons-over-time we are acquainted with. And, indeed again, the absence of this ingredient may make us wonder whether we are really dealing with the same person. But, and that's what I am trying to bring to the fore, there is a basic ontological concept of personhood that does not by itself compel us to deny personal identity in cases of abrupt and vast psychological discontinuity. That's what I mean by calling the concept psychologically noncommittal: it is, as it were, silent about these cases. In focusing on this basic concept, I don't mean to deny that there are other legitimate concepts of personhood (e.g., the concept of a *human* person) — concepts that may be "more psychological," in the sense just adumbrated. And it may well be that our most familiar concept of a person is not the ontological one. But I think that the ontological one is fundamental, and a powerful source of our conceptual bewilderment.

The second clarification concerns the realism/anti-realism issue. An important question in this context is whether *person* is an ascriber-relative (or recognition-dependent) concept. I shall call the whole family of such concepts *CAC*-concepts, because in their case the mere counting as a so-and-so is constitutive of being a so-and-so. The mark of a CAC-concept can be roughly characterized as follows: It applies to the items to which it applies in virtue of the fact that these items count as falling under the concept. That x counts as a C may be spelled out in various ways, for example as "Given appropriate information about x, the vast majority of normal people who have mastered concept C ascribe — or would ascribe, if they encountered x — to x the prop-

---

8. One may be tempted to assume that at least the more specific concept of a *human* person involves having a personality. But I am not so sure about this either; maybe only our concept of a *normal* (or a nondeficient) human person contains personality as a feature.

erty of being a *C*," or as "A sufficient majority of relevant experts or authorities[9] accept, or would accept, *x* as a *C*."[10]

It is fairly uncontroversial that many common concepts are of the CAC variety: *piece of art, fruit, disease, car, jail,* etc. (*Fashion* is, I think, a particularly clear example of a CAC-concept: If *x* counts as fashionable — i.e., if a sufficient majority of the relevant *magistri elegantiarum* accept, or would accept, *x* as fashionable — then *x* is fashionable.) Many concepts of philosophical interest, however, are highly controversial in this respect. If one considers the concepts of, e.g., beauty, goodness, truth, happiness, and justice to be CAC-concepts, this almost inevitably makes one an anti-realist about beauty, goodness, truth, happiness, and justice. That is to say, whoever takes concept *C* to be of the CAC-kind is strongly susceptible to the assumption that, concerning *C*-issues, there is no fact of the matter — no fact, that is, beyond those facts that are about what is, or would be, the considered judgment of a certain range of people about such issues. Whereas a realist about *C*-ness, who deserves this denomination, holds that, may be subject to some sophisticated qualification, facts about *C*s are "genuine" facts. Genuine facts are not just states of affairs corresponding to beliefs that have been formed by a "relevant" bunch of people, however impeccable the conditions of forming these beliefs. I shall say a little more about this presently.

My above remarks, about the particular ontological concept I have in mind, may have already made it clear that my metaphysical sentiment about personhood is downright realistic: Facts expressed by sentences, as used in an ontological discourse, of the type "*x* is a person" (or "so-and-sos are persons") are genuine facts. The concept of a person, at least the ontological one, does not function as a CAC-concept.

Let me try to explain what I mean. Let's assume for a moment that I'm a person and that you're a person. So far, no commitment to realism is implied. Here is what *any* realist about personhood is prepared to add: If this assumption is true, then our personhood is a genuine fact. But realism comes in various stripes; among them are disappointingly soft ones. (As it happens, I am a soft realist about fashion. I'm prepared to accept it as a fact that, for example, certain sorts of belts are fashionable. But for me, this fact is merely a CAC-fact: a fact constituted by such belts' counting as fashionable.) Now

---

9. "Relevant majority" may sound inappropriate whenever there are very few experts or authorities. And this happens often enough. (In a soccer match, e.g., there's only one ultimate "authority" on fouls, goals, etc.) But let that go.

10. However crucial they may turn out under closer inspection, I am not going to care about differences between various sorts of counting-as here.

that's not the attitude of a downright, or hardboiled, realist. He is eager to up the metaphysical ante. As a downright realist about personhood, I am prepared to strengthen the soft realist claim above considerably: "Given that our personhood is a fact, it's an objective fact as hard as they can get. They don't come any harder anywhere — not in physics, not in mathematics, not in logic."

With regard to the epistemological position, accompanying such a strong metaphysical tenet, even a hardcore realist has various options. My own option is this: Don't confuse facts that are metaphysically first-rate with those that are our epistemological darlings: with plain, obvious, undeniable facts, facts that (if need be) can even be proven, in some widely accepted logic calculus, from premises whose *a priori* truth can be recognized by way of intuition. To put it differently: The sheer hardness of a fact doesn't entail a corresponding degree of its obviousness; even some of the hardest facts may be rationally put in doubt. Harking back to the issue at hand, that is to say: By our above assumption, you and I are persons, and, by my hardcore realism, this is an adamant fact, but it is not beyond intelligible doubt.

How could this be? For one thing, others may have their doubts about us and take you and me for zombies, aliens, cleverly designed robots — all of which they presume not to be persons. But more than this, each of us may have doubts about his or her own personhood. If you have such doubts, and if you assume that doubts can be had by persons only, you should, in all consistency, also doubt that whatever it may be that you're having are genuine doubts. So you should be prepared to consider it as possible that what you have are merely your "nonpersonal" substitutes for genuine doubts, let's call them oubts. Oubts feel (or "eel") to, and function for, nonpersons just like doubts do to real persons.

This may sound crazier and crazier, but I tend to think that one isn't immune to such doubt. To illustrate: Assume that Mr. Deckard (Harrison Ford), in the movie *Blade Runner,* is a genuine person (in this fiction) and that he himself assumes androids, or replicants, not to be persons. Even if we assume this, as the movie invites us to do, then nevertheless, from a certain point on, Deckard begins, and he does so for understandable reasons, to doubt his very own personhood. Deckard is part of a fiction, but in the story told by the movie, he, a person by assumption, really doubts his own personhood.[11] He

11. In Philip K. Dick's novel (*Do Androids Dream of Electric Sheep,* New York: Doubleday, 1968) on which the movie is based, Deckard's doubt comes out much more clearly. Moreover, at the end of chapter 20, Dick describes Deckard as being aware of the fact that "reasons" of nonpersons have to be distinguished from reasons proper.

does not merely oubt it. And his reasons for doubting are fairly good ones, and not just airly ood easons to oubt, whatever this may be. The example is from Hollywood and may therefore seem just foolish. I chose it, because the movie is fairly well known and because it may convince you of the coherency, in principle, of genuinely doubting one's own personhood. Moreover, I speculate that there are various mental diseases of actual people (i.e., human persons) that establish the same point: Human persons may in all consistency begin to doubt that they are persons and may begin even to fear that they don't suffer but instead uffer, whatever this may be, and however much it urts.

So the kind of realism about personhood I think to be an ingredient of the sparse ontological concept of a person has nothing to do with "metaphysical" or "absolute" certainty about personhood. I tend to think that, painful as this may be, there is no such certainty to be had. Not even the supposedly special sort of unshakable "subjective" evidence of self-consciousness, in virtue of which we could prove, at least each one of us for himself, his own personhood. But what is crucial for our purposes, is this: Even if we had ways to gain absolute certainty in this respect, such certainty would be nothing in virtue of which we are persons — would not be constitutive of our being persons.

The kind of hardcore realism I take to be appropriate with regard to persons, ontologically conceived, is therefore not wedded to any sort of epistemological fundamentalism. But neither is it hostile towards any such a position: A realist may well believe that his personhood is a fact of which he has, or can have, most certain knowledge *a priori*. This is to say, realism about persons is an ingredient of the ontological conception of personhood, but such realism is epistemologically neutral, or at least is compatible with a wide range of positions concerning the question whether and how facts of personhood could be established.

Let me try to summarize, as straightforwardly as I can, the combination, which I've just tried to rough out, of hardcore realism and epistemological permissiveness:

Personhood is independent of what one takes oneself to be, or what others take one to be. Even if it should be somehow rationally inevitable for a human being to assume that he himself, or she herself, is a person (or, over and above that, that all of his or her fellow creatures are persons), this itself wouldn't be what makes any of us persons. And vice versa, even if all of us came to believe that we aren't persons but merely brains, cleverly designed automata, robots, or androids, this would not affect the fact, granted that it is one, that we are persons.

The crucial "realistic" point in all this seems to me to be simply this: *Person* is not a CAC-concept. Granted, it may well be true that this concept is man-made. Forming it, or eventually hitting upon it, may have been one of the great cultural achievements in human history. Moreover, the ability to responsibly ascribe it, if only fallibly, to others — and, on reflection, to oneself — may be a specifically human talent. But nevertheless, what the concept applies to is not up to us. The fact that an entity falls, or doesn't fall, under this concept is itself fully independent of what humans have achieved, what they are gifted to do, and what they believe.

There's both a sunny and a dark side to such realism. Sunny side: Nobody's personhood depends on anyone's ascription or "recognition" of it, not even his own. Therein lurks something dignifying and consoling. Dark side: No one is immune to doubts, however far-fetched, about his or her own personhood. Why call it a dark side? Because if we ever went so far as to engage seriously in such a doubt, we wouldn't have the slightest idea of what (not anymore: "who") we were. We'd be, as it were, hopelessly lost in the vast ontological zoo. In this lurks something somberly disconcerting.[12]

The two early modern philosophers whose thoughts about our topic we shall consider later are clearly realists about personhood. But, interestingly (I think), the dark side of being a realist seems not to have occurred to them.

2. The Bewildering Conceptual Plenitude of *Person*

One thing that is deeply vexing about personhood is this: Even our fundamental and utterly austere ontological concept of a person seems inexhaustibly rich. And it is quite unclear which of its features are core components and which are peripheral. Which of its aspects should be considered as being fundamental and which as being derived?

It is this deplorable fact that I shall be mainly concerned with in what follows. I shall try to present, very briefly, some evidence that it *is* a fact. I shall venture an explanation for it, which I shall try to support, less briefly, by two examples from the history of philosophy. And I shall air, very briefly again, a suggestion about what to do when the aim is to "regain a complex concept of human personhood."[13]

---

12. What I find so especially outraging about recent pseudo-scientific stupidities, a few examples of which I mentioned above, is that their authors do not seem to be sensitive at all to the depth of such disconcertion.

13. I am borrowing this phrase from Michael Welker's title of the first meeting of our group.

Consider the following random list of characteristics of personhood that have been emphasized by various thinkers as they have employed that concept in their theorizing.

A person, it is said,

1. is an individual capable of rationality
2. is responsible for what it does
3. has dignity
4. is not a something *("quid")* but a someone *("quis")*
5. is free
6. is a unity of a body and a mind (soul)
7. is anything to which words and actions of human beings are attributed
8. is an intelligent agent, capable of a law, and happiness, and misery
9. is an end in itself and an object of respect
10. is an entity to which both mental and physical properties can be ascribed
11. is capable of treating others as persons
12. is capable of verbal communication
13. is conscious and self-conscious
14. is capable of second-order intentionality (in particular, is capable of second-order volitions, which are a precondition of having a free will)

Many of these features themselves do not seem conceptually less demanding than personhood; many of them are somewhat vague. Some of them may appear controversial. (As to #11, for example, there are forms of autism, or so I am told, which disable people from treating others as persons. But we would not be ready to accept without reservation, I presume, that anyone who suffers from such a disease is *ipso facto* not a person.)[14] Arguably, not all of these

---

14. This is not to say that *person* is not a QS-concept, i.e., a concept that essentially involves a certain standard of quality in the following sense: It is part of the mastery of such a concept that one acknowledges, concerning the items subsumable under it, that they can be classified according to how good they are as items falling under this concept. Roughly speaking, if C is an QS-concept, then it is fully mastered only by someone who has also mastered a family of concepts such as "an excellent C," "a good C," "a middling C," "a lousy C," etc. — An example of such a concept would be *argument;* you don't really know what an argument is, as long as you have no idea of how to classify arguments according to their quality as arguments. But you may very well know what a logical proof is, without even being willing to classify such proofs as good or bad ones. So *proof* is not a QS-concept. Three more remarks on QS-concepts: First, they do not need to be evaluative themselves, although their mastery essentially requires the ability to draw value distinctions concerning the members of their extensions. Secondly, it is characteristic of the natural sciences (at least of the more fundamental ones, and clearly of

features go together. (For example, #10 is so wide that it seems to allow for persons who don't exemplify several of the other features.) Clearly, several of these features seem to be dependent on others and so, maybe, this list needs to be reduced. But even more clearly and most importantly for our purposes, there is nothing about this list that gives us reason to assume that it is complete. The list is heterogeneous and it is open; and for all we know, it is essentially open. That is, we have no idea about how, by what kind of argument, we could possibly convince ourselves that it, or some improved variant of it, is complete.

So, on the one hand, personhood appears to be a straightforward matter: As a matter of fact, we can, in normal circumstances, tell a person from anything else with remarkable ease. On the other hand we do not have a clear idea of what the crucial marks of personhood are. The features that come to mind when we think about it are too many and too motley, to elucidate what we really mean by "person"; and we are prepared to admit that ever more features may turn out to be conceptually relevant, as we keep on thinking about it. Moreover, there is no reason to think that the word "person" is ambiguous. It would be absurd to claim that the features listed above specify distinct meanings of the word. "Person" clearly is not like "bank" ("ground beside a river"/"institution offering financial services"). It is exactly the fact that "person" is *not* a homonym which makes the essential openness of any collection of its conceptual features an embarrassing richness.

*   *   *

How is this richness of the concept of personhood to be explained? One answer to this question is historical. Over the centuries, the concept has been used by many thinkers as a conceptual tool for answering quite different questions: metaphysical, theological, and moral. In reaction to these problems, quite different features have been introduced as characteristics of a person. So the word "person," for a very long time, has been a technical, or semi-technical, term in various quite distinct theoretical frameworks, and it has been used in these frameworks for the solution of various quite distinct theoretical problems.

I shall try to illustrate this by two examples from the history of philoso-

---

physics) that their theoretical terms do not express QS-concepts. Third, QS-concepts are not reducible to concepts that do not involve standards of quality.

I am not sure what to say about *person*. But I think it is an interesting question whether it is a QS-concept or not. If it is, or were, one, then it may be difficult to stick to the view (which I have taken here) that there is a "psychologically noncommittal" concept of personhood. That's why I am inclined to assume that *person* is not a QS-concept.

phy, which I take to be quite telling. I hope that they reveal some aspects of the complexity and heterogeneity of our inherited concept of a person, which has been partly formed (reformed and, arguably, deformed) by thinkers like Descartes and Locke.

3. Descartes on Personhood

Let us consider, as a first example, the use Descartes makes of the concept of a person. Although he acknowledges the existence of God and angels, his doctrine is exclusively about human personhood. According to his metaphysics, any human being consists of two entities that are really distinct: the body and the soul, or mind. They are really distinct, because the body is a physical substance and the soul (or mind) is an immaterial substance, and these two substances could exist without each other. It should be noticed that what Descartes calls a *real* distinction between substances is not a factual separateness, but a possible one: two substances are really distinct if they are capable of being separated, "at least by God" (AT VII 78). In the *Sixth Meditation* Descartes presents (the definitive version of) his famous proof that his body and his soul are really distinct. The crucial point of the proof is this. Descartes claims that one can clearly-and-distinctly think of oneself insofar as one is only a thinking thing and not a material (or extended) thing; and one can clearly-and-distinctly think of one's body insofar as it is merely an extended thing and not a thinking thing.[15] Whenever anyone can clearly — and distinctly — understand one thing apart from another, God could have created these things in that way. And this is to say: his or her soul and his or her body are really distinct things. One can, in principle, exist without the other.

Nowadays, Descartes' mind/body dualism is considered by many as an unscientific folly of a clueless and pious philosopher, especially by those who don't know his work. But we should not forget that he was a sober man and an accomplished scientist. In fact (much more than to metaphysics, *prima philosophia*), he was devoted to natural science, *philosophia naturalis,* and spe-

---

15. The hyphens in "clear-and-distinct" are meant to remind you that this is a technical term of Descartes. An idea, or a perception, is *clear,* if it is vivid (like the idea of pain when you suffer from one); it is *distinct,* if it is sharply separated from all other ideas (as the idea of pain is not, according to Descartes, since we have a tendency to mix up the sensation of pain itself with something painful in the cause of the pain). — But the term "clear-and-distinct" has a very special meaning for Descartes: it is reserved for those ideas of which it cannot be assumed, on pain of manifest absurdity, that they are misrepresentations.

cifically to the project of explaining the totality of phenomena in the world as we know it in terms of a mathematico-physical theory. In such a theory matter is hypothesized to consist of nothing but micro-elements (too small to be humanly perceivable), and these elements are ascribed nothing but decent corporeal properties like shape, size, motion, and position. Descartes was a naturalist and reductionist, pretty much in the way that is common among scientists today. But the human mind (specifically *human* cognition, in contrast to animal cognition) he considered as a phenomenon that defies any naturalist-reductive account. In fact, he seemed to have held that no science whatsoever of the human mind is possible. The doctrine that the human mind is scientifically impenetrable wasn't due to some unfounded defeatism on his part. For Descartes, it rather results from a certain speciality of the human mind: the pure intellect (and maybe also from another one: the absolute freedom of will). The *intellectus purus* is a mental capacity completely independent of the others we have (like, e.g., sense-perception, memory, or imagination; these are importantly body-bound and mental, at least in human beings, only in virtue of the fact that they are connected with the intellect). The intellect is our capacity to genuinely understand things and to conceive their essence — our capacity to theorize by employing concepts that have been purified from any sensory, pictorial, or other admixtures. When Descartes claims that animals (most probably) do not have a mind, he does not deny them sense-perception, pains, desires, etc. They have all this, he agrees, but not as genuinely mental phenomena, i.e., not as something that informs an intellect. The right way to understand Descartes' disbelief in animal minds is to understand him as precisely believing that they do not have a pure intellect. For him, the pure intellect is the mind proper, the original and true mind; nothing else is intrinsically mental. Several other human capacities, acts, and processes are mental only in virtue of being appropriately connected with the intellect.

The real distinction between human mind and body is, for Descartes, a fact of metaphysics. But metaphysics is not everything there is in life. Not even for Descartes. As he says during a conversation with the theologian Frans Burman: "A point to note is that one should not devote so much effort to the *Meditations* and to metaphysical questions, or give them elaborate treatments in commentaries and the like. Still less should one . . . dig more deeply into these questions than the author [i.e., Descartes himself] did; he has dealt with them quite deeply enough. It is sufficient to have grasped them once in a general way, and then to remember the conclusion. Otherwise they draw the mind too far away from physical and observable things, and make it unfit for studying them. Yet it is just these physical studies that it is most desirable for people to pursue, since they would yield abundant benefits for life" (AT V 165). And in a letter to Princess Elizabeth he puts this point as follows: "I believe that it is very necessary to have properly understood, once in a lifetime, the principles of metaphysics, since they are what gives us the knowledge of God and of our soul. But I think also that it would be harmful to occupy one's intellect frequently in meditating upon them" (AT III 695).

The metaphysical conclusion that our minds and our bodies are distinct entities is hard to bring into unison with how we experience ourselves. This conclusion is true; it is even shown to be absolutely certain by a metaphysical proof, Descartes insists. But he recommends leaving it at that. The way we experience ourselves, he concedes, is not as consisting of two distinct entities; rather we experience ourselves as the union of our soul and our body. But this union is, in reality, not anything that exists *sui generis*. There is no third entity, over and above our body and our soul.[16] When it comes to taking stock of the basic really existing entities, then, strictly speaking, there are only the two substances of body and soul, which are distinct however intimately they may be interrelated. So, in a sense, when we experience ourselves as a mind/body-union, the way we experience ourselves is not mirrored in the basic metaphysical facts.

It is exactly this union of body and soul that Descartes denotes by the concept of a human person. "Everyone feels that he is a single person [*une seule personne*] with both body and thought [i.e., soul] so related by nature that the thought can move the body and feel the things which happen to it" (AT III 694).

But, as he makes it clear, particularly in his correspondence with Elizabeth, Descartes is prepared to concede that this way of experiencing ourselves as persons is not just due to some sort of negligence or other kind of avoidable mistake. He says, surprisingly, that among our primitive notions which are innate and "can only be understood through themselves," there is

---

16. There are some attempts at terminological appeasement. In a letter from January 1642 to his follower Regius, a professor of medicine at the university of Utrecht who later caused severe trouble for him, Descartes recommended, as Regius' ghostwriter in his dispute with the Dutch theologian Voetius, the following formulations: ". . . human beings are made up of a body and a soul . . . by a true substantial union [*per veram unionem substantialem*]. . . . If a human being is considered in himself as a whole [*homo in se totus*] . . . he is a single *Ens per se*, and not *per accidens;* because the union which joins a human body and a soul to each other is not accidental to a human being, but essential, since a being without it is not a human being" (AT III 508). — This is intended to sound soothing, but the plain fact remains: mind and body are distinct substances, and their union, even if a "true substantial" one, is not a substance.

not only the notion of body and the notion of mind, but also the notion of their union (AT III 665). This is surprising, since — in the final analysis — there is, as we have just seen, no thing to which this notion applies in reality, and therefore the notion of a person is, metaphysically speaking, at least a misleading one. Whereas both the soul and the body can be conceived by the pure intellect, their union, Descartes says, "is known only obscurely by the intellect alone . . . but it is known very clearly by the senses" (AT III 692). This means for Descartes: Although we have very strong and vivid ideas of the senses concerning the union of the body and the soul, these ideas never amount to genuine knowledge, since our senses can *never* give us ideas that constitute knowledge, not even when they are clear (i.e., strong and vivid). Genuine knowledge consists in the intellect's perceiving clear-*and-distinct* ideas. It is only such clear-and-distinct ideas of the intellect that God guarantees to be true. But, to repeat, the ideas we have of the mind/body-union, Descartes insists, are not clearly-and-distinctly perceived by the intellect. So when Descartes says: The union of mind and body is "known very clearly by the senses," we must not forget that the knowledge in question is at best second-class knowledge, or strictly speaking: not knowledge at all. What we do have, when we experience ourselves as *persons,* is nothing but vivid ideas of the senses, but no clear-*and-distinct* ideas of the intellect.

As soon as the intellect, in a metaphysical effort, has brought the ideas both of body and of soul to clearness-and-distinctness, and has achieved the insight that body and soul are really distinct, it faces what we nowadays call Descartes' mind/body-problem: How can there be a causal interaction between these entities, one of them material, the other immaterial? When Frans Burman asked him, in 1648: "But how can this be, and how can the soul be affected by the body and vice versa, when their natures are completely different?," Descartes replied: "This is very difficult to explain; but here our experience is sufficient, since it is so clear on this point that it just cannot be gainsaid" (AT V 163).

So here is why the use Descartes makes of his concept of a person is important for him: Although we have no clear-and-distinct idea of a person, this idea is a primitive innate notion that cannot be reduced to notions that are clear-and-distinct. It is as persons that we experience ourselves quite naturally, as long as we do not philosophize about our nature. And as long as we experience ourselves in this natural way, the mind/body-problem simply does not arise.

That is why people who never philosophize and use only their senses have no doubt that the soul moves the body and that the body acts on the soul.

They regard them as a single thing, that is to say, they conceive their union; because to conceive the union between two things is to conceive them as one single thing. Metaphysical thoughts, which exercise the pure intellect, help to familiarize us with the notion of the soul; and the study of mathematics . . . accustoms us to form very distinct notions of body. But it is the ordinary course of life and conversation, and abstention from meditation . . . that teaches us how to conceive the union of the soul and the body. (AT III 692)

Descartes seems to suggest here, and in other passages,[17] that metaphysics (pure thinking, performed by employing clear-and-distinct notions of the intellect) does not and cannot give us the solution to the mind/body-problem. The way to deal with this problem is rather to *dissolve* it, by recognizing that it simply does not arise as long as we experience ourselves in the way that is most natural for us: as persons. So the concept of a person is used by Descartes as a philosophical tool for the dissolution of a problem — indeed, a mystery — arising in his metaphysics.

The dissolution he hints at seems to be along the following lines: The so-called mind/body-problem cannot be solved theoretically, because we have no clear-and-distinct ideas in terms of which we could explain how an immaterial mind and a material body form an interactive union. It cannot be solved, because no conceptual tools required for a theoretical solution are available. Human cognition is such that it has no access to any category of entities beneath, or beyond, the categories *mind* and *body*. For us, these two categories are rock-bottom. Even our conception of God is within these two basic categories (we have to conceive him as a mind, albeit an infinite one). Don't ask why God didn't give us the conceptual resources to solve this problem theoretically.[18] There is no such problem, except when you philosophize. Apart from this special case, you are dead sure that you are a person. Your assuredness about this is not metaphysical certainty, but it is good enough for all matters of human concern. You enjoy it, except when doing metaphysics, because God was kind enough to let you constantly *feel* that you are a person.

17. E.g., in a letter to Arnauld (July 29, 1648), where he writes: "That the mind, which is incorporeal, can set the body in motion is something which is shown to us not by any reasoning or comparison with other matters, but each and every day by the surest and most evident experience [*certissima et evidentissima experientia*]. It is one of those things which are known by themselves and which we only make obscure when we try to explain them" (AT V 222).

18. In the *Fourth Meditation,* Descartes argues that asking such questions betrays a fundamental misunderstanding.

Don't complain that you are not capable of reaching full-blown ("distinct") understanding of *how* there can be such unions of mind and body. Be grateful for clarity about this issue, for vividly feeling *that* you are a person. This may sound pious, or like a cheap escape. But as far as we can tell, Descartes was fully serious about it. He accepted it as obvious that there are lots of things about which we, as finite minds, aren't capable of reaching *scientia,* knowledge in the strictest sense.

According to the Cartesian account, the concept of a person is not a "theoretical" concept that could help us to gain metaphysical insights into the ultimate structure of reality. It is not clear-and-distinct; it is not one of those concepts by which we can reach genuine knowledge. In the letter to Elizabeth from which I have quoted extensively, Descartes says: "It does not seem to me that the human mind is capable of forming a very distinct conception of the distinction between the soul and the body and, at the same time, of their union; for to do this it is necessary to conceive them as a single thing and at the same time to conceive them as two things; and *this is absurd*" (AT III 693, my italics).

Taking all this together, I suggest that Descartes' thought is this: When you do metaphysics, when you inquire into the ultimate structure of what there is, you are bound to accept that your soul and your body are really distinct; and then, as long as you are engaged in nothing but pure metaphysics, you cannot conceive of yourself as a person (i.e., of the union of your body and your soul). Strictly metaphysically speaking, this is not just too difficult; it would be simply absurd. At the end of the day, the concept of a person is not just confused, but it is in principle so and for a simple reason: the very concept is in tension with an irrefutable metaphysical fact. Nevertheless, this concept (which God was kind enough to put into our souls) is of enormous value. It captures an important aspect of our worldly existence, "which everyone invariably experiences in himself without philosophizing" (AT III 694).

Let me list a few salient features that are characteristic of Descartes' concept of a person as I have just sketched it:

(1) The concept of a person is the concept of the mind/body-union.
(2) This concept is innate and a primitive, i.e. unanalyzable, concept.
(3) It is not clear-and-distinct, and since it is primitive, it cannot be reduced to clear-and-distinct concepts. So we may say that it is essentially not clear-and-distinct.
(4) Nevertheless, it is of enormous value. Not because it helps us to solve the mind/body-problem, but because it helps us to dissolve it.

4. Descartes' Silence on Transtemporal Personal Identity

Assuming for a moment that this sketch of Descartes' doctrine, concededly an unorthodox one (this is a concession, not an apology), is on the right track, there is little wonder that he never cared to raise questions of transtemporal personal identity. I have wondered for many years, if you allow me to intersperse a personal *(sit venia verbo)* remark, why Descartes, otherwise a most subtle thinker on topics concerning the metaphysics of the mind, was apparently never puzzled by the problems about fission and fusion, the body-hopping of minds (or the mind-hopping of bodies, if that makes a difference — I think it does) and all that kind of weird stuff that seems to spring immediately from his substantial mind/body-dualism.

So why was Descartes, of all thinkers, never puzzled by these questions that have occupied metaphysicians ever since Locke's *Essay,* and that seem to be taken bitterly seriously in recent metaphysics — indeed, today seem to be considered more urgent and important than ever? A tempting answer goes as follows: Because, for him, these are all pseudo-problems. A problem that wears its insolvability *in-principle* on its sleeves is a pseudo-problem. To put it in a bunch of slogans: "There's no *puzzle* of transtemporal personal identity. If the relevant questions could be framed at all, they could be framed clearly-and-distinctly; and then they could be answered. But they can't be framed clearly-and-distinctly, since they essentially involve the concept of a person.[19] A question that *in principle* cannot be phrased clearly-and-distinctly is a pseudo-problem; it simply has no answer."

This, I gather, was not Descartes' reason for avoiding issues of transtemporal personal identity. The problems in question would be pseudo-problems for him only if the concept of a person were a ("materially") false idea, i.e., one that is "such as to provide subject-matter for error" (AT VII 231) by not representing anything real, but representing what they represent as something real (AT VII 44). But *person* is not a false idea. What it represents is something real (the mind and the body as a union), so whatever is wrong with it is not that it represents something as real that is not real. What is cognitively inferior about it, in comparison to concepts like *mind* and *body,* is that it essentially

---

19. All these puzzling questions (e.g., "Would somebody, let's call him E.P., who enters, on Earth, a Parfitian Teletransporter be the same *person* as the one who, on Mars, leaves the teletransporter, given that the brain and the body in the cubicle of the Earthian Teletransporter were destroyed in due time?," "If E.P. were teletransported twice over and subsequently destroyed, would any of the two duplicates be the same *person* as E.P.?") involve the concept of a person *essentially* — i.e., they could not be rephrased without this concept.

represents its *repraesentatum* indistinctly (or as Descartes would put it: *"con-fusé,"* which is his technical term for the opposite of *"distincte"*). Yet this, by itself, is not a stain on its conceptual credentials. For its rationale is exactly to represent two-things-considered-as-one. Its appropriate realm of application is outside metaphysics. (Within metaphysics, mind and body demonstrably are to be considered as two distinct things. But as I said: metaphysics is not all there is in life, not even for Descartes.)

For Descartes, the concept of a person is a fine concept, for *the conduct of life*. It is of utmost importance within this realm. It is a concept that captures an important aspect of the human condition.[20] And it would betray a grave intellectual misunderstanding to sneer at it because of its lack of distinctness. A concept's lack of distinctness is not, *per se,* a conceptual deficiency. This sort of lack is the hallmark of many perfectly good concepts. In fact, the vast majority of the concepts on which we have to depend in order to lead our humble human lives are indistinct in not separating their bodily and their mental components: hunger, thirst, love, pain, sweet, soft, red — to mention but a few.

Nevertheless, *person* is merely a second-class concept when it comes to *the contemplation of truth*.[21] The contemplation of truth is to the conduct of life like a move in a game of Blitz chess is to its analysis without time-limit. A perfectly good move in the one context may not live up to the standards of the second.

Therefore, given that the concept of a person can, in principle, not be brought to distinctness, questions about transtemporal personal identity, for Descartes, are fated to imperfect answers (all of them, not only those bizarre cases that are characteristic of our contemporary debate). No answer could possibly possess genuine certainty. True knowledge, *scientia* in the emphatic Cartesian sense, is restricted to the realm of our most clear-and-distinct thoughts. A crucially important philosophical fact about transtemporal personal identity is that no knowledge *sensu stricto* is to be had on the topic — and that therefore, in a sense, personal identity is not a metaphysical topic at all. The only "knowledge" that could be hoped for would be epistemically second-

20. Many things that, as it happens, only human beings can do are things that, for conceptual reasons, only persons could do. Michael could take a stroll, but his dog Carli could do so only in a nonliteral sense of this phrase. Why? I guess it's not because members of the biological species *homo sapiens sapiens* have this ability, and as a matter of empirical fact, members of the species *canis canis* happen not to have it (so that one day a new breed of dogs might turn up whose members literally could take a stroll).

21. For the Cartesian distinction between the conduct of life and the (metaphysical) contemplation of truth, see AT VII 149.

class, knowledge merely "in the moral sense [*moralis sciendi modus*] which suffices for the conduct of life" (AT VII 475).[22]

In a nutshell, Descartes' view might well have been that the questions of transtemporal identity aren't pseudo-problems, but neither are they questions to which a philosophical answer could be given. We would have to try to find answers (or rather: practical decisions about how to deal with the situation), if we were confronted, in practice, with a problem-case. For such cases, we could not bring to bear moral certainty and not even practical knowledge (*connoissance en pratique*), since the latter would at least require a firm habit of belief (AT IV 296), which we could not have acquired concerning novel extravagant situations (body-hopping of souls, etc.). Our guidance would have to be good common sense (*sens commun bon,* AT XI 386; *sensus communis,* in the nontechnical sense, AT X 518, 527), which Descartes mentions occasionally, but does not theorize about.

Now suppose we were to actually confront such a case, e.g., one in which "the Soul of a Prince, carrying with it the consciousness of the Prince's past Life, enter[s] and inform[s] the Body of a Cobbler as soon as deserted by his own Soul,"[23] and had to face the question whether the cobbler now is the same person as the prince. From a Cartesian point of view, no answer could be given with certainty, not even with moral certainty.

A narrow-mindedly straightforward application of the criterion for transtemporal personal identity suggested by Descartes' concept of a person would yield the negative answer: No, the cobbler-now is not the same person as the prince-then. For personal identity, according to Descartes, obviously would have to be identity of the mind/body-union; and the prince's mind and the cobbler's body clearly constitute a union very different from the prince's original mind/body-union. But the strategy of, *first,* concluding that the cobbler is not the ex-prince and *then* drawing whatever consequences from this result as if it were a theorem proven, presumably would not be what our good common sense recommends.

---

22. In this passage of his *Seventh Replies* to (Bourdin's) objections, Descartes adds: "I frequently stressed that there is *a very great difference* between this type of knowledge and the metaphysical knowledge . . ." (AT VII 149, my italics). The very great difference lies in the following: Only metaphysical knowledge has God's truth-guarantee; he would, *per impossibile,* have to be a deceiver, if our alleged metaphysical knowledge turned out to be false belief. But concerning our alleged knowledge in the mere moral sense, God's benevolence does not guarantee the truth of what we believe. Moral certainty inextricably contains an element of epistemic risk.

23. Locke, *Essay concerning Human Understanding,* II.27.15.

It would display more common sense to take into account what concrete practical consequences are at issue. (For example, is there a large sum of money the prince-then owes to somebody, and are we facing now the question whether the cobbler-now or the prince's wife should pay the debt? Or is the question whether the cobbler-now ought to be hanged for a crime, committed by the prince-then? etc.). Get clear about what, *in concreto,* is at issue in this particular situation, and in the light of this and of all that you know, if only with moral certainty, try to discern the best solution[24] to this concrete problem with all of its contingent features. This may sound convoluted, as a piece of advice delivered by common sense. But then again, common sense may be more refined than the scoffers would concede. Its maxims may not be confined to what can be expressed in six-word sentences without hypotaxis. Descartes thought very highly about common sense — where it belongs. And, for him, it indispensably belongs to all matters where problems of personhood are concerned.

*   *   *

Let's turn to something else. It is worth emphasizing that for Descartes mind-identity is not sufficient for personal identity. He has not explicitly formulated a criterion of transtemporal personal identity, but it is quite clear that, given his concept of personhood, his doctrine would yield the following criterion:

Person A, at t, is the same person as B, at t', if and only if (i) the mind of A at t is the same mind as the mind of B at t' **and** (ii) the body of A at t is the same body as the body of B at t'.[25]

It is a common mistake to assume that Descartes is implicitly committed to a purely mental criterion of personal identity. The reason for this mistake, presumably, is this: According to the Cartesian doctrine, I could exist without the body I happen to have; I could even exist without a body; but I could not exist without my mind; and this is to say, my essence is my mind and nothing physical is part of my essence. Therefore: if one's mind is one's total essence, then mind-identity is that which (completely) constitutes personal identity.

But this last step is a *non sequitur:* more specifically, it is a fallacy of equivocation. For Descartes, there are two ways of using the word "I." If it is used, as almost always, in the common way, it refers to the speaker (or thinker) as a person, i.e., as a mind/body-union. But it can also be used in a special, techni-

---

24. Or rather: "one of the best solutions"; for there may be more than one optimal solution.
25. Note that transtemporal body-identity need not be strict "atom-to-atom" identity.

cal sense, in which it refers to some particular aspect of what it usually refers to. In the *Meditations,* Descartes' thinker is for quite a while not in a position to refer to himself as a person, because he cannot yet exclude the possibility that there are no bodies at all in the world, not even his own. In order to make sure that he nevertheless refers successfully, when he uses the word "I," he uses it in a specially narrow sense (roughly, in the sense of "the entity whose existence has been proven with utmost certainty in the *Existo*-argument"). When he uses the word in such an exceptionally restricted way, Descartes speaks of using it *praecise.* It is important to notice that "precisely" here does not mean "in the word's exact (proper, real, strict, or genuine) sense." What it rather signifies is that the word is used *in a technically restricted sense.* Descartes sometimes cares to distinguish between these two uses by applying phrases like *"ego totus,"*[26] in contrast to *"ego quem novi."*[27] The metaphysical result that my mind is my complete essence is a truth exclusively in the second, technical sense of "my." From this, nothing can be inferred to the effect that my mind is my complete *personal* essence.

Descartes is committed to the criterion for human personal identity just mentioned (same mind and same body). But how this criterion would have to be applied to the enormous variety of bizarre possibilities discussed as problems of transtemporal personal identity is a matter about which he, at least in published writing, simply remained silent. And for this, as we have seen, he may have had very good reasons: first, these problems do not have a strictly philosophical or otherwise *a priori* justifiable answer; second, as long as we do not encounter these problems, there is no practical reason for dealing with them; and third, as long as we do not know the practical consequences of our answers, there is not much that could guide our good common sense when we attempt to come up with an answer. And common sense is all we could rely on in such cases.

5. Locke on Transtemporal Personal Identity and Personhood

For Locke, the concept of personal identity is an important one because the justice of all reward and punishment, whether performed by us or performed by God, depends on whether the one who did it is the same person as the one who is rewarded or punished. Our best clue of what we *really* consider

26. E.g., AT VII 81, where he adds "insofar as I am composed of a body and a mind."
27. See for example AT VII 27.

personal identity to consist in does not come from metaphysics ("the same immaterial thinking substance"), physics ("the same material body"), or biology ("the same human being") but rather from how we proceed in applying our laws. The fact that we do not punish (and would not consider it just to punish) "the *Mad Man* for the *Sober Man's* actions, nor the *Sober Man* for what the *Mad Man* did"[28] is of utmost importance. For Locke, this shows that when serious practical decisions need to be made, we treat the sober man and the mad man as different persons (his actual wording is "thereby making them two Persons"). If they are two persons, this is so in spite of the fact that, physically speaking, they are (approximately) the same body, in spite of the fact that they are, biologically speaking, the same human being and in spite of the metaphysical presumption that their immaterial thinking substance is one and the same.

This fact about what we consider just (namely: not punishing somebody, e.g. the sober man, who is physically, biologically, and mind-substantially identical with the wrongdoer) is, I suggest, Locke's *ur*-observation about transtemporal personal identity. Certainly, his conclusion (concerning personal non-identity) is not inevitable. (We may, instead of jumping to Locke's conclusion, prefer to say that in certain circumstances we do not punish the very person who did the deed.) But I am not concerned here with the feasibility of Locke's theory, but with trying to bring to notice what sort of problem he is actually dealing with, how the concept of personhood is meant to be serviceable to a solution, and what is supposed to motivate the proposed solution.

If I am right, Locke's primary target-concept was transtemporal personal identity, not personhood. Where do we actually, and in a serious and responsible manner (not just in the context of idle metaphysical speculation), apply this concept? What is characteristic of this particular sort of application? The answers to these questions pave the way to our best understanding of what personal identity is. Once we have reached such an understanding, the subsequent clarification of a fitting concept of personhood will be light work. Two equations have to be solved, in the right order.

So I suggest the following as the Lockean agenda:

1. Personal identity = that relation, whatever it is, that makes it just to reward/punish someone for something that was done in the past
2. Person = that entity, whatever it is, which is a proper relatum of this relation

28. *Essay concerning Human Understanding* II.27.20.

Famously, Locke offers consciousness (or more specifically, conscious memory) as the solution for the first equation. The rough idea is this: Person *A*, at *t*, is the same person as *B*, at *t'*, if and only if *B*'s consciousness at *t'* could contain a memory of an action consciously performed, or a thought (consciously) had, by *A* at *t*. (If *A* committed crime *c*, then the relation between *A* and *B* that makes it just to punish *B* for *c* is *B*'s (potential) memory of having done *c* — or somewhat more complicated: *B*'s being able to remember a thought θ such that θ was a thought of *A* at *t* in virtue of which *A* was conscious of committing *c*. The crucial point is that the relation in question is a psychological relation obtaining between conscious states: one particular conscious state θ of *A* at *t*, e.g., *A*'s awareness of doing *c*, and another particular conscious state of *B*, θ', which is *B*'s memory of θ. Given this psychological relation, *A* and *B* are "by the same consciousness . . . united into one Person" (*E* II.27.10).

Equally famously, in solving the first equation, Locke starts with what he presents as an uncontroversial specification of personhood:

> . . . what Person stands for . . . , I think, is a thinking intelligent Being, that has reason and reflection, and can consider it self as it self, the same thinking thing in different times and places. . . . (II.27.9)

What is needed, for a solution of the second equation that is satisfactory in the light of the proposed solution of the first equation, is a close connection between this concept of a person and the concept of consciousness (which is all that constitutes transtemporal personal identity). Locke makes the desired connection as close as possible: as consciousness "unites" persons over time, it unites simultaneous mental states into the same person's mental states.

> [consider it self as it self] . . . which it does only by that consciousness, which is inseparable from thinking, and as it seems to me, essential to it: It being impossible for any one to perceive, without perceiving, that he does perceive. When we see, hear, smell, taste, feel, meditate, or will anything, we know that we do so. . . . For since consciousness always accompanies thinking, and 'tis that, that makes every one to be, what he calls self; and thereby distinguishes himself from all other thinking things, in this alone consists personal Identity, i.e. the sameness of rational being. (II.27.9)

Beneath the surface of Locke's account of personal identity, both of the momentary and the transtemporal sort, something is at work that deserves our attention. Locke had a strong dislike for the concept of a substance. He scolds traditional philosophy for "the promiscuous use of so doubtful a term" (II.13.18); in using the word "substance," he says,

> ... we talk like Children; who, being questioned, what such a thing is, which they know not, readily give this satisfactory answer, That it is something; which in truth signifies no more, when so used, either by Children or Men, but that they know not what; and that the thing they pretend to know, and talk of, is what they have no distinct Idea of at all, and so are perfectly ignorant of it, and in the dark. (II.23.2)

So there is at least one completely different sort of *desideratum* for Locke's account: A person should not turn out to be a substance of some sort. It is this, I presume, that makes consciousness so irresistible to Locke: The concept of consciousness, for him, is not the concept of a substance, neither a material nor an immaterial substance which, allegedly, is the permanent, indivisible underlying *substratum* of all mental activities. (Whereas Descartes took the concept of a substance to be metaphysically inevitable and crystal clear, but the concept of personhood to be essentially obscure and merely practically helpful, Locke took the concept of substance to be metaphysically inevitable and hopelessly obscure, but the concept of personhood to be perfectly faultless.)

Let's take stock of some of our findings in Locke; for the sake of perspicuity I arrange them in an order that gives us the Lockean echo to the four Cartesian tenets listed above:

(5) The concept of a person is the concept of an entity that is justly rewarded/punished for its doings (including mental doings).
(6) This concept is neither innate (there are no such concepts, according to Locke) nor primitive, but rather a complex idea that is reducible to the concepts of consciousness and memory.
(7) It is clear and distinct, since it is made of clear and distinct simple concepts. (Whereas our use of the *word* "person" creates obscurity.)[29]
(8) It is of enormous importance. Not because it helps us to solve, or dissolve for that matter, the mind/body-problem, but because it is central to our conceptions of justice and self-care.

---

29. See *E* II.27.28. — It is exactly this alleged linguistic obscurity ("ill use of Names") that makes it necessary for Locke, following a suggestion of Molyneux, to include a separate chapter on these topics in the second edition (1694).

6. Two Ways of Accounting for the Bewildering Plenitude of *Person*

It would be rash to explain the remarkable clash between Descartes' and Locke's tenets as a manifestation of the fact that the two thinkers are not really addressing the same topic (i.e., the same concept of personhood). What I'd rather suggest is something else, namely that the concept of a person, in virtue of its indeterminate richness, lends itself to wildly different accounts; and the accounts that have been developed by various influential thinkers, sometimes within incommensurable theoretical frameworks and inspired by disparate philosophical motivations, additionally have left discordant marks on what we, today, dubiously consider as our "intuitions" about personhood.

As I said, and as the two examples in the excursion are meant to demonstrate, the word "person," for a very long time, has been a technical, or semitechnical, term in various quite distinct theoretical frameworks, and it has been used in these frameworks for the solution of various quite distinct theoretical problems. Moreover, again for a very long time, the word "person" has been in common use as a nontechnical term that is not connected to any particular theory or problem, but has nevertheless surreptitiously incorporated in its meaning an indefinite amount of the semantical complexity just indicated. Maybe what manifests itself as abundant richness inherent in our concept of personhood is only a reflection of the fact that we do not have a shared intuitive grasp of it, but only a common learned tradition, which has bequeathed to us a blend of quite diverse conceptual features that were never meant to go together.

Even if this is true, there may be another explanation for the conceptual richness. It has to do with a certain tension right at the core of our concept of a person:

(1) The concept of a person is **anthropocentric** in its actual application. Leaving God (and angels) aside, the only clear cases of persons we are *familiar* with are human beings.
(2) It is **not at all anthropocentric** in its intension. The concept of a person is not supposed to be the same as the concept of a human being.

There is conceptual leeway both for the possibility of nonpersonal human beings (members of our species lacking exactly those features, whatever they are, that are constitutive of personhood) and for the possibility of nonhuman persons. Any kind of creature could be, or could turn out to be, a person, if it only had that special something, whatever it is, that makes us persons.

Fairy tales, novels, and movies keep reminding us of this nonanthropocentric aspect: Hauff's stork is a person, Shelley's monster is a person, Mathison and Spielberg's E.T. is a person, we are pretty sure that some of the androids or replicants in Dick and Scott's *Blade Runner* are persons, and we are supposed to wonder whether Clarke and Kubrick's computer HAL is a person. If we try to specify what this conceptual leeway comes to, presupposing as we should that any normal human being is a person, we might look at the following two identifications:

> Personhood = that, whatever it is, *without* which a common human being would be only biologically speaking a human being

> Personhood = that, whatever it is, *with* which any being whatever would be, at least, of the same standing as a common human being

These equations may look funny at first sight, but I gather that they capture an important aspect of our concept of a person. And they may explain the embarrassing conceptual richness we found vexing: The list of features by which these two equations can be "solved" may be essentially open.

The first equation makes it quite clear that "common human being" is not to be taken in a biological sense. It is an honorific term for *us* (who happen to be common human beings) and for every possible being that is of the same standing. It is built into the very concept of a person that there is something valuable about common human beings (an accidental feature that each of them may lack) in virtue of which they are, as it were, not *merely* members of the human race. So we should consider the following as another conceptual core fact about personhood:

(3) It is part of the concept of a person that persons are distinctively **valuable**.

And since there is so much about us that can be considered specifically and distinctively valuable, this again may explain why the concept of a person is inexhaustibly rich.

*   *   *

So much for my rather sketchy attempt at a diagnosis of what is vexing about the concept of a person and what may account for its characteristic inexhaustibility!

Now what would have to be done in order to tidy up a bit the conceptual mess? I call it a mess, because (as a result of its richness) we have too many "intuitions" about personhood and almost nothing to give them structure. There are too few universally accepted constraints on this concept in order to make it possible to accept some of our (allegedly) *a priori* assumptions as valid and central and others as questionable or peripheral. I suspect that something like conceptual *analysis* is not what we need in order "to regain a complex concept of human personhood." If we just stare at the concept and brood over its richness, we will drown in a bottomless pit. Rather, something like conceptual construction, or reconstruction, is needed. And for this purpose it is necessary to get clear about what theoretical work we want the concept of a person to do. (Think back to the two examples given above: Descartes knew what theoretical aim he was after. He tried to solve the problem: Given that in reality mind and body are categorically distinct, how come we do not experience ourselves as consisting of two separate entities? He employed the concept of a person in his attempt to answer this specific question. Locke tried to solve a different problem: What is the appropriate subject of punishment and reward? He used the concept of a person for this particular theoretical purpose. Both thinkers had quite determinate ideas of what the concept of a person was supposed to effect within their theories; and this allowed them to attach a determinate sense to it.) So my suggestion is this: Only if we get clear about what kind of theory we are striving for, and what role the concept of a person is supposed to play in it, can we get, or regain, a less vexing concept of personhood.

A final caveat. In this theoretical, constructive endeavor of getting clearer about personhood, we ought not to expect much help from the natural sciences. The best we can hope for is corrective cooperation. The natural scientist may warn us, for example, that given a certain conception of personhood, persons so conceived could not be members of the natural world. But we must not forget that from a strictly naturalist point of view, *person* is just not a category. (*Nota bene,* this is not to say that personhood cannot be accounted for in a naturalist way. David Lewis, for example, has presented an ingenious naturalist account of personhood and transtemporal personal identity, which is based on a psychological concept of person.)[30]

The crucial point here is this: We would have to have reached, independently, considerable conceptual clarity about personhood, before we could reasonably hope for a naturalist characterization of the entities that exemplify

---

30. D. Lewis, "Survival and Identity," (1976), reprinted with a postscript in D. Lewis, *Philosophical Papers,* vol. 1 (Oxford: Oxford University Press, 1983), pp. 55-77.

it. We cannot ask the natural scientist "What is a person?" in the same state of almost complete conceptual ignorance and with the same hope for conceptual elucidation, in which we may ask "What is a magnetic moment?"

Natural science can teach us what human beings (considered exclusively as members of a certain biological species) are; as for storks and computers — and, if there are or were any, extraterrestrials and replicants — science can inform us about their physical and functional similarities and differences. But we must not hope that among the distinctions drawable in naturalist terms, there is one — already drawn, as it were — between those human beings, storks, computers, extraterrestrials, and replicants which (or who) are persons and those which (or who) are not. This would be silly. The natural sciences, with good reason, attach importance to providing no methodological space for value-concepts. This, of course, is not a frivolous narrow-mindedness on their part but a well-considered delimitation of what does, and what does not, fall within their cognitive realm.[31]

31. Thanks to the members of the group, especially to Maria Antonaccio, Philip Clayton, Malcolm Jeeves, Eiichi Katayanagi, John Polkinghorne, William Schweiker, Günter Thomas, and Michael Welker. In developing my ideas about these issues, I have profited a lot from discussing and conversing with them. Many thanks also to my old friends Mark Helme, Rolf-Peter Horstmann, Rainer von Savigny, and Hans-Peter Schütt for support and encouragement. They were kind enough to read earlier versions and spotted several things they found flatly mistaken or just cranky, some of which I have tried to correct or tone down.

Flesh–Body–Heart–Soul–Spirit: Paul's Anthropology as an Interdisciplinary Bridge-Theory

Michael Welker

Several years ago we started our international and interdisciplinary research project titled: "Body–Soul–Spirit: Regaining a Complex Concept of the Human Personhood." The title was — as we now see — a misleading formulation for a program that meant to pursue several goals and connect them.

- One goal was to answer the question: What speaks for and what speaks against the familiar dualizing anthropologies past and present, which invite us to observe the human being and to think about the human person in dual patterns such as "Mind and Body," "Soul and Body," "Spirit and Body," "Self-Consciousness and Consciousness" or "Brain and Spirit"?
- Another goal was to test whether theological talk about "Soul" and "Spirit" was able to grasp phenomena and functions that could also be identified in nontheological, e.g., philosophical or scientific observations and reflections. Would anything be lost when modern philosophies and psychologies tried to replace soul and spirit, for instance by self-consciousness?
- A third goal was the attempt to include the bodily condition of the human being in the discourse between theology, philosophy, and natural sciences and to do so without introducing naturalistic reductionism or an aesthetic impressionism.

Over against the concern to avoid dualistic reductionisms in the search for concepts that could harbor the complexity of the human person, Andreas Kemmerling issued a helpful warning: "What is so deeply confusing about the concept of 'person' is this: its inexhaustible wealth. Even the most basic and meager 'ontological' concept of the person is inexhaustibly diverse. And it is completely unclear which of its characteristics are central — and which ones belong more at the conceptual boundary or perhaps should even be viewed only as derivatives of others."[1] The danger of contemplating human personality via dualistic reductionisms is that one produces a phenomenal blindness that structurally excludes important areas of knowledge. Over against this risk, Kemmerling points to another danger: to "fall into despair over the wealth" of the concept of person and to "sink into a bottomless pit." He suggests that we should lay bare the content-oriented and theoretical interests in our discussion of this concept so that we can attempt "to bring a bit of order into this conceptual muddle."[2]

It was the contribution of Gerd Theissen on the differentiation between *sarx* and *soma,* flesh and body, in Paul's letters, that drew my attention to this anthropology as a candidate to follow Kemmerling's proposal. With Paul's anthropology, however, we seem to have before us a contribution that, with its hard dualism of "flesh and spirit," essentially in the letters to the Galatians and to the Romans, has provided formative theological and theoretical impulses for past and present dualistic and reductionistic anthropologies. On the other hand, Paul's model suggests that we should consider a cohesion of very diverse themes (such as "heart," "soul," "spirit," "reason," "conscience"), all of which have been highly important for theories in which the concept of person has played a central role. Above all, Paul's anthropology is structurally open to topics and questions of both theology and the natural sciences. It does not ignore the complex corporeality of the human being or humanity's difficult relationship to "God's Spirit."

In the following, I should like, first, to illuminate the harsh dualism of "flesh and spirit" in Paul's thought, a dualism that could be regarded as the root of many reductionistic evils in anthropology. In the second part, I will address Paul's thoughts about the multidimensionality of the human body. A third part will deal with the various interrelations between spirit, body, soul, and spirit. In a final part, I will concentrate on Paul's use of the terms "heart" and "conscience" as ciphers for future anthropological research about the complex unity of the human person.

1. A. Kemmerling, "Was macht den Begriff der Person so besonders schwierig?," in *Gegenwart des lebendigen Christus,* ed. G. Thomas and A. Schüle (Leipzig: EVA, 2007), pp. 541-65, 544f.

2. Kemmerling, "Was macht den Begriff der Person so besonders schwierig?," pp. 564 and 563.

1. Flesh and Spirit

In Galatians, Paul speaks of the flesh and the spirit as "enemies," since each sparks off an opposing "desire." This hostile constellation leads to a loss of human freedom that can only be resolved if the spirit is allowed to lead: "Live by the Spirit, I say, and do not gratify the desires of the flesh. For what the flesh desires is opposed to the Spirit, and what the Spirit desires is opposed to the flesh; for these are opposed to each other, to prevent you from doing what you want" (Gal. 5:16-17). Those who are determined by the desires of the flesh are subject to finitude, transience, and decay; those who are determined by the Spirit "reap eternal life" (cf. Gal. 6:8).

We also find this conviction expressed in Romans: "To set the mind on the flesh is death, but to set the mind on the Spirit is life and peace" (Rom. 8:6). Thus Paul's emphatic advice, that "if you live according to the flesh, you will die; but if by the Spirit you put to death the deeds of the body, you will live" (Rom. 8:13). However one is to understand these negatively connoted "actions of the flesh" and their death through the spirit, it is important first to note that Paul does not see the flesh simply as something that must be ignored at all costs.

Though Paul — with his strict differentiation of *sarx* and *soma* (flesh and body) — also repeatedly underlines the bond between the material dimension of the flesh and its transience,[3] the "materiality" of the flesh (over against stone and dust) is in fact an aspect to be valued: by drawing on associations with Exodus 24:12, Ezra 11:19; 36:26, and Jeremiah 31:33, 2 Corinthians stresses: "you show that you are a letter of Christ, prepared by us, written . . . with the Spirit of the living God, not on tablets of stone but on tablets of human hearts" (2 Cor. 3:3). The idea that this might be an accidental or even unfortunate play on words can be dismissed when one takes into account statements (such as 2 Cor. 4:11) regarding the revelatory role not only of the body but also of the flesh: "For while we live, we are always being given up to death for Jesus' sake, so that the life of Jesus may be made visible in our mortal flesh."

Though the flesh represents earthly, frail, and transient existence, it does not fail to receive dignity for having marked out the descent of a human life as well as the seriousness and drama of the divine will for revelation: In Romans, Paul proclaims the gospel of the Son of God "who was descended from David according to the flesh" (Rom. 1:3; cf. 8:3). And Israel is praised on his account,

---

3. See here the essay by Gerd Theissen in this volume; cf. also numerous Old Testament statements such as Isaiah 40:6: "All flesh is grass" and withers (cf. 40:7f.); Job 7:5: "My flesh is clothed with worms."

since "from them, according to the flesh, comes the Messiah, who is over all" (Rom. 9:5). If one takes seriously Paul's often-stressed importance of the divine service — indeed, revelatory power — of the human body (see below, part 2), and if one sees that the earthly body cannot be separated from the flesh (a distinction that Paul clearly makes), then we must do away with all primitive "either/or" conceptions regarding "flesh and spirit." The flesh inalienably belongs to the historical-material basis of the body, and thus (according to Paul) also to the higher level of human existence in heart and soul.

Yet as a notoriously finite and transient basis of existence, it becomes dangerous when its "lusts and desires" are self-directed. In his harsh statements about "the flesh," Paul repeatedly alludes to the elementary fleshly-bodily functions of nutrition and reproduction. If an interest in these functions dominates human existence without placing them in the service of the spirit, then such an existence succumbs to "sin and death." It is well-known that Paul does not hold back in his critique of gluttony, drunkenness, and forms of sexual contact incompatible with the possibility of reproduction (cf. Gal. 5:19ff.; 1 Cor. 5:1; 6:9f., 13ff.; 10:8; 11:21; 2 Cor. 12:21; Rom. 1:26f.; 13:13). If viewed superficially, one might attribute this to Paul's "hostility against the body and desires," to his personal neuroses, or to general canonical homophobias. In fact this harsh critique of the independent interests of "the flesh" grows out of a concern that those who have been won for God and for his gospel might once again be controlled by powers that would surrender them to the futility and transience of human life and block them from the prospects of God's plan for them and from the perspectives of the spirit.

Just as an abstract and totalizing denial of the flesh fails to do justice to Paul's anthropology, an enthusiasm for vague metaphysical and religious ideas such as "pure spirit" and "unmediated relationship with God in the Spirit" also fails to appreciate both the "depth" and the sharply observed and differentiated character of Paul's thought. One can (and should) make this clear with the example of his dispute with the Corinthians regarding their speaking in tongues: "those who speak in a tongue do not speak to other people but to God; for nobody understands them, since they are speaking mysteries in the Spirit. On the other hand, those who prophesy speak to other people for their upbuilding and encouragement and consolation" (1 Cor. 14:2-3). Speaking in tongues obviously fails to impress Paul, even though he affirms that this is speaking directly in the Spirit, speaking even "to God." This is not a singular derailment that could generously be dismissed by mystical enthusiasm for pure religious interiority and ultimate religious feeling. And it is not only public speech, but also prayer and doxologies "in tongues" that are expressly included by Paul in his mild critique as direct contact with God, striven after and achieved in the human "spirit": "For if I pray in a tongue, my spirit prays but my mind [*nous*] is unproductive. What should I do then? I will pray with the spirit, but I will pray with the mind also; I will sing praise with the spirit, but I will sing praise with the mind also" (1 Cor. 14:14-15).

These statements are revealing in many ways. Just as Paul does not condemn "the flesh" en bloc, neither does he present a scathing critique of glossolalic attempts to establish direct contact with God. In 1 Corinthians 14:18, he thanks God before the Corinthians that he speaks in tongues "more than you all" — whatever the measure of comparison may be. However, in this context Paul offers a strong plea for sensible speech in a sensible church service: "If you say a blessing with the spirit, how can anyone in the position of an outsider say the 'Amen' to your thanksgiving, since the outsider does not know what you are saying? For you may give thanks well enough, but the other person is not built up" (1 Cor. 14:16-17). Emphatically, he holds to his position that he "would rather speak five words with my mind, in order to instruct others, than ten thousand words in a tongue" (14:19). And he explicitly warns against a community that loses itself "in the spirit": "If, therefore, the whole church comes together and all speak in tongues, and outsiders or unbelievers enter, will they not say that you are out of your mind?" (14:23).

This clear, though not completely devastating, critique of glossolalia in direct contact with God "in the spirit" connects with a clearly sympathetic declaration of the use of rationality or reason *(nous)* even in spiritual contexts and in church services, and even in prayer and doxology — though this declaration is not directed abstractly against religious emotionalism. Here, rationality and reason are not highly complex entities attainable only through arduous transcendental philosophical training. They do not need to be won via post-pietistic processes of purification against "the naïve" and for "moral faith," as was the case with Kant. Rather, *nous* signifies understandable statements connected with an interest in persuasion and conviction. Even outsiders should be taught and be able, once convinced, to agree ("to say amen"). Cognitive or moral attempts to overpower others — whether they succeed or whether they fail (over against the supposed "lost") — are not a trademark of "the spirit." The profile of the spirit is not recognized in an abstract opposition to "the flesh," and in an essentially numinous or individualistic, "purely spiritual" relationship with God largely disconnected from outside contact. Rather one requires a carefully considered perception and appreciation of the body in order to understand the spirit and the places where it functions both in individual and communal human life.

2. The Multidimensionality of the Body

If one only considers Paul's statements about the decaying, earthly body (1 Corinthians 15) — which leaves us in a life far removed from God (2 Corinthians 5), which is controlled by sin (Romans 6), and which hopes for redemption and salvation from this present forlornness and mortality (Romans 8) — then one might easily be tempted to equate *sarx* and *soma,* flesh and body. Yet although the earthly body is made of flesh and thus shares in the frailties and endangerments of the flesh, they must be clearly distinguished. The body is not only shaped and characterized by flesh but also by a multitude of spiritual forces, and it points to a completely different set of dynamics than the flesh, which aims in a finally futile way at self-preservation.

Paul does not perceive the body merely as a "material entity," the simple bearer of "faculties" of higher value. Rather, the body is a complex organism with many parts, and it connects very different services and functions. As such, it is an area, a sphere in which God "lives" and through which God seeks to be glorified: "Or do you not know that your body is a temple of the Holy Spirit within you, which you have from God, and that you are not your own? For you were bought with a price; therefore glorify God in your body" (1 Cor. 6:19-20).

Paul presents the body even like a place of revelation, as a place where one can perceive the life and death of Jesus (2 Cor. 4:10; Gal. 6:17): "It is my eager expectation and hope that . . . Christ will be exalted publicly now as always in my body, whether by life or by death" (Phil. 1:20). In light of an understanding of the body as an organism composed of many parts, Paul provides a detailed illustration of the existence of the post-Easter, resurrected Christ and the state of his church (cf. especially 1 Cor. 12:12ff.): "For just as the body is one and has many members, and all the members of the body, though many, are one body, so it is with Christ. For in the one Spirit we were all baptized into one body — Jews or Greeks, slaves or free — and we are all made to drink of one Spirit" (1 Cor. 12:12-13). Paul repeatedly demands of the Christians to whom he writes that they understand themselves as the combined and cooperative members of the body of Christ: "Now you are the body of Christ and individually members of it" (1 Cor. 12:27; see also Rom. 12:4f.).

Paul attempts to clarify the activity of the divine Spirit and the great importance of the sacraments of baptism and holy communion in light of the "constitution" and liveliness of this many-membered body. That love which has been "poured out" through the Spirit into the hearts of believers (Rom.

5:5) unites these believers together in the body of Christ.[4] In this way, God is able through the Spirit to work upon each individual. The Spirit "allots to each one individually [his or her particular gift] just as the Spirit chooses" (1 Cor. 12:11). "But as it is, God arranged the members in the body, each one of them, as he chose" (1 Cor. 12:18). The miracle of this organic interplay of individual members in a single body is the achievement of the Spirit.[5] Yet the collective charisma and purposefully directed activity of the members of this body is also an achievement of the Spirit. Paul's stress on this interplay between Spirit and body once again emphasizes Paul's critique of efforts to establish "purely spiritual" contact with God by speaking in tongues.

Finally, the great importance of the body (also in its specific materiality) is stressed in the institution of the holy communion. That bread which is shared, and which symbolically nourishes and "builds up" the congregation is the "body of Christ." The bread that we eat is not identified as the "flesh of Christ" which must pass away. Mediated through gifts of creation — through bread and wine — the resurrected Christ enters into his members not only "in the Spirit" but also manifestly, "in the body," making those members into the carriers of his post-Easter existence.[6] This (difficult to understand) interplay between Spirit and body in the autonomy and cooperation of the body's members, and in that service of the individual members and of the entire body which extends beyond the simple self-maintenance of the organism, represents a sign of hope that points to the eschatological destiny of believers' corporeal existence.

That wonderfully enlivening interplay of the Spirit with the many-membered body is a sign that the body is not finally or completely defined by its corporeality and that it need not be identified with its corporeal frailty and finality. But above all, this wonderful "building up," even of the material, organic community of the "body of Christ," points to the power of the Spirit to create a new reality that awakens in the bodily existence shaped by the Spirit a hope for a life that extends beyond this "fleshly" finitude.[7] In Philippians,

4. On the relevance of the event and the image of the "pouring out of the Spirit," see M. Welker, *God the Spirit* (Philadelphia: Fortress Press, 1994).

5. John Polkinghorne has suggested that we recognize the personality of the Spirit in its context sensitivity: J. Polkinghorne and M. Welker, *Faith in the Living God: A Dialogue* (London: SPCK, 2001); "The Hidden Spirit and the Cosmos," in *The Work of the Spirit: Pneumatology and Pentecostalism*, ed. M. Welker (Grand Rapids and Cambridge: Eerdmans, 2006), pp. 169ff.

6. Cf. M. Welker, *What Happens in Holy Communion?* (Grand Rapids: Eerdmans, second printing 2004).

7. Cf. here J. Polkinghorne and M. Welker, eds., *The End of the World and the Ends of God:*

Paul sums this up with the hope that Christ "will change our lowly body to be like his glorious body, by the power which enables him even to subject all things to himself" (Phil. 3:21). In other texts, he sees this new creative power flowing from the creator, but primarily from the Spirit of God (cf. Rom. 5:5ff.; 8:21ff.; 1 Cor. 15:34ff.; 2 Cor. 3:18). Paul does not simply base his comments here on religious wishes or fantasies. His observations dealing with the inner constitution of the human spirit and other "mental" powers are reinforced in his eschatological views.

3. Spirit–Body–Soul–Reason

Paul closes the first of his letters to the Thessalonians with the wish that "the God of peace himself [may] sanctify you entirely; and may your spirit *(pneuma)* and soul *(psyche)* and body *(soma)* be kept sound and blameless at the coming of our Lord Jesus Christ" (1 Thess. 5:23). For a way of thinking that has become accustomed to omnipresent dualistic anthropologies (from "body and soul," "body and spirit," "mind and material," to that fashionable dichotomy of the late twentieth century: "brain and mind"), this "trichotomous sounding expression" raises a "particular problem of Pauline Anthropology."[8] Normally, New Testament exegesis attempts to "solve" this "problem" by assuring us that Paul is "simply trying to emphasize that God's salvific work touches the whole human being."[9] The claim here, that this is "a plerophoric way . . . of expressing the totality of the human being,"[10] seeks support in part by claiming that *pneuma* "in 1 Thessalonians is for Paul not a component of the human being, but is rather the expression and characteristic of God's new creative action in human beings."[11]

Yet these propositions fail to convince for a range of reasons. Not only does Paul expressly speak in 1 Thessalonians 5:23 of "your spirit," but in other letters as well he clearly distinguishes God's Spirit from the spirit of human beings: according to Romans 8:16, "it is the Spirit himself bearing witness with

---

Science and Theology on Eschatology (Harrisburg, PA: Trinity Press International, 2000); H.-J. Eckstein and M. Welker, eds., *Die Wirklichkeit der Auferstehung* (Neukirchen: Neukirchener Verlag, 2007), esp. pp. 311ff.

8. U. Schnelle, *Paulus. Leben und Denken* (Berlin: De Gruyter, 2003), p. 615.

9. Schnelle, *Paulus*, p. 615; T. Holz, *Der erste Brief an die Thessalonicher*, in *EKK XIII*, p. 265; G. Friedrich, *Der erste Brief an die Thessalonicher*, in *NTD 8*, p. 250.

10. Friedrich, *NTD 8*, p. 250.

11. Schnelle, *Paulus*, p. 615.

our spirit that we are children of God." In almost all letters we find talk of the human spirit or the spirit of particular persons (e.g., 1 Cor. 2:11; 5:5; 2 Cor. 7:13; 12:18; Philem. 1:25). The wish that the community might "be holy in body and spirit" (1 Cor. 7:34), the warnings against "defilement . . . of the spirit" (2 Cor. 7:1) and receiving "a different spirit" (2 Cor. 11:4) as well as the gift of "discerning between spirits" (1 Cor. 12:10) would all be senseless if *pneuma* were "not a component of the human being."

There are certainly statements (primarily in Philippians) that leave it unclear whether Paul — with his encouragements to "stand firm in one spirit" (Phil. 1:27; cf. 2:1) — is referring to the Holy Spirit or is only expressing the equivalent of his wish that the community strive "side by side with one mind (psyche) for the faith of the gospel" (Phil. 1:27; cf. also the statements about "praying in the spirit," 1 Cor. 14:14ff.). References to the "spirit of the world" (1 Cor. 2:12) and the warnings against a "sluggish spirit" (Rom. 11:8, following Isa. 29:10) make it unavoidably clear that one can in no way simply attribute references to *pneuma* in Paul's work only to his doctrine of God.

Nor are reservations about that "trichotomous sounding expression" in 1 Thessalonians 5:23 well grounded exegetically; on the contrary, they must be attributed to anthropological "mental blocks." This becomes apparent when we note that the same interpreters who understand Paul here to be speaking "in a plerophoric way" about the "entire human being" stress that *pneuma*,[12] or ("in the Old Testament tradition") psyche,[13] is also used by Paul to signify "the whole person." If one does not wish to distort the epistemological potential of the Pauline anthropology within a cheap, amalgamated rhetoric, then one must take Paul's differentiation between spirit, body, and psyche seriously.

From both theological as well as anthropological perspectives, the Spirit enables a co-presence and contact with those who are absent. Through his Spirit, the invisible God communicates with the human spirit and imparts to it creative impulses. According to Paul, even those who are absent can have authentic contact with others "in the spirit," despite differences in space and time. By remembering his own visits, his teaching and preaching, and through his petitions before God, but also through the letters and messages of others, Paul is present to the community "in the spirit." This presence is not merely a figment of his imagination. Paul himself can also become "spiritually" present in the community. In 1 Corinthians 5, he describes this process of spiritual communication and co-action: "For though absent in body, I am present in

12. Holz, *EKK XIII*, p. 265.
13. Schnelle, *Paulus*, p. 615.

spirit; and as if present I have already pronounced judgment in the name of the Lord Jesus. . . . When you are assembled, and my spirit is present with the power of our Lord Jesus" (1 Cor. 5:3-4). "The name" and "the power of our Lord," and certainly the Spirit of God (though not expressly mentioned in this passage) play an important connective role here in the connection of the community — even in a very general way, that is, with and without bodily co-presence. However, one certainly does not need to make reference to the Holy Spirit in order to understand the spiritual process of communication between Paul and the Corinthians.

More difficult to understand is the concept of *psyche* in Paul's work. We encounter the term only eleven times in the Pauline corpus, and it has been variously translated, either as "soul," "life," or even "person." Paul takes up the Old Testament expression *nefesh,* which can be translated as "throat, neck, desire, soul, life, person," as well as being used as a pronoun.[14]

It is worth noting that according to 1 Corinthians 2:14 the "person described by the psyche" "is unable to perceive the work of the spirit."[15] The expression, *psyche,* encompasses an individual, earthly life — an earthly, bodily, and spiritual individuality that, while created by God, has not (yet) been filled by God's Spirit. Paul sees the "first Adam" as a "living psyche" and thus as a transitory creature, while Jesus Christ as the "last Adam" is a "life-giving Spirit" (cf. 1 Cor. 15:45). Paul shares not only his preaching with the Thessalonians but also his own bodily-spiritual "psyche," for they have become dear to him (1 Thess. 2:8). He swears to the Corinthians before God upon his own psyche and assures them of his desire to exhaust himself for their psyches (2 Cor. 1:23 and 12:15) — though in these two cases the expression should probably be translated more clearly as "life" (so too in Phil. 2:30 and Rom. 2:9; 11:3).

Furthermore, as for the psyche, only hesitantly would one use the expression "whole" human being — especially if one does not want to overlook the spiritual and theological dimensions. According to Romans 13:1, "each psyche [should] be subject to the governing authorities; for . . . those authorities . . . have been instituted by God." Paul could hardly have said: each person should serve the state "with all your heart and with all the powers of your spirit." In contrast to that assumed set of associations so common in modern Euro-American contexts, Paul's usage of psyche in the sense of "soul, person, and life" is very clearly understood in a secular way. On the other hand, rationality

---

14. H. W. Wolff, *Anthropologie des Alten Testaments,* 5th ed. (München: Kaiser, 1990), pp. 25ff.

15. Schnelle, *Paulus,* p. 615.

and reason *(nous)* is closely connected with prayer and doxology (1 Corinthians 14; see above, part 1). In Romans, the "law of sin," under which the fleshly members of the body stand, is thoroughly opposed by the "law of my mind," which is determined by the spirit (Rom. 7:23ff.). Paul can even speak of God's *nous* (Rom. 11:34) and of a human *nous* that can be renewed by discerning the will of God (Rom. 12:2). At this point, we have now dealt with all the most important instances of this term in Paul's letters. However, before any undue religious-philosophical aspirations arise, it should be noted that Paul also uses a contextually relative *nous* (Rom. 14:5) and considers the possibility that God surrenders some to a "debased *nous*" (Rom. 1:28). How little we should desire prayer, doxology, and the recognition of God's will without rational consistency, and how great should be our wariness of a rational consistency that leads us astray.

4. Heart and Conscience as Ciphers for Areas of Future Anthropological Research

Although the psyche, according to Paul, signifies the earthly, corporeal-mental unity of a person, it is not a soteriological entity. Here Paul is in agreement with the rest of the biblical traditions (except for Tobit), in claiming that "the soul" in and of itself does not receive immortality and other eschatological privileges. The activity of God's Spirit does not penetrate directly into the psyche. Rather its effects flow via the heart in the human body and then indirectly upon the soul. The heart is an exceptionally important entity in Paul's anthropology. As in the Old Testament (861 references for *leb* or *lebab*), it connects "vegetative, emotional, noetic and voluntary functions."[16] If psyche signifies the earthly, corporeal-mental unity of the human person, then the heart, *kardia,* stands for the emotional-voluntary depths. It is via the heart that the divine Spirit reaches the human body and its mental capacities (2 Cor. 1:22; 3:3; Gal. 4:6; Rom. 3:29; 5:5). Yes, God himself can "shine" in the hearts of human beings (2 Cor. 4:6). And it is in the heart that the divine Word arouses faith (Rom. 10:8ff.).

As with the spirit, the heart can also be directed to those who are absent and make them imaginatively present, even in longing: "we were . . . separated

---

16. Bernd Janowski has presented an impressive examination of these functions and their interdependencies: B. Janowski, *Konfliktgespräche mit Gott. Eine Anthropologie der Psalmen,* 2nd ed. (Neukirchen: Neukirchener Verlag, 2006), pp. 166-70.

from you — in person, not in heart — we longed with great eagerness to see you" (1 Thess. 2:17). To those who are absent, the heart can "give room" within a person (2 Cor. 3:2; 6:11; Rom. 7:2f.). However, it is so bound to the body and the "inner" person, that one cannot say: my heart is present with you! Yet it is also the place of hidden intentions and thoughts that can only be revealed with the help of the spirit (1 Cor. 14:25), including also God's Spirit at the eschatological judgment (1 Cor. 4:5; Rom. 8:27). The heart gathers together emotional and moral energies, it bestows "firmness" of character, receives comfort and direction (1 Thess. 3:13; 1 Cor. 7:37; 2 Thess. 2:17; 3:5); it is the location of zeal, firm resolution, and spiritual obedience (Rom. 6:17; 8:16; 9:7). Yet as a human capacity, it can also be foolish, serving the desires of the flesh, fighting against repentance and, in "the simple-minded," allowing itself to be deceived (Rom. 1:21; 1:24; 2:5; 16:18).

Despite all its possibilities for firmness and energy, as an organ bound to an earthly body the heart is still troubled by the melancholy of finitude: "but we ourselves, who have the first fruits of the Spirit, groan inwardly while we wait for adoption as sons [of God], the redemption of our bodies. . . . Likewise the Spirit helps us in our weakness; for we do not know how to pray as we ought, but the Spirit himself intercedes for us with sighs too deep for words. And God, who searches the heart, knows what is the mind of the Spirit, because the Spirit intercedes for the saints according to the will of God" (Rom. 8:23, 26-27).

The revelatory power of the Spirit, which is aimed at recognizing both the divine and the truth, also manifests itself in the human conscience (*syneidesis*). We are dealing here with a dynamic, restless, and sensitive "power of self-judgment,"[17] a consciousness of norms, which also questions itself in light of its fellow human beings and their needs, in which a person's "conflicting thoughts will accuse or perhaps excuse them" (Rom. 2:15). Those persons seized and filled by the Spirit of God, who develop a differentiated capacity for judgment, can on the one hand "commend [them]selves to the conscience of everyone" through the connection of subtle empathy and a steadfastness of their own convictions (2 Cor. 4:2). On the other hand, they are called upon to deal tactfully with others, especially those who cannot mediate the freedom of faith and their tradition-based normative consciousness in their "weak conscience" (cf. Romans 14).[18] In one's conscience, we have a concentration within

---

17. Schnelle, *Paulus,* pp. 606-9; H.-J. Eckstein, *Syneidesis bei Paulus, WUNT 2.10* (Tübingen: Mohr Siebeck, 1983), pp. 242f.

18. On the corresponding processes of moral communication, see M. Welker, *Kirche ohne Kurs?* (Neukirchen: Neukirchener Verlag, 1987), pp. 55-62.

the individual of the cognitive and normative processes of mediation between multipartite social and moral complexity and the search for illumination and cognitive coherence. Paul envisions this balancing between inspirited faith and disciplining reason with regard to the flesh-centered body and the heart-centered human spirit. The human spirit is to be connected with and filled by the Spirit of Christ, and is to be clarified by the *nous,* by reason, a twofold edification that should not become trapped by an anthropological dualism.

Emergence, the Quest for Unity, and God: Toward a Constructive Christian Theology of the Person

Philip Clayton

1. Introduction

Flesh, Body, Mind, Soul, and Spirit — a great catalog of the components of human existence as they have been developed in various forms in the complex history of Christian reflection on the nature of personhood. To define each of these terms and to trace its presence (or absence) in the Hebrew Bible, New Testament, and the subsequent history of Christian thought would require volumes.

Mercifully the author (and the reader) can be spared that laborious task, insofar as the present book focuses primarily on the problem of the unity of these terms. But again, the task quickly multiplies beyond all reckoning, for has there not been an immense number of attempts to specify the unity of these five components? Once again, however, we can greatly limit the horizon. Each attempt to specify the unity of the human person, I suggest, involves an explicit or implicit decision to put one sort of criterion first. The primary criterion might be scriptural exegesis, or faithfulness to the classical creeds, or adherence to a particular school of theology or philosophy, or usefulness for a specific (social or political or ecclesiological) purpose, or, finally, the ability to account for a particular kind of experience or set of

---

I express my gratitude to all members of the four-year research project that produced this book, and especially to the convener and visionary behind the endeavor, Michael Welker. I am also grateful to Steven Knapp of George Washington University for numerous conversations and for his very close reading of the penultimate draft.

data about human experience (anything from physics to philosophy, from mysticism to Marxism).

In the present chapter I approach the question of the unity of the human person from the standpoint of biological evolution, or, to be more precise, from the standpoint of an emergentist interpretation of biological and cultural evolution. I then work to identify the overlap set between contemporary emergence theory and the Christian theological tradition, which means: the set of beliefs about human beings that are compatible with both emergence and Christianity. (A host of other crucial questions beckon, including "Why Christianity?," "Why think Christian theology is true?," and "Why not reinterpret the theological tradition from the standpoint of Christian humanism, Christian Marxism, Christian post-structuralism, or another alternative?" Although these questions deserve attention, I do not attempt answers here.) For those who believe, as I do, that both evolutionary emergence and the Christian theological tradition have something important to say about the nature of human nature, it may be interesting to see what sort of anthropology arises as a result of the intersection of the two.

2. The Emergence of Persons and Spirit beyond Emergence

I assume, all other things being equal (and often they aren't), that an empirically testable explanation is preferable to one that isn't. The most rigorous empirical tests are scientific tests. What makes them rigorous are features such as replicability, intersubjective criticizability, precise quantitative predictions of outcomes, and the formulation and testing of hypotheses about laws-like relations between events. When one designs such tests, one presupposes methodological naturalism, that is, that the world is a closed causal system and that all causes are natural causes. As long as one wishes to use the data resulting from science as guidelines for one's anthropology, one must also accept the framework necessary to produce them. Hence I accept methodological naturalism.

Next, I assume the importance of a bottom-up approach (theology "from below") until it becomes impossible to proceed any further in this fashion. In part this follows from the commitment to allow well-attested empirical results to serve as constraints on theology. But mostly it reflects my desire to write theology not for insiders but for those outside the theological orbit who want to know what a reflective, thoughtful Christian account of the world looks like when it maximizes its contact with contemporary science and philosophy. That

Christian theology cannot be reduced to science and philosophy while still remaining theology should go without saying.

A certain metaphysical minimalism turns out to be a corollary of these two assumptions. One who proceeds in this way is inclined to defer metaphysical or *a priori* pronouncements on the nature of human nature until the scientific constraints are clear, lest one close oneself off from continuing openness to new empirical data and results.[1] Clearly, this approach will affect one's approach to the question of human personhood; it will incline one away from mind-body dualism, for example. If it turned out that Christian theology necessitated a Platonic or Cartesian dualism, Christians would find themselves rather painfully at odds with their colleagues in the sciences. I am not convinced that Christians must be dualists in this sense.

For most of its history, the Christian theological tradition has been heavily metaphysical, and in these pages I do not seek to rid it of all metaphysical remnants. (There are, of course, highly regarded theologians who do.) I further assume that, when one wishes to debate metaphysical questions, one is required to shift to a rather different conceptual and rhetorical framework from that of the natural sciences, viz. a framework that is appropriate to questions of this nature. One can pretend to reduce or explain away metaphysical questions based on an appeal to the authority of science, but one cannot answer them there. Thus, when one pursues theological questions of this type, they must be allowed to downwardly supplement, though not to negate, genuine scientific conclusions. (Generally it's possible to distinguish genuine science from ideology posturing as science. The latter — say, Dawkins's allegedly science-based claims about religion — do not have this same inviolate status.) Finally, I assume that the power of theological responses is increased, not decreased, by in-depth work in the sciences — even when the science, and the associated ways of thinking, challenge or undercut long-held theological conclusions, ways of proceeding, and styles of argument.

3. The Emergence of Persons

Given these assumptions, an adequate theory of persons must begin with and follow the core scientific narrative, which follows the course of cosmic evolution and, within it, biological evolution. I argue that emergent complexity

---

1. In more detail, I assume the importance of descriptive metaphysics but, against Strawson (and Kant), also the possibility of going beyond merely descriptive metaphysics.

offers a meta-framework that helps to link the various scientific disciplines that contribute to this narrative and to summarize the conclusions from diverse disciplines. The concrete details of cases of emergent complexity prior to *Homo sapiens* set the theoretical context for, and are thus indispensable for discussions of, the emergence of personhood in our species. The features of emergent complexity, or emergence for short, differ widely across the organizational stages manifested in natural history, yet not to such an extent that all comparisons are rendered impossible.

The emergence of human personhood shows differences from, but also similarities to, earlier instances of emergence. If on the one hand there were no differences between the different levels of emergent phenomena but all worked in the same way as the standard physics examples (the emergence of the "classical" world from quantum physics, the emergence of superconductivity, the emergence of the quantum Hall effect in solid state physics, the emergence of chemical properties from atomic structure), then nature would manifest at most "weak" emergence. In weak emergence, in contrast to strong emergence, no distinct forms of causation and no new agents are introduced. For weak emergentists, human mental states manifest no causal efficacy of their own but are merely the way that humans "feel" or "experience" the microphysical and neurological causal sequences that are actually doing all the work, including the work of creating those very feelings and experiences!

If on the other hand there were no similarities, no pattern of emergence at all across natural history, then endorsing the emergence of mental qualities would amount to a de facto dualism, for in this case the mental would be the first and only case of an emergent property.[2] In fact, however, the evidence seems to suggest that natural history does include instances of strong emergence prior to mind. Nobel laureate Robert Laughlin cites a variety of examples from physics,[3] and George Ellis presents convincing evidence of emergent dynamics across the levels of evolution.[4] Stuart Kauffman and I have shown that systems on which natural selection can operate are "strongly" or ontologically emergent from physics.[5] Biological systems meet this condition, we

2. See W. Hasker, *The Emergent Self* (Ithaca, NY: Cornell University Press, 1999).

3. R. Laughlin, *A Different Universe: Reinventing Physics from the Bottom Down* (New York: Basic Books, 2005).

4. See e.g. G. Ellis, "On the Nature of Emergent Reality," in *The Re-emergence of Emergence: The Emergentist Hypothesis from Science to Religion,* ed. P. Clayton and P. Davies (Oxford: Oxford University Press, 2006).

5. S. Kauffman and P. Clayton, "On Emergence, Agency, and Organization," *Philosophy and Biology* 21 (2006): 501-21.

argued, if they manifest five features: autocatalytic reproduction, work cycles, boundaries for reproducing individuals, self-propagating work and constraint construction, and choice and action that have evolved to respond to (e.g.) food or poison. Terrence Deacon's groundbreaking work on the "three orders of emergence," which analyzes the irreducible differences between thermo-dynamic, morphodynamic, and teleodynamic systems, helps to identify and explain different types of emergent dynamics in the natural world.[6] As distinct as these three orders of emergence may be, it is arbitrary (*pace* Deacon) to rule out other equally fundamental orders at later stages of natural history. Personhood, I suggest, is one of these.

By their very nature, natural scientific studies of human personhood work to establish maximum continuity with earlier stages of evolutionary history; they seek to explain structures, functions, and behaviors in *Homo sapiens* by establishing parallels with other animals, especially the great apes. I endorse such efforts. Yet the history of emergent systems also leads one to expect dis-continuities, to acknowledge that there are distinctive new properties in hu-mans, and to draw on those disciplines that can explain the theoretically rele-vant features of this new level of emergent complexity. Consider the distinctive features of the human brain. This organ, with its 10^{11} neurons and roughly 10^{14} neural connections, is the most complicated natural system we have yet discovered in the universe. Its evolutionary function is to store and process information, which allows the organism to make more complex and more adaptive responses to its environment. It's no surprise that the rapid evolution of brains in *Homo sapiens* has produced representational ("internal") states of unprecedented complexity. For example, the comparatively simple language-processing capabilities observed in the other great apes have been succeeded in our species by immensely complex language use. As a result of biological and cultural co-evolution, human beings are now able to construct a vast array of diverse symbolic and cultural worlds, engaging in conscious reflection that spans time and distance virtually without limit.

There is no scientific basis to conclude that any of the human capacities could be produced or continue to function without the underlying biologi-cal and neurological systems that produced them. Recent imaging techniques have allowed us to correlate neurophysiological changes with changes in "first-personal" experience to an increasingly high degree of precision, and

6. T. Deacon, "The Hierarchic Logic of Emergence: Untangling the Interdependence of Evolution and Self Organization," in *Evolution and Learning: The Baldwin Effect Reconsidered,* ed. Bruce H. Weber and David J. Depew (Cambridge, MA: MIT Press, 2003), pp. 273-308.

there is every reason to think that our knowledge of the neural correlates of consciousness will increase immensely over the coming decades. As neuroscientific knowledge increases and psychotropic drug therapies are more widely used in medicine, these changes will further revolutionize humanity's understanding of the mind-body relationship. There is no reason, I suggest, that theology must take on the role of opponent to evolutionary biology or neurology.

Nonetheless, nothing in the neural correlates of consciousness supports the reduction of mental states to their physiological substrates, much less to fundamental physics. Brian Cantwell Smith beautifully summarizes the problem with the reductive approach:

> You and I do not exist in [the explanations of physics] — qua people. We may be material, divine, social, embodied, whatever — but we don't figure as people in any physicist's equation. What we are — or rather what our lives are, in this picture — is a group of roughly aligned not-terribly-well-delineated very slightly wiggling four-dimensional worms or noodles: massively longer temporally than spatially. We care tremendously about these noodles. But physics does not: it does nothing to identify them, either as personal, or as unitary, or as distinct from the boundless number of other worms that could be inscribed on the physical plenum. . . .[7]

Thus, assuming that the framework of emergent complexity continues to be supported by scientific results, we should view the first-personal world of the human mental life as another instance of natural emergence — though perhaps the most astonishing instance of all.

4. Emergence and God

But is "natural emergence" all there is? Is reality limited to objects that are composed out of physical mass and are moved by the four fundamental forces described by contemporary physics? Are religious affects such as the longing for immortality or the quest for universal altruism merely "spandrels," pleiotropic side-effects of the complicated neurological structure of our brains? Or is there something in persons that has its source and orientation beyond the framework of the empirical world?

Neither the practice of science nor its results rule out a positive answer to

7. B. Cantwell Smith, *God, approximately,* unpublished paper, p. 3.

the final question. It remains possible that humans are "upwardly open" to a transcendent dimension, which includes something like transcendent mind.[8] People will disagree in good conscience about whether adequate reasons exist for postulating any transcendent reality and about how great (if any) are the negative side-effects of taking such language seriously. (Those on the other side of the aisle from the present author may wish to read the remainder of this chapter as an extended thought-experiment, one that spells out the logic of a position they don't actually believe is true.)

If one introduces the possibility of dimensions of reality beyond the empirical, the discussion is transformed. For now one countenances a type of explanation that is not tied to a downward dependence on lower-level physical systems. One has raised the possibility of a "Before" and an "After"; a nonphysical, hence purely spiritual being or beings; a creative role for that being, at least at the beginning of the cosmic order as a whole; and some correlations between its agency and ours. In short, one has raised the possibility of irreducibly metaphysical explanations.

The theism that I explore in what follows represents one of these metaphysical hypotheses, a possible framework within which to interpret human experience and knowledge taken as a whole. It assumes that the ground or source of the empirical world is not-less-than-personal, eternal, and somehow involved in the origin and perhaps also the subsequent development of the universe as a whole. These theistic assumptions are not incompatible, I suggest, with the emergence picture, just as, more generally, metaphysical explanations of the physical world do not need to be incompatible with the specific laws and regularities described by physics.

5. Anthropology on the Assumption of God

It cannot be our task here to demonstrate the existence of a divine being on the basis of empirical premises. Rather, I want to ask: If both the existence of emergent complexity and belief in God are presupposed, what picture of human nature results?

The scientific perspectives paint a picture of persons as complex bio-

---

8. A minimalist way to do this is to imagine emergent levels that go beyond the level of individual minds, as Samuel Alexander did in his theory of deity as emerging out of the sum total of minds. See Alexander, *Space, Time, and Deity,* 2 vols. (London: Macmillan, 1920); analysis in Clayton, *Mind and Emergence* (Oxford: Oxford University Press, 2004), chapter 1.

Emergence, the Quest for Unity, and God

physical-psycho-social units. We exist only through a continuing "downward dependence" on physical and chemical processes. Human behavior is not fully explained by physics or chemistry or biology — after all, the core message of emergence is that each of these levels in the hierarchy brings new explanatory resources — but it is composed out of and constrained by them. The fact that no emergent level of phenomena, such as consciousness, may contradict the previous levels (say, physics) means that ongoing scientific results continue to be deeply significant for a Christian theology of the person. This is no idle standard. It entails that theological anthropologies not just be open "in principle" to new empirical results, but that they continue to evolve along with the newest scientific data on human physiology, emotion, cognition, and sociality.

This requirement of continuing responsiveness gives us another reason to resist conceiving human beings as mental substances. As complex as natural and social scientific explanations may become, and as complex as the types of causes may be, the principle of downward dependence is in tension with the traditional language of souls and spirits. Theological anthropology, if based on the assumptions outlined above, must accept that the complex properties of and causal relations between persons are organized out of — and to that extent explainable in terms of — the matter and energy of the one natural world. "Persons" — a term currently applied, in fact though not as a matter of principle, only to members of the species *Homo sapiens* — are organisms that possess some collection of mental properties and some (vaguely defined) set of capacities to respond in certain ways in linguistic, social, and cultural situations. We speak of this position as "property emergence," since it does not appeal, as classical philosophy did, to the notion of an underlying substance as the carrier of those properties. True, the concept of "person" cannot be defined or explained at any level lower than the theoretical structure of the social sciences. But nothing that arises at this point removes the ongoing importance of our being natural entities.

Doing theology "from below," as I urged earlier, now suggests that the theological dimension be first introduced on analogy to the way in which the psychological dimension is introduced. Experts argue about exactly when the phenomena first arose that require mental or psychological explanations.[9] Most probably these phenomena were already present when primates began to exhibit a theory of other minds, that is, when they began to use internal representations of the world as another animal would see it to guide their ac-

---

9. For present purposes, psychology is the sum total of psychological predicates, together with the correlations between them and the methods used to describe them.

tions. From that point on we can trace clear patterns of increasing complexity in these representations, greater communal influence on linguistic behaviors (shared language production and elaboration), and decreasing control of the immediate environment over the mental life. Eventually symbolic language became so central for human existence that the biological anthropologist Terrence Deacon has rightly dubbed us "the symbolic species."[10]

Biology continues to hold culture on a leash. Where culture clashes with fundamental biological drives, generally only a minority of the species can oblige, whereas the majority fails to follow (celibacy comes to mind, but so too does socialism). Should a cultural development render one of the two human sexes sterile — say, through air and water pollution, or by means of a new chemical or nanotechnology released into the environment — our species will come to an end in a single generation.

Yet biology's leash on culture is a long one, I suggest — far longer than most evolutionary psychologists seem ready to acknowledge. As Peter Berger writes, "Man, biologically denied the ordering mechanisms with which other animals are endowed, is compelled to impose his own order on experience. Man's sociality presupposes the collective character of this ordering of reality."[11] In the case of most contemporary people in the developed world, our socially and culturally constructed worlds are our primary reality. One has only to travel across cultural boundaries to realize how vastly different are the types of cultural software that can be "run" on the basic hardware of a *Homo sapiens* body and brain. (I write these words in Vishakhapatnam, India, where even the smallest daily interaction brings home the vast cultural differences.)

As biologists of the ilk of Richard Dawkins will claim that biology basically has all the explanatory resources that one needs to explain all psychological phenomena (on the assumption that memes more or less follow the evolutionary logic of genes), so also many nonreligious persons claim that psychology and cultural studies offer all the explanatory resources one needs to explain human religious phenomena. I may not be able to convince them that they're wrong, but I can at least make clear the kinds of claims that Christian theologians have traditionally made. They hold that, as biology is not sufficient to explain the complexities of our cultural existence but must give way to social scientific explanations (psychology, sociology, cultural anthropology, etc.), so also the social sciences are not in the end sufficient to explain all that humans are; a more transcendent dimension of reality must be included as

---

10. See T. Deacon, *The Symbolic Species* (New York: W. W. Norton, 1997).

11. Peter L. Berger, *The Sacred Canopy* (Garden City, NY: Doubleday, 1967), p. 19.

well. Put differently: religious faith is not completely explained by its inner-worldly functions; it is also a response to a Source that precedes the process of cosmic evolution studied by the sciences.

These first two steps of the argument in this section may seem to stand in tension with each other, since the first reflects scientifically based conclusions, the second theological affirmations. I argued in the previous section, however, that there is nothing inherently contradictory about affirming both. Indeed, I'd now like to show that thinking these two dimensions together gives rise to a rather intriguing picture of human personhood, one that may be both attractive and useful.

First, however, the claim needs to be clear: introducing the idea of God can and must have some influence on one's final conclusions about the emergent process. In particular, it allows one to say some additional things about what it is that emerges. Recall that earlier we were not able to go beyond the notion of "property emergence," since the framework of emergent complexity by itself does not allow one to speak of persons as anything more than a set of properties and functions resulting from a particular organization of matter-energy. But anthropology in the context of theism is pushed to take one further step. If there is indeed a divine spiritual reality who is also an active agent, then the notion of spiritual agency is an inherent part of this conception. Each of the three Abrahamic traditions affirms that humans are created by God and are in some sense "made in the image of God" (imago Dei). Thus for these traditions, bearing the image of God contributes in some way to a complete account of human personhood. This affirmation does not mean that the evolutionary account of emergence is false but only that it cannot be the full story.

Thus belief in God and in human persons as imago Dei requires one to supplement the naturalistic theory of the self with some notion of spiritual agency. In addition to the other things that we are, we are agents in some way analogous to the divine agent. Biology and neurophysiology supply content for the term "body," and the social sciences provide content for what the Greeks called psyche or "soul" (though we are more comfortable today using concepts such as "character," "self," or "behavioral dispositions"). But theology cannot proceed without adding to corporeal agency and psychological agency some notion of what a spirit-like agency would involve. As long as theology remains theistic, as long as it continues to advocate the existence of a being whose existence is not dependent on having a body — and, one hastens to add, there are Jewish and Christian theologians who are not theists in this sense — then it must espouse an anthropology that includes the notion of "spirit."

As soon as one formulates that last sentence, however, a dense thicket of difficult and perplexing questions springs up and blocks our path forward. What is this "spirit"? Is it a new and different kind of "thing" in the world, a *res cogitans* to stand alongside *res extensa*? If so, how will such a "thing" interact with physical things? If it is not a thing, what kind of property is it? How far back in evolutionary time before *Homo sapiens,* if at all, can one find hints of the existence of this thing or property?

I must acknowledge that most of the theological tradition was completely comfortable in speaking of spirits as substances, entities existing in their own right. I would prefer to emphasize a different stream of the tradition, which stressed the continuing dependence of all existing things on their Creator (cf. *creatio continua*). This theological tradition resisted the idea of an *ousia* or *substantia* that enjoys independent existence. Werner Beierwaltes, among others, has explored its sources in Neoplatonism and its subsequent influence on the history of theology and on German Idealism.[12] This tradition supported a more radical understanding of created reality as continually participating in that divine reality "in whom we live and move and have our being" (Acts 17:29). Taken in this sense, "spirit" designates finite reality as viewed from the perspective of its existence "in, with, and through" its divine ground.

Following W. Pannenberg, however, I also wish to understand this participation which is spirit in a radically temporalized sense. (It can also be understood in a trinitarian sense, as I will show.) Spirit is not an object we already are or an intrinsically immortal being we've always been. Instead, it is a calling toward a type of existence, and thus a type of being, which we hope someday to enjoy. At present we experience at best a foretaste of that mode of existence. There are in our experience, in our thought, and occasionally in our actions towards others, hints of what it would mean to exist with the property of spirit. Paul writes at one point, "Behold, I show you a mystery; We shall not all sleep, but we shall all be changed" (1 Cor. 15:51, KJV). Spirit, on this view, is not a type of thing or substance, nor even a set of properties that fully characterize our existence here and now. It is (as long as it's not sheer delusion) the first hint of a mode of existence belonging to a deeper dimension of reality, a "sense sublime of something far more deeply interfused," as Wordsworth writes. It is life in and with and through God, life lived in conformity to the nature of God. For this reason, "spirit" belongs more to the not-yet than to the already of anthropology. But, even though it exists only in the guise of hope rather than as present possession, its role as a characterizing feature of human

---

12. See W. Beierwaltes, *Platonismus und Idealismus* (Frankfurt: Klostermann, 1972); and Clayton, *Das Gottesproblem* (Paderborn: F. Schöningh Verlag, 1996), esp. chapter 3.

existence is no less essential. As Paul writes (changing his text to the plural form), "Now we see but a poor reflection as in a mirror; then we shall see face to face. Now we know in part; then we shall know fully, even as we are fully known" (1 Cor. 13:12, NIV).

Of course, there are both advantages and dangers in the idea of agents who are, even to the smallest extent, ontologically more than the set of physical and psychological properties manifested in their behavior. To avoid the dangers inherent in this move, theologians will need to listen much more carefully to the scientific data than they are wont to do. To put the point provocatively: as the entire cultural world remains tethered to a biological leash, so too the success of a religion remains tethered in certain ways to a cultural leash. Neither leash is infinitely long. Should a given religious tradition cease to be credible to contemporary persons, should it no longer be able to make their existence and the cosmos they live in seem meaningful to them, should it (for example) prove to be inconsistent with natural science in an age when core scientific assumptions have become the arbiters for truth, then that religious tradition will cease to have believers — whether it is ultimately true or not.[13]

Conversely, and perhaps more disturbing to some scientific readers, the approach advocated here would require scientists to concede the possibility that a metaphysical framework, in this case a theistic one, can supply further content. In E. O. Wilson's famous attempt at a "consilience" between science and religion, the precondition is that scholars in the humanities grant at the outset that all the knowledge will come from the side of science; they get to add only the coloring, the aesthetics, and the moral evaluations about (what they believe to be) the "good" and "bad" features of this reality.[14] That there might be metaphysical truths that are known through metaphysical reflection, even if they cannot be inconsistent with science — this is the real bone of contention.

---

13. W. Pannenberg emphasized this point brilliantly in a number of passages on the role of meaning or meaningfulness *(Sinn* or *Sinnhaftigkeit)* in religion, e.g., in "Meaning, Religion and the Question of God," in *Knowing Religiously,* ed. L. S. Rouner (Notre Dame: University of Notre Dame Press, 1985), p. 162; "Wahrheit, Gewissheit und Glaube," in *Grundfragen systematischer Theologie,* vol. 2 (Göttingen: Vandenhoeck & Ruprecht, 1980), pp. 226-64; and *Wissenschaftstheorie und Theologie* (Frankfurt am Main: Suhrkamp, 1973). The passionate rejection of science by conservative religious groups worldwide might seem to represent counterevidence to my claims about the importance of science. But one should be highly skeptical that religions that define themselves in opposition to science will be successful on timescales measured in hundreds of years.

14. See E. O. Wilson, *Consilience: The Unity of Knowledge* (New York: Knopf, 1998).

Probably even more controversial is the idea that God's self-revelation in the process of history might be one relevant source in the quest to understand the nature of human nature. It's to that possibility that I now turn.

6. Distinctives of a Christian Anthropology

In the standard science-religion discussions, considering the possibility of the existence of God seems to be just about as far as one is supposed to go. I'd like now to break that convention and consider more specifically Christian contributions to anthropology. I do not claim that any of what follows can be derived from science or philosophy alone; hence this is not an apologetic argument. But I do claim that these possibilities do not conflict either with any specific scientific results or with the assumptions and methods that are presupposed in doing empirical science today.

As we saw above, emergent evolution begins with an understanding of human beings as bio-cultural agents in the context of evolutionary history. Our existence as bio-cultural agents may give us some initial understanding of the nature of God as agent. Such a perspective is supplemented, however, when one affirms that God is the ground and destiny of all things.

A Christian anthropology thus has three stages: (1) understanding human agency through all the forms of empirical (biological and cultural) study that bear on it; (2) deriving what can be known of the divine agent through our own experience of agency; and (3) supplementing both sets of results by means of specifically Christian affirmations about human nature. By the end, theologians have added an ethical (or, more generally, a normative) dimension that natural science by itself cannot supply. Natural science tells us who we now are and how we have come to be this way. Theology, by viewing humanity from the standpoint of a perfect creator, holds out a standard for what we should be, as creatures made in the image of God.

For Christians, this model is inherently Christological; it involves the imperative (and the disposition) to emulate the one who was fully human insofar as he was fully related to God.[15] The teachings of Jesus and the life of Jesus offer the most important dataset for specifying this Christological ideal.

15. Admittedly, not all theologians have held that Jesus' full humanity was the result of his full relation to God; the language of the creeds, for example, does not require one to say this. But nor does the fusing of Christology and anthropology stand in opposition to the creeds, and it remains (to my mind) one of the enduring insights from Karl Barth.

As a result, primacy is given in Christian anthropology to recounting and analyzing highly specific narratives of Jesus' teaching and action, and then adding, "The ideal for human thought and action is something like this." As interested as theologians have been in utilizing philosophical frameworks of one type or another to systematize and interpret the life of Jesus, all such attempts are subject to a sort of hermeneutic of suspicion. Because their source lies (or, I am arguing, should lie) in narratives of Jesus' life and teaching, the door is always open for one to respond to a claim in systematic theology with "yes, but consider again what Jesus did when . . ." or "but what then did it mean that he taught that . . . ?"

No framework better summarizes the Christological narrative that underlies theological anthropology than Philippians 2:5-11. This early Christian hymn contains two moments: a kenosis or self-emptying, and an exalting:

> Your attitude should be the same as that of Christ Jesus:
> Who, being in very nature [form: μορφή] God,
> did not consider equality with God something to be grasped,
> but made himself nothing [emptied himself: εκενωσεν; cf. κενωσις],
> taking the very nature [from μορφην] of a servant,
> being made in human likeness.
> And being found in appearance as a man,
> he humbled himself
> and became obedient to death —
> even death on a cross. (Phil. 2:5-8, NIV)

The idea of a preexistent "equality with God" is not generally applied to other human beings. But the call to become like a servant (doulos) does echo throughout the Gospels, lying perhaps closer to the heart of Jesuanic ethics than any single teaching save the twofold love commandment (Luke 10:27). The assumption is that the human will does not naturally incline toward placing the other above oneself. Indeed, self-affirmation over against others and over against God represents a fairly accurate snapshot of that other famous anthropological assumption: sin or fallenness. In Pauline theology (and later, in Reformed theology), the steps of repentance, salvation, reconciliation with God, and gradual sanctification of "the new person" through the Spirit of Christ (2 Cor. 5:17) are anthropologically central. But the Christological ideal of the Synoptic Gospels is rather simpler. Its essence is captured in that single seven-word prayer in the Garden of Gethsemane, "not my will, but thine be done" (Luke 22:42). To be "in Christ" — Paul's favorite description of the mode of Christian existence[16] — means to subordinate one's own will to the will of the divine, echoing Jesus' phrase, "may your will be done" (Matt. 26:42; cf. Matt. 6:10).

Then follows the second "moment":

Therefore God exalted him to the highest place
and gave him the name that is above every name,
that at the name of Jesus every knee should bow,
in heaven and on earth and under the earth,
and every tongue confess that Jesus Christ is Lord,
to the glory of God the Father. (Phil. 2:9-11, NIV)

Christian anthropology, likewise, has an irreducibly future moment: the hope of the resurrection. The need for hope is deeply ingrained in the human psyche, as is attested by studies in archaeology, psychology, and literature. Science can no more prove that this ever-related hope is vacuous and illusory than it can demonstrate that its longings will one day be fulfilled. Thus hope and faith are Siamese twins, bound at the very center of their being.

There is another, rather less pleasant feature of traditional Christian anthropology, however, which is often derived from this passage. The triumphalism of the last three verses has too often given rise to affirmations that only Christians have any ground for hope. In its crassest form, it's the claim that "we Christians are going to heaven, and the rest of you are going to hell." The exclusivism and intolerance, even misanthropy and hatred, that often lie behind affirmations like this (or that are produced by them) in today's world are only too well known.

To counterbalance these sorts of attitudes, which some critics of Christianity have argued are inherent in Christian theology, it may be helpful to adopt a simple rule. Think of it as an ethical principle that determines when and by whom the language of exaltation may be used, and perhaps even for whom it is true. Here, too, the move is Christological. Jesus insisted that "the kingdom of God" did not belong to the righteous, to the Pharisees and those who "have their reward" in this world. So I suggest: let the language of exaltation belong only to those who are genuinely oppressed and downtrodden. For the "have's," those whom fate has put in places of wealth and privilege, let the anthropological focus be on the opening five verses and their call to self-emptying. In a play on Pablo

---

16. "If anyone is in Christ, he is a new creation; the old has gone; the new has come" (2 Cor. 5:17, NIV). The phrase "in Christ" (en Christo) is used some ninety times in the New Testament epistles.

Friere's "pedagogy of the oppressed," perhaps we could call this "an anthropology of the oppressed." Here, too, we would be faithful to the Jesus of the Gospels, who directed his message preferentially to the poor, the unclean, the "sinners." One thinks also of one of the first interpretations of the significance of his birth, given (according to Luke) by a young uneducated woman, pregnant out of wedlock:

He has brought down rulers from their thrones
but has lifted up the humble.
He has filled the hungry with good things
but has sent the rich away empty. (Luke 1:52-53, NIV)

7. A Multifaceted Unity

The end brings us back to the beginning: the question of the complex unity of the human person in theological perspective. To do justice to the dialectic of the already and the not-yet that flows through most of systematic theology, I stress that every occurrence of the word "unity" in what follows should be read simultaneously as unity (i.e., as an existing reality) and as unification or the process of unifying (that is, as a hoped-for but still-future resolution, as ethical aspiration, as theological or eschatological goal). In this sense, one can speak of the unity of the human person on a variety of different levels and in a variety of different forms. (That nontheological disciplines offer additional forms of personal unity will be amply clear from the other chapters.) The levels, moreover, are deeply interrelated:

- the empirical unity of the actually existing person in his or her actions as an agent in the world. This is not itself a theological notion but is presupposed in the tradition.
- the unity of the person's psyche or "soul" over time. As we have seen, there are other ways to construe this unity for those of us who cannot affirm a substantial soul, including functional and ascriptional unity.
- the unity of body and "soul." This is the spiritual unity of the person. Following W. Pannenberg, I have sought to understand "spirit" in this sense, and not as a disembodied substantial self.[17] Here especially, one must emphasize that spirit is not just a given but also an (eschatological) goal.

17. W. Pannenberg, *Anthropology in Theological Perspective*, trans. M. J. O'Connell (Philadelphia: Westminster Press, 1985).

- the unity of the person as "image of God," in, through, and for which she was created;
- the corporate unity of the "body of Christ" (Ephesians 2; 1 Corinthians 12), which is constituted of many persons under one Head;
- the believer's unity with Christ through the Spirit. Recall again Paul's oft-repeated phrase *en Christo.*
- the unity of the believer's will with the will of God, mirroring Jesus' "not my will, but thine be done" (Luke 22:42).
- the unity of the believer in, with, and through God.

It is not typical for theological anthropologies to end by listing the multiple facets of human unity; single systematic pronouncements tend to be the final word. But a moment's reflection will reveal that an anthropology that would remain a listener to and learner from the sciences and other disciplines cannot rush headlong to the closure of a final conceptual scheme. Existentially as well as theoretically, ours must remain a multifaceted unity. If human being involves the quest to unify the diverse parts of our experience along multiple dimensions, then each axis must remain as a part of the overall project rather than being too quickly *aufgehoben* into a final, undifferentiated unity called "the image of God." Plurality does not always entail relativism.

And yet . . . two deep theological themes do deserve a final word. Several of the unities in this list manifest a threefold structure that evokes the traditional trinitarian belief in the unity of three persons in the one being of God. A theology from below must be cautious about invoking a *vestigium trinitatis* or turning all triadic structures into an apologetic for the trinitarian God. And yet, for those who seek to see how Christian beliefs might help one to conceive the unity of the human person, the trinitarian analogues are certainly not without meaning,

Finally, some Christian authors maintain that the eighth and last form of unity is an eschatological aspiration only. (John Polkinghorne has termed this view "eschatological panentheism.") But, following much of the Christian mystical tradition as well as a significant number of twentieth-century theologians, and deeply influenced by the history of modern philosophical theology,[18] I affirm both the "already" and the "not yet" of this panentheistic unity of the

18. See Clayton, *The Problem of God in Modern Thought* (Grand Rapids: Eerdmans, 2000); *Adventures in the Spirit: God, World, Divine Action,* (Minneapolis: Fortress Press, 2008); *Die Frage nach der Freiheit. Biologie, Kultur und die Emergenz des Geistes* (Göttingen: Vandenhoeck & Ruprecht, 2008); English: *In Quest of Freedom: The Emergence of Spirit in the Natural World* (Göttingen: Vandenhoeck & Ruprecht, 2009).

person in, with, and through God. This is emphatically not to be understood as a pantheistic doctrine, say in the sense of Spinoza or Shankara.[19] Instead, it is the deeply Christian assertion that, in some difficult-to-specify, mystical, or sacramental sense, believers somehow share even now in that unity of the persons that makes up the very nature of the divine being. From this viewpoint — our view of which is partial and obscured (1 Cor. 13:12) — it's clear that all the other seven types of unity must in some sense find their unity in and through this final, theological dimension.

19. I and others have argued the distinction in P. Clayton and A. Peacocke, eds., *In Whom We Live and Move and Have Our Being: Panentheistic Reflections on God's Presence in a Scientific World* (Grand Rapids: Eerdmans, 2004).

II. Scientific Perspectives
in Interdisciplinary Dialogues

Towards an Integrated Anthropology

John C. Polkinghorne

Many dimensions of the rich reality of creation intersect in the human person. We are physical entities, made out of elements that were created in the nuclear furnaces of the stars and in the death-throes of a supernova explosion. We are biological beings, whose evolutionary ancestry implies a kinship with other animals. We are self-conscious beings, aware of ourselves through complex modes of reflexivity and possessing the ability to look into the far future in order to form expectations and hopes of what is yet to come. We are language-users, able to communicate with our contemporaries and with other human generations, both past and yet to come, by means of this almost infinitely subtle and supple resource. We are creative beings, expressing deep feelings and exploring profound delights through participation in the mysterious powers of music, art, and literature. We are intellectual beings, capable of comprehending through science the history and processes of the vast universe that gave us birth. We are religious beings, encountering the sacred reality of God in occasions of awe and worship, obedience and hope. Any adequate anthropology will have to do justice to these multiple dimensions of humanity.

Procrustean reductions are to be rejected when they attempt to diminish complexity by an appeal to some single and allegedly all-sufficient explanatory principle. Humans are not just genetic survival machines. Nor are they simply apprentice angels, temporarily caught in the bodily entrapment of the flesh and awaiting release into a purely spiritual realm that is their true home. Human beings are complex entities, intrinsically embodied but not reducible simply to collections of molecules. In their integrity they unite those diverse aspects of their nature that are referred to under such rubrics as body, mind, and spirit.

The concept of the person is in consequence, as Andreas Kemmerling says in his chapter, "vexingly" complex. Theological anthropology has to accept this complexity, and science is of some help in its doing so. A theology bereft of the worldly curiosity of science would be less than open to all reality, while science on its own, shorn of theological vision, is incapable of attaining the deepest understanding.

The effect of a sharp blow to the head in temporarily erasing conscious mental experience makes it clear enough that human embodiment is to be taken with the utmost seriousness. Yet a merely physicalist approach to human nature, placing absolute emphasis on embodiment and treating the mental dimension of our experience as a kind of epiphenomenal froth on the surface of a fundamentally physical substrate, strikingly fails to match the variety and richness of actual human experience. It leads to those ludicrously impoverished accounts in which the complexity of personhood is replaced by slogan symbols, such as "genetic survival machines" or "computers made of meat."

The insufficiency of the latter scheme was clarified by John Searle's famous "Chinese room" argument.[1] A person sits inside a closed room whose only access to the outside world is through two openings in the walls. Through one of these openings slips of paper are received on which incomprehensible squiggles are inscribed. These are matched with entries in a great book and the squiggle next to the appropriate entry is then copied and handed out through the other opening. The person sitting in the room performs these operations, but has no idea at all about what is going on. In fact, the slips received are questions in Chinese and the slips handed out are the corresponding answers in the same language. The tale is a parable of the workings of a computer. There is no understanding in the room, either in the person (the processor) or in the great book (the program). It lies outside, in the mind of the person who compiled the book (the programmer). Computers are good at syntax, but hopeless at semantics. Human beings are good at both.

If humans were simply finite-state computing machines, what would be the source and guarantee of rational judgment and discourse? What would validate the program? Some have asserted that the evolutionary selection of hardwired neural connections that adequately modeled the environment in which our hominid ancestors had to struggle for survival would have ensured that human brains had programs running on them that related reliably to the world around. There is some plausibility in this claim, but only to the extent that selection could produce a degree of rough-and-ready correspondence of

1. J. Searle, *Minds, Brains and Science* (London: BBC Publications, 1984), chapter 2.

brain activity to the perception of everyday circumstances. However, human rational powers vastly exceed anything as banal as that. Whence has come our ability to comprehend the totally counterintuitive world of quantum physics? Whence the human mathematical ability to explore the properties of non-commutative algebras and to prove Fermat's Last Theorem? These are not survival necessities, or anything that could plausibly be considered a fortunate spinoff from such necessities. Nor does the idea of evolutionary sexual selection (the "peacock's tail" effect of attracting the attention of prospective partners) remove the difficulty. It would be flattering to suppose that nascent human scientific or mathematical abilities would have proved irresistible to the opposite sex, thereby ensuring enhanced reproductive opportunities for their lucky possessors, but it scarcely sounds convincing. Mental life and power have a depth and strength that demands full recognition of the distinctive character of mind in the constitution of humanity, without for a moment denying the reality of our embodiment.

I have suggested elsewhere that the range of human capacities is such that it can only be fully understood if we acknowledge that the context for hominid evolution was much richer than the physico-biological setting that canonical Darwinian theory supposes.[2] Many mathematicians believe that they are engaged in discovery and not merely the construction of intellectual puzzles. They believe that mathematical entities exist in a realm of Platonic ideas. This noetic realm of mathematics would then be part of the context of human evolution, into which our ancestors were drawn, not by survival necessity but by intellectual delight. The mundane utility of developing a brain capable of counting and intuiting a little Euclidean geometry would have given initial access to the gateway to this realm of mathematical ideas, but the subsequent growth of the capacity to explore it fully would have required a different kind of motivation, with the Lamarckian power of cultural transmission ensuring a continually unfolding further development. Similarly, the development of human spiritual capacity and insight can be understood theologically to have arisen from encounter with the sacred presence of God. No doubt, the development of these multiple human capacities was made possible by the plasticity of the human brain, whose immensely complex network of connections is known to be formed largely by experience, with only a comparatively minor role for genetic predetermination, thus affording an epigenetic means for the embodied growth of these human abilities.

2. J. C. Polkinghorne, *Exploring Reality* (London/New Haven: SPCK/Yale University Press, 2005), chapter 3.

The task of formulating an adequate anthropology will require input from a wide range of individual disciplines, covering the various levels of human experience. The separate sciences will certainly have their specialized parts to play in this endeavor. Yet in interdisciplinary discourse of this kind it is general concepts of broad explanatory power that will have the greatest influence in assisting a synthesis. For example, it is certainly the case that contemporary neuroscience is making impressive progress in unraveling the complex neural pathways that are involved in the processing of information received by human organisms from their environment. Such scientific advances are much to be welcomed, but they stand in an ambiguous relationship to wider questions concerning the nature of the human person. The observed correlation of brain activity with mental experience certainly confirms embodiment as being a constituent dimension of humanity, but both dualists and those who take a psychosomatic view of human nature want to take the existence of the body seriously, though in very different ways, and so both can treat these new deliverances of neuroscience with due respect.

The present-day followers of Plato and Descartes regard human beings as made up of flesh and spirit, dual components understood as being distinct substances, the extended matter and thinking mind of the Cartesian scheme. The persistent problem for this point of view has been to understand how these two very different substances are able to interact with each other, as happens when my mental intention of waving is translated into the physical act of moving my hand. Appeal to the pineal gland as the seat of this interaction proved a pretty desperate, and ultimately unsuccessful, strategy. Much more sophisticated was the approach of the Nobel prize-winning neurophysiologist Sir John Eccles, a convinced dualist who believed that quantum effects at the level of synaptic discharges provided the necessary room for maneuver.[3] Eccles would certainly have accepted, and been greatly interested by, contemporary scientific discoveries about the neural pathways of information processing, but he would simply have understood this talk as relating to details on the bodily side of the dualistic divide. By itself, neuroscience cannot settle the dispute between the dualists and the proponents of psychosomatic unity.

Much the same can be said about recent discoveries that have used MRI scanning to show that specific parts of the brain "light up" during specific activities, such as religious meditation. Presumably other parts light up when we think about science. In themselves these observations tell us nothing about the nature and validity of the activities involved. They simply reflect the basic

3. J. C. Eccles, *Evolution of the Brain: Creation of the Self* (London: Routledge, 1989).

fact of human embodiment. It would be truly astonishing if there were any form of human activity that did not have a neural correlate.

The essential point to emphasize is that an integrated anthropology requires concepts of a range sufficiently wide to accommodate all the fundamental forms of human experience. The difficulty of the challenge that this represents can be illustrated by the celebrated problem of qualia, those feelings that are such a basic part of our mental experience. At present a vast gap yawns between neuroscientific talk of patterns of neural activity, however complex and sophisticated this discussion may be, and the simplest mental experiences, such as seeing red or feeling toothache. No one knows how to bridge this gap.

Self-consciousness is constitutive of being human, but the difficulties of understanding it are indeed "hard problems."[4] Attempts to defuse the issue by dismissing accounts of mental experience as "folk psychology" (allegedly induced by the caricature illusion of an internal "Cartesian theater" in which a little homunculus sits watching what is going, a notion clearly unworthy of scientific concern) reject some of our most direct and fundamental experiences in favor of airy and implausible speculation.[5] Despite hubristic claims of success, and talk of consciousness being the "last frontier" that the triumphant armies of a reductionist science are just about to cross, its nature and origin elude our understanding. Indeed, it is not self-evident that the hard problems of human consciousness will ever be open to full scientific treatment. Because consciousness constitutes us as persons, and because we do not have direct access to the consciousness of others, we can never step outside it to regard consciousness from a detached distance, in the way that we can with other profound problems that the scientific method can tackle, from the nature of matter to the nature of life. When I think about my own consciousness, I cannot disassociate that thought from my individual consciousness that contains it. This intrinsic reflexivity of consciousness puts it by itself in the category of a novel kind of private knowledge. This difficulty led some traditions in psychology to be unduly suspicious of using the insights of introspection, a stance most egregiously demonstrated by the now largely forsaken approach of the behaviorists, but this attitude willfully neglects a vital realm of experience. Whether these difficulties put consciousness beyond the reach of full scientific understanding is something that can only be discovered by attempting to pursue exploration as far as it proves possible to do so. This quest should be undertaken with appropriate modesty and with

---

4. D. J. Chalmers, *The Conscious Mind* (Oxford: Oxford University Press, 1996), pp. xii-xiii.
5. D. C. Dennett, *Consciousness Explained* (Boston: Little, Brown & Co., 1991).

the recognition that success is not guaranteed *a priori*. One should never rejoice at ignorance, but it is not dispelled simply by a willful refusal to acknowledge its possibility.

Of course, these aporia affect dualists and psychosomatic unity supporters alike. The latter can argue for their belief by appeal to the persuasiveness of such general considerations as the effects of drugs and brain damage on human personality, and the recognition that hominid ancestry links us to our animal forebears. It certainly seems to be the case that psychosomatic unity is the majority view today about the nature of humanity, and I am content to enroll myself as a member of that persuasion. This contemporary psychosomatic stance would have caused no great surprise or difficulty to the writers of the Bible, for the concept of human beings as animated bodies rather than incarnated souls was also predominant in Hebrew thinking.

Offering a rational articulation of the stance of psychosomatic unity requires the search for some form of metaphysical scheme of a dual-aspect kind, capable of containing the material and the mental within it as intimately interrelated aspects of a single unified reality. According to this view, there is only one sort of created "stuff," but it can be encountered in the complementary modes that we label experiences of matter and of mind. I prefer to use this dual-aspect terminology, rather than that of nonreductive physicalism,[6] because I believe that the latter, despite its balanced intention, is always under pressure to afford an illegitimate degree of enhanced significance to the material. We need constantly to keep in mind that all our knowledge of reality is apprehended and assessed through the perceptive and rational faculties of our minds.

One must admit, however, that in our present state of confused ignorance, dual-aspect monism has much more the character of an aspiration than that of an achieved theory. The philosopher Thomas Nagel says of his own attempts to wrestle with these problems along dual-aspect lines, that it is "probably nothing more than pre-Socratic flailing about."[7] The image is a striking one. Pre-Socratic thinkers, such as Thales, Anaximander, and Anaximenes, had the brilliant idea that the bewildering variety of objects in the world might simply be formed from different states of a single basic stuff — maybe air, maybe water, maybe something else. We might regard these thinkers as having been the first elementary particle physicists! From one point of view, it was a hopelessly

6. W. S. Brown, N. Murphy, and H. N. Malony, eds., *Whatever Happened to the Soul?* (Minneapolis: Fortress Press, 1998).

7. T. Nagel, *The View from Nowhere* (Oxford: Oxford University Press, 1986), p. 30.

ambitious project. The pre-Socratics were two and a half millennia too early to be able to get onto the idea of quarks and gluons. Yet from another point of view, though they were hand-waving, they were doing so in what would eventually prove to be a very fruitful direction. Today, when we talk about psychosomatic human nature and dual-aspect monism, we too cannot manage much more than learned hand-waving. Like the pre-Socratics, we must endeavor to wave in the right direction. I believe that there are some general concepts derivable from science that can help us to do so. One of the purposes of this chapter is to explore two such general ideas.

1. Mind/Body Complementarity

If dualists face the problem of the causal joint between mind and matter, those who espouse psychosomatic unity and dual-aspect monism face a problem of comparable difficulty in attempting to explain how two such different aspects of experience as mind and matter could derive from a common substantial ground. One approach to an answer is that proposed by panpsychism, or pan-experientialism as its process-philosophical supporters prefer to call it. The claim then being made is that there is a "mental" aspect of reality present in all kinds of entities, even if admittedly in very widely varying degrees, so that protons and persons form parts of a single metaphysical spectrum in which the mental finds increasingly explicit (ultimately conscious) expression with increasing complexity of organization. A highly sophisticated scheme of this kind is provided by the process philosophy of Alfred North Whitehead[8] and its theological development at the hands of Charles Hartshorne.[9] The basic metaphysical concept is not substance but events, "actual occasions." These are held to have a two-phase character. First there is "prehension" in which options for possible outcomes are presented that are understood to be open to influence from a variety of sources, including relationship to other actual occasions together with a divine lure seeking to draw process in a particular direction. This is followed by the phase of "concrescence," in which a particular option is selected and occurs. Process thinking pictures a kind of union of the mental and the physical in the marriage bed of actual occasions. The scheme is boldly speculative. Many find difficulty with it. Physics does not determine metaphysics, but it does constrain it, rather in the way that the foundations of

8. A. N. Whitehead, *Process and Reality* (New York: Free Press, 1978).
9. See F. Santos and S. Sia, *Personal Identity, the Self and Ethics* (London: Palgrave, 2007).

a house constrain, but do not determine, the building that can be erected upon them. To a quantum theorist, the edifice of process philosophy does not seem to rest securely on the foundations of what is known about physical process. While there are discontinuities in quantum physics, these occur solely at the isolated events that we label "measurements" — not simply understood as acts taking place in a laboratory, but meaning any irreversible macroscopic registration of a micro-state of quantum affairs. Outside these occasions of measurement, quantum physics proceeds with the smooth continuity described by the Schrödinger equation. This picture does not seem to match well with the punctuated account of the process scheme.

However, there is another concept in quantum thinking that might prove to be of some usefulness to dual-aspect monists. Of course, there cannot be any simpleminded direct transfer of understanding between physics and the profound complexities of anthropological thought, but there may well be a measure of analogical association between the two that could be modestly helpful. A paradigm example of the presence in the same entity of behaviors that at first sight seem irreconcilable is provided by the wave/particle duality of light. After all, a wave is spread out and flapping, while a particle is concentrated and like a little bullet. Yet the same entity can be encountered in these two strikingly different aspects. Physicists understand very well how this apparently oxymoronic combination of wave and particle is actually possible. It is certainly not because particles all have a little bit of undulation in them, which then adds up to make a wave, a suggestion that would be the analogue of the panpsychic idea. Wave/particle duality arises because it is possible to create wavelike states that are composed of an *indefinite* number of particles. This is an option that would not be available in the clear and determinate world of Newtonian physics. There one would simply look and see, counting the exact number of particles actually present. However, quantum theory is based on the superposition principle, the fundamental but counterintuitive premise that quantum states can be constituted by adding together, in a mathematically well-defined way, states that in classical physics would be strictly immiscible. Just as one can have quantum states that mix being "here" with being "there," so one can have states that are mixtures of different numbers of particles. These turn out to be the states that show wavelike properties.[10] This observation may offer a hint of the direction in which to look for the construction of a mind/matter integrated anthropology. The notion would be that it is the presence of

10. See J. C. Polkinghorne, *Quantum Theory; A Very Short Introduction* (Oxford: Oxford University Press, 2011), pp. 73-75.

some form of intrinsic indefiniteness that will permit a rich duality of complementary properties.[11]

Further speculation can suggest a conceivable direction in which to look for this indefiniteness. One of the most important discoveries of twentieth-century science has been the existence of widespread intrinsic unpredictabilities, present in physical process, both subatomically through quantum theory and macroscopically through chaos theory. These are not deficiencies that could be remedied by more precise measurement or more exact calculation, but they represent fundamental properties of nature. It is possible to suppose that these unpredictabilities may at least be a part of what it is that can offer sufficient indefiniteness to allow a subtle and supple duality of mind/matter to be present in such immensely complex entities as human beings. This approach would require an ontological interpretation of the property of unpredictability, regarding it as a sign of openness to the action of further kinds of causal principles beyond those of a reductionist science, rather than merely an indicator of epistemological limitation due to unavoidable ignorance. An interpretation of this kind is certainly a valid metaphysical option to pursue. Moreover, it is one that those of a realist persuasion, for whom what can or cannot be known is a reliable guide to what is the case, should find very natural to take.

It is beyond our present level of understanding to be able to work out this complementarity approach to anthropological theory in any detail, but one can at least claim "the defeat of the defeaters." Contemporary science's account of the causal structure of the physical world is too patchy and open for it to support the assertion that there is no alternative to a crass physicalism.[12]

2. Information

One of the ways in which a system can enter a regime of chaotic behavior is through a proliferating cascade of bifurcating possibilities. Instead of a single path of development, an endless succession of alternative possibilities opens up.[13] For a physical system, these differing paths will correspond to the same energy, but to differing patterns in which the energy flows. On a specific occasion, the actual behavior of the system will correspond to a particular selection from these possibilities. Its specification can be formulated in informational

11. J. C. Polkinghorne, *Science and Creation* (London: SPCK, 1988), chapter 5.
12. Polkinghorne, *Exploring Reality*, chapter 2.
13. See J. Gleick, *Chaos* (London: Heinemann, 1988), pp. 69-80.

terms, the binary coding of "bits," which corresponds to labeling the branches of the bifurcations that are actually realized in this particular case. Considerations of this kind strongly suggest that the adequate discussion of the behavior of complex systems will call for the development of concepts of information able to stand alongside concepts of energy, the two together providing the fundamental basis for a dual-aspect, energy/information scientific description of complexity.

The idea of information that is being appealed to here is rudimentary and comparatively banal. Yet one may reasonably expect considerable expansion of the concept in the course of the development of science in the twenty-first century. The notion of information seems to be on the cusp of significance for contemporary scientific thinking. It is just beginning to become possible in a rather modest way to study the behavior of complex systems considered in their totalities, rather than treated by science's conventional strategy of decomposition into their constituent elements. At the moment this work is at a natural history stage, corresponding to the study of particular examples, and no underlying deep theory has yet been discovered. Nevertheless there are good reasons for supposing that such a theory awaits discovery. Complex systems display astonishing powers of self-organization, by which they spontaneously generate remarkable patterns of dynamic behavior, in a manner totally unforeseeable from the consideration of the properties of their constituents. As the slogan goes, "More is different." This phenomenon of emergent holistic pattern-generating properties has been observed physically in dissipative systems held far from thermodynamic equilibrium by the exchange of energy and entropy with their environment.[14] It is also found in the behavior of logical networks implemented on a computer.[15] It seems reasonable to hope that by the end of the twenty-first century one might expect that a more elaborately defined concept of information will indeed take its place alongside energy as a fundamental category required for understanding the nature of the physical world. The possibility of holistic laws of nature relating to some form of causal influence that one could call "active information" (meaning a top-down influence of the whole upon the behavior of the parts, generating complex behaviors of the total system) seems to be a possibility on the scientific agenda.[16] Here it is important to distinguish dissipative systems from computer models.

14. I. Prigogine and I. Stengers, *Order Out of Chaos* (London: Heinemann, 1984).

15. S. Kauffman, *At Home in the Universe* (Oxford: Oxford University Press, 1995), chap. 4.

16. J. C. Polkinghorne, *Belief in God in an Age of Science* (New Haven: Yale University Press, 1998).

Although the latter can manifest the emergence of self-organized complex behavior, their strictly logical nature means that this is wholly generated bottom-up, arising solely from the deterministic relationships between the elements of the computer program. In the case of physical dissipative systems, however, this need not be the case, because a realistic interpretation of their intrinsic unpredictabilities permits an open room for maneuver in which genuinely top-down causal factors can act. Here might lie a modest clue to why we are more than computers made of meat.

The Nobel prize–winning physicist Robert Laughlin, whose work has lain in the area of collective phenomena in condensed matter physics, has suggested that we are on the threshold of a revolution in physical thinking that will move science from the present Age of Reductionism to a new Age of Emergence. His book *A Different Universe,* has the somewhat ironic subtitle, "Reinventing Physics from the Bottom Down."[17]

If these developments come about, as I expect they will, they will lead to a quite novel physical foundation on which to construct a metaphysical edifice. This would open up promising new directions in which to pursue dual-aspect ideas. Of course, information, even in some new and enhanced sense, falls far short of the rich scope and content that would be necessary to afford adequate accommodation for the mental as human beings experience it, but at least it represents an encouraging direction in which to wave our hands. The duality of energy/information suggests, however faintly, the interesting possibility of an analogical connection with the much deeper duality of matter/mind. There is consequent encouragement to take a new look at a concept of fundamental significance for theological anthropology, the idea of the human soul.

3. The Soul

The concept of the soul, understood as the carrier of individual personhood, plays an important part in theological thinking. Its role is to stand for the essence of each particular human being whose life is precious in the sight of God. So considered, the soul is of the greatest possible significance and value. Furthermore, it is of indispensable eschatological relevance, acting as the carrier of continuity between the life of a person in this world and the life of that same person in the world to come. The dualist can identify the soul with the immaterial component of the human being, believing that it will survive

17. R. Laughlin, *A Different Universe* (New York: Basic Books, 2005).

bodily death, either because its spiritual character makes it intrinsically immortal or because God, in divine faithfulness, will not allow it to perish along with the body. But is there not a danger that the concept of the soul would be lost in psychosomatic thinking, with a corresponding disastrous theological impoverishment?

I do not think so, but some reconceptualization of the soul is certainly required. What is being sought in the use of the idea is a means of speaking of what one might call "the real me," the essential person expressed through a continuing form that corresponds to the abiding significance that that person has in the sight of God. What might be the real me in this sense is at first sight almost as puzzling to understand in this life as it might be in relation to a life beyond death. What could it be that makes the author, an ageing, bald academic, the same person as the schoolboy with the shock of black hair in the photograph of many years ago? It is tempting to say "material continuity," but that is an illusion. The actual atoms that make up our bodies are changing all the time, through wear and tear, nutrition and excretion. We live in a state of material flux. I am atomically distinct from that schoolboy of long ago. What constitutes the real me is not the individual atoms of my body, but the almost infinitely complex information-bearing pattern in which they are organized. I believe that pattern, in its superabundant complexity, is the human soul.[18] Here one is striving to use the notion of "information" in some extremely extended and enhanced sense, beyond the power of adequate contemporary articulation. All that makes up my character must find a lodging in my soul. This, of course, includes the memories that shape and constitute the internal narrative of my personhood. Some of these are consciously accessible, while others are lodged in an unconscious level of the mind, which nevertheless plays an important if veiled role in my life. Because we are embodied beings, the level of conscious access to memory depends upon the state of our brains. Strokes or other forms of brain damage can severely diminish the degree of this access. People may then think that somehow they have lost a part of themselves, but this need not be so. Damage to the brain does not imply diminishment of the soul. One might think of the model of a computer. A deleted file may no longer be readily accessible to the user, but nevertheless it remains impressed upon the hard disk. Another important part of the soul must relate to that web of interpersonal relationships that do so much to constitute us as persons. The pattern that is our soul is not simply confined within our skin.

18. J. C. Polkinghorne, *The God of Hope and the End of the World* (London/New Haven: SPCK/Yale University Press, 2002), pp. 103-7.

Towards an Integrated Anthropology

This concept of the soul, despite its statement having the obvious character of pre-Socratic flailing about, receives at least some mild encouragement from the increasing role that we have seen is being played by information in contemporary scientific thinking, however vast an enrichment of that scientific notion would be needed for it to become relevant to the complexity of human nature. The concept of the soul as information-bearing pattern is also recognizably an ancient idea in modern dress, since it clearly has a close kinship with the Aristotelian-Thomistic notion of the soul as the form of the body. Nevertheless, there are some differences from the Thomistic picture. The modern concept places a greater emphasis on relationality, and it is also much more dynamic in its character. The information-bearing pattern that is me grows and develops as my character forms and my memories accumulate in the course of my life in this "vale of soul-making." This dynamic character of the soul need not preclude its also containing an unchanging component, an invariant signature expressive of my personal individuality.[19] A person's genome would, presumably, be one part of this static dimension of the soul.

The soul understood in this way would possess no necessarily intrinsic immortality. As far as naturalistic thinking is concerned, the pattern carried by the body will dissolve with that body's decay. Yet it is a perfectly coherent Christian hope that the faithful God will not allow that pattern to be lost, but will preserve it in the divine memory. That of itself would not constitute the continued life of the person, for if we are psychosomatic unities, some continuing form of embodiment is also necessary if we are truly to live again. Hence the Christian hope of the great eschatological act of resurrection (rather than spiritual survival), the reembodiment by God of that preserved pattern in the transformed and redeemed "matter" of the new creation.

4. An Integrated Anthropology

These ideas of complementarity and information are but the toys of thought that we can play with as we struggle to think of an integrated anthropology endowed with the richness and complexity that would be adequate to the character of our personal experience. Yet these modest scientific images may give us some encouragement not to succumb to the false assertions of a reductive

19. A toy model would be mathematical invariants, unchanged under groups of transformations.

scientism that seeks to deny the reality of almost all that actually makes human life worth the living.

I have argued that the proposed duality of energy/information can, at least, be seen as bearing a degree of helpful analogy to the much more profound duality of matter/mind. If the line of this argument is the right one to pursue, the resulting understanding of human nature will be a bipartite concept of body and mind. In his chapter, Michael Welker explores a rich range of anthropological ideas drawn from scripture, including the tripartite schema of body, mind, spirit, while considering also the concept of the "heart," understood as the seat of the emotions. From the point of view of this chapter, these valuable refinements of detail are to be understood as elucidating aspects of the extremely rich concept of "information" that would be required to begin to do justice to the profound character of human personhood. For example, Welker's distinction between soul (*psyche,* oriented to the context of nature) and spirit (*pneuma,* oriented to the context of divine reality), would both be understood, from the stance taken here, to be different aspects of the mental pole of human body/mind complementarity.

Brains, Minds, Souls, and People: A Scientific Perspective on Complex Human Personhood

Malcolm Jeeves

This volume exemplifies the variety of approaches that can be taken in any attempts to understand the complexity of human personhood. Any contributions from scientists must, as the Princeton physicist Freeman Dyson has reminded us, be kept in balance. He wrote, "Contemporary discussions of science and religion often have a narrow focus, as if science and religion were the only sources of knowledge and wisdom." He continued, "If we look for insights into human nature to guide the future of religion, we find more such insights in the novels of Dostoevsky than in the journals of cognitive science. Literature is the great storehouse of human experience, linking together different cultures and different centuries, accessible to far more people than the technical language of science."[1]

Some of the areas of contemporary science most relevant to understanding human personhood are psychology, neuroscience, and evolutionary biology. It is research at the interfaces of these in the disciplines of neuropsychology and evolutionary psychology, where significant advances are currently being made.

In his chapter, Warren Brown focuses on how clues from neuroscience may offer fresh insights into evaluating some claims to human neurocognitive uniqueness.[2] For the nonspecialist, however, Brown's chapter may benefit from being set against the general contemporary scientific background of mind and brain research. Things are moving so fast that the nonspecialist may be forgiven

---

1. D. Freeman, "Complementarity," in *Spiritual Information,* ed. C. Harper (Philadelphia and London: Templeton Foundation Press, 2005), pp. 52-55.
2. W. S. Brown, "The Emergence of Human Distinctiveness," this volume.

for, at times, seizing upon what appears to be "the" definitive current scientific story about mind-brain relations, and then too hastily trying to relate it to long-held philosophical and theological views, only to discover that what for a while was the accepted version of the scientific story has already been revised.

1. The Increasing Momentum of Mind-Brain Research

Just how quickly the accepted scientific story changes is illustrated by looking at how some views, firmly held half a century ago, have now been abandoned or radically revised. For example:

1. Fifty years ago few self-respecting North American "scientific" psychologists concerned about their reputations would have dared to speak about the "mind," only about behavior. Behaviorism was dominant and at its peak. It was only with the subsequent "cognitive revolution" that once more it became scientifically respectable to carry out research on the mind-brain relationship that was underlined at a meeting of the Royal Society of London in 2006.[3]

2. Forty years ago it was confidently taught and widely believed that autism was the result of poor relations between the young child and the child's parents. Today, as recent *Scientific American* articles on mirror neurons illustrate, it has become clear that a malfunctioning of specific neural substrates is what results in some forms of autism.[4]

3. Thirty years ago we were teaching our students that you made all your neurons before birth and spent the rest of your life with the supply of nerve cells you obtained during the earliest months. Today we know that the brain actually makes more neurons than it needs and there is a process whereby excess neurons are selectively removed, a process that shapes the adult brain. What we now know is that the brain makes new neurons, a process called neurogenesis, which is regulated by hormones. Professor Joe Herbert, head of the Centre for Brain Repair in the Department of Physiology, Development, and Neuroscience at Cambridge, has noted that "it took until the 1990s for neurogenesis to be accepted as a phenomenon in the adult brain." Herbert has pointed out that a couple of years ago it was discovered that the much-talked-about drug Prozac and some other antidepressants increased neurogenesis.

3. EU Report on Meeting of Minds project January 23, 2006, at www.meetingminds europe.org.
4. G. Rizzolatti, L. Fogassi, and V. Gallese, "Mirrors in the Mind," *Scientific American,* November 2006, pp. 30-37; V. S. Ramachandran and L. M. Oberman, "Broken Mirrors — A Theory of Autism," *Scientific American,* November 2006, pp. 39-45.

This discovery created, and continues to create, great excitement. At the end of his article Herbert concluded: "If you get a feeling of suppressed excitement reading this, then you reflect the optimism of the neuroscientific community, faced by the awesome prospect of studying the most complex structure in the known world, and the knowledge that when it goes wrong it devastates lives."[5]

2. An Increasing Recognition of the Wider Implications of Scientific Research

Today the wider implications of advances in mind-brain research are the focus of major scientific academy meetings and of government inquiries. Here are a few examples that have potential implications for discussions at the psychology, neuroscience, and theology (religion) interfaces.

In May 2008 the UK's Academy of Medical Sciences published a report on "Brain Science, Addiction and Drugs." It underlined both the rate of advance of research in neuroscience and its relevance to contemporary social problems. It also, almost as an aside, by implication raised key questions about the nature of human nature in its discussion of cognitive enhancers. It comments: "[O]ur grasp of the molecular events underpinning learning and memory do suggest that cognitive enhancement should be taken seriously by bodies such as the Food Standards Agency and the Medicines and Healthcare Regulatory Authority."[6] A July 2008 major review paper in *Nature Reviews: Neuroscience,* titled "Brain Foods: The Effects of Nutrients on Brain Function," indicates that the possibility of such enhancement is not speculative scientific hand-waving.[7] It is here-and-now science. Some will quite naturally ask, why then limit it to cognitive enhancement? Given the accumulating evidence for the embodiment of spirituality, should we also seek to apply such research in order to restore normal spirituality, at times lost in some forms of Alzheimer's disease, or to enhance it by using suitable foods? Nothing new in this. Ancient religious rituals used plants to facilitate ecstatic and mystical states — for example, mushrooms (by the Aztecs), peyote cactus (by the Huicol of Mexico), and ayahuasca (by the natives of northwestern South America), as well as substances from water lilies, mandrake, opium poppies, morning glories, and marijuana

5. C. Herbert Joseph, *Journal of Gonville and Caius College, Cambridge* (2006): 23.

6. "Brain Science, Addiction and Drugs," Academy of Medical Sciences, May 2008 Report, London.

7. F. Gomez-Pinilla, "Brain Foods: The Effects of Nutrients on Brain Function," *Perspectives: Nature Reviews: Neuroscience* 9 (2008): 568-78.

plants. Since these drugs act on the brain to bring about their effects, study of these effects on various brain systems can reveal brain mechanisms relevant to understanding more about experiences that people often describe as religious.[8]

In the USA, the National Research Council deemed the wider impact of developments in neuroscience sufficiently far-reaching that they published "a guide . . . on how developments in cognitive neuroscience are likely to affect national security." The authors are some of America's most highly regarded neuroscientists and psychologists, such as Michael Gazzaniga and Elizabeth Loftus. In an October 2008 interview with *The Psychologist,* Elizabeth Loftus commented, "In addition to psychologists there were experts in pharmacology, medicine, molecular biology, human-machine interactions, brain imaging, and more. We were trying to anticipate where the world might be in the next 20 years . . . how we can prepare ourselves to respond for the safety of our society."[9] Is neuroscience really putting our society, including the freedom of religious societies, at risk? Watch this space.

An October 2008 report compiled by a team of more than four hundred scientists assembled by Foresight, the UK government think tank, underlined yet again that when thinking about the mind-brain relationships any overemphasis on the brain to the exclusion of the mind may be seriously misleading.[10] This report is generating controversy, but it underlines the importance of top-down effects that pay proper attention to what it calls our "mental capital" and to the social contexts in which we live.

One final reinforcing cautionary tale is noteworthy at a time when our media so often show striking colored pictures indicating which parts of our brains light up when we are engaged in everything from seeing faces, listening to music, looking at art, or expressing romantic or maternal love.[11] In an October 2008 paper titled "The Truth about Brain Science," Robert Epstein, a contributory editor to *Scientific American Mind,* says that "[c]laims are being made about brain research that just aren't true, and they're being accepted uncritically by the press, the public policy makers and even the courts." Specifically, and this is very relevant to the increasing numbers of studies of the brain

8. A good summary of this information can be found in D. E. Nichols and B. R. Chemel, "The Neuropharmacology of Religious Experiences: Hallucinogens and the Experience of the Divine," in *Where God and Science Meet,* vol. 3: *The Psychology of Religious Experience,* ed. P. McNamara (Westport, CT: Praeger, 2006), pp. 1-34.

9. "Neuroscience for Spooks," *The Psychologist* 21 (2008): 834.

10. "Mental Capital and Wellbeing," http://news.bbc.co.uk/1/hi/health/76077.stm.

11. A. Bartels and S. Zeki, "The Neural Correlates of Maternal and Romantic Love," *NeuroImage* 21 (2004): 1155-66.

correlates of spirituality, he comments, "The vast majority of brain studies being conducted these days are correlational." "The problem," he says, "with many headlines these days is that they automatically claim, based on the latest correlational brain study, that we have identified the cause of . . . this or that." "But," he concludes, "finding correlations isn't the same as finding causes, and finding causes is often quite difficult."[12] This is something we teach our first-year students but is easily missed by the general public.

It is clear that advances in mind and brain research will continue at an ever-accelerating pace. At the same time we must be prepared for many more surprises and upsets to some of our currently widely held views. We shall be wise therefore to pause and carefully and critically evaluate the emerging scientific data and not rush too hastily to seek to integrate it with some of our traditional philosophical and theological views of the human person.

In the following section I shall briefly highlight, for the nonspecialist, some salient features of the contemporary neuroscientific landscape, with the aim of giving the flavor of the portraits emerging of how mind and brain are related. In the remaining sections I shall deal specifically with two sets of issues where an understanding of mind-brain relations are relevant, first to our understanding of the spiritual dimensions of our lives, and second to evaluating a variety of views held down the millennia of what constitutes the imago Dei.

3. Mind and Brain — Salient Features of the Contemporary Landscape

A century and a half of steadily accumulating evidence has shown that there are regions of the brain selectively specialized for specific abilities. This remarkable specificity of function applies both to brain regions and to brain systems. Studies of localization of function within the brain, until relatively recently investigated mainly through so-called "bottom-up" approaches, have given rise to the widespread belief that there is a fixity about the neural embodiment of cognitive and conceptual abilities. This fixity has frequently been described as specificity, which, while substantially correct, nevertheless has in some instances (see below) been misleadingly overstated in a way that fails to do justice to the more recent evidence for plasticity.

More recently advances in the development of brain scanning techniques have led to a fresh awareness of how cognitive processes and the social, as well

12. R. Epstein, "The Truth about Brain Science," *The Skeptical Psychologist, Skeptical Inquirer* (September/October 2008): 32-33.

as the physical environment, including habitual ways of behaving, can "mold" or "sculpture" the brain (see for example Ian Robertson's *Mind Sculpture*[13]). Studies such as those reviewed by Robertson give new prominence to the actual and potential importance of so-called "top-down" processes.

Advances in understanding the possible power of top-down effects have been so fast that what leading researchers such as Grabowski and Damasio in 1996 could see as "only a dream" have already been partially realized by researches such as those by O'Craven and Kanwisher.[14]

Changes in our brains may be reflected in changes in our spiritual awareness. There are well-documented changes in the spiritual dimensions of life, loosely called spirituality, which are clearly dependent upon the intactness and the normal functioning of the neural substrates of behavior. Detailed studies of distressing changes in spirituality in Alzheimer's patients graphically illustrate this. The spiritual dimension to life is embodied. At the same time we must recognize the importance of cognitive processes such as beliefs and expectations, as well as the social context in which these are held, and which underline the importance of recognizing that spirituality is firmly embedded in contexts of relationships both horizontal with one another and vertical with the God we worship.

4. Bottom-Up Approaches to the Study of Mind-Brain Links

In the bottom-up methods that dominated for a century and a half, typical experimental procedures were to make changes in selective neural and/or biochemical substrates of the brain and then observe how behavior or cognitive capacities changed as a result. Soon it was not necessary to produce surgical lesions, since, following on the pioneering work of Hubel and Wiesel, there was a rapid expansion in methods, which depended upon implanting very small electrodes in columns of cells in the brain. Researchers then monitored the activity in those cells, as the subjects, usually animals, were presented with a variety of sensory stimuli.

Typical of the discovery of the remarkable specificity of some aspects of neural processing are the researches dating back twenty-five years by David

13. I. H. Robertson, *Mind Sculpture* (London/New York: Bantam, 1999).
14. T. J. Grabowski and A. R. Damasio, "Improving Functional Imaging Techniques: The Dream of a Single Image for a Single Mental Event," *Proceedings of the National Academy of Sciences* 93 (1996): 14302-3; K. M. O'Craven and N. Kanwisher, "Mental Imagery of Faces and Places Activates Corresponding Stimulus — Specific Brain Regions," *Journal of Cognitive Neuroscience* 12 (2000): 1013-23.

Perrett and his colleagues, who used single-cell recording techniques to map regions in monkeys brains that responded selectively to the sight of human faces.[15] Every new study seemed to tighten the links between what the monkey was seeing and how the cells of the brain were responding. There was a remarkable specificity in the cells' responses to facial stimuli. Among other things, Perrett found, for example, that changing the view of a face in its horizontal orientation from side profile to full face and back had a dramatic effect on the level of activity of face-responsive neurons. All this suggested to Perrett that one of the key functions of these neurons may be to determine the direction of another's gaze. He proposed that the information provided by the eyes, the face, and the body was selectively processed by different columns of neurons, all part of a processing hierarchy for attention direction or social attention. Other researchers demonstrated this was a part of a larger system.

Links between brain and mind are not confined to perception and cognition but also to the understanding of differences in human personality and behavior. Occasional reports of such changes appear in the clinical literature and have a long and checkered history. Most who tell the story start with the account of how Phineas Gage, working as foreman on a New England railroad, accidentally suffered damage to the frontal part of his brain and thereafter was a changed person.

A dramatic example of a similar change was reported recently.[16] It described how a schoolteacher had begun collecting sex magazines and visiting pornographic websites and focusing his attention on images of children and adolescents. This was something that, according to him, he simply could not stop himself doing. He was arrested for child molestation, convicted, and underwent a rehabilitation program that was unsuccessful. The day before his final sentencing he went voluntarily to the hospital emergency department complaining of a severe headache. He was distraught and contemplating suicide and was aware that he could not control his impulses, so much so that he propositioned the nurses in the hospital. An MRI scan of his brain revealed a large tumor pressing on his right frontal lobe. The surgeons removed it and the lewd behavior and pedophilia faded away. Sadly, after a year he began to manifest pedophilia afresh. New MRI scans showed that the tumor was beginning to regrow. It was removed and once again his urges subsided. This case,

15. D. I. Perrett, P. A. J. Smith, D. D. Potter, A. J. Mistlin, A. S. Head, A. D. Milner, and M. A. Jeeves, "Neurons Responsive to Faces in the Temporal Cortex: Studies of Functional Organisation, Sensitivity to Identity and Relation to Perception," *Human Neurobiology* 3 (1984): 197-208.

16. J. M. Burns and R. H. Swerdlow, "Right Orbitofrontal Tumor with Pedophilia Symptom and Constructional Apraxia Sign," *Archives of Neurology,* 60, no. 3 (March 2003): 437-40.

not surprisingly, received wide publicity and comment. One thing, however, is clear: it demonstrated the remarkably tight links between what is happening in the brain and how we behave.

When evidence from brain damage in adult humans is the only or even the main source of evidence about the remarkable specificity of localization of functions within the brain, it can lead to a failure to recognize the plasticity of the developing brain. Such an overemphasis has been given wide publicity by Steven Pinker, drawing mainly on data from adult neuropsychology and genetic disorders.[17] However, other leading workers in the field, such as Karmiloff-Smith, have pointed out that Pinker's interpretation of the data is flawed. She notes that it is based on a static model of the human brain that ignores the complexities of gene expression and the dynamics of postnatal development (for more details, see for example Michael Rutter's 2006 book *Genes and Behaviour: Nature-Nurture Interplay Explained*[18]). Karmiloff-Smith's critique again reminds of how rapidly the "accepted" views may change.[19]

The citation for Professor Karmiloff-Smith's award of the 2004 Latsis Prize by the European Science Foundation aptly sums up the importance of her corrective remarks. It observed that, "Her research aimed to show that the brain is neither hardwired nor a blank slate, but that both genes and environment interact in complex ways and that the actual process of post-natal development plays a crucial role in this dynamic interaction," further adding that "this highlights the fact that the adult neuropsychological model is inappropriate for explaining developmental disorders."[20]

Thus, while there is a remarkable specificity in the neural mechanisms for some of our most important perceptual and cognitive functions in social interactions and for daily living, at the same time there is also plasticity.

5. Top-Down Approaches to the Study of Mind-Brain Links

As the cognitive revolution spread, along with the use of ever more sophisticated brain imaging techniques, research reports appeared pointing to the

17. S. Pinker, *Words and Rules: The Ingredients of Language* (London: Weidenfeld & Nicolson, 1999).

18. M. Rutter, *Genes and Behaviour: Nature-Nurture Interplay Explained* (Oxford: Wiley-Blackwell, 2005).

19. A. Karmiloff-Smith, *The Psychologist* 15, no. 12 (December 2002).

20. Latsis Prize citation in A. Karmiloff-Smith, *The Psychologist* 15, no. 12 (December 2002).

importance of top-down effects. "Top-down effects" refers to changes in cognition being paralleled by localized changes in the brain. Two striking examples of top-down effects illustrate their potency.

First, Maguire and his colleagues noted that licensed London taxi drivers are renowned for their extensive and detailed navigation experience and skills. They collected structural MRI's of the brains of a group of taxi drivers and of matched controls, and discovered that, as a result of two years of intensive training in navigation, the anterior hippocampi of the taxi drivers were significantly larger. Moreover, the volume of grey matter in the right hippocampus correlated significantly with the amount of time spent as a taxi driver. The researchers concluded: "it seems that there is a capacity for local plastic changes in the structure of the healthy adult human brain in response to environmental demands."[21]

The second example is a study by O'Craven and Kanwisher, which illustrates how the mind can selectively mobilize specific brain systems.[22] They asked volunteers to look at pictures of faces or houses or to imagine these pictures. They demonstrated how imagining faces or houses selectively activated the same areas of the brain as when the subjects were seeing the pictures of houses or faces. Specifically, seeing or thinking about faces activated the fusiform face area, while seeing or thinking about houses activated the parahippocampal place area. The experimenters in effect showed that they could actually "read the minds" of their subjects by observing their brain activity. They could tell whether the subjects were thinking about faces or houses by measuring activity in respective brain areas.

6. The Emerging Picture

The picture emerging points to the intimate relationships between mind, brain, and behavior. We described some of these as "bottom-up" and some as "top-down." There is now an emerging consensus about how to portray these intimate relationships. The neurologist Antonio Damasio wrote that "the distinction between diseases of brain and mind and between neurological problems

21. E. A. Maguire, D. G. Gadian, I. S. Johnsrude, C. D. Good, J. Ashburner, R. S. J. Frackopwiak, and C. Frith, "Navigation-Related Structural Change in the Hippocampi of Taxi Drivers," *Proceedings of the National Academy of Sciences* (2000): 4398-4403.

22. K. M. O'Craven and N. Kinwasher, "Mental Imagery of Faces and Places Activates Corresponding Stimulus-Specific Brain Regions," *Journal of Cognitive Neuroscience* 12 (2000): 1013-23.

and psychological/psychiatric ones, is an unfortunate cultural inheritance that permeates society and medicine. It reflects a basic ignorance of the relation between brain and mind."[23] A similar view was expressed by Robert Kendell, a past president of the Royal College of Psychiatrists in Britain. "Not only is the distinction between mental and physical ill-founded and incompatible with contemporary understanding of disease," he wrote, "it is also damaging for the long-term interests of patients themselves."[24]

What is the relevance of the foregoing evidence to our discussions of the spiritual dimensions of personhood? Briefly, it emphasizes that our mental processes are not free-floating somewhere out in space but are firmly embodied in our physical makeup. At the same time it prompts us to remember that the researches of cognitive scientists presented in terms of psychological processes will not vanish and are not explained away as we begin to understand something about how such processes are dependent upon the normal functioning of the human brain.

Sarter has argued that an effective strategy in trying to ensure that any inferences we make about the relations between psychological processes and their neural substrates are soundly based is to remember that "the integration of methods and data from bottom-up and top-down approaches provides a means of circumventing some of the thornier interpretative problems of either approach alone and thereby permits strong inferences in cognitive neuroscience."[25] In this way we can simultaneously remember that cognitive processes are embedded within the brain and at the same time sculpture the brain. It is clear that while there is a remarkable specificity about how some of our most fundamental perceptual and cognitive processes are embodied in our brains, there is also striking evidence of how cognition and behavior sculpture our brains, demonstrating equally remarkable plasticity.

7. Mind and Brain: Body and Soul Relationships of Irreducible, Intrinsic Interdependence?

It is one thing to demonstrate the intimate interrelationship between what is happening at the conscious mental level and what is happening at the level

23. A. Damasio, *R. Descartes' Error* (New York: G. P. Putnam & Sons, 1994), p. 40.

24. R. E. Kendell, "The Distinction between Mental and Physical Illness," *British Journal of Psychiatry* 178 (2001): 490-93.

25. M. Sarter, G. G. Berntson, and J. T. Cacioppo, "Brain Imaging and Cognitive Neuroscience," *American Psychologist* (January 1996): 13-21.

of the brain and the body, but the unanswered question is: How can we most accurately characterize this intimate relationship without making claims or assumptions about the connection between the two that have not yet been demonstrated? What is clear is that there is a remarkable interdependence between what is occurring at the cognitive level and what is occurring at the physical level. We could perhaps describe this as a relationship of intrinsic interdependence, using the word "intrinsic" to mean that, as far as we can see, it describes the way the world is in this regard. Could we perhaps go further than this and say that on our present knowledge it is an irreducible intrinsic interdependence, by this meaning that we cannot reduce the mental to the physical any more than we can reduce the physical to the mental? In this sense there is an important duality to be recognized, but it is a duality without dualism.[26]

Some will recognize that the position suggested here is similar to that of P. F. Strawson.[27] As far as people are concerned, the prime ontological term is "person," the individual subject of whom we assert two types of predicates, mental and physical. There is thus a duality, but not dualism: the ontological reality of "person" is primary, and is neither mental nor physical.

In attempting to think further about this irreducible intrinsic interdependence which manifests duality without dualism, an analogy some have found helpful is in terms of computer software and computer hardware — an apt analogy when so many of us make daily use of our computers. Even here, however, there are traps for the unwary. All too easily analogies of the relationship between mental events and physical events, or software and hardware, are smuggled in as if they were explanations.

8. Neuropsychology, Evolutionary Psychology, and the Imago Dei

In a multidisciplinary symposium such as this, a relevant question is whether there are wider implications of advances in neuroscience, cognitive psychology, and evolutionary psychology that could prompt us to reexamine views of the human person that have been held within the Christian church over the last two millennia. An example of such implications can be illustrated by looking

26. Cf. P. Clayton, "Emergence, the Quest for Unity, and God: Toward a Constructive Christian Theology of the Person," this volume.

27. P. F. Strawson, *Individualism: An Essay in Descriptive Metaphysics* (London: Methuen, 1959), 1.3.78-116.

at the variety of views held by the church down the centuries on what is meant by saying that the human person is made in the image of God.

Consider three of the views of the imago Dei that at various times have been prominent in the church's history and that are challenged by scientific advances.

1. The Imago Dei as the Capacity to Reason

This is exemplified by the following extract from a catechism of the Catholic Church, which states that "God . . . can be known . . . by the natural light of reason. . . . Man has this capacity because he is created 'in the image of God.'"[28]

This Catholic view is firmly embedded in the works of Descartes, who wrote, "The human mind, by virtue of its rationality, provides evidence both of a kind of image of God and at the same time a criterion of radical discontinuity from the rest of creation. The animals are merely machines, and it is said that some of the enlightened believe that their cries of pain are no more than the squeaks of unlubricated machinery."[29] How do such views stand in the light of research into the cognitive capacities of animals and more especially of nonhuman primates? There is now a large body of evidence pointing to the conclusion that animals also think. There is an expanding research literature discussing whether or not chimpanzees have a "theory of mind," for example the two volumes on so-called Machiavellian Intelligence.[30] Further evidence is available of behavior that, if it were seen in humans, would be described as imagination and as involving inventiveness and means-end reasoning. Studies at the interface with neuroscience indicate how these emerging capacities may be related to the development of the brain. The implication is that in each instance any attempt to set down a clear demarcation between the reasoning abilities of nonhuman primates and humans is found to have become blurred.

This, of course, is not to deny that there are definitively distinctive capacities in humans, witnessed for example in remarkable human developments

28. *Catechism of the Catholic Church*, 111. *The Knowledge of God according to the Church*, 36.

29. Descartes as quoted in C. Gunton, *The Promise of a Trinitarian Theology*, 2nd ed. (Edinburgh: T. & T. Clark, 1997).

30. R. W. Byrne and A. Whiten, *Machiavellian Intelligence: Social Expertise and the Evolution of Intellect in Monkeys, Apes and Humans* (Oxford: Clarendon, 1988); R. W. Byrne and A. Whiten, *Machiavellian Intelligence II: Extensions and Evaluations* (Cambridge: Cambridge University Press, 1997).

in learning, philosophy, literature, music, art, religion, and science. The point is simply that evidence for reasoning and thinking abilities in nonhuman primates is available. While rudimentary, they are today seen to overlap with similar abilities in developing small children. It therefore becomes increasingly difficult to seek to anchor a belief in the uniqueness of humans created in the image of God in terms of reasoning.

2. The Imago Dei as the Capacity for Moral Behavior and Moral Agency

The illustrious North American theologian Jonathan Edwards wrote, "herein does very much consist that image of God wherein He made man . . . viz in those faculties and principles of nature whereby he is capable of moral agency."[31] If Edwards was claiming that this capacity was unique to humans, then we may ask how such a claim stands today in light of developments in evolutionary psychology. Over the past three decades evidence has been steadily accumulating of behavior, which if we were to witness it in humans, we would attribute to the possession of a moral sense and moral agency. Thus for example Frans de Waal has written, "Aiding others at the cost or risk to oneself is widespread in the animal kingdom." He adds that "[t]he fact that the human moral sense goes so far back in evolutionary history that other species show signs of it plants morality firmly near the centre of our much maligned nature."[32] Clearly self-giving is found not just in God's human work.

De Waal and other leaders in the field are at pains to point out the dangers of sloppy thinking in this area. De Waal writes, "Even if animals other than ourselves act in ways tantamount to moral behaviour, their behaviour does not necessarily rest on deliberations of the kind we engage in. It is hard to believe that animals weigh their own interests against the rights of others, that they develop a vision of the greater good of society, or that they feel lifelong guilt about something they should not have done."

There are good arguments for believing that some aspects of self-giving and self-limiting behavior have developed over our evolutionary history and become more pronounced among nonhuman primates. For those who begin from theistic presuppositions, it means we can see embedded within creation

31. J. Edwards, "On the Freedom of the Will," part 1, section 5, "Concerning the Notion of Liberty, and of Moral Agency."

32. F. de Waal, *Good Natured: The Origin of Right and Wrong in Humans and Other Animals* (Cambridge, MA, and London: Harvard University Press, 1997), pp. 216-17.

the seeds, development, and fruits of self-giving behavior. We do not need to deny the emergence of self-giving altruism in primates in order to defend the unique self-emptying sacrifice of Christ. That, we believe, was a unique and ultimate act that sets Christ apart from all others in heaven and on earth.

3. The Imago Dei as a Capacity for Personal Relatedness

To focus on the capacity for personal relatedness is another way of describing what in the past has been alluded to in discussions of the societal nature of the divine image. Sinclair Ferguson has pointed out that some of the leading theologians of the last century, such as Brunner and Barth, emphasized that the image of God is not the possession of the isolated individual but of the person in community.[33] Barth developed the idea in a characteristically Christocentric manner. More recently, the theologian Colin Gunton has stated quite explicitly that "to be a person is to be made in the image of God. . . . [I]t is *in our relatedness to others that our being human consists.*"[34] It is interesting that a similar focus on relatedness is found today in the writings of neuropsychologists and evolutionary psychologists. Warren Brown has developed this further in his chapter. But the capacity for relatedness is not some capacity free-floating above the head or out there in space. Evolutionary psychologists Byrne and Corp have written that "learning in social contexts may be constrained by neocortical size," and "neocortical expansion has been driven by social challenges among the primates."[35]

The evidence from neuroscience and evolutionary psychology both point to the beginnings of an understanding of the neural substrates required to be functioning normally for the possession of a full capacity for personal interrelatedness. We noted earlier that one of the most significant neuroscience discoveries in the last decade was the identification of a small, specialized group of neurons in the frontal part the brain. These "mirror neurons," discovered by Giacomo Rizzolatti and his colleagues, seemed to be part of the essential substrate for interpersonal interactions.[36]

33. S. B. Ferguson, entry on "The Image of God," in *New Dictionary of Theology*, ed. S. B. Ferguson and David Wright (Downers Grove, IL: IVP, 1988).

34. C. Gunton, *The Promise of Trinitarian Theology*, 2nd ed. (Edinburgh: T. & T. Clark, 1997), p. 113; my italics.

35. R. B. Byrne and N. Corp, "Neocortex Size Predicts Deception Rate in Primates," *Proceedings of the Royal Society of London* (2004).

36. G. Rizzolatti, L. Fadigo, V. Gallese, and L. Fogassih, "Premotor cortex and the recog-

Ramachandran has predicted "that mirror neurons will do for psychology what DNA did for biology: they will provide a unifying framework and help explain a host of mental abilities that have hitherto remained mysterious and inaccessible to experiments . . . and thus I regard Rizzolatti's discovery as the most important unreported story of the last decade."[37]

It is already evident from further research that these mirror neurons are part of a wider network upon which the capacity for personal relatedness depends. The evidence for this comes from ongoing studies of the brains of autistic individuals. It is widely known that one of the difficulties experienced in some forms of autism is the capacity to relate to other people. It is already evident that in certain autistic individuals the brain is functioning abnormally as compared with controls when they are performing tasks that are known to normally mobilize the so-called mirror neurons. It will be some time before the full details have been worked out experimentally, and they will undoubtedly turn out to be far more complicated than at the moment we suspect. However, the important point here is that the capacity for relatedness, if this is to be seen as the key to understanding the imago Dei, is itself dependent upon our wholeness as persons and intimately dependent upon our biology. It is an embodied capacity.

9. Conclusions

Recent developments in neuroscience and evolutionary psychology are relevant to our understanding of human personhood. A holistic model of the human person does most justice to the scientific understanding of ourselves. Dualisms of parts or substances will not do. There is no scientific evidence for them, and there is no biblical warrant for them. Our unity is central. We know each other, not as brains ensheathed in bodies, but as embodied persons. We are people who relate to each other as beings created in the image of God, but this image is not a separate thing. It is not the possession of an immaterial soul, it is not the capacity to reason, and it is not the capacity for moral behavior.

Fine philosophical distinctions are not the business of the biblical authors. Joel Green has remarked, "the Bible's witness to the nature of human life is at once naïve and profound. It is naïve, not in the sense of gullibility or primi-

---

nition of motor actions," *Cognition, Brain Res.* 3 (1996): 131-41. See also V. S. Ramachandran, *The Third Culture*, 1 June 2000, www.edge.org/3rd.

37. Interview with Tom Stafford, *The Psychologist* 17, no. 11: 636-37.

tiveness, but because it has not worked out, in what we may regard as a philosophically satisfying way, the nature of physical existence in life, death, and afterlife. It is profound in its presentation of the human person fundamentally in relational terms, and its assessment of the human being as genuinely human and alive only within the family of humans brought into being by Yahweh and in relation to the God who gives life-giving breath."[38]

38. J. B. Green, "Eschatology and the Nature of Humans: A Reconsideration of Pertinent Biblical Evidence," *Science and Christian Belief* 14, no. 1 (2002): 33-50. See also A. Schüle, "'Soul' and 'Spirit' in the Anthropological Discourse of the Hebrew Bible," this volume.

The Emergence of Human Distinctiveness

Warren S. Brown

When I look at your heavens, the work of your fingers, the moon and
the stars that you have established; what are human beings that you
are mindful of them, mortals that you care for them?

Psalm 8:4 (NRSV)

1. Introduction

The psalmist asks an important question (Ps. 8:4, above) that is relevant to modern concerns regarding science and Christian faith. Within the specific context of twenty-first-century neuroscience, one might rephrase the question as follows: "Given the rapidly growing knowledge in neuroscience regarding human brain function and its relationship to behavior, cognition, and subjective mental life, what, if anything, about human nature has theological significance (i.e., 'that [God] would care for them')?" Clearly the creation passages in the Bible suggest a unique and distinctive place of humankind in God's creation. What is to be made of this? In what ways are we humans nested within the biological world and to what extent do we transcend biology? Does a theologically robust understanding of human nature demand a nonphysical part — a soul, mind, or spirit — that exists independent of the physical body and brain; or is it possible to understand the rational, moral, religious, and spiritual attributes of humanness as emergent from our physical embodiment and social embeddedness?

This paper will explore the thesis that a theologically adequate theory of human distinctiveness can be constructed within the context of our physical continuity with other animals and the scaffolding of a rich interpersonal culture. In pursuing this thesis, we will see that the neurologically embodied aspects of human nature that are critical for Christian theology can be understood as the deep sense of interpersonal relatedness and sociality that emerges from enhanced brain and cognitive capacities that develop (self-assemble) within the complex fabric of social and cultural systems.[1]

2. The Cartesian Paradigm for Human Uniqueness

A traditional solution to the problem of the theological significance of humankind has traditionally been to presume that we have a nonphysical part that is not subject to physical laws and limitations — such as a soul. René Descartes is most responsible for the huge impact of body/soul dualism on modern secular and Christian thinking. However, Descartes was mostly a physicalist in that he did not believe that the body was inhabited by many souls, as was commonly believed in Descartes' time.[2] Rather, Descartes believed that all basic bodily functions were aspects of a physical "machine," and that the functioning of animals did not transcend these mechanisms. The problem for Descartes was figuring out how such a biological mechanism could result in human consciousness, will, and rationality. So, Descartes solved this problem by retaining one soul. Thus, humans were considered to be unique in having a soul (only one) that is immaterial and interacts with the physical body through the pineal gland.

It is reasonable to ask: "What might Descartes have concluded had he had before him the current body of neuroscience literature?" Would he have found it easier to imagine how rationality might be embodied if he was presented with the recent fMRI evidence regarding the activity of the brain during moral decision making, for example?[3] Descartes' imagination regarding the possibilities for physicalism was limited by a lack of sophisticated neuroscience. He could not have concluded otherwise.

1. Portions of this material can also be found in W. S. Brown, "Nonreductive Human Uniqueness: Immaterial, Biological, or Psychosocial?" in *Human Identity at the Intersection of Science, Technology, and Religion,* ed. N. Murphy and C. C. Knight (publisher pending).

2. This perspective on Descartes is taken from C. Zimmer, *Soul Made Flesh: The Discovery of the Brain — and How It Changed the World* (New York: Free Press, 2004).

3. J. Greene et al., "The Neural Bases of Cognitive Conflict and Control in Moral Judgment," *Neuron* 44 (2004): 389-400. See also J. Greene et al., "An fMRI Investigation of Emotional Engagement in Moral Judgment," *Science* 293 (2001): 2105-8.

However, we have now a great deal of knowledge, still rapidly accumulating, regarding the ways brain activity provides the basis for not only moral decision making, but also various forms of religious experiences and very human interpersonal experiences such as empathy. In the face of this science, it is increasingly difficult to maintain a Cartesian view of human nature. As theologian Wolfhart Pannenberg has said, "When the life of the soul is conditioned in every detail by bodily organs and processes, how can it be detached from the body and survive?"[4] But can a theologically significant person be found within the modern scientific understanding of humankind?

3. The Uniqueness of Human Relatedness

Evolutionary psychologist Andrew Whiten has recently theorized that what distinguishes humankind from the rest of the animal world is "a deep social mind."[5] Whiten's claim is "that humans are more social — more deeply social — than any other species on earth, our closest primate relatives not excepted. . . . by 'deep' I am referring to a special degree of cognitive and mental penetration between individuals."[6] Thus, for Whiten, what makes humans distinctive is not primarily something inside a person (although enhanced brain-based cognitive and social capacities are critical), but how these capacities are used in interactions with other persons. The specific attributes of humankind that Whiten believes come together to allow for the emergence of such deep sociality include a Theory of Mind, culture, language, and cooperation (or altruism).

In a similar vein, I have previously argued that the unique quality that might be referred to as "soul" is a quality of humanness, not a thing.[7] Human "soulishness" (as I called it) is best understood as the capacities for, and experiences of, interpersonal relatedness. From the perspective of human psychology, this would involve both relatedness to other human beings and the ability to relate symbolically to oneself. With respect to theology, "soulishness" would include relatedness to God.

4. W. Pannenberg, *Systematic Theology,* vol. 2 (Grand Rapids: Eerdmans, 1991), p. 182.

5. A. Whiten, "The Place of 'Deep Social Mind' in the Evolution of Human Nature," in *Human Nature,* ed. M. A. Jeeves (Edinburgh: The Royal Society of Edinburgh, 2006), pp. 207-22.

6. Whiten, "The Place of 'Deep Social Mind' in the Evolution of Human Nature," p. 212.

7. W. S. Brown, "Cognitive Contributions to Soul," in *Whatever Happened to the Soul? Scientific and Theological Portraits of Human Nature,* ed. W. S. Brown, N. Murphy, and H. Newton Malony (Minneapolis: Fortress Press, 1998), pp. 99-126.

As with Whiten, I also made the point that deep and rich forms of human interpersonal relatedness are dependent upon, and emergent from, a basic set of human neurocognitive capacities. The cognitive capacities that I outlined included language, a Theory of Mind, forethought, an episodic memory, and socio-emotional responsiveness. Complex interactions between these basic neurocognitive capacities, as they are used in dealing with the social environment, result in the emergence of new higher-level human properties and capacities that cannot be entirely explained by the activity of any of the lower-level cognitive processes. Thus, deep and "soulish" forms of personal relatedness emerge from the dynamic interaction of many cognitive and emotional capacities within the context of human relationships.

My speculations about "soulishness" and interpersonal relatedness are resonant with Whiten's description of human uniqueness as manifest in a "deep social mind." From this perspective, what is distinctive about humankind is not a matter of the uniqueness of particular physical or cognitive abilities; our distinctiveness emerges from the dynamic outcome of our embodied interactions as we are embedded within social relationships and human culture, and within the presence of God.

4. Human Neurocognitive Distinctiveness

It is the primary thesis of this paper that unique human characteristics arise from what emerges in the interaction of various distinctly enhanced, but not unique, cognitive capacities. Nevertheless, it is helpful to consider a few of the basic cognitive capacities that are enhanced in human beings. It would be impossible to cover all of the various neurobiological and neuropsychological ways in which we humans are different from our closest primate cousins. The scientific topic of comparative cognitive neuroscience encompasses a very large literature. Thus, I have chosen to focus on the following topics: uniqueness of the human frontal lobes and their role in foresight, Von Economo neurons and interpersonal emotional attunement, language and symbolic capacities, and a "Theory of Mind."

5. The Human Frontal Lobes

Humans do not have the largest brains — that distinction is held by dolphins, whales, and elephants. However, critical to the power of human versus animal cognition is the relatively larger size of the cerebral cortex, and particularly in the size of those parts of the cortex that are not directly involved in sensory or motor functions. There are three such cortical areas — all referred to as "association cortex." Of these three cortical areas, the most significant evolutionary change has been expansion of the relative size of the prefrontal cortex. This area is roughly 12 percent of the total cerebral cortex in a monkey (a macaque) and 17 percent in a chimpanzee, but enlarged to occupy 29 percent of the total cerebral cortex in a human being.[8] With increased size of the frontal lobe comes much greater influence on processing in other brain areas via extensive two-way interactions with all of the motor, sensory, memory, and affective areas of the cerebral cortex.

Given the enhanced size of the frontal lobes in humankind, it is worth noting the specific functional capacities of the prefrontal cortex — that is, what enhanced cognitive capacities are allowed by this brain area and how might these contribute to human cognitive distinctiveness? Neuroscientist Joaquín Fuster summarizes five capacities for which the frontal cortex is essential: (1) integration of behavior over time; (2) establishment and manipulation of information in working memory; (3) maintenance of attention; (4) preparation for action; and (5) inhibitory control of behavior.[9] In the most general terms, the prefrontal cortex allows for adaptability over time, incorporating both retrospective and prospective aspects into the control of behavior. With respect to human distinctiveness, an exponentially enlarged prefrontal cortex allows for dramatically enhanced temporal regulation of behavior, expanded working memory, better control over attention, longer-term preparation for action, and greater behavioral inhibition and constraint.

Thus, prospective regulation of behavior (i.e., foresight and planning) are important human capacities made possible by our large prefrontal cortex. However, this capacity is not unique to humankind. Recent research reported in *Science* demonstrated the existence of a form of foresight in chimpanzees.[10] This research showed that apes can, in some cases, anticipate the future need for a tool — in one case an apparent anticipation extending over fourteen hours. This research makes the point that foresight is not exclusively (uniquely) present in humankind, but that a rudimentary form of foresight is present in nonhuman primates. Nevertheless, human foresight is distinctively robust.

8. J. M. Fuster, "Frontal Lobe and Cognitive Development," *Journal of Neurocytology* 31 (2002): 374-76.

9. J. M. Fuster, *Cortex and Mind: Unifying Cognition* (Oxford: Oxford University Press, 2003).

10. N. J. Mulcahy and J. Call, "Apes Save Tools for Future Use," *Science* 312 (2006): 1038-40.

The functional importance of the frontal lobes for characteristic human behavior is suggested by the correlation between the slowly maturing frontal cortex and the progressive emergence of adult cognitive skills and adult behavior. In human development, the cerebral cortex is remarkably slow to reach maturity.[11] Whereas a chimpanzee has an adult-like brain by the end of the second year, a similar degree of development is not reached until four to five years later in humans. Remarkably, the frontal cortex in humans is still maturing near the end of the second decade of life. Thus, the differences in cognitive power and flexibility between humans and apes is attributable not simply to the size of the prefrontal cortex, but also to the significantly extended opportunity for social learning to influence the organization of the frontal cortex due to its slow maturation in humans from infancy to adulthood. We shall return later to consider in greater depth the importance of this prolonged physical maturation of the human cerebral cortex for the emergence of human distinctiveness.

6. Von Economo Neurons

Recent research in the laboratory of neuroscientist John Allman at the California Institute of Technology has focused on a unique neuron called a spindle cell, or more typically, a Von Economo neuron.[12] Von Economo neurons are large neurons that have very long axons that project throughout much of the cerebral cortex. The cell bodies of these neurons are only found in the limbic cortex (specifically, the anterior cingulate cortex on the medial surface of the prefrontal cortex, and the insular cortex). The frontoinsular cortex receives information about the visceral/emotional state of the body (that is, information about things like heart rate, blood pressure, peripheral blood vessel dilation, muscle tone, etc.). This visceral information is processed in the insular cortex (and the anterior cingulate), and then spread throughout the rest of the cortex via the axons of Von Economo neurons. According to the hypothesis of Allman, these neurons provide a way of informing cognition about bodily states. Integration of information about bodily states with higher cognitive processing is important for the comprehension and integration of bodily emotional responses into thought, and thus is critical in signaling the emotional and social

---

11. Mulcahy and Call, "Apes Save Tools for Future Use," p. 376.

12. J. M. Allman, K. K. Watson, N. A. Tetreault, and A. Y. Hakeem, "Intuition and Autism: A Possible Role for Von Economo Neurons," *Trends in Cognitive Science* 9 (2005): 367-73.

significance of actions and perceptions (current or anticipated). The anterior cingulate cortex and the insular cortex, where Von Economo neurons arise, are structures that have been found in neuroimaging studies of humans to be markedly active during states of empathy, shame, trust, detecting the mental and emotional states of others, and moral decision making.

Most important for our current discussion, Von Economo neurons are relatively unique to the human brain. This type of neuron is found in great abundance in the adult human brain and in the brains of children as young as four years, but they are few in number in newborn human infants and in apes, and nonexistent in lower primates. Thus, besides having large frontal lobes, the human limbic cortex is supplied with a large quantity of relatively unique neurons that communicate subtle properties of bodily emotional reactions to the entire cerebral cortex. As a consequence, humankind has a relatively unique system for incorporating information about the subtleties of bodily reactions into awareness, thinking, and behavioral regulation. Allman has hypothesized that abnormality in the development of Von Economo neurons may be a cause of the deficits in social interaction characteristic of individuals with autism.[13] In a similar manner, Antonio Damasio has argued for the importance of "somatic markers" (i.e., feedback information regarding bodily emotional reactions) in the regulation of social and moral behavior. Absence of somatic-marker information is (in Damasio's account) the cause of the social inappropriateness, behavioral capriciousness, and amoral behavior of individuals with damage to the medial portion of the prefrontal cortex (adjacent to the anterior cingulate).[14] Damage to Von Economo neurons would diminish the availability of somatic-marker information to the rest of the brain.

7. Language

An obvious and very significant domain of human cognitive distinctiveness is the capacity to use language. Language processing is served by a particular functional brain architecture that is unique to the human brain. Even in newborn human infants it can be shown that there is both anatomical and functional specialization of the left cerebral cortex for language.[15] Thus, while

13. Allman et al., "Intuition and Autism," pp. 367-73.

14. A. R. Damasio, *Descartes' Error: Emotion, Reason, and the Human Brain* (New York: G. P. Putnam's Sons, 1994), p. 118.

15. G. Dehaene-Lambertz, L. Hertz-Pannier, and J. Dubois, "Nature and Nurture in Lan-

language is to some degree a developmental achievement, it rests on what appears to be a genetically endowed neural organization.

It is clear that gorillas and chimps in the wild do not use a language system, although they certainly communicate with vocal and gestural codes. Nevertheless, a large research literature over the last thirty years has suggested that the language gulf between humans and chimpanzees is not as wide as once imagined. Studies abound illustrating the ability of apes to learn various language-like communication systems. The most remarkable example of progress in mastering language is a chimpanzee (Bonobo) named Kanzi studied by Sue Savage-Rumbaugh and her colleagues.[16] Particularly notable was Kanzi's ability to understand a modest vocabulary of spoken English, including simple grammatical properties of sentences. With respect to arguments that are to follow regarding the social scaffolding of human intelligence, we should note the fact that the linguistic achievements of Kanzi occurred not in the wild, but in the context of intensive training and a rich human language environment beginning at infancy.

Terrence Deacon, in his book *The Symbolic Species*,[17] argues that a "symbolic threshold" has been crossed somewhere in human evolution. This threshold is crossed anew by each child via a "symbolic insight" that must be achieved during early development.[18] It is uncertain whether chimpanzees that have been taught language communication systems in laboratory experiments have achieved a symbolic insight. Perhaps Kanzi is remarkable among other examples of chimpanzee language learning in having come to a symbolic insight. Nevertheless, as Deacon rightly argues, the insight necessary for the development of fully symbolic language largely exceeds the capacity of chimpanzees.

With respect to what language might contribute to human uniqueness, we might consider what Deacon suggests as important contributions of language to human thought and behavior. He suggests the following: distancing of action from the demands of immediate motivations and needs; the ability to form a self-concept; expanded empathy; a virtual common mind among

---

guage Acquisition: Anatomical and Functional Brain-Imaging Studies in Infants," *Trends in Neurosciences* 29 (2006): 367-73.

16. S. Savage-Rumbaugh and R. Lewin, *Kanzi: The Ape at the Brink of the Human Mind* (New York: Wiley, 1994).

17. T. Deacon, *The Symbolic Species: The Co-evolution of Language and the Brain* (New York: W. W. Norton, 1997).

18. Deacon, *The Symbolic Species*, pp. 73ff.

groups of people; and the development of ethics.[19] To the degree that these aspects of thought and behavior are dependent on language, and to the degree that a symbolic insight is extremely difficult, if not impossible, for a chimpanzee, then these cognitive characteristics are uniquely human.

8. Theory of Mind

Much research has been done over the last decade on metacognition and the concept of a Theory of Mind (ToM). Metacognition is "thinking about thinking" — the awareness of the workings of one's own mind.[20] Theory of Mind is an understanding of the knowledge, beliefs, and mental states of other persons.[21] The ability to accurately attribute mental states to other people is illustrated by statements such as "I think she thinks" or "I think she thinks that he thinks." ToM also includes the imputation of intentionality and purpose to observations of the actions of other persons during social interactions.

At issue in much of this research has been the process of development of a ToM in children, as well as the possible role of an absence of a ToM in the disabilities of children with autism. There has also been much work done on the degree to which apes have a ToM, and on the extent of that ability. The summary message seems to be that a ToM can be demonstrated in apes — albeit in a less-sophisticated form, perhaps constituting a proto-ToM.[22] Whether present or absent in apes, the capacity to accurately infer the mental states, thoughts, and intentions of other individuals is an important contributor to the uniquely deep sociality of humankind.

9. Other Reflections on Neurocognitive Distinctiveness

Stories about human versus primate cognition populate the scientific literature, academic textbooks, and popular journalism. On the one hand, there seems to be nothing particular that humans can do (be it language, ToM, foresight . . .

19. Deacon, *The Symbolic Species,* chap. 13.

20. J. T. Jost, A. W. Kruglanski, and T. O. Nelson, "Social Metacognition: An Expansionist Review," *Personality & Social Psychology Review* 2 (1998): 137-54.

21. J. Perner and B. Lang, "Development of Theory of Mind and Executive Control," *Trends in Cognitive Sciences* 3 (1999): 337-44.

22. C. M. Heyes, "Theory of Mind in Nonhuman Primates," *Behavior and Brain Sciences* 21 (1998): 101-14.

whatever) that does not have at least some rudimentary form in apes. At the same time, the expression of these cognitive abilities in humankind is many orders of magnitude more sophisticated, to the point that comparing humans and primates seems like comparing apples and oranges — both are edible fruits that grow on trees, but they are nevertheless unique and not the least bit confusable. So, at the level of basic cognitive skills, "uniqueness" is in the eye of the beholder (or the philosophical commitments of the scholar).

It is equally clear from a long history of clinical observations within the medical field of neurology that failure of brain development, or brain disease, or traumatic brain injury can eliminate or seriously reduce any one of these capacities and (in most cases) the person remains unmistakably human, although generally not quite the same person. Thus, however unique or distinctive any one of these individual capacities may be, none of them alone seems to carry the full weight of our humanness.

10. Personhood, Emergence, and Scaffolding

Perhaps the human uniqueness that we intuitively understand is not in either the biological or the cognitive particulars. Perhaps it is a nonreducible quality of being that emerges in the interaction of all of these particulars as we relate to one another, and to the culture in which we live. This section will attempt to show that the quality of being that we call human emerges from brain systems in a manner that is consistent with theories of self-organizing dynamical systems. However, the nature of what emerges is subject to the scaffolding of culture. Thus, we encounter the individual and communal stories of the emergence of humanness and, by implication, of a theologically significant person.

11. Dynamic Systems Theory and the Emergence of Humanness

The theory and descriptions of dynamic systems give the best account of emergence — that is, how new, nonreducible, higher-level, causal properties arise within complex, nonlinear, near-chaotic, interactive systems.[23] The massively interconnected neuronal network of the human cerebral cortex is beautifully

23. For a good description of dynamic systems theory with respect to the human brain and the philosophy of human action, see A. Juarrero, *Dynamics in Action: Intentional Behavior as a Complex System* (Cambridge, MA: Bradford, 1999).

suited for emergence of the highest-level human characteristics via the processes described by the theory of complex dynamic systems.

When pushed far from equilibrium by environmental pressures, highly interactive aggregates self-organize into large functional systems that are constituted by patterns of constraints between the elements. Thus, the elements of the aggregate (which could be molecules, neurons, or a collection of smaller neural networks) come to work together in a coherent and coordinated manner to create a large-scale functional system. This larger system operates internally by restraining (or entraining) the future possibilities of each constituent element. Once organized into a system, the lower-level properties of the constituent elements interact (bottom-up) with the relational constraints created by the higher-level patterns (top-down), without implying any exceptions to lawfulness at the level of the elements.

In such systems, ongoing interactions with novel aspects of the environment cause repeated reorganizations that create increasingly more complex and higher-level forms of system organization, and consequently more complex forms of environmental response and interaction. Thus, multiple smaller systems can be organized into even larger systems. In this way, the process of repeated reorganization can result in a nested hierarchy of more and more complex functional systems. Such organizations and reorganizations of a system in order to meet pressures from its interaction with the environment mean that the system organization embodies meaning in the form of a pattern capable of meeting that particular aspect of the environment. The state of organization carries forward a memory of previous interactions and is prepared to deal with similar situations in the future.

In addition, establishment of patterns of constraints between the elements of a system results in the emergence of higher-level system properties that manifest greater freedom. The system has a substantially greater number of possibilities with respect to its interactions with its surrounding environment than it had prior to each new level of self-reorganization. As Alicia Juarrero expresses it, "The higher level of organization, whether thermodynamic, psychological, or social, possesses a qualitatively different repertoire of states and behaviors than the earlier level, as well as greater degrees of freedom."[24]

As already mentioned, one of the most significant structural characteristics of the prefrontal cortex is its massively recurrent networks of interactions with the perceptual, motor, and memory areas of the brain. From the perspec-

24. Juarrero, *Dynamics in Action*, p. 145.

tive of complex dynamic systems theory, the functioning of such a network of widespread recurrent interactions would result in emergent functional properties that would be both nonreductive and causal in human behavior. In this light, neuroscientist Joaquín Fuster writes:

> [A]s networks fan outward and upward in associative neocortex, they become capable of generating novel representations that are not reducible to their inputs or to their individual neuronal components. Those representations are the product of complex, nonlinear, and near-chaotic interactions between innumerable elements of high-level networks far removed from sensory receptors and motor effectors. Then, top-down network building predominates. Imagination, creativity, and intuition are some of the cognitive attributes of those emergent high-level representations.[25]

Thus, dynamic systems theory specifies how truly emergent, nonreductive properties are possible in complexly interactive physical systems. Such emergence is particularly likely within the hypercomplex human brain with its prolonged maturation and developmental plasticity, allowing for manifold rounds of organization and reorganization when continually pressed by the complex social networks in which persons are embedded.

12. Cultural Scaffolding

There are many factors to consider in giving a reasonable account of human uniqueness. If the idea from dynamic systems theory is true regarding the self-assembly and self-organization of our humanness as we interact with our social and cultural environment, then our embeddedness in culture must be included in thinking about human uniqueness.

Andy Clark, in his book *Being There,* goes so far as to argue that some of the most important aspects of human intelligence are not within the brain or body at all.[26] Clark points out the importance of "external scaffolding" in the emergence of the highest forms of human mental processing. "Scaffolding" refers to all of the ways that an organism relies on external supports for augmenting internal mental processing. Clark writes:

---

25. Fuster, "Frontal Lobe and Cognitive Development," p. 53.
26. A. Clark, *Being There: Putting Brain, Body, and World Together Again* (Cambridge, MA: MIT Press, 1997).

We use intelligence to structure our environment so that we can succeed with less intelligence. Our brains make the world smart so that we can be dumb in peace! . . . It is the human brain plus these chunks of external scaffolding that finally constitutes the smart, rational inference engine we call mind.[27]

Thus, some of the most important elements of human mental capacities arise from that which the long cultural history of the human race has built into our environments to augment our cognitive processes.

Human culture involves a vast array of artifacts that scaffold cognitive processing, the most remarkable of which is language. According to Clark, language symbols pre-structure thinking and problem solving such as to allow later generations to accomplish tasks that could not be mastered by previous generations. Language is, in Andy Clark's words, "a computational transformer that allows a pattern-completing brain to tackle otherwise intractable classes of cognitive problems."[28]

So, our embeddedness in a social and cultural context serves not only to influence the self-assembly and continual reorganization of our bodily neuro-cognitive systems, but it also offloads much of the cognitive work that allows us to act intelligently and creatively and to flourish as persons and as societies. We become more intelligent as human beings by learning to use "tools" that we did not have to invent.

We could also reasonably argue that human social intelligence — our deep sociality — is scaffolded by cultural systems within which we learn to negotiate the social world: families, nurseries, schools, universities, clubs, businesses, governments, etc. Our process of self-assembly in becoming uniquely human is a matter of learning to marshal the benefits of interpersonal and social systems that we do not need to invent.

13. The Augustinian/Cartesian Error[29]

It is characteristic of Augustinian and Cartesian thinking to look for the essence of human uniqueness inside versus outside of persons. Theological

27. Clark, *Being There,* p. 180.
28. Clark, *Being There,* p. 194.
29. This section follows a similar section in W. S. Brown, "The Brain, Religion, and Baseball: Comments on the Potential for a Neurology of Religion," in *Where God and Science Meet: How Brain and Evolutionary Studies Alter Our Understanding of Religion,* vol. 2: *The Neurology of Religious Experience* ed. P. McNamara (Westport, CT: Greenwood Press, 2006), pp. 229-44.

thinking about human nature has been dominated by this view for many centuries. However, study of the neuroscience of important, high-level, uniquely human capacities is also still influenced by the remnants of this Augustinian/Cartesian worldview.

St. Augustine linked Platonic body-soul dualism to a spirituality of inwardness and radical reflexivity (that is, looking inward for the source of spiritual life). He also gave Western culture and Christian theology the idea of an inner self that is often identified with the soul. In this formulation of human nature, our true selves were no longer our whole physical being, but became nonmaterial souls that reside inside our bodies. Philosopher René Descartes sharpened the distinction between body and soul (or body and mind). As described earlier, Descartes believed that the body was a physical machine. However, unable to imagine how rationality could be manifest by a machine, Descartes argued that humans have a distinct nonmaterial entity — a soul or mind. As the seat of rationality, the soul was presumed to be hierarchically superior to, and more important than, the body. In addition, as with Augustine, this hierarchically more important soul (or mind) was presumed to reside inside the body.

Many scientists, philosophers, and theologians these days would argue against Descartes in favor of an embodied (nondualistic) view of human nature. However, even within a nondualist (and thus physicalist) understanding of persons, it is hard to avoid the idea that the most important and unique aspects of humanness reside inside the head. In most theories within neuroscience, the mind is still considered to be an entity that exists entirely inside the head in the form of brain functions that are distinct from the rest of the physical person and also distinct from the social environment. This is the view that Daniel Dennett (1991) has referred to as "Cartesian materialism." Instead of a body and an inner soul (or mind), we have a body and inner brain functions (i.e., brain-body dualism). From this point of view, we implicitly assume that all that is important and unique about human nature must be identified with functions or properties that reside inside individual human persons. This view relegates interpersonal relations and social systems to a secondary status with respect to our understanding of the most unique and important aspects of human nature. Within the Cartesian worldview, everything that is important about humanity must be both inner and individual.

A major change in modern thinking about the human mind has been to move away from the cognitivist view that mental activity is composed of internal computations performed on abstract representations.[30] This cognitiv-

30. R. W. Gibbs Jr., *Embodiment and Cognitive Science* (New York: Cambridge University

ist or computational view is essentially Cartesian in the dissociation of mind from embodied life in the world. The mind stands apart as an abstract symbol manipulator. The current view is of an embodied mind that works via either direct interaction with the environment, or via simulations and emulations of embodied experience in the world. Thus, even when a person is disengaged from current activity and merely thinking, the activities that go on are versions of embodied interactions with the world (i.e., simulations, rehearsals, and memories). Thus individual persons and the social environments that they inhabit are nonautonomous and constantly interactive systems. The mind is not exclusively inner or individual.

An example of this tendency can be found in neuroscience research on religiousness. Consistent with the philosophical commitment to a physicalist understanding of human nature, religiousness is presumed in this research to be embodied in some manner. However, an additional implicit assumption has been the Augustinian/Cartesian idea that any important property of humanness, such as religion, must be resident inside individual human persons (presumably in some unique form of brain functioning). If religion is a unique aspect of humanness, then (in this view) it must be the case that religion resides inside each individual person — within neural systems that are uniquely responsible for one's religiousness and religious experiences . . . perhaps in a "God module."[31]

An alternative view that gains more distance from the Cartesian view is that, while humans have significantly enhanced neural machinery and cognitive capacities, what is most unique about humankind is the way the machinery is used to interact with the physical and social environment. The uniqueness of humankind does not lie in the neural machinery *per se* (which, after all, can be viewed as "merely" an extension and expansion of biological machinery that is also found in apes). Rather, human uniqueness resides in emergent properties elicited by interactions with our social environment — an environment that, in turn, we create and modify. Thus, when studying uniquely human capacities, the critical questions are not about the machinery itself (that is, about brain systems), but about how, when we are embedded in the social processes of human culture, there emerge remarkably more complex forms of behavior and experience, notably increased degrees of freedom in thought

---

Press, 2006). Also see P. J. Marshall, "Relating Psychology and Neuroscience," *Perspectives on Psychological Science* 4 (2009): 113-25.

31. V. S. Ramachandran et al., "The Neural Basis of Religious Experience," *Society for Neuroscience Abstracts* (1997): 1316.

and behavior, and unique forms of behavior such as religiousness and moral responsibility.

14. Final Theological Reflections

What has been presented suggests that the following propositions are reasonable. First, whatever is unique about humankind is not immaterial, as in a nonmaterial soul or mind. Rather, human cognitive neuroscience strongly suggests that all aspects of human functioning are embodied within neural systems. Similarly, these embodied higher cognitive abilities of humans are enhancements of similar structures and capacities found in other primates. Second, whatever is unique about humankind is emergent — that is, the properties and qualities of humanness emerge from the interactive use of basic capacities that are shared in some form with lower primates. Third, these high-level capacities of individuals are not entirely genetically determined, but self-assemble and self-organize within the context of interactions with the social and cultural environment. Thus, human uniqueness is a nonreductive property of the whole person in much the same sense as the nonreductive and causal properties manifested by complex dynamic systems. Finally, the most uniquely human property to emerge is our "deep social mind."[32]

This paper began with the following question: "Given the rapidly growing knowledge in neuroscience regarding human brain function and its relationship to behavior, cognition, and subjective mental life, what, if anything, about human nature has theological significance (i.e., 'that [God] would care for them')?" Thus, the challenge has been to find a description of human nature that is theologically robust (that is, compatible with Christian theology), yet that is resonant with modern neuroscience. It has been argued that humans are not particularly biologically or cognitively unique, nor do they possess a distinct nonmaterial substance or part, but are nevertheless distinctive due to the emergence of a deep sense of social relatedness.

However, in the final analysis, perhaps we should admit that we human beings are theologically unique in the cosmos not due to anything about us (whether nonmaterial, neurocognitive, or socially emergent), but due to the fact that we have been designated to stand in a unique relationship to God.

32. Whiten, "The Place of 'Deep Social Mind' in the Evolution of Human Nature."

Hierarchical Selection and the Evolutionary Emergence of "Spirit"

Jeffrey P. Schloss

"We thus arrive at the conviction of the last importance, that all natural bodies with which we are acquainted are equally endowed with life (gleichmäßig belebt sind); that the distinction between living and dead matter does not exist. When a stone is thrown into the air and falls by certain laws to the ground, or when a solution of salt forms a crystal, the result is neither more nor less a mechanical manifestation of life, than the flowering of a plant, the generation or sensibility of animals, or the feelings or the mental activity of man."[1]

"But if we accept, as I do, the view that living beings form a hierarchy in which each higher level represents a distinctive principle that harnesses the level below it (while being itself irreducible to its lower principles), then the evolutionary sequence gains a new and deeper significance. We can recognize then a strictly defined progression, rising from the inanimate level to ever higher additional principles of life."[2]

In this paper I wish to explore recent developments in evolutionary theory that bear upon our understanding of the crucial tensions in the above quotes, which involve debate not only over the adequacy of mechanistic accounts of

---

1. E. Haeckel, *Natürliche Schöpfungsgeschichte*, Zweite Auflage (Berlin: 1873), p. 21; cited in C. Hodge, *What Is Darwinism?* (New York: Scribner, Armstrong & Co., 1874), pp. 93-94.
2. M. Polanyi, "Life's Irreducible Structure," *Science* 160 (1968): 1311.

life, but over whether there even is a meaningful distinction between animate and inanimate, whether life is a quality or state that admits to hierarchical scaling, and whether human beings can be fully explained by the same fundamental principles that explain the behavior of plants or, for that matter, molecules. The terms that have informed the conversation of this project — flesh, body, mind, soul, and spirit — however imperfectly formulated by theological and scientific discourse of the past, highlight this tension. I will suggest that the reductionist paradigm (championed in the above quote by Haeckel), while it has been immensely fruitful for biology, entails important predictions in the area of evolutionary theory that turn out to be challenged by empirical data. The most recent and unanticipated conclusion is that Polanyi seems to have been right in asserting a progressive and irreducible sequence of living organisms, culminating (but by no means necessarily terminating) in human persons.

I will focus on three hallmark postulates of reductionism in twentieth-century biology. First, is the ostensible triumph of mechanism over vitalism, after three centuries of debate (and I will comment only briefly on this). Second, is the proposal that the gene (and not the cell or the organism) is the "atom" of biology: it is the fundamental particulate actor in the drama of life, as the primary if not the sole level at which natural selection acts. Third, is the claim that not just the origin but also the operation of the human mind — the central tendencies of cognition, affect, and most important in my treatment, the behaviors they induce — can be fully or at least adequately accounted for in terms of contribution to reproductive fitness.

1. Mechanism, Vitalism, and the Extrusion of Spirit

"Soul" and "spirit" (and for many, mind; for some, even body)[3] have fallen into hard times in biology. This is understandable because of their association with substance dualism, and more ambiguously with vitalism — concepts that appear neither warranted by nor fruitful for scientific understanding of biological processes.

With respect to dualism, these notions have not always been nor are they intrinsically metaphysically dualist. The notion of spirit refers, both metaphorically and literally, to "breath of life": Latin *Spiritus,* deriving from *spirare,* to

3. E.g., see Richard Dawkins's reconceptualization of the organism in *The Extended Phenotype* (New York: Oxford University Press, 1983).

breathe.[4] The dictionary definition of "spirit" is simply "the vital principle or animating force within living things." Logically, this can involve anything from a metaphysically distinct vital substance to the mere homeostatic (entropy-resisting) employment of oxidative metabolism evident at the macroscopic level, for example, in metazoan breathing. The term "soul" may have a similar derivation (*psyche, ψυχή* from ψύχω, "I blow"). Of course it has been used in varying and ambiguous ways, including as a synonym with spirit or animating principle, or as mind or rational substance, but a longstanding and important employment in biology — from Aristotle through Hans Driesch and Hans Jonas — is that of form (not morphology, but formational capacity) or entelechy, a naturalized teleology of "holding its end within itself."[5] Interestingly, these two characteristics — roughly conceived of as metabolism and development (including reproduction) — correspond to hallmark energetic and informational attributes of life proposed by Schrödinger and numerous contemporary evolutionary biologists.[6] Aristotle even seems to anticipate if not assert this, in his distinction between entelechia (ἐντελέχεια) and *energeia* (ἐνέργεια) as formative and active principles.

Perhaps more important than (and sometimes conflated with) the metaphysical dispute over dualism engendered by notions of spirit and soul, is the associated ontological debate over mechanism and vitalism. This debate is rendered turbid by two sources of ambiguity. First, while the notion of mechanism is relatively straightforward, the concept of "vitalism" as an alternative involves a wide spectrum of proposals.[7] It has been postulated, or criticized, as

4. It entails a similar etymology both in Hebrew employment of *ruach* and Greek *pneuma* as breath or spirit.

5. C. Cosans, "Aristotle's Anatomical Philosophy of Nature," *Biology and Philosophy* 13 (1998): 311-39; D. Balme, "Teleology and Necessity," in *Philosophical Issues in Aristotle's Biology*, ed. A. Gotthelf and J. G. Lennox (Cambridge: Cambridge University Press, 1987), pp. 275-85.

6. E. Schrödinger, *What Is Life?: with "Mind and Matter" and "Autobiographical Sketches"* (Cambridge: Cambridge University Press, 1991); J. M. Smith and E. Szathmáry, *The Origins of Life: From the Birth of Life to the Origins of Language* (New York: Oxford University Press, 1999); R. Michod, *Darwinian Dynamics: Evolutionary Transitions in Fitness and Individuality* (Princeton: Princeton University Press, 2000).

7. One of the clearest analyses of different meanings of "vitalism" and of the impact of these differences on experimental and philosophical analysis — as scientific debate was reaching its twentieth-century climax — is A. O. Lovejoy's essay, "The Meaning of Vitalism," *Science* 847 (1911): 437-41, which precipitated a lively and perhaps "last gasp" exchange. See H. Jennings, "Vitalism and Experimental Investigation," *Science* 859 (1911): 927-32; H. Jennings, "Driesch's Vitalism and Experimental Indeterminism," *Science* 927 (1912): 434-35; A. O. Lovejoy, "The Import of Vitalism," *Science* 864 (1911): 75-80; A. O. Lovejoy, "The Making of Driesch and the Meaning of Vitalism," *Science* 933 (1912): 672-75.

JEFFREY P. SCHLOSS

involving (a) the existence a vital substance; (b) a teleological or end-directing causal property; (c) a naturalistic animating force akin to gravity or other fundamental forces; (d) Lebensautonomie — the often-critiqued as but not always self-professedly vitalistic notion that life is fully constrained by but not reducible to or predictable from the laws of physics, and therefore needs its own laws;[8] and (e) the comparatively modest assertion that life is explainable by physical laws — but we need to supplement "ordinary" laws of physics derived from observations of inanimate nature with ones we have yet to derive from exploring the special case of life.[9] Range of meanings notwithstanding, the term "vitalism" has become a virtual epithet in modern biology.[10]

The second issue of ambiguity involves not an explanatory but merely a descriptive distinction of living from nonliving things. The attribution of life or agency constitutes a crucial and universal category of human judgment, but it is rendered ambiguous because it is both prescientific in terms of cultural history and preconceptual in terms of cognitive development.[11] Indeed, the detection of agency appears to be fairly promiscuous and unparsimonious

8. Polanyi, "Life's Irreducible Structure"; R. Rosen, *Life Itself: A Comprehensive Inquiry into the Nature, Origin, and Fabrication of Life* (New York: Columbia University Press, 2005).

9. E. Schrödinger, *What Is Life?* Schrödinger makes this point repeatedly in the last chapter of his essay, "What Is Life?": "What I wish to make clear in this last chapter is, from all we have learnt about the structure of living matter, we must be prepared to find it working in a manner that cannot be reduced to the ordinary laws of physics. And that not on the ground that there is any 'new force' or what not . . . but because the construction is different from anything we have yet tested in the physical laboratory" (p. 76). And "We must therefore not be discouraged by the difficulty of interpreting life by the ordinary laws of physics. For that is just what is to be expected from the knowledge we have gained of the structure of living matter. We must be prepared to find a new type of physical law prevailing in it" (p. 80).

10. Some thinkers who are sympathetic to the latter two perspectives but wish to rescue them from the pejorative charge of "vitalism" distinguish them as being "holistic" integration of both mechanism and vitalism (e.g., Ernst Cassirer and J. B. S. Haldane). This may be true of the latter proposal, but we don't know, because the hypothetical new laws are not yet discovered. However, it is definitely not true of the former proposal, and Michael Polanyi, for example, explicitly disavows it: "Irreducibility must not be identified with the mere fact that the joining of parts may produce features which are not observed in the separate parts. . . . Such cases of holism are common in physics and chemistry. They are often said to represent a transition to living things, but this is not the case. For they are reducible to the laws of inanimate matter, while living things are not" ("Life's Irreducible Structure," p. 1310). Philip Clayton (this volume) makes a similar point.

11. Considerable empirical support exists for the existence of innate cognitive mechanisms for attributing agency and distinguishing animate from inanimate, which operate long before the acquisition of language in cognitive development. J. Barrett, *Why Would Anyone Believe in God?* (Lanham, MD: AltaMira Press, 2004).

128

in early stages of both cultural and psychological development. The process of rationally constraining this innate and often overly exuberant or magical imputation of spirit characteristic of early developmental stages is seen in both individual ontogeny and the history of science. It is in this context that the reductive methodology of science has progressively delimited, then reconceptualized, and finally omitted the notion of spirit from our ontology altogether.

The extrusion of spirit from early history through nineteenth-century biology is a story that is told to the point of cliché, if not idealization. But it is often recounted in ways that involve both melodramatic oversimplification and factual inaccuracies that foreclose conversation.

Just as the ascendance of monotheism may represent a constraint on the extravagant attribution of supernatural spirit by shamanistic, pantheistic, and polytheistic religions, so the development of Aristotelian biology — with its distinction between the nonliving and living, the latter entailing vegetative, animal, and rational souls — may represent an analogous constraint on the indiscriminate imputation of living spirit in animistic or idealistic traditions. At the same time, it not only constrained but also nuanced understanding of the living soul or animating principle with an ontology that, while not substantively dualistic, was both hierarchical and teleological in its notion of entelechy.[12]

Cartesian dualism both supplemented and diminished this understanding by, on the one hand, the addition of a metaphysically distinct substance or rational soul, and on the other hand, the elimination of biotic souls and hierarchical distinctions between other living organisms, all of which were simply viewed as machines (Discourse V). The Aristotelian duality of form and substance was replaced by the substance dualism of body and mind; and all nonhuman organisms (and human bodies) were understood monistically and reductively. Anticipating evolutionary theories of abiogenesis, he held that no soul was necessary for the functioning or the origin of organisms, which could arise spontaneously and be operationally explained by the principles of matter in motion. Moreover, just as the origin and the operation of living organisms could be explained mechanistically, so too could their development. Breaking with the epigenetic views of Aristotelian biology which understood organisms to generate themselves progressively under the auspices of a formative principle not understandable in terms of the material parts, Descartes held that "[i]f

12. A. Gotthelf, "Aristotle's Conception of Final Causality," in *Philosophical Issues in Aristotle's Biology,* ed. A. Gotthelf and J. Lennox (Cambridge: Cambridge University Press, 1987), pp. 204-42.

we possessed a thorough knowledge of all the parts of the seed of any species of animal (e.g. man), we could from that alone, by reasons entirely mathematical and certain, deduce the whole figure and conformation of each of its members, and, conversely, if we knew several peculiarities of this conformation, we could from these deduce the nature of its seed."[13]

This provoked a fascinating debate between mechanists and vitalists, which lasted the better part of two and a half centuries. The essence of this debate was not strictly metaphysical, but also empirical: it turned on whether living organisms did things that were qualitatively different than nonliving things, and whether they were therefore necessary to produce these effects (e.g., to give rise to living things, to generate organic form or compounds). The alternative was that the behavior and character of living things is entirely explainable — and presumably predictable — by chemistry. This debate has become something of an icon of the popularized history of biology. The vitalists are often stereotyped as superstitious or pseudoscientific, the mechanists are portrayed as committed to empiricism, and the controversy is frequently depicted as being conclusively resolved by one or several decisive experiments in an epic duel.[14] The truth of the matter is that the debate was complicated, genuine, ongoing, and it spilled across a wide variety of questions and subdisciplines.[15]

A major theater of this drama entailed disputes over spontaneous generation.[16] Interestingly, and contrary to many contemporary textbook presentations, the view of mechanism or strict materialism, now universally accepted,

13. R. Descartes, *Discourse on Method* (1637), cited in B. Burt, *A History of Modern Philosophy,* vol. 1 (Chicago: A. C. McClurg and Co., 1892), p. 98.

14. J. Strick, *Sparks of Life: Darwinism and the Victorian Debate over Spontaneous Generation* (Cambridge, MA: Harvard University Press, 2002); also "New Details Add to Our Understanding of Spontaneous Generation Controversies," *American Society of Microbiology News* 63 (1997): 193-98.

15. D. Dix, "A Defense of Vitalism," *Journal of Theoretical Biology* 20 (1968): 338-40; J. Farley, *The Spontaneous Generation Controversy from Descartes to Oparin* (Baltimore: Johns Hopkins University Press, 1977); P. Sloan, "Descartes, the Skeptics, and the Rejection of Vitalism in Seventeenth-Century Physiology," *Studies in History and Philosophy of Science* 8 (1977): 1-28; N. Roll-Hansen, "Experimental Method and Spontaneous Generation: The Controversy between Pasteur and Pouchet 1859-64," *Journal of the History of Medicine and Allied Sciences* (1979): 273-92; F. Burwick and P. Douglass, eds., *The Crisis in Modernism: Bergson and the Vitalist Controversy* (New York: Cambridge University Press, 1992); P. J. Ramberg, "The Death of Vitalism and the Birth of Organic Chemistry: Wohler's Urea Synthesis and the Disciplinary Identity of Organic Chemistry," *Ambix* 47 (2000): 170-95.

16. Farley, *The Spontaneous Generation Controversy*; J. Strick, *Sparks of Life: Darwinism and the Victorian Debates over Spontaneous Generation* (Cambridge, MA: Harvard University Press, 2002).

was associated (as per Descartes' proposal) with spontaneous generation, now soundly rejected. A jingoistic popular history of science now matches the "winners" by erroneously coupling spontaneous generation with vitalism. For example, a contemporary microbiology textbook states: "Spontaneous generation was a widely held belief throughout the middle ages and into the latter half of the 19th century. . . . The idea was attractive because it meshed nicely with the prevailing religious views of how God created the universe. There was a strong bias to legitimize the idea because this vital force was considered a strong proof of God's presence in the world."[17] Actually, quite contrary to this, in many quarters spontaneous generation was understandably "perceived as a threat to the belief in a providential Creator."[18]

The question of spontaneous generation turned out to be very difficult to resolve empirically, and contrasting experimental results supported each hypothesis without easy, successful resolution. In the seventeenth, eighteenth, and nineteenth centuries respectively, Redi, Spallanzani, and Pasteur each produced experimental demonstrations that challenged spontaneous generation, but it was so tied to the ascendance of mechanistic understandings that alternative explanations were proffered and often preferred. In some current biology textbooks, Pasteur is represented as opposing vitalism and settling the issue of spontaneous generation with his famous *Experimentum crucis* using goose-necked flasks. But neither is the case.[19] He vigorously supported vitalism, and his experiments did not settle the issue of spontaneous generation. (Moreover, had they discredited spontaneous generation, that would have counted as evidence for vitalism.) T. H. Huxley's advocacy for Pasteur and against spontaneous generation in English biology education may have done more than the experiments themselves.[20] Fascinatingly, although the idea of spontaneous generation had been associated with a strict materialism since Descartes, proponents of the new and culturally debated theory of evolution were themselves divided on whether spontaneous gen-

17. T. Paustian and G. Roberts, *Through the Microscope: A Look at All Things Small,* 2nd ed. (Textbook Consortia, 2008). G. Geison, *The Private Science of Louis Pasteur* (Princeton: Princeton University Press, 1995).

18. G. Geison, *The Private Science of Louis Pasteur.*

19. J. Strick, "Pasteur & Tyndall on Spontaneous Generation: The Role of Biology Textbooks in Creating an Experimentum crucis," *SHiPS Resource Center for Sociology, History and Philosophy in Science Teaching,* 2005. http://www1.umn.edu/ships/updates/pasteur1.htm

20. Strick, *Sparks of Life;* also "Darwinism and the Origin of Life: The Role of H. C. Bastian in the British Spontaneous Generation Debates," *Journal of the History of Biology* 32 (1999): 51-92.

eration was consistent with advocating the theory.[21] Huxley ultimately won out with his distinction between abiogenesis and biogenesis, linking the latter to evolution.[22]

A second major empirical question associated with the mechanism-vitalism debate — and lasting nearly as long as that over spontaneous generation through a comparable series of "dueling experiments" — is the debate over epigenesis (the view that form is generated from or "on" matter according to teleological principles not resident in the matter) and preformationism (the mechanistic view that form is precontained in the properties or structures of matter and develops according to physical law). The philosophical roots of epigenesis go back to Aristotle, and the most direct philosophical roots of preformationism are Cartesian.[23] Indeed, by the eighteenth century it seemed that a commitment to metaphysical materialism required preformationism, since it was not clear how form could emerge from undifferentiated matter without a teleological principle.[24] Haeckel, for example, appears to have advocated preformationism "based not on additional embryological observations but on adherence to his own metaphysical adherence to both his monistic materialism and to his desire to provide evidence for evolution."[25] On the other hand, while vitalism did not require epigenesis, the converse — that epigenesis required vitalism of some sort — did seem to many to be the case.

Famously in this regard, Hans Driesch conducted a series of experiments with sea urchin eggs designed to confirm earlier work by Wilhelm Roux that supported preformationism by showing that cells separated from an early developing embryo would not each develop into a full organism but only into that part of the organism that they each were "preformed" to become.[26] But con-

21. Strick, "Darwinism and the Origin of Life" pp. 51-92.

22. C. Sagan, "On the Terms 'Biogenesis' and 'Abiogenesis,'" *Origins of Life and Evolution of Biospheres* 5 (1974): 529; Strick, "Darwinism and the Origin of Life."

23. J. Maienschein, "Epigenesis and Preformationism," *Stanford Encyclopedia of Philosophy* (2005), ed. E. N. Zalta, http://plato.stanford.edu/entries/epigenesis/.

24. S. Roe, *Matter, Life, and Generation* (Cambridge: Cambridge University Press, 1981); J. Maienschein, "Competing Epistemologies and Developmental Biology," in *Biology and Epistemology,* ed. R. Creath and J. Maienschein (Cambridge: Cambridge University Press, 2000).

25. Maienschein, "Competing Epistemologies and Developmental Biology."

26. Roux and other preformationists of the time held to a mosaic rather than homuncular view — that rather than a fully formed little organism, the fertilized egg had precursors of form that were found in different parts of the cell and divided into differentiating parts of the organism. Thus, if a cell was split off from a recently fertilized egg, it could not become an organism, as might be the case epigenetically. Using a two-cell stage of a recently fertilized frog egg, Roux was not able to split off one cell, so he killed one, left it attached, and watched the

trary to his expectations and Roux's earlier results, "Instead, the next morning I found in their respective dishes typical, actively swimming blastulae of half size."[27] These findings and other results from additional experiments drove him to take an epigenetic interpretation of development, though one that initially relied on purely materialistic and widely regarded proposals. However, his ideas of epigenesis led him to posit a modest vitalism of *Lebensautonomie*: biology "must be placed not as a new discipline within physics, but rather as an 'independent basic science' at the side of all physics. . . ."[28] Ultimately, Driesch came to advocate a teleological life force, *Lebenskraft,* denying "specific causal laws for the process of life" and — in a letter published in *Science* — that a biologist cannot "predict what will happen even after he has observed it. This is indeed a consequence of my vitalism."[29] Driesch developed the philosophical implications of his views at Heidelberg and presented them in the Gifford Lectures of 1907.[30]

Notwithstanding the respect accorded (and later forfeited by) Driesch, by the early part of the twentieth century vitalism was entirely abandoned.[31] But ironically, so were preformationism and belief in spontaneous generation — the two views believed to be necessary entailments of mechanism!

As with many scene changes in the drama of science, the transitions are not entirely evidentially determined. I would like to comment on two issues.

---

other develop — into only "half." Using sea urchin eggs, first at the two-cell stage but later with four, Driesch was actually able to separate the eggs, which all developed into normal larvae.

27. H. Driesch, "Entwicklungsmechanische Studien I. Der Werth der beiden ersten Furchungszellen in der Echinodermentwicklung. Experimentelle Erzeugen von Theil- und Doppelbildung," *Zeitschrift für wissenschaftliche Zoologie* 53 (1892): 160-78, translated in B. Willier and J. Oppenheimer, *Foundations of Experimental Embryology* (Englewood Cliffs, NJ: Prentice-Hall, 1964), pp. 38-50.

28. K. Sander, "Hans Driesch's 'philosophy really ab ovo', or Why to Be a Vitalist," *Development Genes and Evolution* 202 (1992): 1-3.

29. H. Jennings, "Driesch's Vitalism and Experimental Indeterminism," *Science* 927 (1912): 435.

30. H. Driesch, *The Science and Philosophy of the Organism,* vols. 1 and 2 (London: Adam and Charles Black, 1908).

31. Another significant bastion of belief in vitalism was the observation that the origin of organic molecules required life. Wohler's synthesis of urea was important, but here again though, the debate was complicated, and not settled simply by Wohler's work. For example, also important was the debate over whether fermentation required an intact cell, or could be accomplished in a cell-free extract. Eduard Buchner's successful 1897 demonstration of the latter contributed substantially to turning the tide against vitalism. R. Kohler, "The Reception of Eduard Buchner's Discovery of Cell-Free Fermentation," *Journal of the History of Biology* 5 (1972): 327-53.

First, the term "vitalism" and the questions associated with it came to be used as an epithet in an ideological dispute: the concept's pejorative connotation was clear but the denotative content of the concept was not. And what twentieth-century biology has rejected is an extreme characterization, if not a caricature, of the perspective (although to the extent such views have been proposed, they deserve rejection). However, the central questions of physical irreducibility, and even teleology (in the form of self-organization) are unsettled and remain on the table. In his Walter Arndt Lecture, evolutionary biologist Ernst Mayr observes:

> It would be a historical mistake to ridicule vitalists. When one reads the writings of one of the leading vitalists like Driesch one is forced to agree with him that many of the basic problems of biology simply cannot be solved by a Cartesian philosophy, in which the organism is considered nothing but a machine. . . . The critical logic of the vitalists was impeccable. But all their efforts to find a scientific answer to all the so-called vitalistic phenomena were failures. Generations of vitalists labored in vain to find a scientific explanation for the Lebenskraft until it finally became quite clear that such a force simply does not exist.[32]

And yet, "rejecting the philosophy of reductionism is not an attack on analysis."[33]

Second, even the debates over spontaneous generation and epigenesis are not fully resolved. There is still some discussion about whether abiogenesis is thermodynamically feasible on earth, and — as with debates between Huxley and Bastian[34] — there is considerable disagreement about whether the origin of life is an *explanandum* or a precondition of the Darwinian *explanans*. And although homuncular preformationism is sometimes understood as having been replaced by epigenetic understandings, since the mid-twentieth century genetic preformationism — the view that the complete structure of the organism is preformed in the code of the genes — has in fact been the reigning paradigm.[35] And within just the last few years, in both developmental biology and evolutionary theory, there has been a reconsideration of epigenetic factors in heredity and development.[36] Elements of both views seem to be true.

32. E. Mayr, "The Autonomy of Biology," *Ludus Vitalis* 12 (2004): 15-27, 16, 24.

33. Mayr, "The Autonomy of Biology," p. 24.

34. Strick, "Darwinism and the Origin of Life."

35. R. Lewontin, *The Triple Helix* (Cambridge, MA: Harvard University Press, 2002); Maienschein, "Competing Epistemologies and Developmental Biology."

36. E. Balon, "Evolution by Epigenesis," *Biology Forum* 97 (2004): 269-312; S. Carroll,

2. Evolutionary Reductionism and Emergence

If mechanism is seen to have excised vital forces from biology at the level of organismic function and development, Darwinism is seen to have excised teleology at the level of their origin. Indeed, Darwinian explanation surely did replace the attribution of intelligent design or final causation as explanations of biological structures. But while it did not employ intelligent causes, it did implicitly entail a distinction between proximal causes (the mechanical principles by which bodies work) and ultimate causes (the purposes for which bodily features exist). In this sense, while opposing natural theology, Darwin can be seen as quasi-Aristotelian.[37] The difference is, in Aristotle the purpose of a biological feature is the reason for, the cause of, its generation — causality looks forward.[38] For Darwin, the "purpose" of a feature is the result of its selective retention. That is, organs (and organisms) are not only effects; they also have ends or functions, but they do not come to be in virtue of or in order to achieve those ends. The function of biotic characters in Darwin's view — and in this respect he did not break ranks with Aristotle or even natural theology — is to enable an organism to flourish in the context for which it was fashioned. Thus although there was no soul or entelechy in organisms, and no force or spirit animating them, and no designing intelligence that created them, there nevertheless was a place for purpose or function in accounts of living organisms.[39] Telos is understood at the level of the organism.

After the union of Darwinian selection and Mendelian genetics in the

---

Endless Forms Most Beautiful: The New Science of Evo-Devo (New York: W. W. Norton, 2005).

37. Darwin's contemporaries assumed his views were irreconcilable with Aristotle's. Gotthelf argues that this involves a misconstrual of Aristotle as advocating intelligent causes similar to natural theology. It turns out that Darwin himself had never read any of Aristotle, until near the end of his life when he was sent a translated copy of the *Parts of Animals*. Darwin's response was stunning: "Linnaeus and Cuvier have been my two gods, though in very different ways, but they were mere school-boys to old Aristotle." A. Gotthelf, "Darwin on Aristotle," *Journal of the History of Biology* 32 (1999): 3-30.

38. Gotthelf, "Darwin on Aristotle"; A. Gotthelf, "Aristotle's Conception of Final Causality," in *Philosophical Issues in Aristotle's Biology,* ed. A. Gotthelf and J. Lennox (Cambridge: Cambridge University Press, 1987).

39. This has been disputed by some philosophers (but not many biologists). While "function" may be a helpful heuristic device for describing the behavior of living systems or their organs, the actual notion of function, indeed the notion of a "system" itself, is claimed by some to lack coherence in the absence of intentional design: e.g., the heart is chemical-electrical activated tissue that has the effect of moving blood, but it is not rightly considered a "pump," the function or purpose of which is to transport nutrients.

synthetic theory of evolution, and its subsequent elaboration by mathematical population genetics, this notion of telos was not so much extruded as reconceptualized as a property of genes rather than organisms. This was a tremendously powerful breakthrough for two reasons. First, it grew out of rejecting an incipient version of untenable, "old school" teleology, positing that traits might be established for the "good of the species" by a process that — like the most vitalistic versions of epigenesis — seemed to require a forward-looking final cause. Second, it solved a problem for traditional Darwinian notions of fitness as a property of individual reproduction posed by sacrificial cooperative behavior on behalf of nonprogeny. "Inclusive fitness" reconceptualized fitness itself not as a property of organisms but of genes (indeed, of a single gene, with each gene having its own selective value).

This move has at least three major implications. First, the organism itself is viewed not just as the product of genes, but merely as the instrument by which genes achieve their purpose of replication: "an organism is just a gene's way of reproducing itself." Moreover, organismal identity is reconceptualized in terms of an extended phenotype[40] or "skinless organism," a statistical construct involving any impact of a gene on the environment, that increases the fitness of that gene. Note that teleology has not been entirely extruded from description; it has been reduced to the level of individual genetic replicators. In that sense, it has been removed from "biology," i.e., the science of the organism, and relocated in the statistics of replicating particles.

In fact, it may have been removed from the empirical domain altogether and constitutes, perhaps for the first time in modern natural science, a case where an *a priori* or apparently necessary truth — a population of replicating entities will change composition in the direction of those entities that replicate more of themselves — occupies a central explanatory role. This entails two additional implications, on which I will comment. One, there is no reason to believe that evolutionary history will display any trends or directionality in organismic structure or function, not even "that organisms will get better at surviving and reproducing . . . [but] at least that they will not get worse."[41] Second, because the primary level of selection is taken to be the gene, with no emergent and certainly no "forward-looking" processes available, the conflicting interests of individual replicating particles will render difficult the appearance of any functional holism that involves overcoming the barrier of costly cooperation between component parts.

40. Dawkins, *The Extended Phenotype*.
41. Smith and Szathmáry, *The Origins of Life*, p. 15.

Like notions of preformation and spontaneous generation, which seemed to be plausible if not necessary entailments of mechanism, these conclusions are perfectly logical implications of the new evolutionary reductionism. The fascinating prospect of science, though, is that the world pushes back to reform ideas. In light of recent work it seems that both of the above anticipations have turned out not to be the case.

Darwin construed the evolutionary process as not just directional but progressive, so that "all corporeal and mental endowments will tend toward perfection."[42] This idea has been vigorously debated since Darwin[43] but has recently been supported by important theoretical and empirical work on the topic currently referred to as major evolutionary transitions.

Of course evolutionary history displays a series of significant "advances" or innovations: air breathing, homeothermy, flight, viviparity (bearing live young), etc. What we have more recently discerned, in part from knowledge unavailable to Darwin, is that underlying these advances is a series of transitions in how biological information is packaged and transmitted, resulting in progressively aggregated functional units that form new levels of individuality.[44] The following are several such transitions:[45]

- Interacting molecular replicators aggregating to form cells
- Individual genes aggregating to form chromosomes
- Prokaryotic cells aggregating to form eukaryotic cells with organelles
- Individual cells aggregating to form multicellular organisms
- Individual asexual reproducers to sexual reproducers
- Solitary individuals to social populations
- Primate to human societies (with extrasomatic information)

There are a number of significant commonalities to all or most of the above

42. C. Darwin, *On the Origin of Species by Means of Natural Selection* (London: J. Murray, 1859), p. 489.

43. M. Ruse, *Monad to Man: The Concept of Progress in Evolutionary Biology* (Cambridge, MA: Harvard University Press, 1996).

44. J. M. Smith and E. Szathmáry, *The Major Transitions in Evolution* (New York: Oxford University Press, 1995); E. Szathmáry and J. M. Smith, "The Major Evolutionary Transitions," *Nature* 374 (1995): 227-32; Michod, *Darwinian Dynamics*; T. M. Lenton, H. J. Schellnhuber, and E. Szathmáry, "Climbing the Co-Evolution Ladder," *Nature* 431 (2004): 913; R. G. Reid, *Biological Emergences: Evolution by Natural Experiment* (Cambridge, MA: MIT Press, 2007); D. Batten, S. Salthe, and F. Boschetti, "Visions of Evolution: Self-organization Proposes What Natural Selection Disposes," *Biological Theory* 3 (2008): 17-29.

45. Smith and Szathmáry, "The Major Evolutionary Transitions."

transitions. First, each stage involves cooperation between individuals — cooperation that entails cost in the form of risks from defection. Overcoming barriers to cooperation is essential for the emergence of each stage.[46] Second, the cooperation often involves functional specialization of parts, out of which new efficiencies or functions emerge.[47] Third, in many cases the cooperative transition results in obligate interdependence, where previously autonomous individuals can no longer function apart from the aggregate; thus, in a sense, a new kind of individual is formed.[48] In fact, the transitions are also referred to as evolutionary transitions in individuality (ETI). An ETI "creates new units of selection because it trades fitness at the lower level for increased fitness at the group level."[49] Thus contrary to an ultimately reductive scenario, we have the emergence of new levels of individuality. Moreover, "Individuality requires more than just cooperation . . . individuality depends upon the emergence of higher level functions that restrict the opportunity for conflict within and ensure the continued cooperation of the lower level units."[50]

Fascinatingly, Aristotle seemed to anticipate this logic of reconciling disparate parts in a shared functional end. When Empedocles posited that plant stems grow up and roots grow down because they have fire and earth respectively, Aristotle did not see how they could cohere in a single organism if they had such conflicting tendencies. He proposed they were held together by a common purpose, which he attributed to a soul, but conceived of as "holding an end within itself." In another context perhaps, "the emergence of higher-level functions" *à la* Michod.

Transforming our understanding of life is the realization that evolution occurs not only through[51] mutational change in populations but also during evolutionary transitions in individuality (ETIs) — when groups of individuals become so integrated that they evolve into a new higher-level individual. Indeed, the major landmarks in the diversification of life and the hierarchical

46. R. Michod and D. Roze, "Cooperation and Conflict in the Evolution of Multicellularity," *Heredity* 86 (2001): 1-7.

47. D. Queller, "Cooperators Since Life Began," *Quarterly Review of Biology* 72 (1997): 184-88; Smith and Szathmáry, *The Origins of Life*; Michod and Roze, "Cooperation and Conflict in the Evolution of Multicellularity."

48. R. Michod, "On the Transfer of Fitness from the Cell to the Multicellular Organism," *Biology and Philosophy* 20 (2005): 967-87; R. Michod, "Evolution of Individuality during the Transition from Unicellular to Multicellular Life," *PNAS* 104 (2007): 8613-18.

49. Michod, *Darwinian Dynamics*, p. 9.

50. Michod and Roze, "Cooperation and Conflict in the Evolution of Multicellularity," p. 6.

51. Cosans, "Aristotle's Anatomical Philosophy of Nature," p. 331.

organization of the living world are consequences of a series of ETIs: from genes to gene networks to the first cell, from asexual to sexual populations, and from solitary to social organisms.[52]

This calls to mind the Polanyi quote with which this chapter began. Indeed, Sigmund and Szathmáry observe that we now understand that Polanyian "progress" is due to serial evolutionary transitions in individuality.[53] Moreover, although we are beginning to make sense of how lower levels are incorporated into higher levels, we cannot predict the emergence of the latter from the functional properties of the former. This corresponds very much with Polanyi's prescient description of irreducibility: ". . . the analytic descent from higher levels to their subsidiaries is usually feasible to some degree, while the integration of items of a lower level so as to predict their possible meaning in a higher context may be beyond the range of our integrative powers."[54]

3. Evolution and Human Identity

While we might not predict the emergence of humans and the nature of human identity on the basis of extrapolating the above processes, are they fully understandable in light thereof? Yes and no. It turns out that our understanding of what it is to be human is greatly enriched not only by what is fully transparent to but also by what seems somewhat opaque to contemporary evolutionary explanation.

Other contributors to this project will reflect on theories of consciousness and the human mind. Being a mere biologist, I want to reflect on what we can directly observe at the organismic scale: behavior. As it happens, human behavior has constituted an ostensible anomaly for evolutionary theory that has both driven it forward to new understanding and revealed limits of its explanatory potency as presently formulated.

A distinctive, if not somewhat anomalous, feature is this: human beings cooperate more intensively and extensively than any other animal. "We are more deeply social than any other species on earth. . . ."[55] Moreover, it is not

52. Michod, "On the Transfer of Fitness from the Cell to the Multicellular Organism," p. 967.

53. K. Sigmund and E. Szathmáry, "On Merging Lines and Emerging Units," *Nature* 392 (1998): 439-41.

54. Polanyi, "Life's Irreducible Structure," p. 1312.

55. A. Whiten, "Primate Culture and Social Learning," *Cognitive Science* 24 (2000): 477.

JEFFREY P. SCHLOSS

just a case of being the "most" social. Cheetahs are the fastest, elephants are the largest, shrews are the most metabolically intensive terrestrial animals. For any characteristic, some individual species has to be the superlative example, and natural selection can readily account for such characters. What distinguishes human sociality from an evolutionary perspective is that cooperation extends far beyond the domains of kinship or direct reciprocity. In his seminal work, *Sociobiology*, E. O. Wilson identifies the quandary posed by this distinctive move:

> Man has intensified the vertebrate traits while adding unique qualities of his own. In so doing he has achieved an extraordinary degree of cooperation with little or no sacrifice of personal survival and reproduction. Exactly how he alone has been able to cross to this fourth pinnacle, reversing the downward trend of social evolution in general, is the culminating mystery of all biology.[56]

This in fact is one possible reason for postulating the transition from primate to human societies as a "major evolutionary transition." Recall that the emergence of new levels of integration involves new forms of cooperative information transfer and also new ways of resolving conflicts of interests between individual participants in the emerging level. There have been two general approaches to explaining the unusual degree of cooperation evident in human sociality.

One approach proposes unique biological adaptations for cooperation that are either found only in or most distinctively in humans. There are two major accounts. The first of these is indirect reciprocity (IR), developed by Richard Alexander in his seminal account of morality,[57] posited to be an adaptation underlying the unprecedented ability of humans to cooperate in groups too large for individuals to know each other and to monitor their history of iterative exchange. IR involves conferring a benefit, not for direct compensation by the recipient, but for reputational enhancement that results in indirect compensatory benefit by a third (or further downstream) participant in a cooperative matrix. Requiring both language and copious ability to recognize and recall individuals, extensive IR is ascribed only to humans, and has been validated by numerous empirical and experimental studies.[58] Note that IR can

56. E. O. Wilson, *Sociobiology: The New Synthesis* (Cambridge, MA: Harvard University Press, 1975), p. 382.

57. R. Alexander, *The Biology of Moral Systems* (Hawthorne, NY: Aldine de Gruyter, 1987).

58. M. Nowak and K. Sigmund, "Evolution of Indirect Reciprocity," *Nature* 437 (2005): 1291-98.

still be understood in terms of maximizing fitness benefits to the individual, though via a means unique to humans.[59]

The second of these biological processes is group selection, which involves genuine relinquishment of individual fitness for group members in situations where intra-group decrement is less than the between-group benefit to fitness. While this is not, in principle, restricted to humans, what is necessary for group selection are mechanisms of social control that coordinate cooperation and reduce intra-group defection. The means for accomplishing this (e.g., those described above), plus the distinctive pattern of inter-group conflict, make group selection especially plausible in the case of humans.[60] Group selection involves the emergence of genuine aggregate functions characteristic of the other major transitions, and is driven by the fact that membership in the new aggregate has fitness advantages over not being a member. However, it does not explain, indeed it cannot explain, behaviors that favor other aggregates or individual members of other aggregates at cost to the actor.

Primarily to remedy this deficit, a completely different approach has developed, involving a proposal not just for a new level of selection, but for an altogether new kind of informational replicator — supplementing genetic with ideational information. So-called "dual-inheritance" notions involve not just the attribution of biological uniqueness, but a measure of biological transcendence which for humans, and only for humans, suggests that the "genetic leash" has broken.[61] Indeed, ideational replicators are not only irreducible to genetic information, but may oppose it.[62] Richard Dawkins famously concludes:

> We have the power to defy the selfish genes of our birth . . . cultivating and

59. Nonhuman animals have been observed to cooperate with others based not on prior exchange but on direct observation of interactions with a second party. This may be considered secondary reciprocity; only humans have been observed to have tertiary (or higher) reciprocity, mediated not by observation but by reputation.

60. Group selection has been a highly controversial topic in evolutionary theory for the last generation. Although it has recently been reformulated and is widely considered to be more plausible, in many cases (e.g., in eusocial insects) a high degree of genetic relatedness cannot rule out inclusive fitness (L. Lehmann et al., "Group Selection and Kin Selection: Two Concepts but One Process," *PNAS* 104 [2007]: 6736-39.) Cooperation in human societies clearly extends beyond boundaries of both kinship and direct and indirect reciprocity.

61. H. Plotkin, *Evolution in Mind: An Introduction to Evolutionary Psychology* (Cambridge, MA: Harvard University Press, 1997).

62. W. Durham, *Coevolution: Genes, Culture, and Human Diversity* (Stanford: Stanford University Press, 1991).

nurturing pure, disinterested altruism — something that has no place in nature, something that has never existed before in the whole history of the world. . . . We, alone on earth, can rebel against the tyranny of the selfish replicators.[63]

Given all this, Haeckel's comment of more than a century ago — "Man is not a special creation, produced in a different way, and distinct from other animals" — now seems far too glib. Of course there are continuities, as there are continuities between all levels of evolutionary transition. But there are also discontinuities. In light of expectations from selection theory, in many regards humans do appear both to have been produced in a different way, and to be distinct from other animals. This is what I meant by saying evolutionary theory enriches our understanding of the human by what it is currently both able and not yet fully able to account for. And this provisional description of the distinctively human emerging in a new level of social cohesion is thoroughly concordant with the program Warren Brown (this volume) more fully develops in a neurophysiologic context.

Although there is much to say about these notions that is beyond the scope of this brief treatment, I want to close with two comments.

First, the rather dramatic dual-inheritance proposal constitutes an acknowledgment but not an explanation. To posit the existence of unseen and undefined "ideational replicators" (or memes) that leverage genes by unspecified means, does not actually explain anything at all, though the postulate does reflect a concession that human behavior appears to involve inputs that are not reducible to maximizing reproductive success. For example, ideas of an internalized morality rooted in the transcendent are posited to "thwart the self-serving thrust of the gene . . . the concept of the soul has to some extent modified the genetic action of natural selection."[64] In a way, this is quite ironically not unlike the vitalistic attribution of nonmaterial forces existing outside the domain of material or "natural" causes, enabling matter to do what it could not do on its own.

Second and finally, although ideational replicators or "memes" represent an irreducible level of information, there nevertheless remains an attempt to recapture dual-inheritance theory for the most reductive forms of evolutionary explanation. This is pursued by treating memes as discrete "particles" of information that are infectiously transmitted, with the same replicating imperative as genes, and for whose "sake" the mind exists as passive host. In the

63. R. Dawkins, *The God Delusion* (New York: Houghton Mifflin, 2006), p. 201.

64. J. Lopreato, *Human Nature and Biocultural Evolution* (Boston: Allen & Unwin, 1984), p. 24.

old Darwinian reductionism, a body is just a gene's way of reproducing itself. In the new reductionism, a "mind is just a meme's way of reproducing itself."[65] At the very point where one might attribute the emergence of mental agency, we have its reductive deconstruction.[66]

I do not wish here to critique the intrinsic problems with this reductionistic formulation of memetics (although such critique has been extensively developed).[67] What I do wish to suggest is that even if the proposal of infectious memes overcoming genes is a plausible explanation, and even if it turns out to be a necessary one, we have no empirical warrant for believing it is sufficient. If social behavior (along with its underlying cognitive and affective motivations) is not wholly reducible to or constrained by genetic selection, there are several options that might enable this. Consider for example the notions of a transcendent moral reality, a soul, and the sacrificially cooperative behaviors that Lopreato suggests attend them. They may indeed be socially imitated or infectiously transmitted.[68] Or they may reflect innate but pleiotropic dispositions of the developing mind — analogous to preformationism — and while they of course require a social context, they may not require (and may even resist) social instruction.[69] Or they may be neither transmitted nor innate, but — analogous to epigenesis — involve emergent results from the teleological process of free and rational inquiry.[70] (This

65. S. Blackmore, *The Meme Machine* (New York: Oxford University Press, 2000).

66. One might wonder if anyone really lives as if they believe this. Susan Blackmore has commented: "It is possible to live happily and morally without believing in free will. As Samuel Johnson said, 'All theory is against the freedom of the will; all experience is for it.' With recent developments in neuroscience and theories of consciousness, theory is even more against it than it was in his time, more than two hundred years ago. So I long ago set about systematically changing the experience. I now have no feeling of acting with free will, although the feeling took many years to ebb away. . . . As for giving up the sense of an inner conscious self altogether — this is very much harder. I just keep on seeming to exist. But though I cannot prove it — I think it is true that I don't." S. Blackmore, in *What We Believe but Cannot Prove: Today's Leading Thinkers on Science in the Age of Certainty*, ed. J. Brockman (New York: Harper Perennial, 2006), pp. 40-41.

67. R. Aunger, *Darwinizing Culture: The Status of Memetics as Science* (New York: Oxford University Press, 2001); K. Distin *The Selfish Meme: A Critical Reassessment* (Cambridge: Cambridge University Press, 2004).

68. D. Dennett, *Breaking the Spell: Religion as a Natural Phenomenon* (New York: Penguin Group, 2006); Richard Dawkins, *The God Delusion*.

69. J. Barrett, *Why Would Anyone Believe in God?*

70. R. Dawkins thinks science is arrived at by precisely this kind of process and — unlike religion — is not an infectious meme. Daniel Dennett thinks science too is memetic, though it is benevolent, unlike religion, which is parasitic.

appears to be just how Platonist, Aristotelian, and Cartesian understandings of souls emerged.)

All of these options involve irreducibility to genetic fitness,[71] each alternative account is empirically assessable, and none are mutually exclusive. Finally, a fourth option is not empirically assessable, but is a distinct logical possibility. Perhaps some ideas are not (merely) transmitted, or intuitively innate, or rationally constructed, but discovered. In this volume Philip Clayton asks "is there something in persons that has its source and orientation beyond the framework of the empirical world?" Of course this is a metaphysical question, and it is difficult to see how it would inform scientific explanation. But as we have seen from the beginning of this essay, science itself suffers if it is formulated or assessed with the *a priori* commitment to ruling out one answer to the question.

71. Actually, in the second category, innate cognitive mechanisms are typically viewed by evolutionary psychology as serving if not maximizing fitness. However, *pleiotropic* dispositions (cognitive byproducts, even if innate) are not understood in this way.

III. Sources of the Christian Traditions in Historical and Global Contexts

"Soul" and "Spirit" in the Anthropological Discourse of the Hebrew Bible

Andreas Schüle

1. Introduction

Whatever one's philosophy about human nature and the human condition might be, the nonnegotiable starting point, at least in modern time, seems to be the physical — "bodily" — reality of human life. We have learned that the physical body is more than just "dumb matter" and as such only a rather primitive vessel for the truly distinctive characteristics of human nature. Reality, as we have come to understand it, is essentially physical, which leaves little to no room for more than a metaphorical use of terms such as "soul" or "spirit." I do not want to concern us here with the question if one is to applaud or rather deplore the modern emphasis on the physical world as the primary reference point of what we consider as "reality."[1] From a theological point of view, however, one has to acknowledge that most of our religious language has been shaped by worldviews that do not endorse the all-embracing character of physicality. To give only one example: in 2 Corinthians 5:1-4, the apostle Paul reflects on the temporary nature of our physical existence and compares it to an earthly tent that we inhabit only for a while but that eventually disappears to give way to a new form of embodiment: "For we know that if the earthly tent we live in is destroyed, we have a building from God, a house not made with

---

1. W. Brown, N. Murphy, and H. M. Maloney, eds., *Whatever Happened to the Soul? Scientific and Theological Portraits of Human Nature* (Minneapolis: Fortress Press, 1998); N. Murphy, *Bodies and Souls, or Spirited Bodies?* (Cambridge: Cambridge University Press, 2006); J. Green, *Body, Soul, and Human Life: The Nature of Humanity in the Bible* (Grand Rapids: Baker, 2008).

hands, eternal in the heavens" (2 Cor. 5:1). Very much along the same lines, the author of 2 Peter anticipates his near end as that point when he will put off "this tent" as Christ has done before him: "Yes, I think it is right, as long as I am in this tent, to stir you up by reminding you, knowing that shortly I must put off my tent, just as our Lord Jesus Christ showed me" (2 Pet. 1:13-14). Note that the language of the "tent" includes but is not limited to the human body. It rather describes one's being connected to and embedded in the physical world, which is, according to Paul, not the only way of being "embodied."

Such an understanding of life and existence presupposes a view of reality that acknowledges the existence of different kinds of realities or "worlds" in which a human person can be embodied at different stages of her physical existence — and beyond. Paul's concept of the body of Christ into which we will be transformed and in which, in a "spiritual" way, we already participate presupposes the existence of such multiple realities and, by the same token, an openness of human nature to being incorporated in more than only the physical universe.

Against this backdrop, Christianity developed a language capable of accounting for different forms of "embodiment."[2] One of the underlying metaphysical assumptions about the human person is that it has an "anchoring" outside the physical word. In other words, a human person is shaped by but not ultimately dependent upon his or her bodily nature. The Old Testament language of "soul" and "spirit," which to explore is the purpose of this paper, expresses this underlying assumption in several distinct ways. By the same token, it is easy to understand why in the modern world with its emphasis on the one physical universe the language of soul and spirit seems to have lost its credibility — or at least its plausibility. If the body is not just a temporary carrier vessel but the essential "stuff" of which a human person is made, then the question arises, if and to what extent the language of soul and spirit is capable of capturing this modern worldview that appears to be so different from its predecessors.

Being a biblical scholar, it is not my intention here to pursue the tension between traditional Christian anthropology and modernity. The simple truth to which I want to draw attention is that worldviews matter when it comes to anthropological concepts such as "body," "soul," or "spirit." This proves to be

2. For an interesting case study on the notion of "hypostasis" in the New Testament see P. Lampe, "Hypostasis as a Component of New Testament Christology (Heb. 1:3)," in *Who Is Jesus Christ for Us Today? Pathways to Contemporary Christology,* ed. A. Schüle and G. Thomas (Louisville: Westminster John Knox, 2008), pp. 63-71.

an important starting point when one approaches Old Testament traditions. I will attempt to show that the Old Testament gives witness to more than one worldview and, consequently, to more than one way of conceptualizing the human person. The need for a historical perspective at this point is self-evident. The transmission history of the Old Testament covers most of the first millennium BCE — a period during which a major cultural paradigm shift occurred: in the wake of the conquests of Cyrus the Great and his successors, Persian culture was on the rise in the ancient world, pushing aside the old Semitic civilizations of Babylon and Assyria. This paradigm shift had a "silent" but nonetheless significant impact on Israelite religion, because it brought about a new way of understanding the cosmos and the place of the individual within the cosmos. It is intriguing to pursue how the Old Testament authors adjusted and recalibrated their anthropological concepts in order to meet the challenges of this new worldview. Even more significant from a theological point of view is that the authors of the Old Testament seemed quite comfortable working with changing worldviews and their respective understandings of the human person as long as they found a basis in them for sustaining a number of key convictions: (1) that a human being was God's creature, (2) that she depended on the presence of her creator in any moment of her life, and (3) that a human being was also able to experience or, put in less loaded terms, to connect with the presence of God in her life. To this effect, the cultic traditions of the OT — most of which precede the Persian era — develop a view of the human being based on the notions of body and *nefesh* (mostly rendered "soul"), whereas especially during the Persian period the human being is increasingly conceived of as body and *ruach* ("spirit"). To be sure, my claim is not that the former simply vanished at a certain point. Historical developments are more complex and, therefore, also "messier" than any reconstructive model can account for. However, it appears that the shift in emphasis from "soul" to "spirit" is characteristic of the developing anthropological discourse of the Old Testament.

2. The Cultic World and the Role of the *Nefesh*

According to the ancient Semitic view, the cosmos had the shape of a disk and dome. The firmament was viewed as a protective shield spanning the surface of the earth. The center of this cosmos was imagined as a mountain with the temple of the highest God at its top.[3] It is well known that the famous

3. S. Maul, "Die altorientalische Hauptstadt — Abbild und Nabel der Welt," in *Die Orien-*

temple tower of Babylon had a pyramidal form that symbolized a mountain touching the sky, which is also what its original name means: Etemenanki (É-temen-an-ki), "house, bond of heaven and earth." This same cosmology shines through in many of the psalms that depict the temple on Mount Zion as the center of the world and as God's dwelling place on earth:

Beautiful in elevation,
The joy of the whole earth,
Is Mount Zion on the sides of the north,
The city of the great King. (Ps. 48:3)

Who may ascend into the hill of the LORD?
Or who may stand in His holy place?
He who has clean hands and a pure heart,
Who has not lifted up his soul to an idol,
Nor sworn deceitfully. (Ps. 24:3-4)

It is quite remarkable that such a cosmology was sustained in ancient Judah, given the fact that there was no temple tower whatsoever, and that Mount Zion was, and still is, a rather unimpressive elevation in the Judean mountain line. However, landscapes do not necessarily matter when it comes to mythic geography. The point here is that God's dwelling place on earth marks the center around which all of life is organized in concentric circles and towards which all living creatures gravitate. As the dome- or tent-like firmament was imagined to protect the cosmos from the surrounding chaos elements so did the temple, as a focal point, hold the world together from the inside.[4] The language of "gravity" is quite appropriate here, because it helps to understand one of the major concerns in the background of this cosmology: it was regarded as essential for every living being to be connected to the place of God and so to participate in life itself. In turn, losing this connection, being cut off from the "fountain of life" (Ps. 36:10) equaled dying and being dead.

This is the point where the notion of *nefesh* comes into play. As mentioned above, most Bible translations render *nefesh* as "soul" but sometimes also as

---

talische Stadt: Kontinuität. Wandel. Bruch. 1 Internationales Kolloquium der Deutschen Orient-Gesellschaft, 9-10 Mai 1996 (Halle/Saale: Saarbrücker Druckerei und Verlag, 1997), pp. 109-24.

4. P. Weimar, "Sinai und Schöpfung. Komposition und Theologie der priesterschriftlichen Sinaigeschichte," *Revue biblique* 95 (1988): 337-85; B. Janowski, "Tempel und Schöpfung. Schöpfungstheologische Aspekte der priesterschriftlichen Heiligtumskonzeption," *Journal of Biblical Literature* 5 (1990): 37-70; E. E. Elnes, "Creation and Tabernacle: The Priestly Writer's 'Environmentalism,'" *Horizons in Biblical Theology* 16 (1994): 144-55.

"heart," "innermost being," or "spirit."[5] Whichever rendering one prefers, more important is the concept implied in the term *nefesh* as it occurs especially in the psalms. One of the most illustrative passages in this regard is the opening section of Psalm 42:

> As a deer longs
> for flowing streams,
> so my *nefesh* longs
> for you, O God.
> My *nefesh* thirsts for God,
> for the living God.
> When shall I come and behold
> the face of God?
> My tears have been my food
> day and night,
> while people say to me continually,
> "Where is your God?" (Ps. 42:2-4)

The language of *nefesh* expresses the neediness of a human being for the enlivening presence of God.[6] The image of the deer that longs for "flowing streams" suggests that, without the experience of the divine presence, a human being "dries out" and wastes away. What betrays a cultic background here is the mention of the "face of God": "beholding the divine countenance" is not merely a metaphorical way of speaking; more concretely, it relates to the idea that in approaching the temple and the holy of holies, in which the cultic statue of the deity had its dwelling place, the worshiper entered a sphere that conveyed to her the experience of standing before god and, to that extent, of seeing god's face.[7]

5. The translation also depends on the semantic field in which the notion of *nefesh* occurs; cf. A. Wagner, "Wider die Reduktion des Lebendigen. Über das Verhältnis der sog. anthropologischen Grundbegriffe und die Unmöglichkeit, mit ihnen alttestamentliche Menschenvorstellung zu fassen," in *Anthropologische Aufbrüche. Alttestamentliche und interdisziplinäre Zugänge zur historischen Anthropologie*, ed. A. Wagner (Göttingen: Vandenhoeck & Ruprecht, 2009), pp. 83-199.

6. Still foundational in this respect is W. H. Wolff, *Anthropology of the Old Testament* (Mifflintown, PA: Sigler Press, 1996), pp. 24-36; for a more recent account of the *nefesh* cf. in particular B. Janowski, "Anerkennung und Gegenseitigkeit. Zum konstellativen Personbegriff des Alten Testaments," in *Der Mensch im Alten Testament. Neuere Forschungen zur alttestamentlichen Anthropologie*, ed. B. Janowski and K. Liess (Freiburg: Herder, 2009), pp. 182-90.

7. F. Nötscher and W. W. Graf von Baudissin, *Das Angesicht Gottes Schauen, nach biblischer und babylonischer Auffassung* (Darmstadt: Wissenschaftliche Buchgesellschaft, 1969

ANDREAS SCHÜLE

In many of the psalms the temple area is depicted as a *hortus vitae,* a garden of life, that, although placed in the center of the cosmos, was detached from the material, earthbound world around it. The *nefesh* is that part of a human being that enables her to connect with the cultic sphere as the place of divine presence.[8]

> My *nefesh* longs, indeed it faints
> for the courts of the LORD;
> my heart and my flesh sing for joy
> to the living God. (Ps. 84:2)

What makes the rendering as "soul" problematic is the fact that this term could suggest that the *nefesh* is in fact something immortal, something capable of existing apart from the physical body. The idea of an immortal soul, however, is entirely absent from the Hebrew transmission of the Old Testament. Passages from the Sinai Torah provide insight into how the *nefesh* was regarded as distinct from and yet dependent upon the physical body. The first one is found in the regulations concerning the purity of a nazirite:

> All the days that he separates himself to YHWH he shall not come near to the *nefesh* of a dead person. (Num. 6:6)

One does not find the rendering "*nefesh* of a dead person" in any of the major Bible translations. Ordinarily, this passage gets translated simply as "dead person/corpse." However, as Diethelm Michel has shown, this is not quite what is meant here.[9] Though it is true that physical contact with a corpse would cause

---

[reprint]); F. Hartenstein, *Das Angesicht JHWHs. Studien zu seinem höfischen und kultischen Bedeutungshintergrund in den Psalmen und in Exodus 32–34,* Forschungen zum Alten Testament 2, no. 55 (Tübingen: Mohr Siebeck, 2008).

8. Recent contributions to the anthropology of ancient Near Eastern cultures have highlighted the sense of "belonging" and solidarity that characterizes a human person in relation to his or her social, natural, and cultic environments; cf. E. Brunner-Traut, *Frühformen des Erkennens. Am Beispiel Altägyptens,* 2nd ed. (Darmstadt: Wissenschaftliche Buchgesellschaft, 1992). Brunner-Traut's idea of a human person as composed of different aspects or layers of life has recently been critically revisited by J. Assmann, "Konstellative Anthropologie. Zum Bild des Menschen im alten Ägypten," in *Der Mensch im Alten Testament,* ed. B. Janowski and K. Liess, pp. 95-120, and Janowski, *Anerkennung und Gegenseitigkeit,* p. 183.

9. D. Michel, "Naepaeš als Leichnam?," *Zeitschrift für Althebräistik* 7 (1994): 81-84. For a similar conclusion with regard to Psalm 16 cf. O. Loretz, "Die postmortale (himmlische) Theoxenie der npš 'Seele, Totenseele' in ugaritisch-biblischer Sicht nach Psalm 16,10-11," in *Ugarit-Forschungen* 38 (2006): 445-97.

a nazirite, as any other person, to become impure, this regulation does not say that the nazirite is not supposed to touch a dead body. The point is, rather, that he is not supposed to come close to a recently deceased person because of the *nefesh* of this person. This suggests that there is something dangerous about the *nefesh* at the transition from life to death. Numbers 19:14-15 provides a background for the potential danger that issues from the *nefesh* of a dead person:

> This is the law when someone dies in a tent: everyone who comes into the tent, and everyone who is in the tent, shall be unclean seven days. And every open vessel, which has no cover fastened upon it, is unclean.

The key element here is that even an open vessel that happens to be in the same room with a dead body becomes unclean. "This," as Michel suggests, "explains itself if one assumes that there is something which leaves the corpse and seeks to creep into a vessel. The assumption seems to have been that, after a person had died, the *nefesh* tried to find a new kind of 'body' for itself, even if this was only an open vessel."[10] Eventually, however, also the *nefesh* dies, though not in the same way as the physical body. It loses its "life power" and, consequently, drifts away into the netherworld, the world of shadows and oblivion, far from the world of the living.[11] Different from the Platonic concept of an immortal soul, the *nefesh* is not a self-sufficient entity that continues to exist beyond the life of the body.

Unlike their Egyptian neighbors, the Hebrews did not entertain a concept of multiple worlds through which the human person, via her soul, successively passes and in which it assumes different kinds of embodiment. In the Hebrew Bible, the cosmos is strictly conceived of as the one creation of God, and everything that exists in it — bodies and "souls" — has a definite and, hence, limited lifespan.[12] Nonetheless, this one world divides into two different realms, the

---

10. Michel, *Naepaeš*, p. 83.

11. Of particular interest in this regard is the recently discovered tomb stele of Kuttamuwa, which includes an inscription by Kuttamuwa that his *nefesh* resides in the tomb stone (for a preliminary report on the archaeological campaign at Zincirli as well as on the inscription itself; cf. the website of the Oriental Institute of the University of Chicago: http://ochre.lib .uchicago.edu/zincirli/). This confirms Michel's observation that the *nefesh* tried to find itself a "home," as it were, in order not to disappear in *sheol*. However, the inscription does not suggest that the *nefesh* continued to live on in the stone. The idea seems to be that funeral stele was a place where the *nefesh* remained in a sphere close to the living and as such also close to being remembered by future generations.

12. A. Schüle, "The Divine-Human Marriages (Genesis 6:1-4) and the Greek Framing of the Primeval History," *Theologische Zeitschrift* 65 (2009): 116-28.

earth, the netherworld, and the elevated temple as God's dwelling place. The fact that a human person was thought of as belonging to these realms made it necessary to think of her as including both a body and a *nefesh*.

3. The Persian Period and the Loss of "World Certainty"

With this cultic worldview and its anthropological implications in mind, the major challenge comes into focus that Hebrew culture found itself confronted with when it entered the Persian period.[13] The Persians, unlike their Assyrian and Babylonian predecessors, did not build temple towers symbolizing the midpoint of the cosmos. It is fair to say that the Persians had a concept of the world that was far more universalistic in character than that of the old Semitic empires, largely because their god Ahuramazda was, in the first place, believed in as the creator of the entire cosmos, which included not only the physical world but also the different nations and ethnicities that filled it. Not that the idea of a creator of heaven and earth was new or unique; however, in the Persian belief system, cosmology was not predetermined by the preponderant "location" of the superpower in the natural, ethnical, political, and religious cosmos — as had been the case with virtually all empires that had ruled the ancient Near Eastern world before.[14] Although the Persians certainly maintained that their capital, Persepolis, was the political center of the entire world of nations and therefore also the preferred place to worship Ahuramazda, their religious worldview did not rely any more on the idea of a cultic midpoint with concentric circles around it. The question of god's place in the cosmos could not be answered in any more specific way than by saying "potentially everywhere."[15]

This shift away from a cultic to a cosmic understanding of the presence of god apparently had a tremendous impact on the biblical traditions of the postexilic periods in Israel. To mention only one example: In 1 Kings 8, Sol-

---

13. J. Wiesehöfer, *Das antike Persien. Von 550 v. Chr. bis 650 n. Chr.* (Düsseldorf: Patmos, 2005), pp. 59-89. G. Ahn, "Toleranz und Reglement. Die Signifikanz achaimenidischer Religionspolitik für den jüdisch-persischen Kulturkontakt," in *Religion und Religionskontakte im Zeitalter der Achämeniden*, ed. R. G. Kratz (Gütersloh: Gütersloher Verlagshaus, 2002), pp. 191-209.

14. Wiesehöfer, *Persien*, pp. 65-71.

15. Wiesehöfer, *Persien*, p. 146. For the biblical appropriation of Persian "universalism" see J. Blenkinsopp, "YHVH and Other Deities: Conflict and Accommodation in the Religion of Israel," in Blenkinsopp, *Treasures Old and New: Essays in the Theology of the Pentateuch* (Grand Rapids: Eerdmans, 2004), pp. 67-80.

omon's temple prayer, the temple is envisioned as the place where the worshiping community gathers to pray to the God who resides in heaven (1 Kings 8:27-30):

> But will God indeed dwell on the earth? Even heaven and the highest heaven cannot contain you, much less this house that I have built! Regard your servant's prayer and his plea, O LORD my God, heeding the cry and the prayer that your servant prays to you today; that your eyes may be open night and day toward this house, the place of which you said, "My name shall be there," that you may heed the prayer that your servant prays toward this place. Hear the plea of your servant and of your people Israel when they pray toward this place; O hear in heaven your dwelling place; heed and forgive.

Here, the Jerusalem temple is seen almost as a synagogue, a place for the community to gather and to pray to the god in heaven, but not as a place of cosmological significance.[16] Consequently, in this new understanding, the temple is a far cry from the earlier concept that identified it as the *axis mundi*. The theological implications that the new cosmology of the Persian period brought about were probably more significant than one can see at the surface of the Old Testament texts. However, the fact that in the early postexilic period the so-called "priestly code" (usually simply referred to as "P") was composed gives reason to believe that with the rise of the Persian empire there was need to provide an account of the religion of Israel that would meet the challenges of the new era.[17]

A few words about P seem in order. Most scholars would agree that P is one of probably two major traditions responsible for the final redaction and, therefore, the literary and theological character of the Pentateuch/the Torah. There is also agreement that the final form of the Pentateuch took shape in the late sixth and fifth centuries, a period marked by the return of some of the Judean people from exile and the reconstruction of Jerusalem and its temple, after the Babylonians had destroyed it in 586 BCE.

The name "priestly code" owes itself to the fact that the bulk of the material attributed to this textual layer of the Pentateuch is concerned with the building of the tabernacle — the "desert sanctuary" — and, consequently, with issues of cult and sacrifice. However, P gives us also a report of the primeval

16. For the notion of the temple as a "house of prayer" cf. Isa. 56:7.

17. For a recent overview of the biblical literature of the Persian era cf. K. Schmid, *Literaturgeschichte des Alten Testaments. Eine Einführung* (Darmstadt: Wissenschaftliche Buchgesellschaft, 2008), pp. 140-74.

history of the world and, as part of this, a report of the creation of the cosmos and of humankind (Gen. 1:1–2:3).[18] One would assume that the priestly worldview should be in line with the cultic traditions we have visited above. Somewhat surprisingly, this is, however, not the case. The desert sanctuary, prefiguring the Jerusalem temple, has nothing of the mythic aura of the earlier "mountain of god" tradition. It is a portable "device," ready to be packed up and put up again wherever the Israelites settle on their way to the Promised Land. Its sole purpose is to provide a space where YHWH, the God of Israel, and his people "meet." The rather lengthy instructions of how to build the tabernacle seem to suggest deliberately that this sanctuary is no more than a building made from human hands that serves as an earthly vessel for the *kabod,* the glory of YHWH — viewed against the backdrop of the temple theology as depicted in most of the cultic psalms a rather sobering account of the function and symbolic meaning of the temple of YHWH. According to ancient Near Eastern ideology, the main sanctuary like the Esagila in Babylon was built by the gods themselves into the foundations of the cosmos,[19] which seems to be quite the opposite of a portable tent, temporarily hosting the glory of God.

Given this new understanding of the cosmos in general and the temple in particular, it is only consequent that also the priestly concept of humanity differs a great deal from the view of a human being as composed of a body and a *nefesh.* While P uses the term *nefesh,* the mention of it in Genesis 1:2, 21, 30; 9:4-6 serves in general terms to distinguish living beings, animals and humans, from unanimated bodies like the stars and the firmament. The *nefesh,* located in the bloodstream of every creature, is the life force, which is not specifically mentioned as something that God created but is nonetheless associated with God as the giver of life, since blood must not be consumed by humans but has to be returned to God through proper ritual procedures. However, if one compares P with the cultic theologies of the Psalter, there is no indication that P associates any specific connection between God and humans with the term *nefesh.* However, P offers a different anthropological category that one does not encounter in any of the pre-Persian texts of the Old Testament. In the priestly portions of the primeval history, human beings are called "images of God." One needs to mention that, in the entire Old Testament, this intriguing phrase occurs only in Genesis 1:26-28; 5:1-3; and 9:4-6 and, for this reason, can hardly be considered as a key term of Old Testament anthropology. The

---

18. A. Schüle, *Der Prolog der hebräischen Bibel. Der literar- und theologiegeschichtliche Diskurs der biblischen Urgeschichte* (Zürich: TVZ, 2006), pp. 49-82.

19. Cf. *Enuma elish,* tablet VI.

notion that humans are images of God is certainly not deeply embedded in the religious or cultic systems of the Old Testament, and even P does not mention it again after the primeval history. However, the need for new anthropological categories, like the imago Dei, seems consistent with the fact that the "body/ *nefesh*" anthropology did not necessarily fit into the decentered cosmos of the Persian era. The idea that humans are "images" or, in a more literal translation, "statues" of God,[20] presented one way for the priestly school of the early Persian period to meet the intellectual challenges of their time.

Leaving the relatively marginal imago Dei discourse aside, a different notion seems to have become increasingly important for Judaism in the Second Temple period: the notion of the *ruach,* which in most Bible editions gets translated as "spirit." As a matter of fact, in most of the biblical texts from the Second Temple period, a human being is viewed as a physical body enlivened or empowered by the divine *ruach.*[21] The advantage of this new approach seems obvious: it does not depend on the rather static cultic worldview that located God's presence in only one particular place. Rather, the notion of *ruach* allows speaking of divine presence in a cosmologically comprehensive way. Note how the rhetoric of a *nefesh* gravitating to the center of the cosmos shifts to that of the expansive character of the divine *ruach* from which a human being cannot "flee":

> O LORD, you have searched me and known me.
> You know when I sit down and when I rise up;
> you discern my thoughts from far away.
> You search out my path and my lying down,
> and are acquainted with all my ways.
> Even before a word is on my tongue,
> O LORD, you know it completely.
> You hem me in, behind and before,
> and lay your hand upon me.
> Such knowledge is too wonderful for me;
> it is so high that I cannot attain it.
> Where can I go from your *Ruach?*
> Or where can I flee from your presence?

20. W. Gross, "Gen 1,26.27; 9,6: Statue oder Ebenbild Gottes," *JBTh* 15 (2000): 11-38; B. Janowski, "Die lebendige Statue Gottes. Zur Anthropologie der priesterlichen Urgeschichte," in *Gott und Mensch im Dialog,* ed. M. Witte, Beihefte zur Zeitschrift für die alttestamentliche Wissenschaft 345 (Berlin/New York: De Gruyter, 2004), pp. 183-214.

21. J. Blenkinsopp, *Isaiah 56-66,* Anchor Bible 19B (New York: Doubleday, 2003), p. 221.

> If I ascend to heaven, you are there;
> if I make my bed in Sheol, you are there.
> If I take the wings of the morning
> and settle at the farthest limits of the sea,
> even there your hand shall lead me,
> and your right hand shall hold me fast. (Ps. 139:1-10)

The history and theology of the "spirit" of God in the Second Temple period is still to be written.[22] Here we can accentuate only some of its most essential features.[23] In order to get an impression of the complexity of the discourse about the divine *ruach* we will turn to the primeval history (Genesis 1–11) and than focus on some of the individual traditions of the Hebrew and Greek versions that show particularly marked views of the nature and function of the *ruach*.

4. *Ruach* in the "Primeval History"

One of the more obvious, yet frequently neglected features of the primeval history, is that it hosts a rich and equally diverse discourse about the divine "spirit."[24] The quotation marks are necessary here, because the semantic field of the Hebrew term *ruach* overlaps only to an extent with our common philosophical concepts of spirit that are informed for the most part by the Greek notion of *nous*.

Ruach occurs for the first time already in Genesis 1:2. Here it is a divine *ruach* that moves about above the primordial ground, which is covered with water and darkness. Throughout the history of Bible exegesis there have been extensive debates about the meaning of *ruach* in this verse. There are essentially two positions. According to one, *ruach* is a wind or spirit that is coming from God and therefore somehow connected with the creator god, whose identity and place in the "world" remain undisclosed in this opening chapter.

22. For an attempt in this direction see W. Hildebrandt, *An Old Testament Theology of the Spirit of God* (Peabody, MA: Hendrickson, 1995); and as a systematic contribution M. Welker, *God the Spirit* (Minneapolis: Fortress Press, 1994).

23. Cf. Blenkinsopp, *Isaiah 56–66*, p. 261: "In the Hebrew Bible the expression 'the Holy Spirit' appears only here [Isa. 63:10-11] and in Ps 51:13[11]. The association of the Spirit with the Presence or the Face of God (also in Ps 139:7) indicates that the Spirit . . . has now become the object of theological reflection, a kind of hypostasis similar in that respect to the Face, the Angel, and, later in the Targum, the Word."

24. For the following cf. Schüle, *Prolog*, pp. 134-37.

According to the other position, *ruach* does not have anything to do with the creator at all. Rather, it is a "powerful (godlike) wind" that belongs to the chaos elements that make the primordial world a *tohu-wa-bohu*.

Regardless of the position one favors in this debated issue (and we will return to this in due course), one thing seems clear: looking at the subsequent texts of Genesis 1–11 there is hardly any doubt that these texts understand the *ruach* of the beginning as belonging to the creator. The next text mention of the divine *ruach* is Genesis 6:1-4.[25] In this passage, God limits the human lifespan to 120 years. The *ruach* now is clearly attributed to God as his own "breath" or "spirit." But Genesis 6:3 goes even one step further. Here we get to know something that Genesis 1:2 does not imply: the *ruach* of God is a spirit that enlivens and sustains human life. Once it is taken away from them, human beings die. They participate for a limited period of time in the divine *ruach,* but once this *ruach* departs nothing vital remains in them and they return to dust.

Although expressed with a different terminology, the same idea of the enlivening breath occurs in the creation of Adam according to Genesis 2. Having formed a body from the moist clay of the ground *(adama)* God breathes the "breath of life" *(nishmat chajjim)* into Adam's nostrils, which makes him a "living being" *(nefesh chajja).* This is not, however, the way in which the other creatures come to life. Plants and birds do not receive God's breath, but are simply formed from the *adama,* which seems to provide enough vital energy to enliven them. The *odem* that comes from God and is received by Adam separates human life from the rest of creation. In this initial, physical encounter, God brings Adam in touch with the breath of life. It is the only time that a human being does not die but rather comes into existence when receiving the "kiss of God."

Yet another understanding of "spirit" occurs in the flood narrative.[26] According to 8:21 it is not only humankind but all the inhabitants of the earth that have the *odem* in their nostrils. In other words, in whatever form it comes, life depends on this *odem* that all of creation receives from, and shares with, their creator. This *odem* is what distinguishes living things from dead matter and marks them as created vis-à-vis the chaos elements of the beginning — darkness, the primordial ground, and the waters that cover it.

These brief remarks about the opening section of the Hebrew Bible may already suffice to show that the notion of Spirit and related terms stand at the

25. Schüle, *Prolog,* pp. 239-44.
26. Schüle, *Prolog,* pp. 260-70, 292-99.

very heart of an intense and diverse inner-biblical discussion on theological key issues. What distinguishes living from dead things? To what extent are there not only different forms of life but also different ways of being alive (humans vs. animals)? And finally, how does the presence of the creator himself affect the emergence and unfolding of life?

If one seeks to unpack the discourse that surfaces in Genesis 1–11, the biblical texts lead their reader into the priestly theology of the Pentateuch and, to an even greater extent, into the wisdom literature of the postexilic period. The following remarks are aimed at accentuating the different voices that contribute to the canonical discourse about God's Spirit.

5. *Ruach* in the Priestly Pentateuch

Having dipped into the complex and diverse postexilic discourse about the divine *ruach* that unfolds in the first eleven chapters of Genesis, let us now try to unravel this discourse in historical order and therefore return to P and to the early Persian period.

Reading Genesis 1:1–2:3, a simple question comes to mind: Where in the "world" as depicted in this creation report is God? What is his place and where is he speaking from? An answer to this may be found in verse 2: The divine *ruach* is above the waters that fill the space in which heaven and earth will be furnished. Although the Priestly text never explicitly thematizes where God can be found, the mental image that is created here sees God as surrounded by a breath/spirit that indicates his presence. This *ruach* keeps the chaos elements and their potential for destruction and disorder within their limits. On this reading, the first verses of the Hebrew Bible introduce the boundary line between God and the primordial cosmos, suggesting that wherever the divine *ruach* moves about there cannot be chaos.[27]

The term *ruach elohim* occurs again in the context of the building of the tabernacle at Mount Sinai, God's first dwelling place among his people. Here it is now a person, the craftsman Bezalel, whom God endows with

---

27. A similar motif occurs in the priestly flood narrative and in the Exodus story. After the flood, God sends a *ruach* that pushes back the chaos waters (Gen. 8:1), thus allowing life to spread again over the earth. In the book of Exodus, God sends a wind from the east (*ruach qadim*, Exod. 14:21) that divides the waters of the Red Sea in order for Israel to walk through it on dry ground. There is no explicit connection to the divine *ruach* in Gen. 1:2; and yet, it seems reasonable to assume that the use of the term *ruach* in contexts where God directly interferes to restore creation and save his chosen people is not accidental.

his *ruach* so that he is able to furnish the interior of the tabernacle (Exod. 35:30-31).[28] The meaning of this seems to be twofold. First, no human being can know or imagine how to design and decorate the place that will later be filled with the divine glory. It has to be God himself who gives inspiration to this work. But whereas Moses is given a miniature model *(tabnit)* of the building, Bezalel receives with God's *ruach* an even greater gift. Secondly, it seems that the place itself, the holy of holies, has a certain affinity with the *ruach*. Since this is the only place where God touches the ground of the earth, it follows in the Priestly logic that the *ruach* precedes God's personal presence.

The Priestly texts associate the nearness of God with the presence of his *ruach*. It is this *ruach* that human beings experience as a powerful presence of order and, as in Bezalel's case, of inspiration when God approaches their sphere of life. However, in the Priestly tradition God's *ruach* is not a creating or life-giving spirit. It surrounds God but it doesn't issue forth from God to pervade and sustain the created world.[29]

6. *Ruach* as the "Spirit of Life"

The step to such an understanding of God's spirit as a vital principle in all of creation is taken, however, in postexilic poetic and wisdom literature. Among the most prominent examples of this expanded vision is Psalm 104:

28. Interestingly, the mention of the divine spirit here occurs in a context that uses wisdom vocabulary to describe Bezalel's excellent skills — the craftsman is depicted here as a "wise" person (on this topic cf. A. Berlejung, "Der Handwerker als Theologe: Zur Mentalitäts- und Traditionsgeschichte eines altorientalischen und alttestamentlichen Berufsstands," *Vetus Testamentum* 46, no. 2 [1996]: 145-68). While P does not elaborate on the connection between the divine *ruach* and wisdom, this connection does play a key role in texts and traditions that are influenced by the priestly Torah (cf. Wis. of Sol. 7:21, where wisdom herself is seen as the bearer of a spirit that, in 9:17, is then identified as the spirit of God). While G. von Rad was essentially right when he stated that the (preexilic) "priestly-cultic world allowed no room for activity deriving from inspiration," the Priestly Code of the Torah seems to represent a development that opened priestly theology to the idea of divine presence and activity in the world through the *ruach* (cf. von Rad, *Old Testament Theology* [Louisville: Westminster John Knox, 2001], p. 99).

29. However, the idea of a life-giving spirit is present in the book of Ezekiel, which has close theological parallels to P. According to Ezekiel's famous vision of the dry bones in the valley (Ezek. 37:1-14), God summons a *ruach* to "breathe upon the slain, that they may live." Ezekiel does not suggest, however, that this wind is associated with God's *own* breath.

O Lord, how manifold are your works!
In wisdom you have made them all;
the earth is full of your creatures.
Yonder is the sea, great and wide,
creeping things innumerable are there,
living things both small and great.
There go the ships,
and Leviathan that you formed to sport in it.
These all look to you
to give them their food in due season;
when you give to them, they gather it up;
when you open your hand, they are filled with good things.
When you hide your face, they are dismayed;
when you take away their breath, they die and return to their dust.
When you send forth your spirit, they are created;
and you renew the face of the ground. (Ps. 104:24-30)

The theological connections between Psalm 104 and Genesis 1 have long been recognized,[30] although it remains debated whether Psalm 104 is the older text or if the psalmist here revisits and reenvisions the priestly cosmology of Genesis 1. While this debate does not need to concern us here in any detail, it does seem to be the case that Psalm 104 emphasizes the connection between the creator and his creatures beyond the initial act of creation. All creatures depend on the presence of their creator; it is not only their sheer lives that they receive from God but it is God's presence through his spirit that nourishes and sustains them. The psalmist also emphasized that human beings, if not all of creation, respond gratefully to their existence as creatures (Ps. 104:31-35). In the cosmology of Psalm 104, it is spirit and praise that together fill the earth and make it the "atmosphere" in which creator and creation are joined together. Along the same line, Psalm 104 elaborates on the rhythm of living and dying and, hence, the emergence of new life. God gives his *ruach* and he withdraws it and in so doing he "renews the face of the earth." The spirit does not simply move about above the world as in Genesis 1:2, but rather pulsates through it and links the living history of the world to the vitality of the creator himself.

Against the background of this cosmology, wisdom texts seem to reflect

---

30. J. L. Mays, *Psalms* (Louisville: Westminster John Knox, 1994), p. 331; J. D. Levenson, *Creation and the Persistence of Evil: The Jewish Drama of Divine Omnipotence* (Princeton: Princeton University Press, 1988), pp. 53-65.

on the question whether or not human life makes any difference to the creator, and whether there is anything in particular that distinguishes humans from the rest of creation. Psalm 104 as well as other texts that we have mentioned above describe any living being as composed around two elliptical poles: one that is material and connects them according to their emergence from the dust of the earth, and one that characterizes them specifically as God's creatures. In this view, *ruach* is that which forms matter into a particular living entity. Once this connection dissolves, however, nothing remains. Neither matter nor the *ruach* carry an individual signature of what once was a living being.

Focusing specifically on the human condition, this basic concept is revisited and reworked in different wisdom traditions. Ecclesiastes is probably the most explicit among the biblical voices that take the temporal "fusion" of matter and spirit to highlight human finitude and, in ethical terms, the value of human finitude. Ecclesiastes is adamant in insisting that nothing of a living being survives its temporal demise:

> For the fate of humans and the fate of animals is the same; as one dies, so dies the other. They all have the same breath, and humans have no advantage over the animals; for all is vanity. All go to one place; all are from the dust, and all turn to dust again. Who knows whether the human spirit goes upward and the spirit of animals goes downward to the earth? (Eccles. 3:19-21)

Ecclesiastes does not allow for any speculation as to whether the spirit that dwells in human beings "goes upward," that is to say, returns to God, thus making the individual immortal with God. Some take this to mean that Ecclesiastes has an extremely skeptical and even pessimistic approach to human life, best summed up in the expression "Enjoy what you have for as long as you can." However, Ecclesiastes' position seems in fact to be far subtler than that. In opposing an understanding of the spirit as something that extends human life beyond its natural limits, the author means to emphasize that the material and spiritual constitution of a human being give it space and time within God's creation. According to Ecclesiastes, we are made for this world in which God has allotted everything its proper "moment" but not for any other. Both body and spirit are thus inextricably tied to the world as God's creation.

Within the Greek transmission of the Old Testament, Ecclesiastes' position is challenged especially by the Wisdom of Solomon. The opening section of this text almost reads as a refutation of Ecclesiastes and the tradition behind it (e.g., Psalm 104):

For they reasoned unsoundly, saying to themselves, "Short and sorrowful is our life, and there is no remedy when a life comes to its end, and no one has been known to return from Hades. For we were born by mere chance, and hereafter we shall be as though we had never been, for the breath in our nostrils is smoke, and reason is a spark kindled by the beating of our hearts; when it is extinguished, the body will turn to ashes, and the spirit will dissolve like empty air. Our name will be forgotten in time, and no one will remember our works; our life will pass away like the traces of a cloud, and be scattered like mist that is chased by the rays of the sun and overcome by its heat. For our allotted time is the passing of a shadow, and there is no return from our death, because it is sealed up and no one turns back. Come, therefore, let us enjoy the good things that exist, and make use of the creation to the full as in youth." (Wis. of Sol. 2:1-6)

Wisdom of Solomon modifies the scheme that we have outlined above in several significant ways. In addition to its enlivening power, the spirit here is also identified as the divine wisdom that pervades every part of the world.[31] It is not only in his wisdom that God creates and sustains; as part of his spirit, wisdom is also woven into the fabric of everything that is created. Even more important for our purposes, God's eternal wisdom has a complementary part on the human side: as images of God, humans are given an immortal soul (2:23). This enables Wisdom of Solomon to take the opposite stance to Ecclesiastes: The soul of a righteous person will in fact "go upward" and return to God.

But the souls of the righteous are in the hand of God, and no torment will ever touch them. In the eyes of the foolish they seemed to have died, and their departure was thought to be a disaster, and their going from us to be their destruction; but they are at peace. . . . Like gold in the furnace he [God] tried them, and like a sacrificial burnt offering he accepted them. In the time of their visitation they will shine forth, and will run like sparks through the stubble. (Wis. of Sol. 3:1-7)

It is not entirely clear from where these souls originate. Does God create an immortal soul in every human being or did all souls preexist with God before the world was made? The latter appears to be the more likely solution.

31. "I learned both what is secret and what is manifest, for wisdom, the fashioner of all things, taught me. There is in her a spirit that is intelligent, holy, unique, manifold, subtle, mobile, clear, unpolluted, distinct, invulnerable, loving the good, keen, irresistible" (Wis. of Sol. 7:21-22).

In the view of Wisdom of Solomon, God is not only surrounded by spirit and wisdom, but also by "souls" that in an angelic-like form belong among the vital primordial elements. This in turn means, however, that the core of human nature is not of this world but belongs to a reality beyond our knowledge and experience. And this precisely is Wisdom of Solomon's point: the physical world that holds injustice and pain even for the most faithful and righteous person does not define what is most precious about a human being.

The comparison between Ecclesiastes and Wisdom of Solomon allows us to see differences between a theological anthropology that is essentially based on the concept of "spirit" and one that introduces in addition a concept of an immortal soul. Note, however, that the Greek concept of soul has hardly anything in common with the ancient cultic concept of *nefesh*. One question that needs to be addressed beyond this paper is whether the concept of an immortal "soul" is necessarily tied to a *Weltanschauung* that includes the idea of a world beyond the physical universe. Parts of Greek philosophy obviously suggest this.[32] The fact that Ecclesiastes and Wisdom of Solomon respond differently to the concept of an immortal soul indicates that its compatibility with biblical creation theology and its rootedness in a "one-world" cosmology is a controversial issue already within the Old Testament canon in its Hebrew and Greek versions.

32. For a good overview of the multifaceted discourse about immortality in Greek philosophy see M. V. Blischke, *Die Eschatologie in der Sapientia Salomonis,* Forschungen zum Alten Testament 26 (Tübingen: Mohr Siebeck, 2007).

Sarx, Soma, and the Transformative Pneuma: Personal Identity Endangered and Regained in Pauline Anthropology

Gerd Theissen

Traditional biblical exegesis has argued that Pauline anthropology is principally holistic, which corresponds to Jewish and biblical tradition. In this tradition humans encounter the transcendent God and because of this encounter experience themselves as a whole. No duality exists between an inner self connected to God and an external body far removed from God. The soul and the body exist at an equal distance from the one and only God. A crucial argument for this holistic understanding of human nature is the term *soma* (body), sometimes used as a *pars pro toto* for the whole "person" (e.g., Rom. 6:12-13). Dualistic texts, however, must be reinterpreted in a nondualistic way. I am referring to the contrast between *sarx* and *pneuma* (flesh and spirit) in Romans 8:5-8, of *eso* and *exo anthropos* (internal and external self) in Romans 7:22-23 and 2 Corinthians 4:16, of *palaios anthropos* (the old self) in Romans 6:6 and *kaine ktisis* ("new creature") in Galatians 6:15, and of *nous* and *mele* ("mind and members") in Romans 7:22-23.

A nondualistic interpretation understands such dichotomies as resulting from human behavior: Human beings are flesh, but living according to the flesh *(kata sarka)* gives the flesh an alienating power that ultimately dominates human behavior, although this power derives from human behavior in the first place. According to this view, the devaluation of one element in these polarities (i.e., of *sarx, exo anthropos,* and *mele*) is simply a matter of fact (it is "ontic," not "ontological"), but there is no dualism in principle. From the outset, the human being constitutes a whole, but sinful behavior creates a duality of flesh

---

I would like to thank Jennifer Adams-Massmann for editing my English in this manuscript.

and spirit.[1] This interpretation is often combined with a second argument concerning the history of traditions behind these terms, as dualistic language is traced back to the influence of nonbiblical traditions from Near Eastern or Greek sources.

Two observations reveal problems with this mainstream interpretation. First, while it is true that the term *soma* can be replaced by the personal pronoun in some cases, the term *peritome* can also be replaced in some cases by "Jews." Yet the term *peritome* in Pauline writings generally means only a particular somatic ritual marker of Jewish identity and is not a *pars pro toto* for the whole Jewish person. The synecdochic use of *soma* as *pars pro toto* in some cases cannot be taken to infer that *soma* is always a synecdoche for the whole person. This would be a linguistic mistake.

Secondly, in dualistic Pauline texts the polarity between *sarx* and *pneuma* is the most remarkable phenomenon. In many but not all cases, *sarx* has a negative connotation. *Soma,* on the other hand, often but not always has a positive connotation in ethical, ecclesiological, and eschatological contexts, as we shall see. In keeping with the mainstream interpretation, we should expect the negative connotation of *sarx* to have originated in nonbiblical traditions and the positive connotation of *soma* in biblical traditions. But in fact *sarx* (meaning flesh, in Hebr. *basar*) is an authentic biblical term. Its negative interpretation is documented in the biblical tradition in the Qumran texts where *basar* is connected with sin (1QM 12:12; 1QS 11:9, etc.). *Soma,* however, is a Greek term without an equivalent in the Hebrew tradition.

While some aspects of the exegetical consensus concerning Pauline anthropology may be mistaken, it cannot be completely wrong. According to the traditional exegetical consensus, the dualism of the internal and external self *(eso* and *exo anthropos)* is a remnant of Platonic ideas in Pauline writings.[2] This is the best explanation. According to the mainstream interpretation, however, we should expect Paul to mitigate this dualism in accordance with his holistic anthropology, but instead he actually sharpens this contrast. In the context of the *eso*-and-*exo*-*anthropos* dualism, the term *soma* has an unusually negative meaning: the internal *anthropos* is at war with the members of the body, crying for salvation from this "body of death" (in Rom. 7:23-24). In Romans

---

1. The classical representative of the holistic interpretation of Pauline anthropology is R. Bultmann, *Theologie des Neuen Testaments,* 3rd ed. (Tübingen: Mohr, 1961), pp. 193-203. English translation: *Theology of the New Testament,* trans. K. Grobel (Waco, TX: Baylor University Press, 2007).

2. T. Heckel, *Der Innere Mensch: Die paulinische Verarbeitung eines platonischen Motivs,* Wissenschaftliche Untersuchungen zum Neuen Testament 2:53 (Tübingen: Mohr, 1993).

6:6 the old self *(the palaios anthropos)* is crucified together with the "body of sin." According to Romans 8:13, we must "put to death the deeds of the body." These are strong negative statements about the body. In these cases *soma* is a synonym for *sarx* as used in its most negative sense. The parallelism of the internal and external *anthropos* with the old and new *anthropos* — the term "new *anthropos*" is missing in Paul, but he does speak of a "new creation" in Galatians 6:15; 1 Corinthians 7:19 — shows that Paul's dualism expresses a *transformative* anthropology of deep change within the person, not a static dualistic anthropology of a high and a low stratum within the person. The contrast between the interior and external self is even intensified within this transformative anthropology: the *eso anthropos* must be renewed every day, while the *exo anthropos* is wasting away. With a static dualistic anthropology, it would be enough to say that the "interior self" remains and dominates the external or that the internal survives the external self.

Scholars agree that this transformative anthropology is embedded in a *transformative cosmology.* The whole world is changing. Christians act and are transformed in accordance with this cosmic change. Awaking from sleep in the dawn of a new cosmic day, they put on the armor of light, meaning "they make no provisions for the flesh to gratify its desires" (Rom. 13:11-14). The transformative power to change the world and human nature comes from the crucifixion and resurrection of Christ. Humanity is being transformed in *conformitas* with this fate. The abolishing of the old is symbolized by the cross. The body of sin is *crucified* (Rom. 6:6), the flesh and its passions and desires are *crucified* (Gal. 5:24), and even the world is *crucified* for a Christian (Gal. 6:14). But the crucifixion is followed by a resurrection. Paul speaks therefore of a "newness of life" (Rom. 6:4) or a "new creation" (Gal. 6:15; 2 Cor. 5:17).

Two misconceptions have distorted modern interpretations of Pauline anthropology. The first is that a holistic anthropology includes a positive evaluation of the body, while a dichotomous anthropology involves a devaluation of the body. Yet according to the cultural values of antiquity,[3] the opposite is true: if there is an internal hierarchy of a lower and a higher stratum within each person, the lower stratum is not expected to live up to the same norms as the higher stratum (comparable to slaves in society who were not supposed to behave like free men and women). The body is experienced as distant from the

3. P. Brown, *Keuschheit der Engel: Sexuelle Entsagung, Askese und Körperlichkeit am Anfang des Christentums* (Wien: Hanser, 1991), pp. 39-46, 47-79. English original: *The Body and Society: Men, Women, and Sexual Renunciation in Early Christianity,* 2nd ed. (New York: Columbia University Press, 2008).

ego *(ich-fern)*. Therefore, the body is allowed to behave in a way that would not be as appropriate for the central self. Within a holistic anthropology, the body is a part of personal identity, especially in the encounter with a transcendent God. The weaknesses, deficiencies, and failures of the body are now a crucial problem. The *ego* is identified with the body. Here we encounter a deeply pessimistic anthropology present in some currents of thought and which Paul shares: there is no higher stratum within the human exempted from sin. Furthermore, this pessimism concerning the flesh and the body derives from a particular strand of biblical tradition. Common Judaism and some currents of thought in the New Testament (Matthew, Luke, James) have a much more balanced "ethical anthropology": humans are able to repent, and their anthropological structure does not have to be changed in contrast to the demands placed by Paul's "soteriological anthropology."

The second misconception about Pauline anthropology is the idea that a pessimistic anthropology of the body is not life-negating *per se* and an optimistic anthropology of the body is not life-affirming *per se*. The differentiation between pessimism and a life-negating philosophy comes from Albert Schweitzer.[4] He argued that a pessimistic view of the world can coexist with a positive philosophy of life. If a person affirms life despite living in a dark world, that person's affirmation of life is much stronger than that of someone with an optimistic worldview. This insight can be applied to our problem: although a person may experience the body and the flesh as a source of evil, he or she may nevertheless develop a very positive view of life if convinced that even this poor and sinful body and flesh is able to perform good deeds and fulfill God's will. Indeed, the transformative anthropology of Paul combines a deep anthropological pessimism with a very strong affirmation of life.

We can thus say that Paul advanced neither a holistic nor a dualistic anthropology but a transformative anthropology.[5] While dualistic patterns certainly exist in Pauline thought — he speaks of an antagonism between *sarx* and *pneuma*, "flesh and spirit" (Rom. 8:5-8) — such dualistic statements describe human nature between the old and the new world: *sarx* belongs to the old world, *pneuma* to the new. The external self is replaced by the internal, the old self by the new. Human existence is in a process of change. The whole world is being transformed and human nature is being transformed

---

4. A. Schweitzer, *Civilization and Ethics* (London: Adam and Charles Black, 1946). German original: *Kultur und Ethik* (München: Beck, 1923; 1981).

5. G. Theißen, *Erleben und Verhalten der ersten Christen: Eine Psychologie des Urchristentums* (Gütersloh: Gütersloher Verlagshaus, 2007), pp. 76-109.

in conformity with Christ. Christ is the model of such a change, the spirit is the energy for this change, and the body and flesh are the location where this change is taking place.

In what follows I wish to develop three theses. The first refers to both sides of the dualism of *sarx* and *pneuma*. Both terms relate to transpersonal and personal powers. These transcend human consciousness and deliberate control. At the same time, they are elements of human nature — both within and beyond the human person — and they embrace dissociative parts of the human person.

The second thesis refers only to the bodily aspect of this dualism. The two terms *sarx* and *soma* designate the biological aspect with two complementary points of view: *sarx* represents the energy of life that must be repressed, while the body is the energy that can be sublimated and integrated. We might say that the body designates all aspects to be integrated within the human person, while *sarx* is all those aspects beyond the boundaries of the individual person that need to be overcome.

The third thesis refers to the pneumatic side of the dualism: *pneuma* is the transformative self, which in Paul describes both the human and divine spirit depending on whether this spirit has its center within the person or externally (in God), that is, whether it is attributed to the inner human person or to an external transcendent factor. Thus, we come across the double meaning of *pneuma*: *pneuma* is both within and outside of the human person. Within the human person, it cooperates with the mind *(nous)* and other parts of the person.

1. The Antagonism of *Sarx* and *Pneuma*

My first thesis concerns the opposition between the terms *sarx* and *pneuma*. Both terms express a personal and transpersonal dimension. They designate the intersection between personal and transpersonal realities: *sarx* indicates the biotic-based passions (the *pathemata*), while *pneuma* refers to the counter-passion of God. Humans live in between these transpersonal powers, both experienced as dissociative parts of the human person. Although the *pneuma* overcomes the dissociative states of the person, the flesh remains a dissociative power.

Scholars agree that Paul differentiates between God's *pneuma* and human *pneuma*. The best evidence is Romans 8:16: God's *pneuma* witnesses to the *pneuma* of human persons. God's *pneuma* is more than the human *pneuma*, for the divine *pneuma* speaks to the human *pneuma*. Also in 1 Corinthians 14 Paul differentiates between *pneuma* and another human agency, the *nous* or the human mind. Speaking in tongues is caused by the spirit of God: "Now there are varieties of gifts, but the same Spirit" (1 Cor. 12:4). One of these gifts of the spirit is glossolalia.[6] Human reason does not participate in the act of glossolalia. The *pneuma*, speaking in glossolalia, transcends human consciousness and control. Nevertheless, Paul does not speak of the spirit of God as the subject of glossolalia, but his own spirit:

> For if I pray in a tongue,
> my spirit *(pneuma)* prays
> but my mind *(nous)* is unproductive:
> What should I do then?
> I will pray with the spirit,
> but I will pray with my mind also;
> I will sing praise with the spirit,
> but I will sing praise with the mind also. (1 Cor. 14:14-15)

The pneumatics are undoubtedly "possessed" by the spirit. Their behavior is comparable to those possessed by demons, except that pneumatic possession is a positive possession, causing ecstasy rather than sickness. The *pneuma* speaks through glossolalia, but the person does not know what is happening even if it is her own *pneuma* ("my *pneuma*") that is active. In modern categories this could be called a dissociative experience. The person experiences an internal process but she does not have full access to this process. She neither understands completely what is happening nor is she able to control it, so that an interpreter is necessary. The ideal interpreter is the pneumatic herself, who then acts as a prophet. Concerning prophets Paul says: "The spirits of prophets are subject to the prophets" (1 Cor. 14:32). He speaks about spirits in the plural. So there is no doubt these spirits are not the spirits of individual human beings, but have their own center. Humans should strive to control the energy of the *pneuma*, but in many personal states the *pneuma* controls them.

Similarly, Paul also differentiates between human *sarx* and *sarx* as a tran-

---

6. G. Theißen, *Erleben und Verhalten*, pp. 195-202. H.-J. Klauck, "Von Kassandra bis zur Gnosis: Im Umfeld der frühchristlichen Glossolalie," in Klauck, *Religion und Gesellschaft im frühen Christentum*, Wissenschaftliche Untersuchungen zum Neuen Testament 152 (Tübingen: Mohr, 2003), pp. 119-44. Klauck, "Mit Engelszungen? Vom Charisma der verständlichen Rede in 1 Kor 14," in Klauck, *Religion und Gesellschaft im frühen Christentum*, pp. 145-67. L. T. Johnson, *Religious Experience in Earliest Christianity* (Minneapolis: Fortress Press, 1998), pp. 105-36.

spersonal power. Humans are not able to control the transpersonal power of flesh. Because they are flesh, they are sold into slavery under sin (Rom. 7:14). Flesh and spirit "are opposed to each other to prevent you from doing what you want" (Gal. 5:17). Paul very often chooses the term *soma* in order to designate those aspects of human life that humans can influence: for example, he exhorts Christians "to present your bodies *(somata)* as a living sacrifice, holy and acceptable in God, which is your reasonable worship" (Rom. 12:1).

In Paul's anthropology, *sarx* and *pneuma* are both transpersonal realities — biotic nature, on the one hand, and God, on the other — which intervene in human life either in a disastrous way (in the shape of the *sarx* and its aggressive energy) or in a beneficial way (as with the energy of the *pneuma* and its energy of love). It is a struggle between possession and counter-possession. Compared with the ethical anthropology of Judaism and Jewish Christians, this opening of human beings to transpersonal influences seems to be a regression, but it can also be seen as progress as Paul neither interprets this transpersonal influence in a demonic way nor as a struggle between Satan and God. Rather, he understands it in an anthropological way, as a struggle within the human person. Thus, it is not God or the Devil who are in conflict within the human being but the flesh and the spirit. Both flesh and spirit can become a part of human personality. In addition to their transpersonal dimension, they have a personal dimension. They act as a bridge in both directions.

In the next section we will deal with each part of this "dualism." This second hypothesis concerns the bodily aspect of human nature: the synonymity of *sarx* and *soma* in Pauline writings.[7]

2. The Bodily Aspect of the Antagonism: *Sarx* and *Soma* in Pauline Writings

The second thesis: Both terms, *sarx* and *soma,* designate the bodily aspects of human persons, but there is a difference between them. Humans share the flesh *(sarx)* with all living beings on earth. Being *sarx,* humans are involved in an aggressive and destructive struggle for life. This ought to be overcome by a transformation: humans share the same body *(soma)* with other humans in Christ (as the body of Christ). The *sarx* denotes a conflicting power of life

---

7. Cf. L. Scornaienchi, *Sarx und Soma bei Paulus: Der Mensch zwischen Konstruktivität und Destruktivität,* Novum Testamentum et Orbis Antiquus 67 (Göttingen: Vandenhoeck & Ruprecht, 2008).

within the biotic sphere of life, while the *soma* or body is a uniting power within the human sphere of life. We may interpret this with the help of an "intentional anachronism." In this case, we would understand it as the need to "repress" some biologically rooted energy, i.e., the energy of the flesh *(sarx)* as well as the chance to "sublimate" some of this energy, i.e., the energy of the body *(soma)*. Repression and sublimation of energy are expressed by the different use of *sarx* and *soma*. The *sarx* is repressed, while the *soma* is sublimated.

Let me explain this thesis: What should Christians repress according to Paul? They should repress the flesh *(sarx)*, meaning they should, as Paul says, "crucify the flesh with its passions and desires" (Gal. 5:4). Paul characterizes fleshly behavior in the following way: "If, however, you bite and devour one another, take care that you are not consumed by one another" (Gal. 5:15). The struggle for life should be overcome. The *sarx* represents destructive behavior and aggression against other people and against God. Paul can thus say: The *sarx* is hostility or enmity against God (Rom. 8:7).

What should Christians sublimate? The body (the *soma*). The body is not a positive or neutral term in Pauline anthropology. Rather, we often find a negative evaluation of the body in line with Greek traditions. In Greek texts, the body *(soma)* is often the dead corpse, the dependent slave, or the body as a prison. Paul shares this pessimistic view but he uses the term "body" *(soma)* within three contexts in a very positive way and all three contexts refer to the transformation of humanity.

(a) First, it is an *ethical transformation:* In ethics the *soma* is the medium for performing good deeds: "I appeal to you . . . to present your bodies *(somata)* as a living sacrifice, holy and acceptable to God, which is your spiritual worship" (Rom. 12:1). The *pneuma* is the power of this new life.

(b) Second, it is a *social or ecclesial transformation:* In ecclesiology *soma* means the *soma Christou*, the body of Christ as a metaphor of the church (1 Cor. 12:12ff.; Rom. 12:4-8). Christians share the flesh *(sarx)* with all living beings; they share the same body as members only with other Christians. The *pneuma* is the uniting power within this body.

(c) Third, it is an *eschatological transformation:* In eschatology the earthly *soma* will be transformed into a spiritual body (a *soma pneumatikon*) (1 Cor. 15:44). The spirit *(pneuma)* is the power that gives new life to the dead body (Rom. 8:11).

In these three contexts (ethical, ecclesial, and eschatological frameworks) the body is a transformed body, a body created anew by the spirit or transformed

GERD THEISSEN

by the spirit. Lorenzo Scornaienchi has analyzed the relationship of *sarx* and *soma*. We can summarize his results in the following diagram:

spatial \ temporal	Human beings before salvation and transformation	Human beings after salvation and transformation
Human beings as *soma* (body)	*Passivity and death:* *soma* = slave, dead, corpse, dependency, and mortality	*Constructive activity:* The *soma* is animated by the *pneuma* and causes prosocial behavior.
Human beings as *sarx* (flesh)	*Destructive activity:* The *sarx* is the basis for the passions and for enmity against God and causes destructive behavior.	*Passivity and death:* The *sarx* and its passions are killed.

The following insight is crucial: "body" *(soma)* is not a neutral term designating the whole human being without any negative aspects. This mainstream interpretation is wrong. The body is by nature passive and mortal in Pauline thought. But the body is animated by the Spirit *(pneuma)* and becomes active. When it is animated by the Spirit, it becomes a transformed and renewed body. Flesh *(sarx),* on the contrary, is very active before salvation, but is condemned to be passive and mortal as a consequence of salvation. The *soma* is given new life, whereas the *sarx* is killed and crucified.

It is significant that Paul uses the metaphor of crucifixion to speak of the struggle against the *sarx.* The modern reader may be shocked because "killing" the natural drives and affects seems unacceptable and impossible. But Paul always associates two things with "crucifixion": first, the crucifixion is the place of a hidden revelation. If the *sarx* is crucified, the flesh is the place of God's paradoxical presence in the human sphere and in history. The most positive statements on the flesh *(sarx)* indeed speak in this way about an epiphany of Christ both in the body and in the flesh. Secondly, crucifixion is followed by resurrection, death by life. Both aspects are present in the famous words of Paul:

We are afflicted in every way, but not crushed;
perplexed, but not driven to despair;
persecuted, but not forsaken;
struck down, but not destroyed;
always carrying in the body *(soma)* the death of Jesus,
so that the life of Jesus may also be made visible in our bodies.
For while we live, we are always being given up to death for Jesus' sake,

174

So that the life of Jesus may be made visible in our
mortal flesh *(sarx).*
So death is at work in us, but life in you. (2 Cor. 4:8-12)

The same logic of cross and resurrection is at work in Romans 6. If the old
self is crucified and the body of sin destroyed (Rom. 6:6), then a new life must
follow, according to this logic. Indeed, Paul admonishes the congregation immediately after this statement about the crucified body, telling them to "present yourselves to God *as those who have been brought from death to life* and
present your members to God as instruments of righteousness" (Rom. 6:13).
The *sarx* is crucified, but its energy will be resurrected and transformed. The
power to do this lies in the *pneuma.* What is more, we may say that the power
of the *pneuma* is the transformed power of the *sarx.* The human *sarx* must be
"crucified" so that the energy of the *sarx* can be resurrected as *pneuma.* The
third hypothesis is thus that the *pneuma* is the transformative self, merging
together the creative power of God and the dissociative self of human beings.

3. The Spiritual Aspect of the Antagonism:
Human and Divine *Pneuma* in the New Testament

The third thesis is this: just as *sarx* and *soma* refer to the bodily aspects of human nature, the *pneuma* refers to the spiritual aspect. The human *pneuma* lives
within the human person, while the divine *pneuma* lives outside of the human
person. But whereas the *sarx* must be "destroyed" in order to be transformed
into the *soma,* the human *pneuma* (as well as the heart, mind, and soul) are
preserved within this unity of divine and human *pneuma.* The divine *pneuma*
is an integrative power, establishing a new unity of the person beyond all
antagonisms and dissociative phenomena. The *pneuma* overcomes dissociation. In early Christianity the *pneuma* is the power to regain an endangered
personal identity and integrity.

The transformation of human nature from a fleshly to a pneumatic existence is the work of the spirit. This spirit unifies two spiritual realities: the Spirit
of God and the spirit of individual human beings. The key text is Romans 8:12-17:

So then, brothers, we are debtors,
not of the flesh, to live according to the flesh —
for if you live according to the flesh, you will die;
but if by the Spirit you put to death the deeds of the body,

you will live.
For all who are led by the Spirit of God are children of God.
For you did not receive a spirit of slavery to fall back into fear,
but you have received a spirit of adoption.
When we cry: "Abba! Father!"
it is that very Spirit bearing witness with our spirit
that we are children of God,
and if children, then heirs, heirs of God
and joint heirs with Christ —
if, in fact, we suffer with him
so that we may also be glorified with him.

In this text, divine Spirit and human mind are both called "spirit." They are discerned as separate yet simultaneously united. The divine Spirit is both a motivational power to transform human deeds and a cognitive power of revelation to bear witness to the human mind (= to the "spirit"). The motivating power is described as a creative power. Those who have "killed" the deeds of the flesh will experience the resurrecting power of the creator God, as Paul writes immediately before: "If the Spirit *of him* who raised Jesus from the dead dwells in you, he who raised Christ from the dead will give life to your mortal bodies also through his Spirit that dwells in you" (Rom. 8:11). The cognitive power of revelation is described as a communicative power that makes it possible to address God as "Abba, Father!" The divine Spirit is localized outside the human person; the human spirit is localized within the person.

To understand this duality of a spirit that can be an internal and external reality at the same time or be localized within and outside of the person, we have to sketch the history of the human "dissociative self" in the history of religion where we encounter the same duality.[8]

In ancient times, humans saw their lives as guided by different forms of a "dissociative soul": the external soul and the messenger of death were both localized outside of human persons, while the excursive soul and the soul of death were both localized within human persons. The person was not yet an identity with a clear demarcation from the environment, but was split and porous. The dissociative soul localized outside the human person could be interpreted as the divine Spirit but also as the ecstatic human soul. The dissociative soul localized within the human person could be interpreted as the human spirit but also as an incarnated divine Spirit.

---

8. G. Theißen, *Erleben und Verhalten*, pp. 49-109.

I should say a few words about this odd "thing" called the "dissociative soul" (*Außenseele* or "external soul" in German, also known as the *Freiseele* or "free soul"). I will first address the phenomenon in ancient times and in popular psychology up to the present, and then discuss the disappearance of the dissociative soul in Greek philosophy and Jewish religion (in the Old Testament). Finally, I will comment on the revival of the dissociative soul in early Judaism, early Christianity, and Middle Platonism.

3.1. *The Dissociative Soul in Ancient Egypt and Ancient Greece: Centralizing the Internal Soul and Internalizing the Dissociative Soul*

The term "external soul" is not acceptable to modern minds. We locate the soul within humans. "External soul" is much more an *emic* term describing past beliefs. In our view (that is, in *etic* terms) we would prefer to speak of a dissociative self. We know that our mind can function on different levels and that one part of our mind may have no access to the other part, whether temporarily or for a longer period of time or even forever. I prefer the term "dissociative *soul*" (instead of self) because the term "soul" clearly refers to premodern times. This is important because dissociative states are considered to be pathological disturbances in our culture. They appear as a result of posttraumatic disorders, in which a traumatic situation of abuse or violence in childhood is reenacted at a later time (either in short flashbacks or enduring reenactments). During such reenactments, the dissociative self in the past from childhood has no access to the present mind of the adult person, but feels as guilty or helpless as the child. We also know that dissociative states of consciousness occur during creative work, so that the absentminded professor is a typical example of such nonpathological dissociation. In general, such a professor is able to function in the everyday world within limits because of some access to everyday consciousness, which enables the professor to manage in his or her current environment, although that person may be otherwise totally absorbed in other problems. This suggests that in dissociative states of mind we are often in touch with objective realities, such as the professor who is obsessed with a scientific problem. In antiquity, people were convinced they could touch an objective reality while in a dissociative state of mind.

Since the "invention of the internal man"[9] or "the psychological turn in

9. J. Assmann et al., eds., *Die Erfindung des inneren Menschen: Studien zur religiösen Anthropologie* (Gütersloh: Gütersloher Verlagshaus, 1998).

177

the European history of religion"[10] the boundary separating internal and external reality has been strengthened. A struggle has ensued to identify what is external and what is internal. The concept of an external or dissociative soul exists in a variety of concepts.

The dissociative soul is either localized from the outset beyond human beings, encountering them from outside in extraordinary states of the mind (either in *altered states of consciousness* or *near-death experiences*), or the dissociative soul is localized from the outset within humans but is able to leave for a moment or forever. We can therefore distinguish four forms of the dissociative soul:

(a) The dissociative soul may be encountered as the *external soul* (as the *Außenseele*): People believe in a life power or an external vitality that the Romans called *genius*[11] or the Greeks, the personal *daimon*. This concept of the external soul has survived to today as the guardian angel who accompanies humans during their lifetimes.

(b) The dissociative soul may also be encountered as the *messenger of death and mediator of postmortal existence*. It is an *alter ego*. It appears only once before death in order to announce death. This belief has survived in the idea of an angel of death who carries the soul to heaven.

(c) The dissociative soul may take the form of the *soul of excursion* (the *Exkursionsseele* or the *Freiseele*): This soul is located within human beings, but is able to leave the body during their lifetimes — in ecstasy or at times of extreme danger or stress or in a dream, when the soul visits other places. The phenomenal basis for this belief is the experience of dissociative or *altered states of consciousness*, most remarkably *out-of-body experiences*.

(d) The last form of the dissociative soul is the *soul of death:* In dying the soul leaves the person forever and exists as a shadow outside the body, but sometimes communicates with living people. The phenomenal basis for this belief derives from encounters with dead persons in hallucinatory perceptions, in dreams, or in *near-death experiences*.

So far I have outlined four basic possibilities for conceptualizing the dissociative soul. It is either connected with life or death or is located within human beings or outside of human beings:

10. B. Gladigow, "Bilanzierungen des Lebens über den Tod hinaus," in *Tod, Jenseits und Identität*, ed. J. Assmann and R. Trauzettel (München: Karl Alber, 2002), pp. 90-109.

11. Cf. Solfram Aslan Maharam, Art. Genius, *Der neue Pauly: Enzyklopädie der Antike*, ed. H. Cancik and H. Schneider (Stuttgart, 1996-), 4:915-17.

The four forms of the dissociative soul		
	The domain of life and earthly behavior	The domain of death and postmortal life
External Localization: The soul as a divine reality	The dissociative soul as external soul, as genius, a protecting demon or guardian angel	The dissociative soul as the messenger of death or angel of death, which encounters the person from the outside
Internal Localization: The soul as a humane reality	The dissociative soul as soul of excursion, which leaves the body in dreams and ecstasy during one's lifetime	The dissociative soul as the soul of the dead, which leaves the dead person

I should add that at least one ancient culture, the Egyptians, structured the dissociative soul in a highly systematic way, differentiating between *Ba* (the body self) and *Ka* (the social self). In philosophy we find a system of dissociative souls (demons) in Middle Platonism with Apuleius of Madaura, *De Deo Socratis*.

3.2. *The Disappearance of the External Soul in Classical Times: Plato's Demythologization of the Dissociative Soul and Its Denial in the Old Testament*

The development of an integrative personal center caused the concept of an external soul to disappear. This development took place in Greek philosophy and the Old Testament for different reasons.

Plato was familiar with traditional demonology. He knew about demons serving as guardian gods for peoples[12] or individuals.[13] He was also familiar with demons as the souls of the dead, since the souls of great humans were worshiped as *daimones*. The *daimonion* of Socrates was probably a motive for developing a philosophical demonology that went beyond such popular beliefs. Plato wrote that the demon is the internal center of the human and is responsible for the human's *eudaimonia* (*Tim.* 90a.c). At the end of his *Politeia*, Plato recounts the near-death experience of the Armenian ER. He was believed dead and was supposed to be burned at the stake, but became alive again (*Resp.* 614a ff.). ER tells of his encounter with the realm of death and the Goddess of Fate, Lachesis, who said to him: "The demon will not elect you, but you will elect your demon. . . ." The new message was that the human soul and not God

12. Plato, *Pol.* 271d ff.; 272e f.; 274b; *Tim.* 24c f.; 42e, *Critias* 109b f.; *Leg.* 713c ff.
13. Plato, *Phaed.* 107d ff.; 113d; *Rep.* 617d f., 620d f.; *Leg.* 877a.

GERD THEISSEN

is responsible for the demon who is elected (*Resp.* 617d-e). Plato, speaking in a mythological way of demons, actually demythologizes demons. Humans are responsible for their personal demons, meaning they are responsible for the guiding self and the dissociative parts of the self. As E. Cassirer writes, in this Platonic text the idea of personal responsibility overcomes mythical fate.[14] The dissociative soul is internalized and reappropriated.

The dissociative soul also disappeared in the Old Testament, for different but comparable reasons to Greek philosophy. In Israel each human being has a center which is the heart. In addition to the heart, there are other organs such as the "heart and kidney." But all organs are oriented toward one external center: God, in keeping with the commandment that "you shall love the LORD your God with all your heart, and with all your soul, and with all your might" (Deut. 6:5). The heart is the cognitive, emotional, and motivational center of personality. The four variants of the dissociative soul disappear. One reason is that the topic of death is neglected in the Old Testament. The souls of the dead are only fading shadows in Sheol. There is no belief in a real afterlife. The invocation of the souls of the deceased is forbidden (1 Sam. 28:3-25) and many forms of fortune telling are suppressed. The phenomenon of demonic possession is not an important topic, in comparison with the New Testament. Demons exist but they do not invade the center of human nature. On the contrary, it is the very Spirit of God that disturbs people such as Saul (1 Sam. 16:14; 18:10). Between God and humans there is no place for an independent external soul. The external power is God or God's spirit, the internal power of the human person and mind. We might say that the disappearance of the dissociative soul is due to an ethical monotheism that did not include a belief in the afterlife and emphasized a strong sense of responsibility for one's own life. The law and the prophets ascribe responsibility for life to humans themselves and to God. Nevertheless, while the idea disappeared in the Old Testament, in popular belief the dissociative soul must have survived.

3.3. The Remythologizing of the Person in Hellenistic and Roman Times: The Reappearance of the Dissociative Soul as Belief in Demons and Angels

The belief in a dissociative soul survived in the popular underground and was renewed in Hellenistic-Roman times. There appears to have been a remytholo-

---

14. E. Cassirer, *Philosophie der symbolischen Formen II: Das mythische Denken* (Darmstadt: Wissenschaftliche Buchgesellschaft, 1958), p. 161.

gizing of the internal psychic space by demons (as a negative form of dissociative souls) and by guardian angels (as a positive form of dissociative souls), supported by the new belief in an afterlife. This belief supports the concept of a soul independent of the body. In philosophy at the time we can also observe a revival of demonology.[15] In early antiquity the word *daimon* was often equivalent to God and was seen as a positive being. The *daimonion* of Socrates was a moral voice. But the general development of the word "demon" *(daimon)* resulted in a pejorative meaning of the term, except in philosophy. This may be due to the Socratic *daimonion* and the definition of *daimones* as intermediaries between God and humans in the *Symposium (Symp.* 202e-203a). In Middle Platonism we encounter an elaborate system of demonology (with roots in earlier Platonism: Xenocrates; Philippos of Opus = Pseudo-Plato, Epinomis). This may be due to the Platonic problem of mediating between the sensual and spiritual world. This mediation was personalized: first, the demiurge was given more significance in later Platonism as creator of the world, and then the doctrine of demons as personal mediators between God and humans was developed. In Middle Platonism, they act as mediating powers responsible for conveying human prayers to the gods and sharing revelations from the gods with humans. Like the gods they are immortal but like humans they experience passions and emotions. Unlike the gods they have a body; unlike humans these bodies are not visible except in particular revelations. The demons are also part of a hierarchy:

(a) Some demons are universal superhuman powers such as Somnus and Amor (sleep and love). Both are altered states of consciousness.
(b) Some demons are personal demons, guarding and sheltering individuals. They live within particular humans and are audible as an internal voice (comparable to the *daimonion* of Socrates). But they already existed before the birth of the individual human and continue to exist after that person's death.
(c) Another class of demons is represented by the souls within human beings. The Latin *genius* is interpreted in this way.
(d) The final class of demons is made up of the souls of the deceased (in Latin *lemures*). The demons of very important persons (like Asclepius) are worshiped.

This system of demons covers the four traditional forms of the dissociative soul — partly as functions of the same demons, partly as different demons. I

---

15. M. Baltes et al., eds., *Apuleius, De Deo Socratis: Über den Gott des Sokrates,* SAPERE 7 (Darmstadt: Wissenschaftliche Buchgesellschaft, 2004).

have ignored the first class of demons, Somnus and Amor, which cause altered states of consciousness: sleep and dreams (with reduced activation) and love and ecstasy (with enhanced activation).

The survival of the four forms of the dissociative soul in Middle Platonism		
	The domain of life and earthly behavior	The domain of death and post-mortal life
External Localization	The personal demon sheltering and guiding the individual during his or her lifetime	The personal demon taking the soul to heaven after death
Internal Localization	The demon as the soul within a human being	The demons as the souls of deceased persons

4. The Renewal of an Integrated Concept of Personhood in Early Christianity

In mainstream Christianity, Christ is the external soul that transcends human persons, and all transcendent powers are concentrated in him. The Spirit covers the four functions of the dissociative soul. The Spirit has an external origin and governs humans from outside, but it also dwells within humans and can explain ecstatic phenomena such as glossolalia. It is the power that overcomes death, as the core of human beings is re-created as a spiritual body.

The Holy Spirit and the four forms of the external soul		
	The domain of life and earthly behavior	The domain of death and transmortal life
External Localization	God sends the Spirit into the hearts of people (Gal. 4:6).	The spirit overcomes death: Those who "sow to the Spirit, . . . will reap eternal life from the Sprit" (Gal. 6:8).
Internal Localization	The spirit dwells within human beings and can occasionally leave the person (1 Cor. 5:3). It causes ecstatic phenomena. It makes persons into the temple of God.	The Spirit is an internal power within human beings that causes the resurrection of the dead (Rom. 8:11).

I am quite aware that my idea that the Holy Spirit is the reappropriated dissociative soul — or, to be more precise, the power to overcome dissociation within the human person — is a new and bold idea. Let me provide some supporting arguments for this hypothesis.

(a) Possession by the Spirit is a form of counter-possession in contrast to demon possession. If demons are dissociative phenomena, then positive possession by the Spirit is also a positive dissociative phenomenon. But this counter-possession is not alienation: the center of the person is not excluded, but empowered. It is a counter-possession that overcomes possession by an alienating power.

(b) In the New Testament the Spirit is symbolized in the story of Jesus' baptism by a dove. The Spirit is not a dove but (in Mark) something similar to a dove. Jesus sees "the Spirit descending like a dove on him." We should thus translate it literally: the dove is descending into him: *katabainon eis* auton (Mark 1:10). The Spirit becomes his internal power of life. The dove is a variant of the bird of the soul. Jesus is united with his heavenly external soul, his positive dissociative soul.[16]

(c) In the Gospel of John, the giving of the Spirit recalls the creation of Adam in Genesis 2:7. The resurrected Christ sends his disciples into the world. Then we read: "When he had said this, he breathed on them and said to them, 'Receive the Holy Spirit'" (John 20:22). Adam became a living soul by God's spirit, whereas the disciples are given the Holy Spirit in the same way.

5. The Renewal of an Integrated Concept of the Person through Gnosis: The Human Being as the Earthly External Soul of a Divine Self

In the Gnostic movement we encounter a cognitive restructuring of the relationship between the personal center and external soul. The earthly human being is deemed to be the external soul of the true self in heaven; the heavenly self is the true center of the person. Through gnosis they are reunited. The heavenly self as a part of God recognizes itself in the sparks of the divine soul

---

16. I owe this new interpretation of the dove to cultural anthropologist Thomas Hauschild. See the survey on many interpretations in William D. Davies and Dale C. Allison, *The Gospel According to Saint Matthew,* vol. 1, International Critical Commentary (Edinburgh: T. & T. Clark, 1988), pp. 331-34.

scattered within the world. Mythical speculation argues that the transcendent divine being became estranged from itself in many emanations and alienations within the world, so humans have to start re-collecting the estranged sparks of light with gnosis. All religious traditions are therefore symbols of God's search for God's own self within human beings. The "excarnation" becomes the mythical symbol of this process.

For some Valentinian Gnostics, life is like a nightmare or a dream (cf. *Evangelium Veritatis* 29f.). They interpret their souls on earth as the excursive part of their true souls in heaven. They also expect that when they die their personal guardian angels will act as bridegrooms and take their souls to heaven. These guardian angels are the messengers of death. The excursive soul is again reunited with the true soul in heaven. Therefore, they interpret the Lord's Supper as the sacrament of the bridal chamber, reuniting the dissociative soul on earth with the original true soul in heaven.

The Gnostic self as dissociative soul of the true self in the pleroma (in heaven)		
	Domain of life	Domain of death
External Localization	The internal core of human beings is the dissociative soul of the true heavenly self. This self is a part of the pleroma.	In dying, the internal self is united with its heavenly self — with the angels who are the soul's bridegrooms.
Internal Localization	The internal soul of human beings has access to God by gnosis. Gnosis is resurrection now.	The true self of human beings in heaven is immune against death.

There is a remarkable difference between Gnostic anthropology, on the one hand, and the anthropology of Paul and mainstream Christianity, on the other. Mainstream Christianity argues that God became human in order for humans to be transformed into divine beings. They argue for a transformative anthropology. Gnostic anthropology, however, is not at all a transformative anthropology. In Gnostic Christianity the dissociative soul is the hidden self on earth, while the true self in heaven looks for its earthly counterpart as its lost dissociative soul. The dissociative soul of the true self in heaven returns to heaven. It does not transform the self on earth but discovers its heavenly origin.

In Pauline anthropology the duality of the spirit as *divine Spirit* and *human spirit* corresponds to the duality of *sarx* and *soma*. But it is significant that the duality of *divine Spirit* and *human spirit* uses the same word, *spirit*. The divine Spirit overcomes this duality. Human spirits are filled with the divine

Spirit. The Spirit merges with all parts of the person. Therefore, it is possible to use the same words for two aspects of human spiritual life. At the same time the spirit transforms flesh into body, dissociating the fleshly destructive passions from the human person, but the spirit then reintegrates them after transforming them through crucifixion and resurrection. The divine Spirit does not destroy the human spirit in this way. The human *pneuma* is not crucified in order to merge together with the divine *pneuma,* but is renewed every day in a *creatio continua.* Paul says: "Even though our outer nature *(ho exo anthropos)* is wasting away, our inner nature *(ho eso anthropos)* is being renewed day by day" (2 Cor. 4:16). In the same way the mind *(nous)* is renewed (Rom. 12:2). The Christian is a new creature *(kaine ktisis)* (Gal. 6:15). The divine Spirit is a creative power working in the human spirit, integrating human *pneuma,* the human heart and mind, without destroying them and thus creating a new unity and wholeness.

So we may conclude that the unity of the person was established in Greek philosophy by the rule of reason, while in biblical theology it derives from the rule of the one and only God. This unity was endangered by dissociative forces, by demons outside the person and passions within the person. The New Testament is sensitive to these dangers. Human beings are driven by demons, powers, and the activity of the flesh. But the divine Spirit is an integrating power transforming the energies of the *flesh* and crucifying them in order that they may be resurrected as the energy of the *body.* At the same time the divine Spirit is a creative power renewing the internal self and mind every day. The divine Spirit transcends human spirit. It is a gift from outside, a dissociative experience, but its goal is to fill the human body like a temple and overcome all dissociation. Therefore, we cannot say there is only human reason within the person or that the transcendent God exists solely beyond the person. Rather, the Spirit, a divine power, re-creates human beings so that the endangered personal identity and integrity are regained.

Augustine's Aporetic Account of *Persona* and the Limits of *Relatio:* A Reconsideration of Substance Ontology and Immutability

Volker Henning Drecoll

In the article "Person" of the voluminous *Augustine through the Ages*[1] we find the following assumptions about Augustine's concept of person: "There are two central and intimately connected senses of person" (scil. in the Trinitarian and the anthropological context), but "the sense of 'person' which applies to the members of the Trinity is the fundamental sense." "Augustine never gives the analytical definition of the concept of 'person' we might want," but "in the case of God, personhood is not distinct from essence or existence" and Father, Son, and Holy Spirit are "generically three persons." "Person also applies to the substance of the Trinity," though "relations among persons in the Trinity are neither substantial nor accidental." This short description offers a series of problems and contradictions. It seems to be presupposed that Augustine had a "concept" of person deeply founded in the Trinitarian theology. At the same time a "definition" is missing, and it remains absolutely unclear whether person is identical with essence viz. substance or has to be distinguished from it, whether it is only a generic term or it implies a certain type of relations. How do these different assertions fit together? What is the crucial point in Augustine's "concept" of person?

The reception and tradition of the Augustinian Trinitarian theology in the following centuries includes the term "person." Especially Boethius and then Thomas Aquinas shaped the term "person" as a crucial term of each Trinitarian theology. This tradition became somewhat "classical": "In taking relations as constitutive of divine persons, the classical tradition was quite aware that hu-

1. Cf. S. Katz, "Art. Person," in *Augustine through the Ages: An Encyclopedia*, ed. A. D. Fitzgerald (Grand Rapids: Eerdmans, 1999), pp. 647-50.

man categories do break down when they are applied to God. In the Boethian definition person means 'an individual substance of rational nature'. A person means a substance or subsistent being, not an accident such as relation. . . . In God, however, relations are subsistent . . . ; and a subsistent relation is at the same time his or her own essence."[2]

The following article attempts to once again analyze the impact of the term "person" for Augustine's Trinitarian theology as it can be found in his *De trinitate*. Before moving to this task, however, a few brief remarks may be added about the use of *persona* in Augustine's work in general.

1. Meanings of *Persona* in the Works of Augustine

The noun *persona* has a wide range of meanings in the works of Augustine. If we put aside the use in Trinitarian and Christological contexts (which will be considered later), Augustine uses *persona* with the following meanings:[3]

1. In the context of grammar, *persona* means simply the first, second, or third person of a conjugation (cf. *dial.* 1 etc.).

2. *Persona* means the role that can be played. In an ironic question to Cicero as a supporter of an Academic skepticism he offers the alternative, to put aside *(ponere) personam patroni* and to accept the *personam philosophi (suscipere)* (cf. *Acad.* 3,35).[4]

3. *Persona* may also refer to an important person or a famous personality, e.g., Augustine remarks he has invited *magni cuiusdam hominis personam* (cf. *beata u.* 16).

4. In rhetoric, *persona* may refer to the person whose character, behavior, intentions, or actions are the subject of a speech. A good speech has to deal with *res* (the facts) and the *persona* (cf. *rhet.* 2-5). In a similar way *persona* is simply the designation of a certain person; e.g., the person of Mani is counted among the apostles by the Manicheans (cf. *util. cred.* 7), seventy-seven *personae* wrote the Septuagint (cf. *qu. eu.* 2,6,1), etc.

---

2. A. Kyongsuk Min, *The Solidarity of Others in a Divided World: A Postmodern Theology after Postmodernism* (New York: T. & T. Clark, 2004), p. 125.

3. The most detailed analysis of *persona* in the works of Augustine is H. R. Drobner, *Person-Exegese und Christologie bei Augustinus. Zur Herkunft der Formel una persona, Philosophia Patrum 8* (Leiden: Brill, 1986); the use in Trinitarian contexts however is analyzed only in passing.

4. Cf. T. Fuhrer, *Augustin, Contra Academicos (vel De Academicis) Bücher 2 und 3, Patristische Texte und Studien 46* (Berlin/New York: De Gruyter, 1997), p. 398.

5. That *persona* can refer to the character and behavior of an individual is affirmed by the fact that *persona* can even refer directly to the behavior or lifestyle of a person. E.g., Augustine opposes *duae personae laudabiles,* on the one hand those who have found already the goal of their searching, and on the other hand those who are searching intensively *(inquirere)* *(util. cred.* 25). That the *personae* are mentioned in the plural here without reference to two individuals shows that *duae personae* means "two lifestyles" or "two behaviors."

6. Of course, the behavior of somebody can be only superficial or even deceptive. In this sense, Augustine describes the *hypocritae* as those who cover *sub persona,* i.e., behind a role or mask what they are and show *in persona* only what they are not (cf. *s. dom. m.* 2,64).[5]

7. In exegetical contexts, *persona* occurs in the so-called "prosopographic interpretation," i.e., biblical passages or verses are explained *ex persona alicuius* (*domini, Dei, ecclesiae,* David, etc.). This form of exegesis is already seen in Augustine's early works (cf. *s. dom. m.* 1,44) and he uses it in all his exegetical works (the sermons, commentaries, and even the homiletic-exegetical works like *Io. eu. tr.*).[6]

8. In contexts concerned with the doctrine of grace Augustine uses the combination *personam accipere* from Galatians 2:6, even as a noun in the genitive form as it can be found in Romans 2:11 and Colossians 3:25: *acceptio personarum.* This term recalls the judicial use of the word: A good judge does not favor one party or a person, he passes a judgment *sine acceptione personarum* (vgl. *exp. Gal.* 12, *ep. Rm. inch.* 8, *c. Faust.* 22,67, etc.).[7]

2. The Concept of *Persona* in *De Trinitate*

The most important work for better understanding Augustine's idea of *persona* is his *De trinitate.* In this work, Augustine scrutinizes the biblical testimonies, the concepts of Trinitarian thought, and develops his famous new approach, known popularly as the "psychological Trinitarian doctrine."[8] Even the con-

---

5. Cf. Drobner, *Person-Exegese,* p. 103.
6. Cf. Drobner, *Person-Exegese,* pp. 69-77.
7. Vgl. Drobner, *Person-Exegese,* pp. 88-94.
8. The discussion about the date of *De trinitate* has been resumed by P. M. Hombert: *Nouvelles Recherches de chronologie augustinienne, Collection des Études Augustiniennes. Série Antiquité 163* (Paris: Institut d'Études Augustiniennes, 2000), esp. pp. 45-80, who follows, perhaps too uncritically, R. Kany: *Augustins Trinitätsdenken. Bilanz, Kritik und Weiterführung der modernen Forschung zu "De trinitate," Studien und Texte zu Antike und Christentum 22* (Tübin-

cept of relation belongs to the profile that is reckoned normally among the central issues of Augustine's Trinitarian thought.[9] I will reconsider his understanding of the term *persona* by analyzing some passages of books 5 and 7 of this famous work.

a. De Trinitate *Book 5*

Augustine introduces the concept of relation in *trin.* 5. Here he argues that even if there are no *accidentia,* accidentals in God, this does not mean that we have only sentences about his substance (cf. *trin.* 5,6/24-26). Of course, Augustine refutes an anhomoian theology that started from the diversity of predicates and assumed that this diversity is not only external to the substance, but the difference between some predicates (as unbegotten and begotten, *ingenitus* and *genitus*) shows a difference concerning the substance as well (this type of theology was not really put forward by any Latin theologian, so Augustine introduces this argument only as a fictional sentence, known to him from history, *trin.* 5,4/6-11).[10]

We may remember shortly that Augustine favors *essentia* instead of *substantia,* because *essentia* shows the connection with *esse* (as *sapere — sapientia, scire — scientia*) (*trin.* 5,3). Of course, this *essentia vel substantia* has accidentals (cf. *trin.* 5,3/7-10), the qualities that can be modified or changed (cf. *trin.* 5,5/1f.). Accidentals are not only qualities that can be adopted and abandoned, but there are even permanent ones, the *accidentia inseparabilia,* ἀχώριστα. In the creation even these accidentals will be lost, at the latest if they cease to exist[11]

---

gen: Mohr Siebeck, 2007), esp. pp. 41-46. The chronological method of Hombert is under debate; cf. V. H. Drecoll, "Der Stand der Augustinforschung," *Theologische Literaturzeitung* 134 (2009): 876-900, esp. 895-97. For our purpose it may be sufficient to remember that the texts analyzed here (*trin.* 5 and *trin.* 7) belong to the time before 411 or after 414.

9. Cf. for this, e.g., A. C. Lloyd: "On Augustine's Concept of a Person," in *Augustine: A Collection of Critical Essays,* ed. R. Markus (Garden City, NY: Doubleday, 1972), pp. 191-205; R. Cross: "*Quid tres?* On What Precisely Augustine Professes Not to Understand in *De Trinitate* 5 and 7," *Harvard Theological Review* 100 (2007): 215-32; for the history of research cf. Kany, *Trinitätsdenken,* pp. 198-210.

10. Cf. Kany, *Trinitätsdenken* pp. 495-97.

11. We may put aside the question if this means that all qualities of the created being are accidentals and the substance of created beings is only the *quodditas,* the fact of being. This is probably not the goal of Augustine's argument here; he simply wants to deny that all permanent qualities can be regarded as substantial ones. The question how some qualities can be regarded as qualities belonging to one's substance, some other are only accidentals, is not

(cf. *trin.* 5,5/2-9). Accidentals cannot be assumed in the case of God; expressions like *pater, filius,* or *spiritus sanctus* cannot be regarded as accidentals, nor as expressions concerning the substance *(secundum substantiam).* That's why Augustine introduces the concept of *ad aliquid,* in relation to something (*trin.* 5,6/1-8).[12] The Trinitarian names like Father, Son, or Holy Spirit are a good evidence for the fact that sometimes expressions neither indicate accidentals nor are they said *ad se ipsum.* In fact they are said *ad aliquid,* in relation to something, or *ad invicem,* in relation to each other. And these are both cases of the relations, the expressions said *secundum relativum* (trin. 5,6/10-22).[13] The concepts of *secundum substantiam* and *ad se* on the one side, *secundum relativum* and *ad aliquid* on the other side, are parallel. For the moment we can leave aside the application of this distinction against the anhomoian theology (*trin.* 5,7f.).[14] More important is that Augustine adds that all we can say about the Father, the Son, and the Spirit, in the sense of *ad se,* cannot be said in the plural. If we call the Father, the Son, and the Spirit God, great, good, etc., and these are expressions said *ad se,* related to himself or itself, we have to conclude that there is one God who is great, good etc. (*trin.* 5,9/1-22). What is said *ad se,* in relation to himself or itself, is said about the Trinity as a whole, is said directly about the Trinity, *de ipsa trinitate* — and that's why it is not said in the plural, but *singulariter* (*trin.* 5,9/35-37). Therefore we have to speak of *una essentia, una magnitudo,* etc. (*trin.* 5,9/37-41).[15] The error of the anhomoian argument is not the attempt to state some qualities as being given for God's essence or substance (this is in fact possible for qualities as *magnus, bonus,* etc.), but to have chosen the wrong qualities for doing so, namely qualities that cannot be said *ad se,* in relation to himself or itself (*trin.* 5,7/17-19).

This is the context where Augustine compares the Trinitarian language of the Greeks with the Latin tradition. He observes that *essentia* corresponds to the Greek οὐσία, even if normally Latins prefer to use the noun *substantia* (cf.

---

raised by Augustine here. Augustine introduces the distinction *substantia — accidentia* only for refusing it in the case of God or the Trinity.

12. For the question, whether the distinction between substances and accidentals is called into question, cf. J. Brachtendorf, *Die Struktur des menschlichen Geistes nach Augustinus. Selbstreflexion und Erkenntnis Gottes in "De Trinitate,"* Paradeigmata 19 (Hamburg: Felix Meiner Verlag, 2000), p. 65, note 25.

13. For the philosophical background of discussions in the Platonic schools cf. Kany, *Trinitätsdenken,* pp. 498f.

14. Cf. A. Schindler: *Wort und Analogie in Augustins Trinitätslehre, Hermeneutische Untersuchungen zur Theologie 4,* (Tübingen: Mohr Siebeck, 1965), pp. 152-54.

15. Cf. Brachtendorf, *Struktur,* p. 66.

trin. 5,9/41f.). And this leads him to the famous note that he does not understand the difference between οὐσία and ὑπόστασις in its full sense, especially because we should translate μία οὐσία τρεῖς ὑποστάσεις with *una essentia tres substantiae.* Without any discussion of the problems raised by this translation, Augustine shortens the argument by stating that the Latin use of the words does not permit *substantia* in the plural in the case of God, so we should speak of *una essentia vel substantia* (cf. *trin.* 5,10/47-51).

The gap that emerges by this comparison between the Latin and the Greek terminology, the lack of a precise term for indicating the Father, the Son, and the Holy Spirit, this gap is the place where the term *persona* takes place. Augustine introduces this noun only at this late point of his argument. Many Latins who were intensively thinking about Trinitarian thought and are true authorities, spoke of *tres personae.* Augustine explicitly states that they did so for lack of a better term, simply for indicating what they recognized without words, *sine verbis* (cf. *trin.* 5,10/1-3). In this manner, they expressed the nonidentity of the Father, the Son, and the Holy Spirit, and they were supported by all biblical sentences that include plural forms (e.g., John 10:30: *ego et pater unum sumus* [not *unum est*]) (cf. *trin.* 5,10/4-8). The crucial question, however, is how we can speak of three: *quid tres* — what is it that is three? It is not possible to find an appropriate term or concept for this; the traditional concept of person does not fulfill this function, but the use of *tres personae* is used in the theological tradition only *ne taceretur* (cf. *trin.* 5,10/8-11), for not being silent at all.

So the use of the concept *persona* in Trinitarian contexts is an unbeloved child, a stopgap solution, required for lack of a better term. This means that the concept of person depends on the concept of relation, developed earlier in the argumentation of *On the Trinity.* So, critically, the concept of relationship cannot be understood from the concept of person or personhood. So we may conclude that the term *persona* has only weak and unstable foundations, at least in Augustine's Trinitarian thought and in his perspective on the development of Latin Trinitarian thought before him. This accords well with the fact that the term *persona* is quite rare in *trin.* 5 (next to the mentioned passage *trin.* 5,10/1.10 the term is used only in *trin.* 5,9/35). The term *persona* is a problematic replacement of a better, but missing term, introduced by the tradition without any clarifications.

It therefore becomes clear why the concept of person disappears in the following chapters (this is true of the second half of *trin.* 5 and the whole of *trin.* 6 except one, nearly untechnical use *trin.* 6,11/2). By these chapters, Augustine deals with two issues: first, it is for certain that the Father, the Son, and the Holy Spirit are great, good, etc. not by participation, because then the qualities would be superior to them, but the being of the Father, the Son, and the Spirit is greatness, goodness, etc. The concept of *participatio* is explicitly refused (cf. *trin.* 5,11). Second, the sentences made not *ad se ipsa,* not about themselves, that is, the sentences *ad aliquid* in relation to something else have to be differentiated in those that are referred *ad invicem* to each other, and those that are referred *ad creaturam,* in relation to the creation (cf. *trin.* 5,12/1-3). In doing this, Augustine introduces the difference between the internal relations within the Trinity and the external ones. He concludes that sentences about the external relations of the Trinity, the relations towards the creation, can only be used in the singular (*unum principium* etc.), because the acting of the Trinity is inseparable.

For our purpose the observations about *trin.* 5 lead to the following three points:

(a) For clarifying the concept of *persona* in general, the Trinitarian context is not very helpful; in fact, if we follow Augustine in his arguments of *trin.* 5, the Trinitarian thought is not appropriate for doing this.

(b) Those things that can be called *persona* should be described as relations or (even better) as sentences *ad aliquid,* in relation to something.

(c) Within the relations, we have to differentiate the internal and the external ones. This is the case for the Trinity, too, so we have internal and external relations of the Trinity.

b. De Trinitate *Book 7*

The problems concerning the concept of person are present again in *trin.* 7. Here Augustine comes into heavy aporias where the concept of *persona* begins to break down. Looking for the aim of this book within the context of the whole work, we could conclude that the inconsistency and the problematic applicability of the term *persona* to the Trinity are the reason for Augustine's new approach to the matter from book 9 onwards. The reflections about the traces of the Trinity, the *vestigia trinitatis* in the human mind, are thus the result of the problems raised by the term *persona.*

Persona is used in *trin.* 7 only in the sense that Augustine affirms its value as a stopgap solution. This becomes clear by the manner in which Augustine speaks again about the distinction between *essentia* and *personae.* Augustine first notices that the used tradition only serves for expressing that which can hardly be expressed. This fits the Greek tradition that distinguishes between *una essentia* and the *tres substantiae* (as τρεῖς ὑποστάσεις) as well as the Latin tradition that differentiates between the *una essentia vel substantia* and the *tres personae* (*trin.* 7,7/1-6). Both traditions aim to indicate in which aspect the Father, the Son, and the Spirit are three: *quid tria vel quid tres* (*trin.* 7,7/6-11).

Here Augustine develops an analytical argument. For indicating the three-foldness, a *speciale vel generale nomen* is needed: a specific name and a general one. The human mind, however, does not find appropriate expressions, because the human thoughts cover a wider field than can be expressed by human language — and this is more the case for the Divine Being (*trin.* 7,7/11-15).

First, Augustine deals with the distinction between *speciale nomen* and *generale nomen* in general. Three human beings, cows, or horses are three because the given name is a *nomen speciale,* a specific name. That such a *nomen speciale* can be applied to these three, means at the same time that even the more general *nomen generale,* e.g., *animal,* can be used in the plural. Augustine affirms this even for the categorical names *(superiore genere)* as *substantia, creatura,* or *natura.* So we have to speak of *tres substantiae* or *tres creaturae* or *tres naturae.* If we can use a *nomen speciale* in the plural, this fits always even the *nomen generale.* The fact, however, that a *nomen generale* can be used in the plural does not lead to the conclusion that even the *nomina specialia* must be used in the plural (in the example, the fact that a cow, a horse, and a dog are called *tria animalia* does not lead to the conclusion that there are three horses, cows, or dogs).

Augustine applies these considerations (*trin.* 7,7/16-55) to the Father, the Son, and the Holy Spirit. The question *quid tres* ("in what way are they three?") leads him to the question of whether the Father, the Son, and the Holy Spirit are terms related to each other, used *invicem* (*trin.* 7,7/56f.). Evidently, this is not the case. A term like "friends" *(amici)* is a relation that can be really used in both directions, but of course this is not true in the case of the Father, the Son, or the Holy Spirit (*trin.* 7,7/57-64). So it seems probable that the common aspect for these three, the specific and therefore even general name *(speciale aut generale nomen)* is only *id, quod persona est* (*trin.* 7,7/64-66).[16] These words can be translated in a twofold manner. They can be translated with: "that which a person is" (so the content or the character of a person would be indicated, the Father is so, the Son so, and the Spirit so). Or it can be taken to simply state that he or it is a person. Perhaps at first glance the first possibility seems more probable, but Augustine does not add a consideration about the category "person." The context prevents me from assuming that the Father, the Son, or

---

16. See Brachtendorf, *Struktur,* p. 75.

the Holy Spirit can be understood as *commune*. So I therefore would prefer the second possibility: to be a person is the general or common aspect that allows speaking of three, in the case of the Trinity. Augustine adds that this is true only in common language, *si consuetudinem loquendi respicimus* (*trin.* 7,7/66f.). A detailed explanation of personhood is missing. Only that personhood is a *generale nomen* is evident. This is supported by the fact that even a human being can be called *persona,* so even in spite of the fundamental difference between God and human beings both can be called a person, so person is not a *speciale nomen* (*trin.* 7,7/74-76). According to the rules he established in the beginning of the argument it should be possible to indicate for the Trinity on the one hand the *generale nomen* (that is, the common aspect, e.g., personhood), and on the other hand a *speciale nomen* that can be used in the plural, because there is no difference by nature, but this has not been found, *quod tamen non invenitur* (*trin.* 7,7/67-74).[17]

With this negative result Augustine reaches the crucial problem. If we affirm that personhood could be regarded as common aspect, the question is raised why the terms *deus* and *persona* cannot be used in a similar way. If personhood is a *commune* and this fits even the divinity (or rather: fits to be God), there are two possibilities: We could use both terms in the plural (as a *generale nomen*), or we have to use both terms in the singular (because they indicate the identity of the *essentia*) (*trin.* 7,8/77-89). Even the language of the scripture is not helpful here, because there is no explicit contradiction to calling the Father, the Son, and the Holy Spirit *tres essentiae tres personae* (*trin.* 7,8/90-99). In this sense the term *essentia* would be as common for the Father, the Son, and the Holy Spirit (a *commune nomen*) as it is the term *persona* (and this fits even the term *substantia,* understood according to the Greeks as ὑπόστασις) (*trin.* 7,8/110-17).

That it seems necessary to speak of *una persona* or of *tres essentiae* is a crucial problem not dissolved by Augustine. Instead of this, he affirms that there is a necessity of speaking *(loquendi necessitate).* This necessity *(loquendi necessitas)* is urgent because of the heresies (*trin.* 7,9/118-20). Therefore in lack of appropriate concepts we are not allowed to speak of *tres essentiae* (this would mean: that there is a difference within God). At the same time we have to affirm that there are three in God; otherwise we would agree to the heresy of Sabellius (*trin.* 7,9/120-27). The biblical witness leads to the affirmation that Father, Son, and Holy Spirit are not identical (*trin.* 7,9/127-31). To the question:

---

17. It may be questioned whether Augustine states that such a *speciale nomen* does not exist in general (cf. Schindler, *Wort,* p. 166) or if it cannot be found by human weakness.

what it is that can be called three *(quid tria diceret)* the *humana inopia* (the lack of better understanding, always subject of the sentences) mentions *substantias sive personas*. Of course, in this sentence, *substantia* is used for the Greek ὑπόστασις. Using these terms, we are not assuming a diversity in God nor a simple *singularitas,* but the unity is stressed, if the *una essentia* is affirmed, and at the same time the *trinitas,* the "threefoldness" is maintained, if the *tres substantiae vel personae* are affirmed (*trin.* 7,9/131-35).

The following excursus shows the problems of the term *substantia* and may be mentioned only briefly here. Of course, it proves that Augustine is not familiar with the various aspects and the notion of the Greek ὑπόστασις. He deals with two possibilities: first, we can try to understand the term as something relative, indicating a relation, but this seems not very appropriate, because *substantia* seems to indicate even the *essentia;* or, we may rather understand the term to mean that which subsists to anything else, e.g., the body that has a color or form "subsists" to its color or form. In the case of God, this meaning would deny the simplicity of God, his character as *simplex;* God would subsist *to* his goodness etc., and thus the goodness would be superior to God. So the result of this argument is rather: God can be said to be a *substantia* only *abusive,* i.e., in a wrong manner (*trin.* 7,9/136-7,10/26). Perhaps it is more appropriate to speak of *tres personae* than of *tres substantiae* (always understood in the sense of the Greek ὑποστάσεις) (*trin.* 7,10/27. = 1f.). That's why Augustine advises even the Greeks to speak of τρία πρόσωπα rather than of τρεῖς ὑποστάσεις.[18]

But even if we accept the term *persona,* an aporia emerges. The same argument *(eadem ratio)* as used for the term *substantia* fits even the term *persona* (*trin.* 7,11/6f.). It is difficult to establish a difference between being and personhood in the case of God. To be is said in relation to itself, *ad se,* but to be a person, is said *relative,* in the sense of a relation (*trin.* 7,11/7-9). Augustine does not use the term *ad aliquid* here, but the adverb *relative* that seems to be identical. And the adverb *relative* is interpreted by examples that imply a reciprocal relation, that can be used *ad invicem* (*trin.* 7,11/11f.). The examples of friends, family members, neighbors *(amici, propinqui, vicini)* mean a reciprocal relation where each expression can be used for both sides. This is, however, not true in the case of the Father, the Son, and the Holy Spirit. The Father is not the person of the Son etc. (*trin.* 7,11/9-18). Augustine does not take into

---

18. The Tomos of the Council of Constantinople 381 is lost, but the subsequent council of 382 seems to have affirmed that there we have to confess the μία οὐσία of the Trinity ἐν τρισὶ τελειοτάταις ὑποστάσεσιν ἤμουν τρισὶ τελείοις προσώποις, cf. Theodoret, *Hist. Eccl.* 5,9,11. Augustine does not know this as a rule of the theological language.

consideration a notion of relatedness that implies a kind of "direction" (as is the case for the relation between a cause and the effect). This shortens the argument considerably and makes it appear probable that Augustine does not intend a clear concept of "person" here, but rather wants to stress the aporetic and problematic character of the used terms for showing that the distinction between *una essentia* and *tres personae* is not satisfactory at all.

This aim is pursued in the following passage. Here Augustine states that the being of the Father, the Son, and the Holy Spirit must be identical to their personhood, their being a person. The *substantia patris* is nothing other than the *persona patris* (trin. 7,11/18-20). The personality of the Father does not mean the relation to the Son, but means the Father himself: *Ad se quippe dicitur persona, non ad filium vel spiritum sanctum* (*trin.* 7,11/22f.). If we say "Father," we do not mean: the relation to the Son, but the Father himself directly. So it seems that even the notion of being a person belongs to the sentences said *ad se*. So to be a person seems to become an essential predicate of God that can be compared to classical predicates as great, good, etc. Doing this, Augustine can no longer avoid speaking of *una persona* (as is the case for the *una essentia*, to which the predicates like great, good, etc. belong). So he stops his argument here, concluding in an apodictic manner: we need terms for indicating the threefoldness in order to admit that we are only silent to the question, what do we mean if we confess three — *ne omnino taceremus interrogati quid tres, cum tres esse fateremur* (*trin.* 7,11/28-33).

It is clear that the term *persona* is not used because of his internal evidence or a certain meaning that is quite helpful for a logical argument, but is simply a stopgap solution. Considered in detail, it is a quite problematic term that leads to many contradictions.[19] The result of these passages in books 5 and 7 is very clear: Augustine is not only skeptical towards the notion of *persona*, but he abandons the term *persona*, stating that it may be used for lack of a better term, as part of the tradition, a problematic tradition in this case.[20] He does not develop his own ontological term or concept, but is even skeptical towards the terms *substantia* or ὑπόστασις. *Persona* is only used for indicating that there are three, but being a person is not applicable to the Father, the Son, and the Holy Spirit in its proper sense.

19. The following explanations about the distinction between *genus* and *species* may be left aside here. The hypothesis of Roland Kany (cf. *Trinitätsdenken* 504f.) who unconvincingly presumes a dependence upon Gregory of Nyssa *(Ad Ablabium)* deserves further research but does not address the aporetic character of *trin.* 7,11.

20. This does not imply a "'unitaristische' Tendenz" (B. Studer: *Augustinus, De Trinitate. Eine Einführung* [Paderborn: Schöningh, 2005], p. 188).

c. Consequences for the Use of Persona

The result of the aporetic limitation of the concept of *person* leads to the following two consequences:

1. Augustine begins with his research for a new way of describing the differentiation within the Trinity. Especially the reflection of triadic structures of the loving-knowing *mens* from *trin.* 9 onwards offers such a description. This can be regarded as consequence of the limited value of the concept of *persona*. If it is not possible to develop the Trinitarian theology by ontological concepts or terms, especially because the sentences made *ad aliquid* are difficult to express by an exact term, a new way of describing the relations is needed, even avoiding the term *relatio* as quasi-ontological term.

In fact, the term *relatio* has no significant impact in the theological language of Augustine. Often *relatio* means simply a petition or report in a juridical sense. In the sense of "relation" between two things the term occurs only in *trin.* 5,12: the relation between the Holy Spirit on the one side and Father and Son on the other can be seen in the expression *donum dei*. Aside from this single occurrence in *trin.* the use in *ep.* 170,6 can be compared (here Augustine states that a difference of *relatio* does not imply a difference by nature) as well as *Gn. litt.* 4,28 (the cognition of God is related to the praise of God). So *relatio* normally does not mean relation in the works of Augustine. A close link between *persona* and *relatio* is not given here. This fits the aporetic character of *trin.* 7. Even a clear reduction of the Trinitarian persons to *ad aliquid*-sentences is not the solution Augustine prefers.

2. The statement that the term *persona* may be used for lack of a better term and as a part of a (problematic) tradition leads to an occasional use, e.g., in Christological contexts. Augustine regularly affirms that God and man are closely linked to each other; *filius dei* and *filius hominis* are united. Augustine often calls this unity *unitas personae* and uses regularly the expression *una persona*.[21] The exact meaning of this expression, however, is not explained, and furthermore a crucial impact of the concept of *persona* for establishing this unity is not provided. The term *persona* does not even replace ontological concepts (as can be found, e.g., in Cyril of Alexandria or Boethius). This fits well with the pre-Chalcedonian character of Augustine's Christology in general.

The use of *persona* in this Christological meaning may be illustrated by analyzing two passages of *trin.*: For explaining the appearances and missions of the Father, the Son, and the Holy Spirit, Augustine affirms that the *verbum*

---

21. Cf. Drobner, *Person-Exegese*, pp. 249-53.

dei is linked with a human being and mixed in him *ad unitatem personae*. This shows that the Son of God is sent into the world and is identical to the *filius hominis*. This *persona* is able to show and to announce the *angelica natura* (*trin.* 4,30/149-54). Augustine wants to explain the *inseparabiliter operari* (*trin.* 4,30/1-35), so he therefore distinguishes the appearances before the incarnation (in which God appears *per angelos; trin.* 4,31/36-40) from the incarnation and Pentecost. In his explanation of the incarnation, the concept of *persona* is no longer used; Augustine simply affirms that John 1:14 cannot be understood as proof for a change of the Logos into flesh viz. of the *verbum dei* into a creature; but rather in the incarnate *verbum Dei, hominis caro* and *rationalis hominis anima* are linked to each other, so the incarnate is God *and* man (*trin.* 4,31/40-46).

In a similar way Augustine uses John 1:14 in the context of the distinction between *scientia* and *sapientia*. The *verbum* is the *dei filius,* the *caro* the *hominis filius;* both are like *simul in unam personam dei et hominis*. Augustine finds both aspects expressed in John 1:14b: *gratia* refers to *scientia, veritas* to *sapientia*. It is the best grace if a human being is linked with God *in unitatem personae* (*trin.* 13,24/1-31).[22] Here the term *persona* is used occasionally, although without any further explanation.

In his Christology Augustine often mentions the divine and the human side by side; he often crosses both aspects, but he does not give a terminological concept of how this unity of the divine and the human side in Christ could be understood in detail. This is remarkable, because Augustine had dealt with the concept of incarnation since his days in Milan and Cassiciacum. In his *conf.* he reports that Alypius claimed that Christ was a real human being and was different from other human beings *non persona veritatis,* but by his human and ethical qualities and his perfect participation in *sapientia* (*conf.* 7,25). He mentions the non-Christian Nebridius, whose opinion of Christ assumed that his *caro* was just a *phantasmum* (cf. *conf.* 9,6).[23]

According to Drobner, Augustine started very early with his looking for a term or concept that could express this unity of God and man in Christ, but he abandoned his attempts to use expressions like *dominicus homo* or *persona sapientiae*.[24] Similar approaches may be observed in passages according to

22. Cf. Studer, *De Trinitate*, pp. 217-19.

23. Cf. V. H. Drecoll, B.II.12. *Ambrosius als Taufvater Augustins und der "Mailänder Kreis,"* in *Augustin Handbuch*, ed. V. H. Drecoll (Tübingen: Mohr Siebeck, 2007), pp. 127-43, esp. 142; C.II.2. *Der Christus humilis*, pp. 438-45, esp. 441.

24. Cf. Drobner, *Person-Exegese*, pp. 153-65; *pace* Drobner (*Person-Exegese*, p. 153) *dominicus homo* does not mean "Mensch des Herrn" but rather a human being that is Lord in the

which Christ fulfills *in una persona* the duties of being the king and the priest (cf. *c. Faust.* 12,33, *cons, eu.* 1,5) or Christ has accepted a *persona inferior, id est humana* (cf. *Gn. adu. Man.* 2,37; *persona* means just a human individual here).

In his later works Augustine uses the term *persona* regularly in Christological contexts — but without any further explanation. So the meaning of *persona* is quite open or flexible, rather determined by the arguments of the context than being an important term or concept that determines the argument. E.g., in *pecc. mer.* 1,60 Augustine refers to John 3:13: Nobody ascends into heaven except he who descends from it. Augustine understands this sentence to refer to the believers who are changed and raised *in unitatem Christi.* Christ as the incarnate descends and then the unity of *caput* and *corpus,* i.e., the believers included, ascends. So the unity between Christ and the believers is crucial for Augustine's understanding of the verse (*pecc. mer.* 1,60; 60/9-21). For our purpose it is noteworthy that Augustine compares this unity between Christ and the believers as a parallel case to the unity of divinity and humanity in the incarnate. Neither does Christ regard his *divinitas* as unworthy of being declared *filius hominis,* nor does he avoid the denomination of his *caro* as *filius dei.* Of course, this shows that in the incarnate, there are not two different agents, but just *unus atque idem deus et homo* (*pecc. mer.* 1,60; 60/21-61/4). And just as the divine side, the *filius dei,* remains in heaven and the human side, the *filius hominis,* walks on earth, in the same way, *per unitatem personae, qua utraque substantus unus Christus est,* even so the *filius dei* is on earth and the *filius hominis* in heaven (*pecc. mer.* 1,60; 61/4-8). So just as Christ achieves this for his own person, the believers can also achieve it (*pecc. mer.* 1,60; 61/8-16). In this argument, the term *unitas personae* declares the cause for the crossover of qualities and activities, so the term seems to be important here; the exact meaning of the term, however, remains unclear. Does Augustine mean simply a reciprocal applicability of the predicates of the divine and human side, a real communication viz. exchange, or a new unity? And if so, of what kind? From this passage, where the term *persona* occurs in an important argument, but without any further explanation, the weak precision of the term is confirmed again.

Several other passages, similar to those mentioned, could be added (e.g., *ench.* 36, *c. s. Arrian.* 4.6.7., *c. Max.* 2,20,3, *ep.* 137; *ep.* 140,12; *ep.* 169,8, *ep.* 219), but even in the Christological context the term *persona* seems to be nothing more than a magic formula, a nonfixed and flexible variable. If the term had

---

same moment (the *dominicus* implies more than "zum Herrn gehörig"; cf. Drobner, *Person-Exegese,* pp. 156f.).

a quasi "erlösende Kraft"[25] for Augustine, this can be only said for the flexible use of it, not for the precise and helpful concept expressed by it.

So even the Christological or anthropological context seems to be no help for getting a better grasp on what exactly this concept of *persona* entails, e.g., the way in which the term gets a special, precise meaning in Christological contexts, a meaning that could be helpful for Trinitarian theology. On the contrary, Augustine clearly observes that analogies taken from psychological analysis do not lead to a complete understanding of human personhood as a whole. So at the end of *trin.* he remarks that triads as *mens — notitia — dilectio* (or the triad *memoria — intellegentia — voluntas* that seems to be quite parallel, cf. *trin.* 15,12/23-25) are *in homine,* but not the human being itself. All definitions of human beings (as *animal rationale mortale* or *substantia rationalis constans ex anima et corpore*) and the mentioned triads belong to each individual as *una persona,* but are not a complete representation of it *(hominis vel in homine sunt) (trin.* 15,11/1-10). The realm of the soul is not represented by the famous triads, but rather only the higher part of the soul is the subject of the analysis *(quod excellit).* So it is just this higher part of the soul that may be interpreted as the image of God *(trin.* 15,11/10-18). And at this point, the closest link between human beings and God, there is a profound difference that can be observed exactly in the use of *persona:* In the case of God, *tres personae* belong to the *una essentia,* but in the case of human beings, each individual belonging to the one essence is *una persona (trin.* 15,11/18-22). Augustine affirms a similar difference for the triad *memoria — intellectus — amor (trin.* 15,42/23-43/31); the aspect of personhood cannot be transferred to the Trinity one-to-one (cf. *trin.* 15,43/5-7.20-23). Augustine explicitly denies that the three functions of the *una persona* (of the human being) could be simply parallelized with the *tres personae* of the Trinity (with the effect that the Father is parallel to the *mens,* the Son to the intellect, the Spirit to the will or love). So the aim of the triads is not to deduce three activities of the human mind from a kind of "self-differentiation" within the Trinity (and of course not to deduce the functions of the Trinitarian persons from the triadic structure of the human mind), but the elucidation of the reciprocal crossing of three functions that are one. It is a pity, but Augustine does not reflect on the impact that this difference has for Christology. The relation between anthropological unity of personhood *(una persona)* and the unity of the divine and human side in the incarnate is sometimes explained by a comparison with the unity of soul and body,[26] but these passages do not

25. Both terms can be found in Drobner, *Person-Exegese,* p. 241.
26. Cf. Drobner, *Person-Exegese,* pp. 117-24.

offer any help for the fundamental question of how the profound difference of personhood in anthropological contexts (being true even for the incarnate) and Trinitarian contexts (being true for the Son as part of the Trinity) fit with one another. Even here the obscurity of the term *persona* becomes bearable.

3. Further Reflections

Analyzing the use and the impact of the term *persona* in Augustine's theology leads to negative and disappointing results. Augustine uses the term, but only for avoiding absolute silence. He neither develops a Trinitarian concept of the term (nor a Christological one), nor does he introduce the term as a crucial element of his anthropology. Boethius uses the term *persona* for all rational beings — God, the angels, and human beings[27] — but his famous definition *(persona* as *naturae rationabilis individua substantia)*[28] is clearly composed for Christological purposes[29] and he uses the concept of diversity of the divine *personae* only with prudence.[30] Unlike Boethius, Augustine does not give any definition of *persona;* to the contrary, according to Augustine, personhood, understood as a deep link between being a person and being related to each other, is not an appropriate way of describing the relation between God and human beings. This has consequences not only for the understanding of human "persons," but even for the understanding, if there is one at all, of God, especially the Trinitarian God.

27. Cf. Boethius, *Contra Eutychen 2* (214/152f. Moreschini).

28. Cf. Boethius, *Contra Eutychen 3* (214/171f. Moreschini).

29. Applied to the Trinitarian God, the problem would emerge that the concept of person cannot be distinguished from the substance and nature. God is clearly a substance, and God has evidently a nature that is not irrational, i.e., a rational nature, and of course the substance of this rational nature cannot be divided, so it fulfills the conditions of being a person on the one hand and on the other hand it is clear that only Father, Son, and Holy Spirit should be regarded as persons. The observation may be interesting that Boethius in his explanation of the difference between οὐσία, ὑπόστασις, and πρόσωπον uses the definition for human beings, but then, in the case for God he avoids the term *persona* and introduces it only parallel to the Greek use of ὑπόστασις/*substantia* (Contra Eutychen 3; [218/243-219/264 Moreschini]).

30. Cf. Boethius, *De sancta trinitate 3* (179/314-16 Moreschini): *relatio . . . non faciet alteritatem rerum de qua dicitur, sed, si dici potest, quo quidem modo id quod vix intelligi potuit interpretatum est, personarum.* Of course, the theological tradition uses the term *persona* in a broad sense, linking it closely to the concept of *relatio* (the abstract noun *relatio* may be regarded as a genuine development of Boethius), the most famous explanation of the problems raised by this is Thomas Aquinas, *Summa Theologiae Prima pars,* q. 29 and q. 40.

In fact, the Trinitarian God could be understood as a process of love, including the agent (the lover), the object (the beloved), and the love itself. This would imply that God is "in relation," his substance his love (and this could be supported by texts of Richard of St. Victor — and readers of the New Testament could quickly add 1 John 4). Perhaps it seems attractive to affirm God as such a loving, dynamic, related personhood, and to add: The immanent relation between the Trinitarian persons is the model that shapes the relation between the Trinity and human beings; the dynamic God as love is exactly this relation. God is then no static entity to be described in ontological terms, but is "dynamized," a motion or process. This, at the least, becomes clear from Augustine's concept of *persona*. This raises the question for the appropriateness of relatedness, personhood, and love for describing God. Of course, love is a phenomenon of human life, probably one of the greatest emotions human beings experience. But of course, everybody who has fallen in love remembers even the risk of loving. Is the love accepted and turned back by the beloved? And even if this is the case and common life begins, the love is always in danger. He who starts with loving has to give up a portion of his normal life. Indeed, human beings risk a lot for loving and for their hope of being loved; sometimes human beings do absolutely silly things for this — even things that are clearly against the aims of one's life. So love is an irrational thing that can be hardly controlled by the mind; it is a will, but a special one, always in danger of losing itself. Love is also open and unsure about the future in that being lucky or altogether unlucky are two options that cannot be planned, but only expected or hoped. So, love as human phenomenon includes three aspects: (a) the risk of failure and disappointment, (b) the risk of an open and unsure future, and (c) the special risk of losing some part of one's self, perhaps even the risk of becoming lost in love.

Of course, this explanation is not given for elucidating the whole phenomenon of love, but only for stressing one point that cannot be eliminated from "love" between human beings — a point that becomes problematic, if the concept of love is applied to God. It is not enough to affirm that in God's case love avoids the risky side of love. This would only lead to an equivocal notion of love. Love in the case of God would then be a totally different thing than in human life. And this would raise the question, whether "love" is not exactly the substance of God, but only a term used with a special meaning, a kind of metaphor transferred to God. This process of transfer would imply a kind of change of the concept. So the question of what God is, is not resolved, but only raised again.

The point where the applicability of the concept of love becomes difficult is seen in the following question: Is God changeable in his love? i.e., can he be changed by his love? This would mean that it is not already clear what will happen to God. The will of God would be open to the future, and this is not only a positive, promising chance, but even a danger: God could change his mind. He could decide not to redeem the whole universe, or all human beings or Christians. He could forget his promise given to Noah and destroy the whole of creation.

Therefore, if the affirmation of God being love is to be maintained, it must include a presupposition, namely that God won't be lost in his love, that he is not changed in a way that he gives up his original will, that his being won't be totally transformed, so that in the end — his love could fail, he could be disappointed and hateful. God as love should express that there is a fixed area in God, not changeable by his love and relatedness. God will continue with his love; his love is bigger and stronger than all human mistakes and crimes.

This seems to be exactly the function and the positive impact of the classical predicate of God's immutability. God's immutability is not regarded as a simple lack of motion or action; God acts and accomplishes the history of salvation etc., but God is said to be immutable for making sure that God remains what he has promised to be. Of course, this is a quite static point in God. It must be a static point, a limit of his openness, a kind of determination, of being determinate. The freedom of God has its limits in the necessity of remaining God.

This leads to the fundamental question: What is the relation between the love of God, his relatedness, his loving character — and this fixed area or immutable substance? If the presupposition is accepted that there is a stable point in God, not open to the future, it then must be asked if it is really true that God is "in relation"? Is it really so that his personhood consists in being related, integrating both fixed and open being at the same time and on the same level?

This is not consistent. That's why the assumption is needed that, yes, in God there are both: a limit of his freedom, a static, fixed area, determinate and without openness — and the field of relations, of openness, of actions that have their place in time and space. But these two sides are not equal to, or simply in harmony with each other. For believing that God will remain what he has promised to be, it has to be affirmed that the fixed, determinate area rules the actions and relations. Relations and actions are only secondary to the being in itself. In this sense, exactly the concept of substance or essence, or *ousia* or whatever, could be helpful; a substance notion could be the cornerstone of the concept of God. Therefore God's economic actions can no longer be regarded as having a direct and representative effect on God's being. The distinction between immanent and economic Trinitarian thought should be reconsidered. Of course, the economic action of the Trinity is not totally different from his substance. Every action must fit the substance that is the agent. But the economic action cannot be regarded as a complete and full representation of the agent. Indeed, if God gave himself entirely in his actions, this would raise serious questions about any idea of God altogether and require us, rather than worshiping, to remain silent and to wait for the end of history, if there is one, in order to see what will happen to this God, and to see what he will be in the future. For if he is totally given in his actions — even the actions we have to expect for the future and do not know actually — this God may turn out to be a different God in the end, and it would only be prudent to wait and see if that God is the one he has promised to be. On the other hand, the assumption that human beings are an image of God cannot be related to their personhood or their character as social, interrelated beings, but should be rather understood as their experience of being the receivers of divine revelation and grace. The character of image, then, would be restricted to some aspects of the human mind or soul, and not even the fact of the incarnation changes this (because even the incarnation achieves no bridge between what a person is in the case of human beings and the totally different sense of person in the case of God).

So, the question whether there is a concept of person in Augustine that could be helpful for the description of the exact relation between human beings and God leads to further considerations about the concept of God and the Trinity. Personhood, however, is no bridge that links God and human beings, at least if we follow Augustine. *Persona* is simply a term of a problematic tradition that hardly can be applied to the Trinity; it is not appropriate in itself. That's why Augustine leaves the term in an aporetic discourse, without positive result, looking for new ways of describing the image of God in the human mind, stressing the profound difference between human being and the Trinitarian God.

Augustine's Investigation into Imago Dei

Eiichi Katayanagi

We are concerned with regaining a complex concept of human personhood. In order to do this we must have insight into the characteristic nature of human beings. For this purpose I want to investigate in this chapter the Christian heritage of understanding a human being as imago Dei, especially in the works of Augustine. Augustine's characteristic understanding of imago Dei lies in the thesis that the human mind has in its depth a trinitarian structure; that is, in its memory, its intelligence, and its will. He insists thereby upon the fact that a human being is touched by God in the depth of his mind, that is, that man has in this depth the sense of openness to eternity. For Augustine, imago Dei means this human capacity of openness to eternity.

1. Human Will as the Basic Field in Which the Trinitarian Structure of the Human Mind Can Be Found

In book VIII of his *De trinitate,* Augustine makes a fresh start in his investigations into understanding God as trinity. As he clearly recognized the difficulty of the attempt to directly investigate the trinitarian God, he tries in this work to understand the trinitarian God indirectly through creatures, especially through the trinitarian structure of the human mind. The motive for his investigation is theological, but his method of analysis is philosophical.[1]

---

1. Cf. M. F. Sciacca, "Trinitate et unite de esprit," in *Augustinus Magister* (Paris: Études Augustiniennes, 1954), p. 521. Also L. Hölscher, "Die Geistigkeit der Seele. Augustins Argu-

In so doing, he realizes wherein lies the difficulty in finding the trinitarian God. The difficulty comes from the human way of thinking. Man cannot conceive of things without sensible representation. Therefore man cannot conceive of one God that has three persons. Augustine aims to divest himself of this sort of thinking.

He takes as his starting point the loving activity of human will. He recognizes in the loving activity three elements; that is, the subject of loving, the loved object, and the love itself. The characteristic in this analysis of loving activity is, that in the loving activity one can conceive of the love itself as an independent third term in addition to the subject of loving and the loved object. What does Augustine mean by this third term, the love itself? He knows very well the fact that when one loves an object, he loves not only this object, but also loves the love itself by which he loves the object. This positing of double objects in the loving activity is not contingent for Augustine. He often mentions this double structure of the willing act. In the narrative of his youth in Carthago, the analysis of these double objects of the human will has special importance. "I came to Carthago. Boiled kettles of filthy love affairs surrounded me from every side. I have not yet loved and loved to love *(amare amabam)* . . . and inquired what is to love, loving to love *(amare amans)*."[2] Narrating autobiographically, he accurately describes the reflexive structure of the loving activity.

Also, in his investigations into the liberty of human will, Augustine stresses the reflexive character of the human will in which man can find the ground of the liberty of the will. "For what is so much in the power of the will as the will itself?"[3] He recognizes that the will is nearest to the will itself, and is in its own area, and that the will is therefore at man's disposal.

In *De trinitate* VIII he declares that love itself is nearer to the mind than the loved object and therefore much more known to the lover. The loved object is outside of the lover, and has an unknown and hidden side. But the love by which man loves the object is well known to himself, or at least better known than the object. "Let no one say, 'I don't know what to love'. Let him love his brother, and he will love that love; after all, he knows the love he loves with better than the brother whom he loves."[4] For Augustine,

mente in *De Trinitate*," in *Gott und sein Bild, Augustins De Trinitate im Spiegel gegenwärtiger Forschung*, ed. J. Brachtendorf (Paderborn: Schöningh, 2000), p. 127.

2. Augustine, *Confessiones*, III, 1,1.

3. Augustine, *De libero arbitrio*, I, 12,26.

4. Augustine, *De trinitate*, VIII, 8,12, trans. Edmund Hill, *Saint Augustine: The Trinity* (New York, 1991).

the relation of the mind to his love is the relation of the mind to the lover. In his relation to his loving activity, man relates to himself. This reflexive structure reveals the nature of the mind, which knows clearly and distinctively its own selfness.

Moreover, the relation of the mind to the love itself is for Augustine the relation of the mind to God as the principal standard of the love. He says: "There now, he can already have God better known to him than his brother, certainly better known because more present, better known because more inward to him, better known because more sure."[5] From his Hortensius-experience at age nineteen, by which he decided to investigate the truth, he knew well that it is not enough for a human being that he has the will to live a happy life. One must have the will to live a righteous life. After he had struggled very hard in his investigation into truth, he recognized that man must have God as the standard for the righteous life; that is, the standard for his love. For Augustine, God is not merely the object of his love, but the source and standard of his love, which teaches him what love he should have if he desires to live a happy life. Augustine knows that "[t]herefore those who seek God through these powers which rule the world, or parts of the world, are in fact being swept away from him and cast up a long way off, not in terms of distance but of divergence of values; they are trying to go by an outer route forsaking their own inwardness, where God is present more inwardly still (*interiora sua deserunt, quibus interior est Deus*)."[6] The investigation of God in his *De trinitate* is an investigation of this inwardness of his own, within which God is more inner. When Augustine tries to search for the trinitarian God through human imago Dei, he always feels God's presence in the innermost of his mind as the ground of the mind itself. The reflexive character of the will reveals both the essential nature of the human mind and God as the source of the mind.

Here, in the trinitarian structure of loving act, Augustine arrived at the starting point of his investigations into imago Dei. Augustine says at the end of book VIII: "But here let us rest our effort for a little, not supposing that it has already found us what we are looking for, but as if finding a place where something has to be looked for. It has not yet been found, but we have found where to look for it."[7]

5. Augustine, *De trinitate*, VIII, 8,12.
6. Augustine, *De trinitate*, VIII, 7,11.
7. Augustine, *De trinitate*, VIII, 10,14.

2. Augustine's *Cogito*

Augustine goes further and examines in book IX the case in which the mind loves itself. Here the subject that loves and the object that is loved is the same. Here are only two, the subject of loving act and the love. The loved object is identified with the subject. (The love cannot be omitted.) Does the mind lose its trinitarian structure? Augustine does not think so. He considers carefully the nature of the loving act and concludes that the knowledge of himself is the necessary condition of the love. How can man love an object that is utterly unknown? He finds even here the object that has been absorbed in the loving subject. This object is the knowledge of himself. His research is guided by the principle that man cannot love what is utterly unknown. He finds again the trinitarian structure of the human mind, i.e., mind, love, and knowledge of itself. The love and knowledge do not lie in the mind like color in the body. They are independent and substantial as three. But the expression of the first term, the mind, makes one misunderstand that the mind is superior to the other two terms. After careful consideration, Augustine replaces the expression of the first term, "mind," with "memory." The relational character of memory to knowledge and love is more suitable to express the trinitarian nature of the mind. In considering the nature of the human mind which knows itself, Augustine finds the admirable activity of self-knowledge.

Augustine examines the case in which the mind that does not yet know itself inquires into itself. If the mind has no knowledge of itself, what kind of knowledge guides this investigation? Examining all the cases of investigations of things unknown, Augustine finds that a unique and new kind of knowledge (*novum genus*) guides the investigation into the unknown self. When the human mind inquires into itself, the mind has a knowledge of itself as one not knowing itself. Yet the mind already has an awareness of itself even though it is ignorant of the nature of this self.

> And then when it seeks to know itself, it already knows itself seeking. So it already knows itself. It follows then that it simply cannot not know itself, since by the very fact of knowing itself not knowing, it knows itself. If it did not know itself not knowing, it would not seek to know itself. For it knows itself seeking and not knowing, while it seeks to know itself.[8]

The self-knowledge that Augustine finds here is remarkable and unique. For its nature seems to be unknown, but its presence is apparently already known.

8. Augustine, *De trinitate*, X, 3,5.

The reflexive character of the human mind, which Augustine found in the loving act in book VIII, takes a clearer form on the level of spiritual self-love.

Augustine analyzes this remarkable knowledge very carefully. He stresses the total character of this knowledge of the mind of itself. The mind does not have two parts, one of which is known and the other unknown. When the human mind knows itself, it knows itself totally, though it knows itself as one not knowing itself. Augustine thinks that this remarkable character of the mind comes from the duplicate structure of the mind, that is, constituted by unconscious knowledge *se nosse* and conscious knowledge as *se cogitare*. He gives an example. A cultivated man knows geometry though he at one moment has not this in mind, because at that moment he is thinking of rhetoric. With this distinction Augustine obtained insight into the unique and deep structure of the mind (X,5,7).

Augustine interprets the ancient precept "Know yourself" as the recommendation to "Know yourself consciously *(se ipsum cogitare)*." He uses here the term *cogito* very carefully. The *cogito* has the function of distinguishing itself from other things. The term *cogito* has here the meaning of stripping the cover that prevents humans from discerning the nature of the mind. Augustine uses here the two terms, *cogito* and *intelligere,* differently. The mind has understanding *(intelligentia)* as its essential nature, as "being." Augustine puts it this way: "So the mind knows that it is and that it lives, in the way intelligence is and lives *(sic ergo se esse et vivere scit, quomodo est et vivit intelligentia)*."[9] This statement resembles the Stoic notion of three strata of being: that is, to be, to live, and to understand. In the Stoic notion, to understand is the upper stage, under which strata of living and being are based. Understanding is thereby merely additional. Yet, according to Augustine, the human mind is and lives as understanding.[10] Understanding is the way of being and living of the human mind. In this sense understanding belongs to the nature of the human mind as being. Man must distinguish this mind's way of being as understanding from others. Augustine's *cogito* takes this distinguishing function. He takes the understanding of the mind not merely as a faculty but as substance. For Augustine the mind is the self-knowing, active reality that indicates itself by its direct perception of certain evident knowledge. For him the nature of human mind is something certain and evident that is directly present to human beings. Augustine concentrates his attention on this reality.

9. Augustine, *De trinitate,* X, 10,13

10. Cf. E. Bermon, *Le cogito dans la pensée de saint Augustin* (Paris: Vrin, 2001), pp. 93-99; S. Menn, *Descartes and Augustine* (Cambridge: Cambridge University Press, 1998).

Nobody surely doubts, however, that he lives and remembers and understands and wills and thinks and knows and judges. At least, even if he doubts he lives; if he doubts, he remembers why he is doubting; if he doubts, he understands he is doubting; if he doubts he has a will to be certain; if he doubts, he thinks *(si dubitat cogitat);* if he doubts he knows he does not know; if he doubts he judges he ought not to give a hasty assent. You may have your doubts about anything else, but you should have no doubts about these; if they were not certain, you would not be able to doubt anything.[11]

Human beings find themselves only in this certain evident knowing activity, i.e., the understanding *(intelligentia)*, and exclude all other uncertain things from the essence of the thinking mind. Augustine says,

> And so when it (mind) thinks, for example, that it is air, it thinks *(putat)* that air understands *(intelligere),* it knows *(scit)* that it understands itself; and it does not know but only thinks it is air. Let it set aside *(secernere)* what it thinks it is, and mark *(cernere)* what it knows it is.[12]

According to Augustine, the way of being of mind is this understanding *(intelligere)* of itself, and Augustine's *cogito* is this distinguishing *secernere* function.

With this conclusion, however, Augustine does not think that the question as to the nature of human mind has been completely solved. He knows very well the difficulty of the questions about the human mind. The main difficulty consists in the double construction of the self-knowledge of the human mind, that is, the relation between *nosse* and *cogitare*.

Augustine showed in book X that the human mind has a perpetual and hidden self-knowledge *(se nosse),* which is unconscious to the ordinary self and is in opposition to *se cogitare,* which is clearly conscious knowledge. Yet Augustine's distinction between *se nosse* and *se cogitare* does not refer to the distinction between *memoria* and *intelligentia.* Rather, Augustine asserts that *se nosse* differentiates itself into *memoria* and *intelligentia.* He points out the problem, which the following books of *De trinitate* should solve:

> We were in the process, you remember, of bringing the mind to light in its memory and understanding and will of itself, and discovering that since it was seen always to know itself *(se nosse)* and always to will itself, it must at the same time be seen always to remember itself *(sui meminisse)* and always

11. Augustine, *De trinitate*, X, 10,14.
12. Augustine, *De trinitate*, X, 10,13.

to understand *(se intelligere)* and love itself, although it does not always think about itself *(se cogitare)* distinctly from things that are not what it is. And thus it seems to be difficult to distinguish in it between its memory of itself and its understanding of itself. That these are not in fact two things, but one thing called by two names, is the impression you might get in this case where they are joined together very closely and one is not prior at all in time to the other.[13]

Augustine claims that as we have discovered perpetual self-knowledge, we must also acknowledge a double structure of self-knowledge, that is, *sui meminisse* and *se intelligere*. These two seem to be one thing that has two names. Deep human self-consciousness seems to lie hidden in memory. Here nothing seems to be other than memory. Yet Augustine wants to distinguish memory *(meminisse)* and consciousness *(intelligere)* even here. The reason why he distinguishes *se intelligere* from *sui meminisse* is that he wants to clear up the misunderstanding that human deep self-knowledge belongs only to an unconscious memory *(sui meminisse)*. He has a keen insight into the fact that this deep self-knowledge has its own clear consciousness *(se intelligere)*, which is always actual and does not slumber.[14] Modern men, however, think that only *se cogitare* has this sort of clear and distinctive self-knowledge. Augustine aims at elucidating the complicated relation between *se cogitare* and *se intelligere*. In this enterprise can be seen the difference between Augustine's concept of *cogito* and that of Descartes.

In the following books Augustine gives examples of the mind's trinity. To begin with, he mentions the trinity of sense perception. To see a sense-object involves three things: a perceived object, the vision of this object, and the seeing subject. The case of memory-trinity also involves three things: a vision in the memory of the once-perceived object, the reminded vision, and the reminding person. The faith-trinity also involves three things: what man believes in, the vision of the faith, and the person who believes. The focus of this investigation is always on the way the second term comes from the first, and how the third combines these two. Augustine's attention is always directed toward the formation of the second; that is, the formation of *cogito*.

After this preliminary investigation Augustine arrives in the fourteenth book at his main theme; that is, the trinitarian structure of the self-conscious human mind. He here acknowledges imago Dei. He finds here in the human

13. Augustine, *De trinitate*, X, 12,19.
14. J. Brachtendorf, *Die Struktur des menschlichen Geistes nach Augustinus, Selbstreflexion und Erkenntnis Gottes in "De trinitate"* (Hamburg: Felix Meiner Verlag, 2000), p. 192.

mind something everlasting. "But it is intolerable to suppose that while the soul is by nature immortal and from the moment of its creation never thereafter ceases to exist, its very best attribute or possession should not last out its immortality."[15] But it is precisely this everlasting quality of human mind that causes difficulty, because this everlasting trinity lies profoundly deep in memory, separate from momentary consciousness (cogito). Imago Dei seems therefore to belong only to memory. How can it be said that this imago Dei involves trinity; that is, not only memory but also intelligence and will? How, in other words, does "cogito (clear consciousness)," which manifests the essence of the thinking mind, relate to the imago Dei, which lies deep in the human mind?

In the beginning of this investigation Augustine stresses the great power of *cogito*:

> Such however is the force of thought *(cogitatio)* that the mind can not even set itself in some fashion in its view except when it thinks about itself. Nothing is in the mind's view *(conspectus)* except what is being thought about, and this means that not even the mind itself, which does the thinking about anything that is being thought about, can be in its own view except by thinking about itself *(se ipsam cogitando)*. Though as a matter of fact, how can it not be in its own view when it is not thinking about itself, seeing that it can never be without itself, as though it were one thing and its view another, I can not really fathom.[16]

Augustine resolutely identifies the mind with its view. Mind's being is equal with its view *(conspectus)*. But this identification causes difficulty. In what way is it not in its own view when it is not thinking of itself *(se cogitare)*? This question is one that Descartes did not solve. Distinguishing self-reflection from the case of looking at one's own face in a mirror, Augustine reasons: "So the only alternative left is that its view is something that belongs to its own nature, and that when the mind thinks about itself *(se cogitat)* its view is drawn back to itself not through an interval of space, but by a kind of nonbodily turning round *(incorporea conversio)*."[17] Augustine here again asserts his conviction that the nature of human mind is the thinking reality which is called here *conspectus,* and that the mind enters into this reality by the act of *cogitare*.

15. Augustine, *De trinitate,* XIV, 4,6.
16. Augustine, *De trinitate,* XIV, 6,8.
17. Augustine, *De trinitate,* XIV, 6,8.

Augustine asks afresh the relation between *intelligere* and *cogitare*. Behind this question lies a perplexity as to the relation between our momentary *cogitatio*, which first forms our self-consciousness, and the memory that precedes this self-consciousness.

> We said toward the end of the tenth book, however, that the mind always remembers, always understands and loves itself, even though it does not always think about itself *(se cogitare)* as distinct from things that are not what it is. So we must go on to inquire in what way understanding belongs to thought *(quomodo ad cogitationem pertineat intellectus?)* while awareness *(notitio)* of anything that is in the mind even while it is not being thought about is said to belong only to memory. If this is so, then it did not always have these three in such a way that it remembered, understood, and loved itself, but it only remembered itself, and then came to understand and love itself when it began afterward to think about itself.[18]

Analyzing several examples of external trinity of the mind he concludes:

> For if we refer to the inner memory *(interior memoria)* of the mind with which it remembers itself and the inner understanding *(interior intelligentia)* with which it understands itself *(se intelligit)* and the inner will *interior voluntas)* with which it loves itself, where these three are simultaneously together and always have been simultaneously together from the moment they began to be, whether they were being thought about or not, it will indeed seem that the image of that other trinity belongs only to the memory. But because there can be no word in it without thought *(sine cogitatione)* — we think everything we say, including what we say with that inner word that is not part of any people's language — it is rather in these three that this image is to be recognized, namely memory, understanding, and will. And here I mean the understanding we understand with as we think *(Hanc autem nunc dico intelligentiam qua intelligimus cigitantes),* that is, when things are brought up that were to hand in the memory but were not being thought about, and our thought is formed from them.[19]

There are two main interpretations of the relation between the inner trinity and *cogito*-trinity. A French scholar, J. Moingt, gives in his comment on Augustine's *De trinitate*[20] positive evaluation of the function of *cogito*. He con-

---

18. Augustine, *De trinitate*, XIV, 6,9.
19. Augustine, *De trinitate*, XIV, 7,10.
20. J. Moingt, "Oeuvres de Saint Augustin," *Bibliothèque Augustinienne* 16 (1955): 634.

tends that here in the fourteenth book, Augustine duplicated in fact the trinity of the tenth book. By emphasizing the function of *cogito* as discriminating the mind from other things, he distinguishes the interior trinity as primary and primitive, separate from "*cogito*-trinity," as secondary and explicitly refined. J. Moingt is correct when he stresses the function of *cogito* as completing the imago Dei of the human mind. But he misunderstands Augustine when he asserts that the interior trinity is imperfect, because this trinity does not yet have explicit intelligence, that is, *cogito*. His misunderstanding may be caused by his high estimation of *cogito*-trinity as a conscious state and underestimation of the interior trinity as unconscious, primitive, and imperfect. This is a modern prejudice. Augustine did not think so. For Augustine the inner trinity is the authentic imago Dei.

On the other hand, J. Brachtendorf stresses the perpetual character of the interior trinity and underestimates *cogito*-trinity as outward.[21] He distinguishes the everlasting interior trinity as the authentic imago Dei, separate from temporal *cogito*-trinity. He is correct when he highly estimates the inner trinity as imago Dei, which is always active in its profundity. But his underestimation of *cogito*-trinity as secondary is not correct. Augustine declares decisively that imago Dei should be found in *cogito*-trinity.

What should be corrected in the interpretation of both scholars is the way in which they distinguish interior trinity from *cogito*-trinity. Both scholars distinguish *cogito*-trinity from interior trinity as something separate. J. Moingt describes *cogito*-trinity as more perfect than interior trinity, while J. Brachtendorf condemns it as derivative, and does not acknowledge it as

---

"Dans la première trinité, l'âme est en fait 'infirme et enténébrée'; son amour, 'perverti', la divise plus qu'il ne l'unit; sa mémoire, 'assoupie', ne se rapelle plus de qui elle est (19). Les trios puissance sont bien là, mais à l'état inchoative, récapitulées dans l'élément de la mémoire (13; velut in memoria sua constitutam); élément informe, image voilée. Mais qu'une sage psychagogue excite l'amour, éclaire l'intelligence, réveille le souvenir. Le verbe caché est 'mis au jour'; l'image, dévoilée."

21. J. Brachtendorf, *Die Struktur des menschlichen Geistes nach Augustinus*, p. 225: "Es ergibt sich somit eine innere und eine äußere Dreiheit. Die innere, gebildet aus 'interior memoria', 'interior intelligentia', 'interior voluntas', ist stetig, d.h. sie wechselt ihren Gegenstand nie, und sie ist gleichursprünglich mit der 'mens'. Daher kann Augustin sagen, daß 'diese drei immer zusammen sind und zusammen waren, seit sie zu sein anfangen'. Die äußere Dreiheit wird gebildet aus, 'memoria', 'cogitatio' inclusive der durch diese entstehenden, äußere 'intelligentia' sowie dem Willen, der 'memoria' und 'cogitatio' eint."

Cf. L. Hölscher, *Die Realität des Geistes, Eine Darstellung und phänomenologische Neubegründung der Argumente Augustins für die geistige Substantialität der Seele* (Heidelberg: Universitätsverlag C. Winter, 1999), pp. 271-78.

the authentic imago Dei. Both J. Moingt and J. Brachtendorf, however, in common set *cogito*-trinity outside of the interior trinity. The former identifies *cogito*-trinity as a perfect form of imago Dei separate from the interior trinity as an inferior form. The latter cuts off *cogito*-trinity as derivative from the authentic everlasting interior trinity. But Augustine sees in *cogito* the activity of *intelligentia* of the interior trinity. Both scholars overlook the fact that *cogito*-trinity contains in itself the interior trinity and the fact that interior trinity persists itself in *cogito*-trinity. One must acknowledge that when he thinks *(cogitat)* he does not stand outside of the perpetual interior trinity, but rather that he sets himself inside of the interior trinity and he thus finds himself inside the perpetual interior trinity. When I think, in other words, I am conscious that I have always been aware of myself. It is not that now, for the first time, I know myself.

What Augustine strives to elucidate is the relation of *cogit* to the interior trinity, or the role of *cogito* in imago Dei. Augustine asks: "In what way does understanding *(intellectus)* belong to thought *(Quomodo ad cogitationem pertineat intellectus)*?" His answer is found in the statement: "And here I mean the understanding we understand with as we think *(Hanc autem nunc dico intelligentiam qua intelligimus cigitantes)*." Augustine found that *cogito* has in itself *intelligentia*. *Cogito* does not stand outside of interior *intelligentia*. J. Brachtendorf wants to place the interior trinity somewhere deep in memory outside of *cogito;* that is, outside of the now-thinking ego. The moment when I think *(cogito)* does not belong, according to Brachtendorf, to the everlasting interior trinity. That is absurd.

The question that Augustine raised in the last chapter of book X is the difference between *sui meminisse* and *se intellegere*. Augustine answers this with the help of the notion of the act of *cogito*. When I think myself *(cogito)*, I distinguish my *intelligentia* as *cogito* from my *memoria* as that of which my *intelligentia* is born, and I stand just in this interior trinity. I do not go outside of this interior trinity to, as it were, a secondary derivative trinity of *cogito*. But it is just inside of this interior trinity that I know the difference between *intelligentia* as the thinking ego and *meminisse* as the ground on which the thinking ego stands.

Both J. Moingt and J. Brachtendorf set *cogito* outside of the interior trinity. I claim that Augustine sets it inside of the interior trinity. With *cogito,* one goes into the inside of the interior trinity and knows for the first time that one has always been aware of this interior trinity.

3. Imago Dei as the Place Where the Human Being Finds Himself Already Touched by God

Augustine found imago Dei in the trinitarian structure of the human mind, that is, in his *memoria, intelligentia,* and *voluntas.* But he knows very well that human mind itself is not enough to be called imago Dei if it does not participate in the reality of the trinitarian God. Nevertheless, he undertook his inquiry into imago Dei in the human mind independently of its participation in God. What is the reason for this? It seems to me that Augustine sees in the trinitarian structure of the human mind itself the possibility of the participation in God (*capax Dei,* XIV, 12,15). What is this possibility? He explains:

> The human mind, then, is so constituted, that it never does not remember itself, never does not understand itself, never does not love itself. But if you hate someone you are dead set on doing him harm, and so it is not unreasonable to talk about the mind of man hating itself when it does itself harm. So the man who knows how to love himself loves God; and the man who does not love God, even though he loves himself, which is innate in him by nature, can still be said quite reasonably to hate himself when he does what is against his own interest, and stalks himself as if he were his own enemy.[22]

Augustine declares resolutely that he who loves himself rightly loves God, and he who does not love God hates himself. He says: "By forgetting God it was as if they had forgotten their own life, and they turned back to death, that is, to hell."[23] For human beings God is, according to Augustine, in a way his own very life. He who does not love his own life, therefore, hates himself. We have already shown that for Augustine, God is the standard and the spring of the loving activity of human beings. The human mind knows this standard, though it may be misdirected and wretched.

> Then where are these standards written down, where can even the unjust man recognize what being just is, where can he see that he ought to have what he does not have himself? Where indeed are they written, but in the book of that light which is called truth, from which every just law is copied and transferred into the heart of the man who does justice, not by locomo-

22. Augustine, *De trinitate,* XIV, 14,18.
23. Augustine, *De trinitate,* XIV, 13,17.

tion but by a kind of impression, rather like the seal which both passes into the wax and does not leave the signet ring.[24]

Augustine sees in the trinitarian reflexive structure of the human mind immediate presence of self. This presence of self makes it possible to choose accession to God or separation from God. In the profound depth of this self, however, the mysterious presence of the trinitarian God can be felt, says Augustine, notwithstanding the fact of distant separation from God.

> Not that it (the human mind) remembers him (God) because it knew him in Adam, or anywhere else before the life of this body, or when it was first made in order to be inserted into this body. It does not remember any of these things at all; whichever of these may be the case, it has been erased by oblivion. Yet it is reminded to turn to the Lord, as though to the light by which it went on being touched in some fashion *(quoddam modo tangebatur)* even when it turned away from him.[25]

24. Augustine, *De trinitate*, XIV, 15,21.
25. Augustine, *De trinitate*, XIV, 15,21.

The Affects of the Soul and the Effects of Grace: On Melanchthon's Understanding of Faith and Christian Emotions

Markus Höfner

1. Introduction

One can dispute whether William James was right in claiming that "feeling is the deeper source of religion."[1] However, the statement that feelings and emotions form one important dimension of religious experience in general, and of the Christian faith in particular, will raise little controversy. Evidence for this can easily be found in the canonical texts of the Judeo-Christian traditions. In the Psalms, to name just one very clear example, the believer's relation to God is perceived and expressed as a phenomenon that is deeply shaped by emotions such as joy and gratitude, grief and contrition: "My soul . . . is struck with terror" (Ps. 6:3) — "You have turned my mourning into dancing; you have taken off my sackcloth and clothed me with joy" (Ps. 30:11).[2] Such observations could easily be multiplied.

Of course, any attempt to integrate these observations into a systematic understanding of religion or the Christian faith will not only have to answer

1. W. James, *The Varieties of Religious Experience: A Study in Human Nature* (1902), ed. M. E. Marty (New York: Penguin, 1985), p. 431; emphasis added.
2. Biblical quotes follow the New Revised Standard Version. For the affective modeling of the relation to God in the Psalms and its anthropological context, cf. the highly informative reflections offered in B. Janowski, *Konfliktgespräche mit Gott. Eine Anthropologie der Psalmen* (Neukirchen: Neukirchener Verlag, 2003).

My thanks to Dr. Stephen Lakkis, Taipei, for his careful language correction of the English manuscript.

the — anthropological — question of what emotions are and how we can account for them in a complex understanding of the human person; it will also have to explain why religious or Christian emotions are so special — if indeed there is something special about them — and how these emotions can be related to the affective dimensions of human experience in general. Two strategies can be adopted in an attempt to deal with these questions. Whereas the first would attempt to identify one emotion as the defining center of religion — such as the "feeling of absolute dependence" (Schleiermacher)[3] or the affective awareness of the "mysterium tremendum et fascinans" (Otto);[4] the second would attempt a phenomenological inquiry into how different emotions shape and are shaped by religious experience and understanding. If one wants to avoid essentialist assumptions, this second strategy would be more promising — and it is certainly the one given more credit in the current debate. Thus, for example, Robert C. Roberts has outlined a "Christian psychology of emotion," which builds on the conviction that emotions are central to the formation of a "Christian character." This approach results in a phenomenological attempt to describe the specifically Christian content of emotions such as contrition, joy, gratitude, or compassion.[5] And Mark Wynn has studied how religious emotions both inform and are informed by the perception of value and religious understanding, thereby highlighting their importance for directing moral action.[6] Apart from emphasizing a preference for a nonessentialist, phenomenological approach, these recent contributions also show that a sound understanding of religious emotions today can hardly be achieved without the help of general philosophical theories of emotion and the findings of neurobiology. To understand religious or specifically Christian emotions, it is essential to examine whether, and to what extent, emotions themselves possess rationality and how they are to be related to bodily processes.[7]

---

3. Cf. F. D. E. Schleiermacher, *Der christliche Glaube nach den Grundsätzen der Evangelischen Kirche im Zusammenhange dargestellt* (1830/31), ed. M. Redeker (Berlin: De Gruyter, 1999), §4.

4. Cf. R. Otto, *Das Heilige. Über das Irrationale in der Idee des Göttlichen und sein Verhältnis zum Rationalen* (1917) (München: Beck, 1963).

5. Cf. R. C. Roberts, *Spiritual Emotions: A Psychology of Christian Virtues* (Grand Rapids: Eerdmans, 2007), esp. pp. 3-31.

6. Cf. M. R. Wynn, *Emotional Experience and Religious Understanding. Integrating Perception, Conception and Feeling* (Cambridge: Cambridge University Press, 2005), esp. pp. 123-48.

7. In the current philosophical debate, a central question is whether emotions are (just) "upheavals of thought" (cf. M. Nussbaum, *Upheavals of Thought: The Intelligence of Emotions* [Cambridge: Cambridge University Press, 2003]) or whether they are marked by a "cognitive impenetrability" (cf. P. Goldie, *The Emotions: A Philosophical Exploration* [Oxford: Oxford Uni-

From a theological perspective, these reflections on emotion and religion are important, as they contribute to an understanding of faith. If faith cannot be reduced to a set of cognitive beliefs — as important as they are — or to a certainty located in religious subjectivity, but must rather be thought of as a complex way of life or *Lebensform,* then its affective dimensions need to be theologically articulated.[8] And if faith is not a human possibility or result of human efforts, but a gift of God's grace, then such an articulation will have to consider how God's grace relates to and shapes the emotions of believers.

In order to pursue this theological interest, this paper will take up and consider the reflections on emotions, faith, and human personhood developed by the Reformation theologian Philipp Melanchthon. Melanchthon is helpful here since he does not simply discuss emotions within a profiled theological framework, and thus he promotes the conviction that theology can never be content to speak about God if it fails to explicate salvation as a reality on the human side. Instead he also strives to relate his theological reflections to both the anthropological thinking and the sciences of his time. In this way, he provides us with a good example of an interdisciplinary approach in theology. And in both respects, he offers important impulses for contemporary theological reflection. In this paper I will sketch out the development of Melanchthon's theological interpretation of emotions — or "affects," to use his preferred term.[9] I will do this by contrasting his early *Loci communes* (1521)[10] with his later *Loci praecipui theologici* (1559). This will be followed by a brief survey of the problems and perspectives discernible in this line of development, which will then lead into an investigation of the relation between emotions and rhetoric as outlined by Melanchthon in his *Elementa Rhetorices* (1531). The main

versity Press, 2000], p. 76). The importance of neuroscientific findings for the understanding of religious experience is highlighted by Rebecca Sachs Norris, "Examining the Structure and Role of Emotion. Contributions of Neurobiology to the Study of Embodied Religious Experience," *Zygon* 40, no. 1 (2005): 181-99. For further discussion in this area, see the contributions by Warren Brown and Malcolm Jeeves in this volume.

8. For an example from recent discussions cf. J. Cottingham, *The Spiritual Dimension: Religion, Philosophy and Human Value* (Cambridge: Cambridge University Press, 2005), pp. 1-17.

9. It is worth reminding readers that our modern psychological notion of emotion had not yet been developed in Melanchthon's time (for the history of the concept, cf. T. Dixon, *From Passions to Emotions: The Creation of a Secular Psychological Category* [Cambridge: Cambridge University Press, 2006]). However, the phenomenological parallels still allow us to learn from his reflections on affects, and will still be valuable for the contemporary discussion.

10. References to Melanchthon's works will follow the *Corpus Reformatorum,* ed. C. G. Bretschneider (Halle/S., 1834-1860) [hereafter CR].

argument I hope to present in this paper is that this rhetorical perspective on emotions allows us to conceive of the mutual dependence of affects, will, and understanding in the medium of speech. Some final concluding remarks will move on from this basis to highlight what we might learn today from Melanchthon's thought both with regard to the "specialness" of Christian emotions and for an understanding of faith as a complex form of life.

2. The Affects of the Soul and the Effects of Grace in Melanchthon's *Loci*

2.1. A First Sketch: The Battle of Affects in the Loci Communes (1521)

In his 1521 *Loci communes* — which stands as the Reformation's first comprehensive systematic theology — Philipp Melanchthon begins to outline the basic concepts of the Christian faith. But he does so in a rather unusual way. Before considering questions of sin and grace, or justification and faith, he presents an anthropological reflection on the human person's abilities and powers *(De hominis viribus adeoque de libero arbitrio)*.[11] The central point of this view of the human person — a view that profoundly shapes his following theological considerations — is summarized by Melanchthon himself:

> [I]nternal affections are not within our power. For by experience and practice we have found out that the will of its own accord cannot assume love, hate or the like affections; but that one affection is conquered by another.[12]

A brief terminological gloss is needed here to understand what Melanchthon is saying in this passage. The Greek term "pathos" has been translated into three Latin concepts: *perturbatio, affectus,* and *passio;* and there has been a long tradition of differentiating perturbatio and affectus on the one hand, as signifying sudden emotional upheavals, from passio on the other, which is used to designate longer-lasting emotional habits.[13] Yet Melanchthon himself

---

11. Cf. *Loci communes*, CR 21, 86-97.

12. "[I]nterni affectus non sunt in potestate nostra. Experientia enim usuque comperimus non posse voluntatem sua sponte ponere amorem, odium aut similes adfectus, sed adfectus adfectui vincitur" (Loci communes, CR 21, 90). English translation in: *The Loci Communes of Philip Melanchthon* (1944), trans. C. L. Hill (Eugene, OR: Wipf & Stock, 2007), p. 76.

13. Cf. J. Hengelbrock, *Art. Affectus I., Historisches Wörterbuch der Philosophie,* vol. 1 (Darmstadt: Wissenschaftliche Buchgesellschaft, 1971), pp. 89-93.

uses the term "affect" in a broader sense that cuts across this difference, as it becomes clear from the two examples he gives in the quotation above: Love and hate can be sudden emotions, just as they can be emotional habits. At the same time, they are complex emotions when compared, for example, to feelings of pleasure or pain. It is these complex emotions that Melanchthon focuses on in his reflections on affects.

Now Melanchthon's central claim in the above quotation is that the "internal affections are not within our power" and that human persons are not capable of freely determining which affects — be it love or hate, hope or fear, mourning or anger[14] — will shape their lives and actions. In order to prove this claim, Melanchthon considers the anthropological place of affects, and thereby discusses the different powers of the human soul *(anima)*. Following a dualist anthropological scheme that understands the human person as a unity of body and soul — and reserves the term "spirit" for the Spirit of God[15] — Melanchthon differentiates two powers within the soul: the power of reasoning *(vis cognoscendi)* and the power to follow or refuse what reason has discerned *(vis, qua vel persequitur vel refugit, quae cognovit).*[16] It is already clear from this description that, for Melanchthon, the power of reasoning is dependent on the second power of the soul, which follows or refuses what reason has discerned. At first sight, we might be tempted to accuse Melanchthon of conceptual vagueness, since he describes this second power both as an ability of the will *(voluntas)* and as the power of the affects *(adfectus).*[17] But a closer reading reveals that we have here the precise point he is trying to make: by locating both the will and the affects in the second power of the soul, Melanchthon implicitly criticizes the idea — prominent in the Scotist tradition — that confines the affects to the sensitive capability *(appetitus sensitivus)* of the soul, and consequently ascribes to reason and will the ability to dominate and control these affects. For Melanchthon, affects do not represent an entity in addition to the will but rather the manner or way in which the will acts in its determination either to follow or not follow the power of reason.[18] This means that affects are not simply "sentiments," but rather the decisive impulses that direct human action and life. And as the affects of the

14. These are Melanchthon's own examples (cf. *Loci communes,* CR 21, 90f.).

15. Cf. *Loci communes,* CR 21, 207.

16. Cf. *Loci communes,* CR 21, 86f.

17. Cf. *Loci communes,* CR 21, 87f.

18. For this interpretation, cf. K. H zur Mühlen, "Melanchthons Auffassung vom Affekt in den Loci Communes von 1521," in *Humanismus und Wittenberger Reformation,* ed. M. Beyer (Leipzig: Günter Wartenberg, 1996), pp. 327-36.

soul are not just a part of human nature, but determine the human person as a whole, a change in the direction of human life can only be effected in the realism of the affects themselves: *adfectus adfectui vincitur* — one affection is conquered by another.[19]

Building on this anthropological introduction, Melanchthon's theological deliberations then aim to sketch out the Reformation insight that the reestablishment of a salvific relation to God is not a human possibility, but must be thought of as an exclusive effect of God's grace. Furthermore, this claim, Melanchthon argues, implies a concept of human sin that — against the position of Erasmus and the Scotist theologians[20] — negates the possibility of a free will *(liberum arbitrium)* that can approach grace voluntarily. Instead of restricting sin to the sensual part of the human person, Melanchthon therefore describes original sin — which in his view inevitably results in actual sin[21] — as a power that dominates human life in its totality. In taking up this position, he draws on his theory of affects: If the human person is subjected to sin as he or she is subjected to affects such as love and hate, then sin can and should be understood as an affect itself: "Sin is a depraved affection, a depraved motion of the heart against the law of God."[22] Thus for Melanchthon, describing sin as a depraved affect does not rule out, but rather implies that the reality of sin becomes manifest in human life in different sinful affects, such as "blasphemy, hatred of God, self-love, [and] diffidence toward God."[23] With this explanation in place, Melanchthon argues that the basic insight of his theory of affects becomes applicable to the reality of sin: Sin, as with all affects, is not under human control; and as a "depraved affect" it can only be conquered by another affect *(adfectus adfectui vincitur)* — another affect that has to be understood theologically as an effect of grace.

Analyzing grace in terms of this theory of affects, Melanchthon affirms — as did Luther — that grace is grounded in Christ as savior and that by faith only does his justice become ours.[24] However, without negating this Chris-

---

19. *Loci communes,* CR 21, 90.

20. Cf. *Loci communes,* CR 21, 87, 92.

21. Cf. *Loci communes,* CR 21, 99.

22. "Pravus adfectus, pravusque cordis motus est contra legem dei, peccatum" (*Loci communes,* CR 21, 97; Hill, p. 82).

23. "Blasphemiam, odium dei, amorem sui, diffidere Deo" (*Loci communes,* CR 21, 113; Hill, p. 106).

24. Cf. *Loci communes,* CR 21, 159-81. For a detailed account of Melanchthon's notion of justification in the *Loci communes,* cf. A. Peters, "Rechtfertigung," in *Handbuch Systematischer Theologie 12* (Gütersloh: Gütersloher Verlagshaus, 1984), pp. 64-73.

tological basis, Melanchthon places great emphasis on depicting the Spirit of God as the gift of grace which is poured out into the human heart.[25] While he refutes all attempts to see grace as a new quality of the human soul,[26] he stresses that it is by the work of the Spirit that the benefits of Christ become the reality of salvation within the lives of believers. As this reality of salvation overcomes the reality of sin, and since sin for Melanchthon is to be understood as a "depraved affect," salvation as an effect of grace must also become manifest in the realm of the affects. The Spirit of God as the gift of grace creates spiritual affects *(spiritualis affectus)*[27] in the believer and thus enables that believer to trust and love God, and to act towards other human persons according to God's will in a way that is spontaneous and joyful *(sponte et hilariter).*[28] Of course, Melanchthon knows that such a change in this life will never be complete, so that the life of faith is to be seen as a dynamic process of growth in faith *(profectus),* in which the spiritual affects are deepened by the Spirit of God.[29] But nevertheless, he holds that sinful and spiritual affects are mutually exclusive, and the clearest expression of this (not unproblematic) assumption can be found in Melanchthon's statement that while the affect of sadness is a mark of sin, the affect of joy is an effect and an expression of grace.[30]

By contrasting in this way the "depraved affects" of sin with the spiritual affects that are created by the Spirit of God as the gift of grace, Melanchthon intends to explain in anthropological terms what Paul in Romans 8:5f. describes as the power of the flesh *(sarx)* as opposed to the power of the spirit *(pneuma).*[31] The presupposition that underlies this attempt is Melanchthon's conviction that affects are at the center of the human person, determining human life in its totality — a conviction that is emphasized all the more by his habit of substituting the term "affect" with the biblical notion of "heart," denoting the inner center of the human person.[32]

25. Cf. *Loci communes,* CR 21, 158.
26. Cf. *Loci communes,* CR 21, 157f.
27. Cf, *Loci communes,* CR 21, 185.
28. Cf. *Loci communes,* CR 21, 163. For Melanchthon, it is only on the basis of such good affects that good works become possible at all (cf. *Loci communes,* CR 21, 179f.).
29. Cf. *Loci communes,* CR 21, 178. 206f.
30. Cf. *Loci communes,* CR 21, 181f.; Liber de anima, CR 13, 53-57.
31. Cf. *Loci communes,* CR 21, 105f. For an explication of this Pauline contrast and its anthropological context cf. the analyses presented by Gerd Theissen and Michael Welker in this volume.
32. Cf. *Loci communes,* CR 21, 90.

2.2. A Different Picture: Free Will and "Natural" Affects in Melanchthon's Loci Praecipui Theologici (1559)

When we move from Melanchthon's early systematic work to his late *Loci praecipui theologici* (1559),[33] we see that the picture he draws of the human person, its affects, and its encounter with grace changes dramatically. At the center of this change lies Melanchthon's revised understanding of the human will.[34] In the *Loci communes,* Melanchthon's aim was to negate the freedom of the will by referring to affects "not within our power." Yet in the *Loci praecipui* he affirms the freedom of the will, reassuring us that remnants of the imago Dei still remain intact after the fall, so that man does not cease to be a responsible counterpart of God.[35] Sin, Melanchthon now stresses, does not abolish the capacity of the human intellect to discern ontological and logical axioms or the God-given ethical rules of natural justice.[36] When he comes to the discussion — already familiar to us from his early *Loci* — of the differences and the cooperation between reason *(mens)* and will *(voluntas),* he now highlights the freedom of the will either to follow or refuse the judgment of reason. Suddenly, according to the *Loci praecipui,* the human will is now able to make responsible decisions and to effectuate moral action.[37] This reassessment of human free will is motivated by Melanchthon's intention to overcome the danger of determinism apparent in his early thinking. Yet it also manifests his deep humanistic convictions, which have now become more clearly integrated into his theological reflections.[38] And it is this Christian humanism

33. With regard to the dynamic development of Melanchthon's thought between the early and late *Loci,* only those aspects that appear in the *Loci praecipui* are of systematic interest here.

34. This new framework has an impact on the structure of the two books. In 1521, the reflections on affects are found in the first chapter, thus setting out the frame for the following elaboration of sin and grace. In contrast, in 1559 the chapter "De humanis viribus seu de libero arbitrio" is a part of the doctrine of sin and is preceded by reflections on human free will (cf. *Loci Praecipui,* CR 21, 662-65).

35. For an instructive overview on Melanchthon's notion of the imago Dei, cf. A. Peters, "Der Mensch," in *Handbuch Systematischer Theologie 8* (Gütersloh: Gütersloher Verlagshaus, 1979), pp. 64-68.

36. For Melanchthon's concept of such *notitia naturales,* cf. Günter Frank, "Philipp Melanchthons 'Liber de Anima' und die Etablierung der frühneuzeitlichen Anthropologie," in *Humanismus und Wittenberger Reformation,* ed. M. Beyer (Leipzig: Günter Wartenberg, 1996), pp. 313-26, 317-21.

37. Cf. *Loci praecipui,* CR 21, 654f.

38. There is a tendency to view Melanchthon as a thinker located somewhere between humanism and the Reformation, implying that he was neither a "real" humanist nor a "real" Reformation theologian (such as Luther). However, the originality of Melanchthon's thought

that also prompts Melanchthon to engage extensively with the scientific and philosophical theories of his time.[39]

Clearly, these new presuppositions also demand a revised concept of sin. In the *Loci praecipui,* when Melanchthon understands sin as "a defect, an inclination or action that is opposed to God's law,"[40] he is quick to assert that this defect of sin does not revoke the goodness of human personhood as created by God. Rather, it has to be understood as a weakness *(imbecillitas)*[41] which manifests itself both in the lack of a true knowledge of God and in wrong affects *(vitiosi affectus)* that impede the will's ability to follow the judgment of reason.[42] Thus for Melanchthon, sin, as a weakness, does impair the freedom of the will, but it does not negate it. Yet at the same time, the human will is not capable of overcoming this weakness through its own power.[43] This is why a life in accordance with God's will can only be initiated through God's grace.[44]

In his discussion of grace, Melanchthon emphasizes the prevenient character of God's grace not only by linking it to the preaching of the gospel and the work of the Holy Spirit,[45] but also by describing its content as the forgiveness of sin and the imputation of Christ's righteousness *(imputatio iustitiae).*[46] However, at the same time, Melanchthon takes into account the effects of grace in the lives of believers, describing those effects under the title of reconciliation *(reconciliatio).*[47] Such reconciliation, Melanchthon argues, includes the redirection of a believer's life into alignment with God. That such a redirection

---

(which is systematically downplayed in this tradition of interpretation) rather seems to lie in his thoughtful integration of humanism and Reformation theology. Good arguments for such a reading are provided by C. Strohm, "Philipp Melanchthon — Reformator und Humanist," in *Philipp Melanchthon. Exemplarische Aspekte seines Humanismus,* ed. G. Binder (Trier, 1998), pp. 9-46. For the current articulation of a Christian humanism, cf. the contribution of William Schweiker in this volume.

39. Cf. the analyses of his *Liber de Anima* (1553) and *Elementorum Rhetoricis Libri Duo* (1531) below.

40. "Peccatum est defectus vel inclinatio vel actio pugnans cum Lege Dei" (*Loci praecipui,* CR 21, 667; English translation mine).

41. Cf. *Loci praecipui,* CR 21, 684f.

42. Cf. *Loci praecipui,* CR 21, 655f.

43. "Hic certum est, homines non habere libertatem deponendi hanc pravitatem nobiscum nascentem aut deponendi mortem" (*Loci praecipui,* CR 21, 655).

44. We can say this even though Melanchthon's strategy of depicting human will both as the basis for moral action and as a power that, in a certain way, cooperates in justification does at times seem to obscure the sola gratia (cf. *Loci praecipui,* CR 21, 658f.).

45. Cf. *Loci praecipui,* CR 21, 751-61.

46. Cf. *Loci praecipui,* CR 21, 1037f.

47. Cf. *Loci praecipui,* CR 21, 1037f.

actually includes all dimensions of the human person becomes clear in Melanchthon's description of faith, which presents the only way we can receive the grace of God. For Melanchthon, in faith the human intellect discerns the prevenient grace of God in Christ *(notitia),* the human will then assents to salvation *(assensus)* and the affects are directed by trust in God *(fiducia).*[48] And when Melanchthon goes on to detail the concept of fiducia as including both the reverence *(timor)* and love *(dilectio)* of God, he affirms — against the stoic ideal of apatheia — that the Christian life does not only consist in knowing God and assenting to his grace, but also possesses an affective dimension.[49]

However, Melanchthon's account of how this affective dimension is to be understood differs significantly in the *Loci praecipui* from his description in the *Loci communes:* While the treatment in the *Loci communes* suggests that sinful affects have to be replaced by spiritual affects, in the *Loci praecipui* Melanchthon acknowledges the reality of "natural" affects that are part of God's good creation and not destroyed by sin.[50] Thus, for example, the heroic rage of Achilles, Melanchthon argues, is not a vice, but rather something good, although it is contaminated by Achilles' ignorance of God.[51] And on this basis, Melanchthon can describe the "new" affects shaping the life of believers not as a replacement, but as a transformation of such "natural" affects which, in the life of believers, are shaped by love of and trust in God.[52]

Melanchthon's interest in such "natural" affects, which by grace are transformed rather than replaced, is reflected in his account of their placement within the human being. Whereas in the 1521 *Loci* the affects are eventually equated with the human will *(voluntas)* as the second power of the soul in addition to reason *(mens),* in the later *Loci* affects are the lowest part of the soul, clearly subordinated to the power of the will.[53] Thus whereas the *Loci communes* proposes a unidirectional dependence of the will and understanding on the affects, in the *Loci praecipui* this is reversed to a unidirectional

48. Cf. *Loci praecipui,* CR 21, 742-51 and for a detailed analysis M. Seils, "Glaube," in *Handbuch Systematischer Theologie 13* (Gütersloh: Gütersloher Verlagshaus, 1996), pp. 119-46.

49. Cf. *Loci praecipui,* CR 21, 697f.

50. Cf. the instructive analysis in P. Bartmann, *Das Gebot und die Tugend der Liebe. Über den Umgang mit konfliktbezogenen Affekten* (Stuttgart: Kohlhammer, 1998), pp. 217-22.

51. "In Achille ira Heroica est res bona, quia vere opus Dei est, sed contaminatur, quia non regitur agnitione Dei" *(Loci praecipui,* CR 21, 677).

52. In contrast to his description of Achilles' rage, Melanchthon sees the rage of David as an example of such transformed affects: "Econtra similis ira in Davide purior est, in quo accedunt agnitio, timor, invocatio, fiducia Dei" *(Loci praecipui,* CR 21, 677).

53. Melanchthon now adopts a threefold scheme of the human person, consisting of intellect *(mens),* will *(voluntas),* and the appetitive drive *(locomotiva)* *(Loci praecipui,* CR 21, 653).

dependence of the affects on the will and understanding. When Melanchthon goes on to say that the affects are located in the human heart, this term takes on a meaning significantly different from its use in the *Loci communes*. Whereas in the early *Loci* Melanchthon draws on the biblical notion of "heart" as the innermost center of the human person, in his later *Loci* he now understands the term "heart" as denoting primarily the organic entity. Therefore the anthropological placement of the affects, as far as the later *Loci* is concerned, is no longer at the "inner" center of the soul; they have been shifted to the "outer," bodily condition of the human person. Affects, Melanchthon now stresses, are bound to bodily, organic processes.

In his 1553 *Liber de anima,* Melanchthon develops a detailed account of the correlations between bodily processes and human affects, relying extensively on theories taken from classical and Renaissance physiology.[54] Thus, for example, Melanchthon aims to explain joy and sadness by tracing them back to physiological movements in the human heart *(motus cordis):* joy corresponds to a dilation of the heart *(dilatatio),* but in sadness the heart contracts *(constringitur);* and due to the neural connections between the heart and brain, these movements of the heart effect the pleasantness of joy as well as the bitterness of sadness.[55] While we might be hesitant to affirm Melanchthon's attempt here directly to connect these physiological ideas to theological convictions (by linking the organic spirit of life to the Spirit of God),[56] we should acknowledge the way in which these physiological considerations served Melanchthon's theological reflections in an indirect — and more plausible — manner.[57] This becomes clearer in Melanchthon's summary of his findings, which he contrasts with his understanding of the Stoic account of the affects. While the Stoics, in Melanchthon's view, understand affects as mere opinions and as intrinsically negative phenomena that virtuous persons should strive to erase in order to approach the ideal of apatheia, Melanchthon's own physiological findings, he argues, show the opposite: that affects are not opinions, but bodily processes,

---

54. For the traditions underlying Melanchthon's argument in the *Liber de Anima,* cf. J. Helm, "Zwischen Aristotelismus, Protestantismus und zeitgenössischer Medizin. Philipp Melanchthons Lehrbuch De anima (1540/1552)," in *Melanchthon und das Lehrbuch des 16. Jahrhunderts,* ed. J. Leonhardt (Rostock: Universität Rostock, 1997), pp. 175-91.

55. Cf. *Liber de Anima,* CR 13, 126f.

56. Cf. *Liber de Anima,* CR 13, 88f.

57. For an overarching examination of Melanchthon's theologically informed reception of natural philosophy, cf. the thorough analysis in S. Kusukawa, *The Transformation of Natural Philosophy: The Case of Philipp Melanchthon* (Cambridge: Cambridge University Press, 1995), esp. pp. 75-123.

and that they are an essential part of human nature that cannot and should not be negated.[58] Together, Melanchthon sees these insights underlining a conviction that Christian affects be understood as a transformation rather than as a replacement of "natural" affects.

2.3. The Affects of the Soul and the Effects of Grace: Preliminary Results

At this point, we can take the common trait running through Melanchthon's reflections and summarize them in the following simple thesis: affects form an integral and indispensable dimension of the human person. Thus for Melanchthon, to overcome our affects altogether represents an absurd and potentially dangerous goal. It is this insight, he maintains, that distinguishes his own account from Stoic philosophy and its ideal of apatheia. Since, for Melanchthon, the Christian faith redirects the life of the whole human person, faith must also be seen as an intrinsically affective reality that cannot be reduced to its cognitive contents. It is not that we should surrender these cognitive contents, but in Melanchthon's view they have to be integrated into a complex concept of faith that connects *notitia, assensus,* and *fiducia.* With this basis in place, Melanchthon can then explain both sin and grace as affective realities, thus spelling out the Pauline contrast between flesh and Spirit in terms of a theory of affects. Necessary criticism notwithstanding, we can certainly appreciate this approach as an anthropological hermeneutics of faith, one that intends to illustrate and substantiate theological concepts by reference to human experience.

At the same time, when we compare Melanchthon's 1521 and 1559 *Loci,* we notice crucial differences that arise from his theological reassessment of human free will. These differences present us with opposing alternatives: either affects determine the will and understanding, and therefore the whole human person (the position of the early *Loci*), or the will and understanding regulate the affects and therefore steer human life as a whole (Melanchthon's opinion from the late *Loci*). When moving from the first to the second position, we also note another shift in Melanchthon's account of human affects, namely from "inner" to "outer." This shift is particularly visible in his concept of the human heart. Whereas the 1521 *Loci* follows the biblical use of the term in understanding the heart as the inner center of the human person, the 1559 *Loci* uses "heart" to refer to the bodily organ. This shift allows Melanchthon to align his theory of affects to the medical thinking and natural philosophy

58. Cf. *Liber de Anima,* CR 13, 131f.

of his time. While we can concede that this strategy risks obscuring his earlier insights regarding the impact of the affects on the center of the human person, we can still appreciate his intentions here — his reassessment of human free will — since they reflect the deep humanistic motives at work in his thinking.

However, as to the question of what is special about Christian emotions, the later *Loci* indisputably moves beyond the apparent problems of Melanchthon's early work. For in focusing on the contrast between sinful and spiritual affects, the early *Loci* conceives of specifically Christian emotions as replacing the sinful emotions that occupy the human heart and thus leave no room for the perception and appreciation of those affects "natural" to the human being as God's creature. The problems here become obvious when Melanchthon correlates sin with the affect of sadness, and grace with the affect of joy. While we might appreciate Melanchthon's conviction that peace with God can positively shape the lives of believers, the claim that faith liberates us from sadness and that joy can count as an indicator of a Christian life appear both deeply unconvincing from a phenomenological perspective and dangerous due to the rigid moralism that such a claim obviously supports. In contrast, in his 1559 *Loci,* Melanchthon affirms that there are good "natural" affects in the human person which, as remnants of the imago Dei, have not been totally destroyed by sin. Melanchthon describes these affects as good predispositions, bestowed on us by God the creator. These "natural" affects are then transformed — not replaced — by grace as they are ordered and directed by faith in God. With this insight in the late *Loci,* which finds an early parallel in Augustine's reflections on Christian affects,[59] Melanchthon arrives at a more plausible account of Christian affects, one that avoids the pitfalls of his earlier reflections.

Yet up to this point, just how such a transformation of the affects takes place has remained an open question. One reason for this may lie in the fact that Melanchthon — in both *Loci* — considers the affects as the "counterpart" of reason and will, as phenomena that have no rational structure themselves. This amounts to a dichotomization of emotion and reason in a way that can be rightly objected to from both philosophical and neurobiological perspectives.[60] To further investigate the possibilities of such a transformation of the affects,

59. An impressive example is Augustine's contrast between a *tristitia mundi* and a *tristitia secundum deum,* in *De civitate Dei,* IV, 4-12 and IX, 11-13. For an interpretation of this contrast and its context, cf. J. Brachtendorf, "Augustinus. Die Ambivalenz der Affekte zwischen Natürlichkeit und Tyrannei," in *Klassische Emotionstheorien. Von Platon bis Wittgenstein,* ed. H. Landweer and U. Renz (Berlin: De Gruyter, 2008), pp. 142-61.

60. For a philosophical perspective, cf. M. Heidegger, *Sein und Zeit* (1927) (Tübingen 1993), §§29-34. Neurobiological arguments against the traditional dichotomy of emotion and

we can look at two contexts where the affects have classically been discussed, namely in ethics and in rhetoric.[61] Melanchthon himself dedicated extensive studies to both.[62] The following section will concentrate on his reflections on rhetoric — reflections that promise to deliver a productive solution to the alternatives provided in the 1521 and 1559 *Loci*, specifically: instead of proposing a unidirectional impact (of the affects on will and reason, or of will and reason on the affects), Melanchthon will unite affects, will, and reason in the medium of language, a step that might help us to conceive of their interrelatedness in mutual dependence.

3. Moving the Soul: Rhetoric and the Shaping of Affects

Melanchthon's work in the field of rhetoric, which started early in his career,[63] finds its mature expression in his *Elementa Rhetorices* (1531). Building on classical authors such as Aristotle and Cicero as well as on Renaissance discussions,[64] Melanchthon's approach gains its specific profile through his conviction that rhetoric is inseparable from dialectic.[65] Perceiving that in his own period the separation of both disciplines had reduced dialectics to an "artless" game of logical definitions, and transformed rhetoric into a means of "writing insincere praises of princes,"[66] Melanchthon's strategy to reintegrate rhetoric into dialectic has a double aim: Dialectic, Melanchthon argues, must stay related to the fundamental questions of human life, while rhetoric must build on dialectic in order to express its questions and arguments in proper speech.[67]

---

reason are presented in A. Damasio, *Descartes' Error: Emotion, Reason and the Human Brain* (New York: Putnam, 1994).

61. For a classic example, cf. Aristotle, *Rhetorica II*, 2-11, 1378a-1391b and *Ethica Nicomachea II-IV*, 1103a-1128b.

62. For Melanchthon's work on rhetoric, cf. section 3 below; for his ethical studies, cf. his *Ethicae Doctrinae elementa* (1550) CR 13, 165-276 and H. Ziebritzki, "Tugend und Affekt," in *Der Theologe Melanchthon*, ed. G. Frank (Stuttgart: Thorbecke, 2000), pp. 357-73.

63. For an overview of the various editions of Melanchthon's treatise on rhetoric, cf. O. Berwald, "Philipp Melanchthons Rhetoriklehrbücher," in *Melanchthon und das Lehrbuch des 16. Jahrhunderts*, ed. J. Leonhardt (Rostock: Universität Rostock, 1997), pp. 111-22.

64. Cf. J. Knape, *Philipp Melanchthons "Rhetorik"* (Tübingen, 1993), pp. 1-16.

65. Cf. *Elementa rhetorices*, CR 13, 419-21.

66. Cf. J. R. Schneider, "Melanchthon's Rhetoric as a Context for Understanding His Theology," in *Melanchthon in Europe*, ed. K. Maag (Grand Rapids: Baker Academic, 1999), pp. 141-59, 150.

67. Cf. Schneider, "Melanchthon's Rhetoric," pp. 146-53.

Therefore, when Melanchthon defines rhetoric as "the art which teaches the method and the theory of speaking appropriately *(recte)* and with distinction *(ornate dicendi),"*[68] it is clear to him that this *recte* and *ornate dicendi* are not a mere play with words, but refer to the linguistic form given to those questions and arguments discussed in dialectics and systematic philosophy and which are basic for human life. And this linguistic form, Melanchthon argues, is necessary both for achieving semantic clarity in thinking and for making semantic truths operative for the addressees of rhetorical speech. The goal of rhetoric "is to persuade, or better, to move souls powerfully and to set souls in motion *(permovere atque impellere animos)."*[69] However, such a "moving of souls" in Melanchthon's view is inconceivable without rhetorical speech having an impact on human affects.

Linking rhetoric and affects as Melanchthon does is certainly not a new idea. In Aristotle's *Rhetoric* we already find extensive reflections on how rhetorical speech can and should influence the affects of an audience.[70] Building on this classic example, Melanchthon discusses the way rhetorical speech can "move the soul" by shaping human affects. To clarify how rhetorical speech can shape human affects, Melanchthon develops what may well be called a "physiology of persuasion," which examines how the sounds of words enter the human ear, are then judged by intellect and will, and finally lead to affects that motivate action.[71] Yet of vital importance for Melanchthon is the observation that semantic content and affective content are themselves inseparably connected in the words *(verba)* of rhetorical speech. For Melanchthon, this can be illustrated by the correlations between specific topics, words, and affects: just as virtuous speech corresponds to the affects of love, and talk of vices corresponds to the affects of hate, so too mild words are suitable to express mild affects *(ethe),* while harsh words must be used to articulate dramatic affects *(pathe).*[72] Yet the interconnectedness of semantic content and affective importance also becomes clear, he argues, when we attend to the acoustic sound of

68. "Rhetorica vero est ars, quae docet viam ac rationem recte et ornate dicendi" (*Elementa rhetorices,* CR 13, 419; English translation mine).

69. *Elementa rhetorices,* CR 13, 420; English translation mine.

70. Cf. Aristotle, *Rhetorica II,* 2-11, 1378a-1391b.

71. Cf. *Liber de Anima,* CR 13, 112-48 and L. D. Green, "Melanchthon, Rhetoric, and the Soul," in *Melanchthon und Europa,* vol. 2, ed. G. Frank and K. Meerhoff (Stuttgart, 2002), pp. 11-27, 14-19.

72. *Elementa rhetorices,* CR 13, 454. Melanchthon relates here to the classical differentiation of affects in accordance with the distinction between ethos and pathos (cf. O. Berwald, *Philipp Melanchthons Sicht der Rhetorik* [Wiesbaden: Harrassowitz, 1994], pp. 51f.).

words and sentences: words, like music, can have an immediate impact on the human soul, but unlike music they also possess semantic content.[73] Finally, for Melanchthon this connection between thoughts and affects is also evidenced by the rhetorical technique of *amplificatio,* which does not only aim at creating affects corresponding to semantic arguments, but also to sustain them in order to set and keep souls in motion.[74]

Melanchthon's insight into the interconnectedness and mutual dependence of understanding, will, and the affects also has theological implications. For when Melanchthon says that faith is created "through listening to and understanding the voice of the Gospel,"[75] it is clear to him that the theological task of making the voice of the gospel heard cannot be achieved without the help of rhetoric — a conviction impressively reflected in his own theological work.[76] That such a use of rhetoric is appropriate for unfolding the message of the gospel can be seen, he argues, in the fact that scripture (as the authentic witness of God's word) is itself a rhetorical text.[77] Therefore, for Melanchthon, rhetoric is as indispensable for understanding scripture as it is for the theological explication of the gospel.[78] It is for this reason that in his discussion of rhetoric in the *Elementa Rhetorices,* Melanchthon inserts a passage defending the Reformation reading of scripture against the concept of the fourfold modes of scriptural exegesis.[79]

I can only briefly note a further consequence of Melanchthon's reflections on the affects in the context of rhetoric: To explain rhetorical speech as a means of shaping the affects and thus of moving human souls implies that although affects may well be described as bound to organic, bodily processes, they are also simultaneously cultural and social phenomena in the same way as rhetorical speech is a cultural and social phenomenon. On this basis, Melanchthon

73. "Neque musica duleior aut iucundior auribus, aut mente pereipi ulla potest, quae aequabilis oratio, constans bonis verbis ac sententiis" (*Elementa rhetorices,* CR 13, 460). Cf. for this aspect also Green, "Melanchthon, Rhetoric, and the Soul," p. 23.

74. "Ducuntur autem ex omnibus loas dialectices amplificationes, ad impellendos animos, exaggerata vel dignitate, vel turpitudine rei" (*Elementa rhetorices,* CR 13, 454, cf. 479-83). Cf. Green, "Melanchthon, Rhetoric, and the Soul," pp. 24f.

75. "Spiritum sanctum efficacem esse per vocem Evangelii auditam seu cogitatam" (*Loci praecipui,* CR 21, 658; English translation mine).

76. For the rhetorical background, especially of the *Loci communes,* cf. Schneider, "Melanchthon's Rhetoric," p. 153.

77. Cf. Schneider, "Melanchthon's Rhetoric," pp. 154f.

78. Cf. M. B. Aune, *To Move the Heart: Philipp Melanchthon's Rhetorical View of Rite and Its Implications for Contemporary Ritual Theory* (San Francisco: Christian Universities Press, 1994), pp. 17-29.

79. Cf. *Elementa rhetorices,* CR 13, 466-74.

is able not only to underline the political importance of rhetoric,[80] but also to describe the Christian church as *coetus scholarum,* in which faith and its affects are educated by the rhetorical exhibition of God's word.[81]

In his *Liber de anima,* Melanchthon outlines two alternative ways in which human affects can be shaped and directed. The first he calls despotic, because just as in a despotic state the ruler forces his subjects to obey, so too here the attempt is made to subdue affects by the force of the will and intellect. However, Melanchthon sees the second way as both more effective and more appropriate when it comes to the affects of faith. This is the political way in which the affects are shaped so as to agree with the will and intellect, just as in the Greek polis free citizens used public deliberation to reach agreement. This "political" way of shaping affects is the task of rhetoric, both in public discourse and in theology, which must explain the word of God so it can shape the affects of believers for a life of faith.[82]

4. Conclusion

"Hoc est Christum cognoscere, beneficia eius cognoscere"[83] — to know Christ is to know the benefits of Christ. To be sure, this programmatic sentence from Melanchthon's *Loci communes* can be dangerous. It may encourage us to make humanity rather than God the center of theological reflection. However, its positive implication can be seen in the conviction that theology is not only God-talk, but that it also must spell out what salvation means for human life in all its dimensions. And this, as Melanchthon's work impressively shows, includes theological reflection on emotions or "affects." Believers experience the benefits of Christ, Melanchthon writes, both in peace of conscience and in a reshaping of affects by God's grace.[84] As the preceding analyses have shown, for

80. Cf. here N. Kuropka, "Melanchthon between Renaissance and Reformation. From Exegesis to Political Action," in *Melanchthon in Europe,* ed. K. Maag (Grand Rapids: Baker, 1999), pp. 161-72.

81. Cf. *Loci praecipui, CR* 21, 834-40 and the analysis in M. Wriedt, "Pietas et eruditio," in *Dona Melanchthoniana,* ed. J. Loehr (Stuttgart: Frommann-Holzboog, 2001), pp. 501-20, 510-16.

82. Cf. *Liber de Anima, CR* 13, 130f.

83. *Loci communes, CR* 21, 85.

84. "Duo imprimis sunt beneficia, quae Christum orbi commendant, pacata conscientia et animus compos affectuum suorum" (*Declamtiuncula in Divi Pauli doctrinam* [1520], in *Melanchthon Werke,* Studienausgabe, vol. 1, ed. R. Stupperich [Gütersloh: Gütersloher Verlagshaus, 1951], p. 38 [missing in CR]).

Melanchthon such a theological reflection on emotions can only be successful if it adopts an interdisciplinary approach, including theological, physiological, and rhetorical perspectives. And in this respect, Melanchthon's work can serve as a model for contemporary debate, though many of his empirical assumptions will no longer stand up to modern science. But if Melanchthon is correct that emotions are both bodily and cultural phenomena, then their analysis (even today) should never be reduced to a single perspective.[85]

However, even more important for contemporary reflection is Melanchthon's concept of specifically Christian emotions, which result not from a replacement, but from a transformation of "natural" emotions — an insight he articulates in his 1559 *Loci,* thus overcoming a crucial problem in his earlier 1521 *Loci.* Yet to fully understand this insight we need to turn to his discussion of affects in the context of rhetoric from his *Elementa Rhetorices* (1531). Here Melanchthon moves beyond establishing a unidirectional dependence of understanding on emotions (as in the early *Loci*) or of emotions on understanding (as in the late *Loci*) by expressing their interconnectedness and mutual dependence in the medium of rhetorical speech. On this basis, one can envisage the shaping and transformation of emotions as a "political" process that aims at the correspondence of emotions, will, and understanding — a correspondence that is central for the Christian faith as created and shaped by grace through the word of God, which is written and preached rhetorically. If we follow Melanchthon's insight into the interrelatedness of emotion and understanding, then we cannot subscribe to William James's claim that emotions are "the deeper source of religion," while "philosophic and theological formulas are secondary products."[86] But to follow Melanchthon does mean that we recognize the role and articulation of emotions as one dimension of complex human personhood and of faith as a comprehensive form of life.

---

85. Rather, as Robert C. Roberts rightly states, "religious emotions in particular call for the fullest range of investigative strategies. They vary widely across cultures and are highly sensitive to disciplined formation; they are strongly associated with sets of beliefs about the nature of the universe and human nature and are often a response to verbal communication. They are associated with ritual and in many traditions are subject to rather strict criteria of legitimacy. Yet, despite the salience of these cultural conditions, religious emotions are no less physiological than other kinds" (Roberts, "Emotions Research and Religious Experience," in *The Oxford Handbook on Religion and Emotion,* ed. J. Corrigan [Oxford: Oxford University Press, 2008], pp. 490-506, quote 502f.). For a recent attempt to integrate philosophical, psychological, and neuroscientific accounts of emotion into an understanding of religious emotions, cf. N. P. Azari and D. Birnbacher, "The Role of Cognition and Feeling in Religious Experience," *Zygon* 39, no. 4 (2004): 901-17.

86. James, *The Varieties of Religious Experience,* p. 431; emphasis mine.

The Concept of "Body" in Indian Christian Theological Thought

Origen V. Jathanna

We live in a world in which we see both the cult of the body and disparaging of the body. We are familiar with both rarefied spiritual notions of the human person and gross materialistic understandings of it. This of course is not new. At the same time, the perceptions of these contrasting views do not remain the same, but present themselves in a variety of modifications and combinations at different times and in different places.

In Indian Christian theological thought thus far, what stands at the center has been Christology. In Christology again it is the question of the meaning and significance of Jesus Christ in relation to religious plurality, which presents various ultimate goals and different means to reach them, on the one hand, and, on the other, the possibilities that Jesus Christ offers in terms of fullness of life for all, in the context of multiple bondages and forms of oppression. Christology, of course, cannot be dealt with in isolation from other aspects of Christian faith, such as the understanding of God, theological anthropology, and soteriology. Christian faith has to take the creational, incarnational, staurological,[1] and resurrectional dimensions seriously, to which "body" is integral, if Christian faith has to remain faithful to its foundational vision of reality. This truth finds pointed expression particularly in 1 Corinthians 15. The resurrection of the body/flesh is an important aspect of Christian belief as expressed in the Niceno-Constantinopolitan Creed and the Apostles' Creed. The basic question in this regard, therefore, has to do with the ultimate significance of the embodied historical life and hence, of

---

1. This deals with the meaning and significance of the death of Jesus Christ on the cross.

the body. In view of this, this paper seeks to reflect on the concept of body in Indian Christian theological thought.

1.

Any systematic theology worth its name has to be contextual, and contextual theology has to be systematic. This has been the case in the history of Christian theological thought, though not always equally self-consciously. The Indian context is wide and varied. In view of this, theological anthropology has to take various context-related factors into account, while theologically reflecting on, and giving expression to, the concept of body in Christian faith.

It may be noted that in classical Indian philosophy, all schools hold the view that souls or *jiivas*[2] are not created and are eternal, if terminologically these refer to Self/self. The body's role is acknowledged as the vehicle of the embodied life, during the transmigration of the soul, i.e., during the *karma-samsaara.* The series of embodiments are linked by the continuity provided by *suukshma shariira* or *linga shariira,* which broadly speaking refers to the psychic entity, consisting of *manas* (mind), *buddhi* (intellect), and *ahamkaara* (ego). The ultimate liberated state, which is called *mooksha* or *mukti,* can be attained only by coming out of the cycle of *karma-samsaara,* i.e., of births and rebirths. All this implies that the body, both gross *(sthuula)* and subtle *(suukshma),* has only an instrumental value and is not integral to the human being, seen from the point of view of the ultimate goal. This state of affairs does not change whether the soul as self is understood to retain its distinctness from the Self (understood either as *Paramaatman* or *Brahman*) or not.[3] M. Hiri-yanna, a well-known authority on Indian philosophy, states that the body,

2. Though an attempt is made in this paper to indicate long vowels by repeating the same vowel, a practice that is followed by some lexicographers, strict consistency could not be maintained, as the spelling in the quotations would either use diacritical marks or just ignore the difference between the long and the short vowel. Other phonetic aspects, using the diacritical marks, could not be taken up. This is also not indicated in the case of the terms that are commonly used in current English, as well as in the case of a number of proper names.

3. S. Datta, "Karma and Rebirth," *Indian Philosophical Annual* 1 (1967): 103-7; S. Chennakesavan, "Critique of the Doctrine of Rebirth," *Indian Philosophical Annual* 1 (1965): 143-47; S. Iswarananda, "Does the Soul Reincarnate?" Indian Philosophical Annual 1: 9-15; T. P. Meenakshisundaram, "Common Folk of Tamilnad and Theory of Karma and Rebirth," Indian Philosophical Annual 1 (1965): 24-31; K. Mishra, "Person in the Light of Pratyabhijna Philosophy," *Indian Philosophical Annual* 8 (1972): 206-12; H. Narain, "The Microcosmic Concept of Person," *Indian Philosophical Annual* 8 (1972): 187-93; S. S. Sastri, "Does the Soul Reincarnate?"

praana (vitality, breath), and *manas* (mind) provide a sort of "empirical home" for the soul.[4] This, however, may seem not to be the case with Vishishtaadvaita of Raamaanujaachaarya (1017?-1137), for whom the self-body analogy, or what is called *shariira-shariirii-bhaava*, is of crucial importance for understanding the God-world relationship, in which, though the world is contingent, it is said to be related to God through all eternity.[5] The difficulty, however, is that for Raamaanujaachaarya the ultimate state of liberation is *videeha mukti* (*mukti* without the body), and he does not accept the possibility of *jiivanmukti*, i.e., the ultimate liberation while still being in the body.[6] This then would mean

---

Indian Philosophical Annual 1 (1965): 160-63; R. J. Singh, "Karmic Idealism of the Jainas," Indian Philosophical Annual 1 (1965): 20-23.

4. M. Hiriyanna, *Outlines of Indian Philosophy* (London: Allen & Unwin, 1949), pp. 68-69. He further observes that in the Upanishadic thought both cosmic and acosmic views of the relationship between Brahman and the world are present — according to the former the Absolute is all-comprehensive *(Brahma-parinaamavaada)* and as per the latter the Absolute is all-exclusive *(Brahama-vivarta-vaada,* i.e., Brahman merely appearing as the world; pp. 62-63). See also p. 419. J. Arapura, "An Approach to the Indian Belief in Rebirth," *Bangalore Theological Forum* 26, no. 2 (June 1994): 35-48.

5. E. J. Lott, *God and the Universe in the Vedantic Theology of Ramanuja: A Study in His Use of the Self-Body Analogy* (Madras: Ramanuja Research Society, 1976). Lott, *Vedantic Approaches to God* (London and Basingstoke: Macmillan, 1980), pp. 27-65. Lott, "Finite Self and Supreme Being: Vedantic Types of Analogical Method," *Bangalore Theological Forum* 11, no. 1 (January-June 1979): 2-35. In this regard, Lott writes: "For Ramanuja, *Brahman* understood as the 'whole' is the point of reference for determining how the constituent 'parts' are related. This position seems to preserve for Ramanuja both the real and integral character of the universal whole, and also the substantial dependence of all the 'parts' upon the being of *Brahman,* and thus his supremacy in every way. This ontological viewpoint corresponds exactly with the organic analogy." Lott, *God and the Universe,* p. 223. See also his article, "The Ecological Body: An Epiphanic Image for Mission," in *Mission with the Marginalized: Life and Witness of Rev. Dr. Prasanna Kumari Samuel,* ed. S. W. Meshack (Tiruvalla: Christava Sahitya Samaj, 2007), p. 337; see also pp. 324-45. Lott, after dealing with the understanding of body in various religious traditions in the Indian context, including in Christian thought, concludes that "no tradition, therefore, seems to be without some degree of body-ambivalence." While this would be, in broad terms, acceptable, this overlooks the nature and extent of body-ambivalence in different traditions. See further A. H. Overzee, *The Body Divine: The Symbol of the Body in the Works of Teilhard de Chardin and Ramanuja* (Cambridge: Cambridge University Press, 1992).

6. For a discussion on this, see S. S. Raghavachar, *Introduction to the Vedarthasangraha of Sree Ramanujacharya* (Mangalore: The Mangalore Trading Association, 1957), pp. 134-38. A. S. Gupta, *A Critical Study of the Philosophy of Ramanuja* (Varanasi: The Chowkhamba Sanskrit Series Office, 1967), pp. 131-32. Eric J. Lott holds that in view of the *shariira-shariirii bhaava* of Raamaanuja, the body-soul relationship has significance also in the soul's final state (email responses from E. Lott, dated October 17 and 27, 2005, for which I am thankful). While this would be true at the cosmic level, it is rather doubtful whether body is organically integral

that, while at the macrocosmic level God has the world of sentient and non-sentient beings as God's body, which is understood in terms of instrumentality

---

to the individual soul/self in its final state, i.e., *mooksha*, as per Raamaanuja. In this regard, the following points may be noted: (1) In the body-soul analogy/model, Raamaanuja lays the emphasis on the relationship between the supreme Self and the individual selves. (Anne H. Overzee clearly states that in Ramanuja the primary category in terms of ontological reality is the self, "and not the body, and that the Supreme Self and its relation to the individual self is referred to first. This is the primary 'analogue,' not the human body-self relation. . . ." *The Body Divine*, p. 99). (2) The main purpose of this analogy is soteriological (i.e., the Self-realization, in which the distinction between the Supreme Self and the individual selves would remain) and not cosmological, though this has important cosmological implications. (3) Insofar as Raamaanuja clearly denies *jiivanmukti* and thinks in terms of *videehamukti,* the prakritic body does not seem to have any ultimate significance in his thought at the microcosmic level and does not seem to be organically integral to the continued being of the individual souls in the state of *mukti,* though the souls in this state may express themselves through *sattva/shuddasatva,* which is an element of matter. (For *Sattva/Suddhasatva* see: *To Christ through the Vedanta: The Writings of P. Johanns,* compiled by T. de Greeff, series ed. Joseph Patmury [Bangalore: United Theological College, 1996], pp. 100-108.) According to Dr. Wilson Edattukaran, who holds the view that for Raamaanuja the body is something constitutive of the *jiiva,* it need not be the *prakritic* or material body, but can be the pure transparent *(suddhasatva)* body of the liberated soul (email dated December 11, 2007, for which I am thankful). On the question of *Prakriti* and its two forms, see M. R. Sampathkumaran, *The Gitabhashya of Ramanuja* (Madras: Prof. M. Rangacharya Memorial Trust, 1969), p. xi (VII.4-5); also: pp. xiii-xiv and 199-200. In this light, one might argue that it is only the gross material body, the body of *karma,* that would not be integral to the *jiiva*/self in the liberated state of final *mukti,* but a body made of a different kind of substance still would be integral. This, however, does not seem to be the case, when one reads Ramanuja carefully: The body seems to have only an instrumental, which too is dispensable, role in the liberated state. R. D. Karmarkar points out, in the "Introduction" to *Sribhashya of Ramanuja,* edited by him (Poona: University of Poona Sanskrit and Prakrit Series, vol. 1, part 1, 1959), p. xxxi: "The 'Liberated Soul' can enjoy all that he wishes for, in the *Vaikuntha* in any form which he commands at will or even without a body." This point becomes clear in Raamaanuja's *Sri Bhashyam,* trans. V. K. Ramanujachari, vol. 2 (Kumbakonam: Published by the translator, 1930), IV, 4, 5, pp. 907-8. Here one may note that the freed jiiva can either have a body or can be without a body; it can create a body for itself for its enjoyment or can be without a body; it can also remain in one body and pervade all other bodies. These are the various possibilities for the freed jiiva. All this makes the above point clear that for Ramanuja body is *instrumental but not constitutive in the ultimate liberated state.* In a way, it might appear a little strange that, though for Raamaanuja both sentient and nonsentient beings together constitute the body of God, the *prakritic* dimension of reality does not have any ultimate and organically integral and constitutive significance at the microcosmic level of the individual soul. But, then, we need to realize that he has a distinct definition of the "body" that lends itself to understand the self also as the "body" of God, and to use the "body" in his analogy for understanding the relationship between Brahman and the selves/souls/*jiivas,* as well as Brahman and the world.

— body, analogically speaking, is that which is dependent on the soul and is wholly controlled by the soul for its purpose,[7] — at the microscopic level of the individual selves the body is not constitutive as an integral dimension of the soul/self in the ultimate liberated state. Sri Aurobindo Ghosh of Pondicherry (1872-1950), who was also influenced by modern Western thought, adopted an evolutionary frame of reference in developing his understanding of Indian philosophy. For him matter, life, mind, and spirit stand in an evolutionary ascending order. This needs a radical change of the entire human nature, leading from mind to supermind, and nature to supernature. Though Aurobindo holds on to the identity of Brahman and Self, for him the ultimate goal is not just the liberation of the soul, but the mastery over nature and the transformation for a greater perfection in the earthly existence itself. According to him, future evolution will effect the necessary mutation of the body. He also thinks of matter in terms of higher *prakriti* or nature.[8] We also need to note that the Indian subaltern traditions, particularly the Dalit tradition, suggest that they take the bodily dimension of the human being seriously.[9]

7. A. J. Appasamy is here referring to Raamaanuja's *Sri Bhashya*, II, I, 9. Appasamy, *The Gospel and India's Heritage* (London: SPCK, 1942), p. 206. According to Ramanuja, a proper definition, which will cover all cases is: "A body is that substance, which an intelligent person in every way supports, controls and uses for his own purposes, and which exists only to serve him." Raamaanuja, *Sri Bhashyam,* translated by D. B.Ramanujachari, vol. 2, chapters 2-4 (Kumbakonam: Published by the Author, 1930), pp. 458-59. Lott quotes Raamaanuja: "Any entity that an intelligent being is able completely to control and support for its own purposes, and the essential nature of which is entirely subservient to that self, is its body." Lott, *Vedantic Approaches to God,* p. 48.

8. S. Aurobindo, *The Future Evolution of Man: The Divine Life upon Earth,* compiled with a summary and notes by P. B. Saint-Hilaire (Pondicherry: Sri Aurobindo Ashram, 1963), 11, pp. 147-48.

9. V. Devasahayam, *Doing Dalit Theology in Biblical Key* (Madras: Gurukul, 1997), pp. 39-40. (This originally appeared in V. Devasahayam, ed., *Frontiers of Dalit Theology* [New Delhi/Madras: ISPCK & Gurukul, 1997]; Devasahayam, *Outside the Camp: Bible Studies in Dalit Perspective* [Madras: Gurukul, 1997], p. 54.) Referring to the Tamil classical literature, in the conclusion of his book on Indian Christian anthropology, D. W. Jesudoss makes the following remark: "The author has tried to write his anthropology in which attempt he has used many Indian terms — both Sanskrit and Tamil. Usually he has criticized the Indian view of man as that which does not treat the body of man as God's 'good' creation but is only a prison of the soul. Though this may be the general trend in India, there are exceptions also. It is surprising to note that the early Dravidian literature, namely Tirukkural of Tiruvalluvar, seems to show another strand of thought, i.e., that the body of man and his soul are like bride and bridegroom. The following Kurals support such a view, viz. Kural 330, 940, and 1122." D. W. Jesudoss, *What Is Man? Theological Attempts and Directions Towards the Formation of an Indian Christian Anthropology Today* (Madras: Gurukul, 1986), p. 223. For an Indian Christian

The Indian socio-economico-political life is characterized by a secular, democratic, and socialist pattern of society, on the one hand, and a stratified society, in which, at the people's level, the caste-structure continues to pervade the Indian psyche in various subtle and not-so-subtle ways. In this context, militant communal forces seek to establish their power and impose their ideology. While the middle class is growing, urban population is increasing, and in some of the economic spheres of life India is doing well, the gap between the rich and the poor is not narrowing, and in fact is understood to be increasing. In this context, poverty continues to be a serious challenge. So also is the lack of adequate healthcare. As the agricultural sector is not given due importance, there is an increasing number of suicides among the farmers (also among the weavers), due to the debt-trap. Women, in spite of the constitutionally guaranteed equal rights and some significant improvement in certain spheres of life, still face, both socially and culturally, various kinds of discrimination. All this has serious implications, especially for the bodily dimension of life.[10]

2.

Against this background, we shall now turn to consider the concept of body in Indian Christian theological thought. First, we shall take a look at a few select attempts in the nineteenth and the twentieth centuries, and then take into account select subaltern theologians in the present-day Indian context.

A. S. Appasamy [Appaasaamy] (1848-1926), with his background in Shaiva

anthropology, Jesudoss suggests the following components: Man as *Yogi,* Man as *Bhaktayogi,* Man as *Karmayogi,* Man as *Gnanayogi,* and Man as *Anban,* i.e., Man in Love or Man Come of Age. Jesudoss understands the term "Yogi" in its etymological sense, and uses it to refer to Man as Body-Spirit/Soul unity; see pp. 146-222. K. P. Aleaz presents a "convergence" of Advaita Vedanta and Eastern Christian thought, in *A Convergence of Advaita Vedanta and Eastern Christian Thought* (Delhi: ISPCK, 2000); see esp. pp. 288-98.

10. B. N. Banerjee, *My Great India: Economic Development and Glaring Disparities* (CBS Publishers, 2001). S. Bayly, *The New Cambridge History of India: Caste, Society and Politics in India from the Eighteenth Century to the Modern Age* (Cambridge: Cambridge University Press, 1999). C. T. Kurien, *Poverty, Planning and Social Transformation* (Bombay: Allied Publishers, 1978). J. Mattam and P. Arockiadoss, eds., *Malayalam Manorama Year Book 2009; Hindutva: An Indian Christian Response* (Bangalore: Dharmaram Publications, 2002). Amartya Sen, *The Argumentative Indian: Writings on History, Culture and Identity* (London: Penguin, 2005). K. L. Sharma, ed., *Social Inequality in India: Profiles of Caste, Class and Social Mobility* (Jaipur and New Delhi: Rawat Publications, 1999, Reprint 2001). Y. Singh, *Social Stratification and Change in India,* revised ed. (New Delhi: Manohar, 1997, reprint 2002).

Siddhaanta, thought of Jesus Christ as the Son having the original form of pure light, who, for the sake of granting *darshana* (vision) to his devotees, assumed a spiritual body, which he calls *suukshma shariira*. This according to him is the prototype and origin of Jesus' physical body that he assumed at his incarnation.[11]

Brahmabandhab Upadhyaya [Brahmabandhab Upaadhyaaya] (1861-1907), who was well versed in Veedic and Veedantic thought and was influenced by Thomistic theology, first sought to interpret Christian faith in relation to the Veedic and later to Veedantic thought. He in fact took over the composite nature of human being, adopting the Indian philosophical view of five sheaths or *kooshaas,* presided over by a personality, which is a reflected spark of the Supreme Reason.[12] Though a basic dualistic understanding of body and soul is present in his thought,[13] as a Christian thinker he has a positive view of the human body: though defiled by sin, the body can become the temple of the Spirit of God by virtue of the sanctifying grace infused into the soul by God. After death it is buried, so that it may rise as a spiritual body.[14] He also holds the view that souls are immortal not by nature but by the will of God.[15]

Sadhu [Saadhu] Sundar Singh (1889-1929) came from the Sikh religious background and contributed towards the Christian *bhakti* strand of thought. With a strong mystical-spiritual inclination, his anthropology has some dualistic traits. At the same time, he holds that the Spirit pervades the whole body. His positive view of the human body becomes evident when he asserts that "Christ rose in the same body in which He was crucified. It is sin alone that brings corruption to the body and makes it unfit for entering heaven. But Christ's body was without fault and spotless, and after He had conquered death it was changed into a glorious body; and, in that glorious body, He is seated with God on His throne (Rev. 3:21)."[16] This has implications for his theological

11. K. Baago, *Pioneers of Indigenous Christianity* (Bangalore/Madras: CISRS & CLS, 1969), p. 116.

12. J. Lipner and G. Gispert-Sauch, eds., *The Writings of Brahmabandhab Upadhyay*, vol. 1 (Bangalore: UTC, 1991), pp. 190, 293.

13. Lipner and Gispert-Sauch, eds., *The Writings of Brahmabandhab Upadhyay*, vol. 1, p. 252.

14. Lipner and Gispert-Sauch, eds., *The Writings of Brahmabandhab Upadhyay*, vol. 1, p. 290. In this connection, Upadhyay's view of burial and cremation is interesting — the former showing a positive view towards the body and the latter a negative view.

15. Lipner and Gispert-Sauch, eds., *The Writings of Brahmabandhab Upadhyay*, vol. 1, pp. 290-91.

16. F. T. Dayanandan, ed., *The Christian Witness of Sadhu Sundar Singh: A Collection of his Writings* (Madras: CLS, 1989), p. 166. M. Biehl, *Der Fall Sadhu Sundar Singh: Theologie zwischen den Kulturen* (Frankfurt am Main: Peter Lang, 1988), pp. 200-203.

anthropology. The objective of the incarnation is to "bring again" those whom he created in his own image into glorious bodies like his own, whom he can admit into his fellowship and eternal kingdom.[17] This clearly indicates that the body in its glorified form is included in the heavenly life.[18]

Vengal Chakkarai (1880-1958) was a prominent member of the Madras Rethinking Group. For Chakkarai, physical resurrection of Jesus Christ is very important. Though he makes use of the Indian philosophical term *suukshma shariira* (subtle body), he takes care to make the distinction clear as regards what it refers to in Christian faith:

> The Hindu idea is not analogous to the Pauline anthropology; the former asserts a *sukshma sarira* behind or beyond every *sthula sarira* in every man; it is a natural endowment, that is, a ghost or wraith with certain forms. When a man ceases to live, it is this subtle body that goes with him. Now in the Pauline view — it is only he that discusses this somewhat mysterious body — the body of the spirit — or body given by the spirit — is a new creation, or gift conferred on the believer. . . . It is a supernatural, not an existing reality — but a reality yet to be. That is why Jesus died and rose again; it is through Him that such a body is to be given — He is the first fruits. This change is the supreme manifestation, even the redemption of the body — the transformation of this lowly body (not vile as the Authorized Version has it) changed into His glorious body.[19]

According to Chakkarai, this is very different from the belief in the natural immortality of a human being. "Therefore the Resurrection is an addition to life, not elimination or extinction of the essential humanity that is now embodied into the Divine Nature by the ascended Lord."[20]

17. T. Dayanandan Francis, ed., *The Christian Witness of Sadhu Sundar Singh: A Collection of His Writings* (Madras: Christian Literature Society, 1993), p. 166.

18. At the same time, Sundar Singh also expressed his view, while speaking about Christians, that there is a spiritual body within, which comes out after death and then goes to the Second or the Third Heaven. In a few cases of those who have lived very close to Christ, their physical body itself will be transformed into a spiritual body and will be taken up to heaven. In the case of Jesus Christ also his physical body was transformed into a spiritual body in which he went to heaven. Here, in the former case, the idea of the spiritual body seems to come close to *suukshma shariira* of the Indian philosophical thought, with the difference that in the Indian philosophical thought, generally speaking, *suukshma shariira* does not partake in the ultimate state of liberation. Moreover, there is also the element of transformation. The eschatological dimension, however, seems to be weak. See K. Baago, *Pioneers of Indigenous Christianity*, p. 162.

19. P. T. Thomas, ed., *Vengal Chakkarai*, vol. 2 (Bangalore: UTC, 1992), pp. 307-8, 306.

20. Thomas, ed., *Vengal Chakkarai*, vol. 2, pp. 310-11. It may be noted that the Syrian

Pandipeddi Chenchiah (1886-1959) was another very prominent member of the Madras Rethinking Group. He contributed substantively to Indian Christian theological thought. The Incarnation and the Resurrection of Jesus Christ stand at the very center of his theological thought. Over against Advaita Veedanta, he stressed that ultimate salvation is to be found not by bypassing or going behind the created order of being. It has to be understood in terms of the creation reaching its ultimate goal by becoming a new creation, through the new cosmic energy, the Holy Spirit, which entered the created order of being through the incarnation and the resurrection of Jesus Christ, the Son of Man. In Jesus, the entire creation mounted a step higher, and he is the first fruits of the new creation and all are invited to become "Christs" in and through him. For this, what is needed is a new Saadhana, i.e., a new yoga [*yooga*], in order to avail oneself of the new cosmic energy and thereby become a part of the new creation. In this connection, Chenchiah strongly emphasizes the permanent nature of the incarnation and of the humanity that was assumed by Jesus. According to Chenchiah, the human body of Jesus has entered the sphere of the Spirit, and the Second Person in the Trinity is hereafter Jesus, the Son of Man. For Chenchiah salvation is not merely liberation from sin, but also from death, and this is central to Christian faith.

In view of this, he sought to develop a Christian Yoga called "Amrita Yoga" (yoga of immortality) or "Parishuddaatma Yoga" (yoga of the Holy Spirit). Its purpose is "to reproduce Christ in men, to beget Christians, to temple [the] Holy Spirit in the body of Man."[21] This shows how significant and integral the body was for Chenchiah's theology.[22] "The New Man, the

---

Orthodox Indian Christian thinker Paulos Mar Gregorios (1922-1996) emphasizes that new humanity, which is the incarnate humanity, is inseparably united with the whole creation and to the Creator. P. M. Gregorios, *The Human Presence: An Orthodox View of Nature* (Geneva: WCC, 1978), p. 8. Surjit Singh, coming from the Sikh background, focuses on the issue of the individuality in relation to the Absolute in critical interaction with the thought of S. Radhakrishnan. S. Singh, *Preface to Personality: Christology in Relation to Radhakrishnan's Philosophy* (Madras: CLS, 1952), pp. 92-110.

21. Chenchiah, "Problems of Indian Christian Community," *The Guardian*, 1942, p. 391.

22. O. V. Jathanna, *The Decisiveness of the Christ-Event and the Universality of Christianity in a World of Religious Plurality* (Bern/Frankfurt am Main/Las Vegas: Peter Lang, 1981), pp. 386-404. It may be noted that Chenchiah developed his theological thought in critical interaction with the Vitalist Philosophy of Henri Bergson, *Vishuddaadvaita of Vallabha and the New Yoga Experimenters, Sri Aurobindo Ghosh and Master CVV of Kumbakonam*. See also D. A. Thangasamy, *The Theology of Chenchiah* (Bangalore: CISRS and YMCA, 1966). On Vallabha see T. de Greeff (compiler), *To Christ through the Vedanta: The Writings of P. Johanns*, vol. 1, pp. 207-360; see esp. pp. 282-84. Vallabha held the view that God himself owns a body and that

Son of God, is not a spirit but also body — the body being a transfigured body like the resurrection-body of Jesus."[23] According to Chenchiah, the human being is still in the making. In his "revolutionary evolution," the lower is not canceled or dissolved. "Matter," for example, is not dropped but transformed.[24] In fact, Chenchiah's emphasis on the integral nature of the human body in all eternity in a manner appropriate to the new creation comes to focus in his discussion on yoga, in critical dialogue with the traditional forms of yoga. He finds all forms of traditional yoga, namely Raaja Yoga, Hata Yoga, and Tantra Yoga, not to be helpful as all these have one ultimate goal, namely that of seeking ultimate liberation from and beyond the created order of being. With great insight, he pointed out that not only Raaja Yoga, but also Hata Yoga and Tantra Yoga, which take the human body seriously in the process of yogic practice, in fact have as their goal the cutting off of all retreat back to life, by burning all the karmic residues. Hence, only their starting points are different, not their goal. Chenchiah was attracted to Sri Aurobindo Ghosh [Goosh] and Master CVV of Kumbakonam because they sought to develop a new and different kind of yoga, with a different goal, which, as Chenchiah saw, took the physical and the material dimension seriously without neglecting the Spirit.[25] It is in view of this, as was pointed out, Chenchiah sought to develop a Christian yoga, which would take the material, physical, and the historical dimensions seriously. Hence, he says: "redemption is the clothing of the spirit within immortal body and not merely the negative escape from sin or sins. . . . A yoga of annihilation of creation does not suit the aspiration to perfect creation. We do not desire to move backwards into the origin. We march onwards to an end which is a consummation and perfection."[26]

A. J. Appasamy (1891-1975) interpreted the Christian faith in relation to Raamaanujaachaarya's Vishishtaadvaita and is a prominent Indian Christian thinker, standing in the *bhakti* strand of thought. He was also influenced by

---

he is the subject and object of spiritual senses, which, however, are beatific and immaterial, unlike our own senses. According to P. Johanns, this theory of the spiritual body may be the most important part of Vallabha's system. To see God we need to assume a *nirguna* body, which works within a mental frame, made all of *aananda* or of divine matter, and not the coarse body or the subtle body. De Greeff (compiler), *To Christ through the Vedanta*, pp. 282-84.

23. Chenchiah, "Sri Aurobindo — His Message," p. 52.

24. Chenchiah, "Sri Aurobindo — His Message," p. 52.

25. D. A. Thangasamy, *The Theology of Chenchiah* (Bangalore: CISRS and YMCA, 1966), pp. 268-88.

26. Thangasamy, *The Theology of Chenchiah*, pp. 282-83.

Sadhu Sundar Singh. As we have noted earlier, for Raamaanuja the self-body analogy was important in understanding the relationship between God and the world. Appasamy holds the view that God assumes four kinds of bodies: the world of nature; the fleshly organism of Jesus Christ; the eucharistic bread and wine; and the church.[27] He uses the terms *mind, soul,* and *spirit* synonymously.[28] He takes "historicality" of human existence seriously and in this connection sees the importance of the body.[29] For him the continuation of the human personality into eternity is important.[30] In his view, the resurrection of Jesus Christ primarily has to do not with the glorified body, but with his messiahship and divinity.[31] Appasamy stresses the supremacy of the spirit over the body and acknowledges the instrumental nature of the body.[32] At the same time, what is important for us to note is that, in the light of the resurrection of Jesus Christ, Appasamy comes to the conclusion that transition from the physical to the spiritual is not impossible and there is no chasm between them.[33] In fact, they are closely related, though having their own characteristic features.[34] This transition, however, does not mean rejection of the human body, but the surmounting of the limitations of the ordinary physical body, while remaining within reach of the senses.[35]

Paul D. Devanandan [Deevaanandan] (1901-1962) stressed, as noted by M. M. Thomas, the need for a new anthropology with its concepts of personality and of justice in community and in history, which is capable of providing an adequate basis for the renewal of the society, both at personal and corporate

27. A. J. Appasamy, *The Gospel and India's Heritage* (London/Madras: SPCK, 1942), pp. 206-8.

28. Appasamy, *The Johannine Doctrine of Life: A Study of Christian and Indian Thought* (London: SPCK, 1934), p. 168.

29. Appasamy, *The Gospel and India's Heritage,* p. 263.

30. Appasamy, *Christianity as Bhakti Marga: A Study of the Johannine Doctrine of Love* (Madras: CLS for India, 1926), pp. 76, 79.

31. Appasamy, *The Gospel and India's Heritage,* p. 244.

32. Appasamy, *The Gospel and India's Heritage,* pp. 204-6. This resembles Raamanuja's view. On Appasamy, see also R. H. S. Boyd, *An Introduction to Indian Christian Theology* (New Delhi: ISPCK, 1989), pp. 138-43. At this point, we may note that Manilal Parek, who came from the Jain religious background, held the view that, though the human body is integral to the human being, it is secondary. He identifies the risen body of Jesus Christ with the subtle body and expressed his view that the resurrection of the body with the soul is a queer idea. R. H. S. Boyd, *Manilal C. Parekh 1885-1967, Dhanjibhai Farikbhai 1895-196* (Madras: CLS, 1974), pp. 140-41, 165-66.

33. Appasamy, *Christianity as Bhakti Marga,* p. 141.

34. Appasamy, *The Gospel and India's Heritage,* p. 152.

35. Appasamy, *The Gospel and India's Heritage,* pp. 141-42.

levels. Devanandan found this basis in the new creation that emerged from the crucified and the risen Christ, because of God's identification with humans in all human struggles for perfecting and realizing the true human nature. Devanandan developed his theology of the new creation in critical dialogue with the Indian renascent religious thought and secular ideologies in India.[36] The human being is essentially a being-in-community, and one can be truly a human being only in a new order of human relationship. He says: "Wrong ideas about the high caste and the low caste, the silly notions about man's superiority over woman, and the like had to go. . . . What is really needed is a change of heart, a new spirit, a new way of thinking about man and about life in this world. A somewhat high-sounding phrase commonly used by Indian people today is 'socialistic pattern of society.' Whatever else it may mean, it certainly stands for 'a new order in human relations in which man can be truly man.'"[37] Devanandan's theological anthropology is derived from his Christology and ecclesiology. His basic concern, thus, was with human beings in the context of life together, life in the human community. The importance of the human body must be understood in this context and in the context of the reality of God's purposeful creation, which is destined to be renewed into a new creation.

M. M. Thomas (1916-1996) in his own way further developed the insights of P. D. Devanandan. M. M. Thomas's theological anthropology may be described as a Christ-centered humanism. His main concern is the struggle for fuller humanity, and fuller humanity is understood in the light of the incarnation, death, and resurrection of Jesus Christ, which provide the struggle for fuller humanity not only with the needed basis but also with the needed criteria. The building up of a just and participatory society is integral to fuller humanity. In Thomas's thought, humanization and salvation are related in terms of what is penultimate and ultimate. For him, person-in-community, sense of historical purpose of self-fulfillment, a realistic relation between power, justice, and love, and open secularism are the elements of a new humanism.[38] With this theological concern, Thomas has developed a theological frame of

36. M. M. Thomas and P. T. Thomas, *Towards an Indian Christian Theology: Life and Thought of Some Pioneers* (Tiruvalla: The New Day Publications of India, 1992), pp. 188-90.

37. J. Wietzke, ed., *Paul D. Devanandan*, vol. 2 (Bangalore: UTC, 1987), p. 49. Devanandan, *Preparation for Dialogue: Dialogue: A Collection of Essays on Hinduism and Christianity in New India* (Bangalore: CISRS, 1964), pp. 148-49.

38. H. T. Wolters, *Theology of Prophetic Participation: M. M. Thomas' Concept of Salvation and the Collective Struggle for Fuller Humanity in India* (New Delhi/Bangalore: ISPCK & UTC, 1996), p. 214. Thomas also describes self-understanding of the human being in terms of creativity, self-identity, historical mission, and ecumenism (p. 216); see also pp. 172-231.

reference in active dialogue with the renascent religious thought in India, with various ideologies both in India and outside India, and with ecumenical Christian theological thought. While the human being is a part of nature, he/ she also transcends nature by way of a faith-response to the ultimate. Thus, Thomas asserts: "Man's selfhood is poised between nature and spirit."[39] For Thomas's understanding of the human being, the body is integral. He is critical of Mahatma Gandhi [Mahaatma Gaandhi], who equated the essential self of the human being with the aatman and consequently rejected the body and matter as the source of all selfishness, without being able to see the sources of evil present in spiritual self-righteousness.[40] Thomas makes the important point that the physical body can be understood only in relation to the total human person: "It is not possible to deal with the physical body unrelated to the total human person. The body is an integral part of the personality. The humans express the social character of their personhood through the needs of the body. It is through the body that they either glorify God or serve as slaves of devilish forces; that means the body is certainly a spiritual reality."[41] For him the personality or personhood is a combination of body, mind, and spirit, as well as its social relationships.[42] He firmly holds the view that the Christian's ultimate hope is not unrelated to the body, and this comes from the knowledge of the cross and the resurrection of Jesus Christ.[43] Thomas is equally emphatic on the integral nature of the human body for the human being, as well as on the need for the transformation of the body by putting on the immortal spiritual body in Christ: "It is neither humans with mortal bodies

39. M. M. Thomas, *Man and the Universe of Faiths* (Madras: CLS, 1975), p. 148; see also pp. 21-26.

40. M. M. Thomas, *The Acknowledged Christ of the Indian Renaissance,* 2nd ed. (Madras: CLS, 1970/1976), p. 224. In Thomas's view, Gandhi was not able to move from principles to the person, because of not taking seriously the dimension of sin and the need of divine forgiveness (p. 239); see also pp. 222-39.

41. M. M. Thomas, *Spiritual Body: I Corinthians,* trans, T. M. Philip (Tiruvalla/Bangalore: CSS Books & BTTBPSA, 2005), p. 22.

42. Thomas, *Spiritual Body,* p. 22.

43. Thomas, *Spiritual Body,* p. 22. See also T. M. Philip, *The Encounter Between Theology and Ideology: An Exploration into the Communicative Theology of M. M. Thomas* (Madras: CLS, 1986), esp. pp. 67-70. T. M. Philip quotes M. M. Thomas: "The bodily resurrection of Jesus indicates the glorification of the personhood of Jesus who is crucified in his physical body. There is no personhood without body. The resurrection of Jesus marks the inauguration of a new humanity in the midst of history" (p. 68). Again: "The new being, the new self, denotes a new human nature itself. It involves the renewal of heart and mind. . . . It involves also renewal of *the body,* as part of man's personality. No doubt as in all else, we wait for the resurrection of the body, when our vile bodies will be fashioned like unto His glorious body (Phil. 3:21)" (p. 69).

nor souls having no body that inherit eternity, but the humans who have discarded natural body of perishable nature and put on immortal spiritual body, in Christ. That means body is an integral part of human personhood in the present as well as in the future (today, tomorrow and in eternity)."[44] It is clear that for Thomas this is not identical with *suukshma shariira,* which is hidden behind the *sthuula shariira* as a given, but it is a gift of God.[45]

Sebastian Kappen [Kaappen] (1924-1993), a Roman Catholic theologian, representing a radical "liberationist" strand of theological thought, understands body and soul in the light of Hebrew thought — soul and body "each standing for the person as the whole." What we refer to as "body" (corresponding to *basar*) is the outwardness of what we call the "soul" (corresponding to *nepes*), the inwardness of the body.[46] *Ruach* is spirit, understood as "the power of God that has become the power of man in the measure in which the latter is open to the call of the Divine," which as power is contrasted with flesh as powerlessness."[47] For him, "bodily functions have meaning only inasmuch as they are drawn into the orbit of man's dialogue with God."[48] "If the body can occasion man's estrangement from God, so can estrangement from God rob the body and the senses of their authentic function . . . (Mk. 8:17-18)."[49] He sees the alienation of the body at various levels, and understands the ministry of Jesus as that of bringing wholeness and integration to human persons, "renewing the within and the without of man," which includes the power to commune with nature, with men, and with God.[50] Kappen calls it "humanization."[51]

In the contemporary Indian Christian theological scene, there is a renewed interest in, and concern for, the human body. It is not just the embodied nature of human existence, but also its social, economic, ecological, gender, and caste-ethnic-class dimensions that are taken into account. J. Jayakiran Sebastian, for example, while reflecting on the care of HIV/AIDS survivors, looks at the

44. Philip, *The Encounter Between Theology and Ideology,* p. 23.

45. Thomas notes that, while in the ancient Hindu *Veedantic* thought the entire emphasis was on the soul, and the state of ultimate salvation was entirely unrelated to the realities of day-to-day living, in the modern times there are reinterpretations in this regard, under the impact of Christian thought and Western civilization, as well as under the pressure of the democratic socialistic politics of modern India (p. 25).

46. S. Kappen, *Jesus and Society: Selected Writings of Sebastian Kappen, S.J.,* vol. 2 (Delhi: ISPCK, 2002), p. 21.

47. Kappen, *Jesus and Society,* p. 22.

48. Kappen, *Jesus and Society,* p. 24.

49. Kappen, *Jesus and Society,* p. 25.

50. Kappen, *Jesus and Society,* pp. 26-27.

51. Kappen, *Jesus and Society,* p. 27.

human body not in isolation but in the societal context. In this connection, in order to take cognizance of "all that has been imbibed and which informs our existential present," he looks at the understanding of the human body in the early church, considering the body of the martyr, the body of the ascetic, and the body of the celibate.[52] We shall now briefly consider the understanding of the body in the present-day Indian subaltern theological streams of thought.

One of the leading contemporary Dalit Christian theologians, V. Devasahayam [Deevasahaayam], expresses his opinion that traditional theologies, both in India and in the West, did not give adequate importance to the redemption of the body, because of the dualistic understanding of the constitution of the human being, emphasizing the spirit.[53] He derives his understanding of the body from Christology: "Christian faith is built on the Word's assumption of the body. . . . He took care of his body. . . . He was concerned about feeding the hungry ones and healing the sick of their bodily ailments. Paul says that the process of New Creation is characterized with groans against bodily violations while waiting for the redemption of the body."[54] For Paul, the body is the temple of the Holy Spirit.[55] Devasahayam notes that the body is still the vehicle of oppression,[56] and he draws the attention of the reader to the contemporary reality of the human body, particularly of the Dalit woman's body, and says: "Abortion, female infanticide, neglect of females in provision of food, dowry deaths, genital mutilation, sexual exploitation, torture, murder, hard work, and treatment as the property of the other are some of the glaring violations against the sacredness of human person and of the human body."[57] He demands that "theology should endeavour to create a sense of reverence for human body, especially of women, as if it were Christ's own body."[58]

Shimreingam Shimray deals with the issue of human rights in tribal Christian theology. Though he does not deal with the body as such, it is clear that human rights violation is also violation against the body, including muti-

---

52. J. Jayakiran Sebastian, "The Wounded Body in Early Christian Thought: Implications for the Care of HIV/AIDS Survivors," *Bangalore Theological Forum* 33, no. 1 (June 2001): 151-57.

53. V. Devasahayam, *Doing Dalit Theology in Biblical Key* (Madras: Gurukul, 1977), p. 39. This view, of course, has to be qualified.

54. Devasahayam, *Doing Dalit Theology in Biblical Key,* p. 39.

55. Devasahayam, *Doing Dalit Theology in Biblical Key,* p. 40.

56. V. Devasahayam, *Outside the Camp: Bible Studies in Dalit Perspective* (Madras: Gurukul, 1997), p. 54.

57. V. Devasahayam, *Doing Dalit Theology in Biblical Key,* p. 40.

58. Devasahayam, *Doing Dalit Theology in Biblical Key.* See also V. Devasahayam, ed., *Frontiers of Dalit Theology* (Delhi/Madras: ISPCK and Gurukul, 1997).

lating the human body.[59] Nungshitula, a tribal woman theologian, expresses her view that the present Ao Naga [Aaoo Naaga] Christian Anthropology is dichotomous as regards the body and the soul, the spiritual and the material, this world and the other world. In this context, she shows her concern for developing a holistic and integrated Christian anthropology with the help of the traditional Ao Naga anthropology, which she presents as being relational, integrating, and evolving.[60] O. Alem Ao stresses the wholeness and the permanence of the person and the community dimension of life, with special emphasis on the relationship with God and with fellow human beings, as well as with other "creations."[61] For the Mizo [Mizoo] tribal Christian theologian K. Thanzauva, what is central to humanity is communitarianism. He understands the act of creation "not as what a potter or an artist does, but as 'bodying forth' as the mother does."[62]

Gabriele Dietrich, a naturalized Indian of German origin, speaks of the spirit being housed in matter, permeating all of nature, both in animated and nonanimated form. She also takes the community dimension seriously. For her the spirit is housed not only in matter but also in the human community, which implies that the human community is also seen as the body of the spirit. She holds that neither nature nor the human community can be reduced to the other, and, therefore, while human beings cannot subjugate nature, the human community also cannot be subsumed under nature. She thus sees the body as a comprehensive term that comprises both nature and the human community.[63]

59. S. Shimray, "Tribal Theology and Human Rights," *Tribal Theology: A Reader,* ed. S. Shimray and J. Assam (Tribal Study Centre, Eastern Theological College, 2003), pp. 152-65.

60. Nungshitula, *The Naga Images of the Human Being: A Resource for a Contemporary Theological Anthropology* (Jorhat: Tribal Study Centre, 2001); see esp. p. 146. Here, I think, the question is not whether the traditional Ao Naga "anthropology" is as holistic and integrating as the author has presented or not (since the interpretation sometimes seems to go beyond what one can find in the myths and stories that are presented), but the basic theological concern for developing a relational and integrating Christian anthropology in the given context.

61. O. Alem Ao. *Tsungremology: Ao Naga Chrsitian Theology* (Mokkokchung, Nagaland: Clark Theological College, 1994), p. 100.

62. K. Thanzauva. *Theology of Community: Tribal Theology in the Making* (Aizawl, Mizoram: Mizo Theological Conference, 1997), pp. 106-19. It may be noted that here we have briefly looked at only the Ao Naga and the Mizo writers, though there are different hill tribes and tribes from the plains in India, who have been contributing to tribal Christian theological thinking. I am thankful to Sangtemkala for drawing my attention to some of the resources on the subject matter in tribal Christian theological thought in the northeast Indian context.

63. G. Dietrich, "The World as the Body of God: Feminist Perspective on Ecology and Social Justice," in *A New Thing on Earth: Hopes and Fears Facing Feminist Theology (Theological Ruminations of a Feminist Activist)* (Delhi: ISPCK, Madurai, 2001), pp. 173-202. Also in *Journal*

Evangeline Anderson-Rajkumar [Raajkumaar], an Indian Christian woman theologian, looks at the body of a woman as a defining aspect of womanhood in the context of gender, physical, social, and economic oppression and discrimination, shaped and dictated by patriarchal ideology. She points out: "A woman's body serves as an excellent epistemological tool to analyze the experiences of women. The body has an identity; it is shaped by ideologies. The specific ideologies of casteism, capitalism, and colonialism play a vital role in the process of definition of the identity-ideology of a woman's body. The body of woman is undeniably the site of inscription, oppression, exploitation and violence. At the same time, it is also the instrument that women use, to show resistance, spirit of combat, solidarity, celebration and victory."[64] She notes that woman's identity is linked to the inscribed meanings and expectations on her body because of the dominance of patriarchy. The woman's body stands at the center of all experiences of violence against women, and she underlines the importance of the affirmation of the body. There is need to redefine the freedom, rights, and responsibilities of a woman over her body and sexuality, in order to reconstruct women's identity. This, however, cannot be done in abstraction, but only by taking the wider socio-economic and other factors into account.[65] Lalrinawmi Ralte [Lalrinoomi Raalte], reflects on the world as the body of God from an eco-feminist theological perspective in the context of tribal women in Mizoram, in light of the metaphor for the world as the "body of God" used by Sallie McFague, and concludes that "the metaphor of the world as the body of God leaves room for ecological responsibility."[66]

---

of Dharma 18, no. 3 (1993): 258-84. I am thankful to Dr. Monica Melanchthon for drawing my attention to this article.

64. E. A.-Rajkumar, "Significance of the 'Body' in Feminist Theological Discourse," *Bangalore Theological Forum* 33, no. 2 (December 2001): 98-99.

65. E. A.-Rajkumar, "Significance of the 'Body' in Feminist Theological Discourse," pp. 80-98. In a more recent article, Evangeline Anderson-Rajkumar seeks to embark upon a new basis for feminist Christology, by depoliticizing the ideologies of the body as an inscribed, lived, raced, and sexed body, and then by resignifying the body and rearticulating Christology in context within the body framework, in the light of the whole life and ministry of Jesus Christ as the fundamental resource for depoliticizing, as well as for resignifying/repoliticizing the body. A.-Rajkumar, "Politicizing the Body: A Feminist Christology," in *Asian Faces of Christ: Theological Colloquium*, ed. V. Tirimanna (Bangalore: Asian Trading Corporation, 2005), pp. 143-75. S. J. Samartha, in his article, "Images of the Human: A Search for Wholeness," *Asia Journal of Theology* 8, no. 2 (October 1994): 261-70, stresses the need to seek ways of living together as human beings in the global community. He presents the emerging new images of the male and the female, and the demand for the acceptance of the feminine as an essential part of the human, in the context of male-female relationship in society.

66. L. Ralte, "The World as the Body of God: Eco-feminist Theological Discourse of the

3.

After having taken into account the concept of body in the various strands of Indian Christian theological thought in the context of its thought-world, we shall now move on to reflect on it further, and make a few theological observations and suggestions, in view of formulating an Indian Christian understanding of the body in the present-day context.

In the Indian context, though there is a strong tendency to lay the emphasis on the soul/spirit, almost all the Indian Christian theological thinkers, representing various strands of theological thought, have taken the body to be integral to being human, including in the consummated state of salvation. At the same time, they underline the need for the transformation and glorification of the body, which is offered as a gracious gift of God in and through Jesus Christ.

In the contemporary theological scene, the body is increasingly considered, not in isolation, but in the context of interpersonal, communitarian, gender-relational, societal, economic, structural, and ecological dimensions of human existence. This has a salutary corrective as well as enriching value, as it helps bring to conscious level the exploitation, oppression, trampling on human dignity, violence, and the like, and calls for a concerted struggle against such a state of affairs. At the same time, in view of the rapidly secularized and economically globalized world, aggressively promoting consumerism, the emphasis on the body should not be worked out within a narrowly conceived "this-is-all-that-there-is" worldview, losing sight of a holistic view of the human person, created in and for the image of God. While the body is constitutively integral to the human person, it is significant precisely as an integral dimension of the wholeness of human personhood. Human personhood can neither be reduced to the body, nor appropriately conceived apart from the body. This manner of understanding of the human being would also help keep human beings from abusing others, including God's wider creation, as well as from abusing themselves. Thus, the cult of the body, on the one hand, and the rejection or denigration of the body, on the other, both need to be eschewed from a Christian faith perspective.

There is still further need to thematize, in the present-day Indian context, the integral nature of the human person in the light of the Christian understanding of the human and to work out the bodily, vitalist, psychic, spiritual,

---

South and North with Special Reference to Tribal Women," a paper presented in November 2007 at the Faculty Research Seminar, UTC, Bangalore (mimeographed typescript), p. 15.

interpersonal (including gender-related and age-related), societal, cosmic, and transcendental aspects of the human person in critical dialogue with Indian religio-cultural and socio-political life and thought, on the one hand, and insights from the natural and human sciences, on the other. What is needed is to develop an understanding of the complex human person as a created subject, whose identity is formed *coram Deo* in responsive interaction with God, on the one hand, and, simultaneously, responsible "convivence" with fellow human beings and the wider creation, on the other, without reducing personhood simply to a divine spark, a manifestation of the divine Self under name and form *(naama ruupa),* or an eternal soul-self, related to the bodily and psychic aspects only temporarily in the state of bondage, but essentially a bodiless reality in its supposedly true being.

Christian theological anthropology, for which new creation in Jesus Christ is pivotal, has to take the creation, the incarnation, the cross, and the resurrection seriously. This theological understanding, in turn, necessitates the making of the physical and the historical dimensions of life integrally constitutive to our understanding of the human person. In this light, an adequate concept of the body has to be worked out, holding together the aspects of both continuity and discontinuity, in light of the hope of the resurrectional transformation and new creational fulfillment.

Taking the bodily dimension seriously as integrally constitutive to the ultimate meaning and reality of human life, i.e., both here and now and hereafter, provides a strong basis and impetus to engage oneself with the struggle for the integral liberation and all-round well-being of all.

While there is need to uphold respect for all sentient and nonsentient beings in God's wider creation with a new vigor and resolve, the biblical understanding of the special dignity and responsibility of the human being as an embodied living person should not be lost sight of.

IV. Contemporary Theological, Ethical, and Interdisciplinary Challenges

The Dignity of Human Personhood and the Concept of the "Image of God"

Bernd Oberdorfer

"Denn auch der Einzelne vermag seine Verwandtschaft mit der Gottheit nur dadurch zu betätigen, dass er sich unterwirft und anbetet."[1]

1. "Image of God" — A Theological Equivalent to the Concept of the Dignity of Human Personhood?

The idea of a "human dignity" that is common to every human individual simply because it is a human individual and upon which are based "human rights," has been broadly acknowledged in the European mainline churches only since the end of World War II.[2] This might be surprising, because today the churches preferably declare themselves as being advocates of human rights and insist on their "Christian roots," and even law scholars regard the idea of "human dignity" as an import from theological or philosophical sources and discuss whether and how it can be consistently integrated into the law system.[3] For a long time, however, according to the churches the idea of human rights epitomized the spirit of secularization, representing an anthropology that focuses on the individual without reference to God, defining the human

---

1. "The individual, too, is only capable to operate his relationship to the Godhead by submitting and worshiping." J. W. von Goethe, *Dichtung und Wahrheit,* part 1, book 5, in Goethe, *Werke* Hamburger Ausgabe (München: DTV, 1998), vol. 9, p. 202 (my translation).

2. Cf. Ulrich H. J. Körtner, *Evangelische Sozialethik* (Göttingen: Vandenhoeck & Ruprecht, 1999), pp. 141-74.

3. Cf. the chapter by Stephan Kirste in this volume.

being as an autonomous subject instead of a dependent creature. The idea of human rights seemed to display an individualism that all too easily was morally disqualified as egoism neglecting the commandment of brotherly love and declining any social commitment.

Most certainly, this distrust is partly caused by the historical origins of the idea of human rights, which are strongly linked to the fight for freedom of religion. Basically, the individual should be given the right to choose his or her religious belief without being forced by church or state. The individual's religious confession should have neither negative nor positive impact on his or her social status (profession, marriage, public posts, etc.). By this, the churches' influence on people's lives has greatly decreased. The churches had to learn to accept the right of publicly articulating convictions that were "heretic" from their own perspective. This started with the Augsburg Religious Peace of 1555, which, however, restricted the right of free choice of religion only to two options: Roman Catholics and Lutherans. These two groups, albeit reluctantly, agreed to tolerate each other but, as is well known, were eagerly concerned about excluding any other groups from this right. Not incidentally, the first declaration of human rights originated in a country that had given refuge to many of these "excluded thirds": the United States of America. Presumably, this "heretic" origin hindered the "import" of this idea into "old Europe." Obviously, however, the churches' resentment heavily increased when the French Revolution picked up the idea with a strong anti-clerical emphasis. Now, the churches saw themselves confronted with the challenge of tolerating not only other forms of religion but also explicit atheism. The freedom of "believing differently" was supplemented by the right of "believing nothing."

I omit the well-known fact that the idea of individual human rights restricted the influence not only of the churches but also of the state, and focus on the question of what this development meant for the churches. Crucially, the challenge was to accept an anthropology, according to which religion — or, more exactly: "true religion" — is not essential to attributing the full dignity of personhood to a human being. Translated into the internal language of church dogmatics, the challenge consisted in the following: The idea of a common, unalienable, inviolable human dignity can only be theologically acknowledged, if there is a theological concept that characterizes human beings simply as human being, i.e., that allows the ascribing of full human dignity also to persons who are not (or no longer, or not yet) Christians.

It is the concept of the "image of God" that appears to be perfectly appropriate to that challenge, and there are good reasons to call it the key concept of modern theological anthropology.[4] Its occurrence in the first narrative of creation in Genesis 1 (Gen. 1:26f.) seems to qualify it for the most common theological characterization of humankind, compared to which any other descriptions are only second-order specifications. This is even underlined by the exegetical observation that the priestly narration adapts the concept from Israel's religious environment, but whereas in the ancient Near East the term is exclusively used for the king, in the OT it is as it were democratized and applies to every human being. Its exposed position in the beginning of the narratives of God's commitment to the world seems to make it an ideal category for conceiving the specific dignity of human beings — of every human being — before (and thus independent of) any ethnic differentiation, before (and thus independent of) any moral distinction (the "Fall"). Even more clearly, any gender discrimination is excluded when explicitly the creation of humankind as "image of God" is complemented by the phrase "and created them male and female."

But a closer examination of the use of the term in the Bible and the theological tradition displays a more ambivalent picture and gives rise to many questions. This starts with the meaning of the concept in the context of Genesis 1 itself; I will come back to this. The problems, however, increase when we survey the Bible as a whole. Quantitatively, the term "image of God" does not play a major role in the OT. It is conspicuous, still, that human persons are addressed as "image of God" even after the Fall (Gen. 5:1; 9:6); this serves as an argument for the prohibition of murder and for the inviolability of any individual human life.[5] Apparently, in the OT, the terminology does not include the possibility that human beings might lose or damage or decrease their qualification for being "image of God." In the NT, however, specifically Jesus Christ is called "image of God." Only "in Christ," mediated through Christ, in communion with Christ, other individuals can be spoken of as "images of God." But the question emerges whether this goes for any human being — or exclusively for believers. There are even a few passages where we find a kind of hierarchy of images: Only the male is the image of Christ who is the "image of God" — the female, however, is dependent on the male in this regard (cf. 1 Cor. 11:3, 7).

---

4. Cf., e.g., G. Ebeling, *Dogmatik des christlichen Glaubens I* (Tübingen, ²1982), p. 376: "The concept of image of God . . . is a point of intersection of all crucial dogmatic topics" (my translation). But also cf. the more skeptical remarks in O. H. Pesch, *Frei sein aus Gnade. Theologische Anthropologie* (Freiburg, 1983), pp. 376-81.

5. This goes also for Genesis 4:15 (Cain), albeit without explicit reference to the concept of "image of God."

This Christological concentration of the concept allows two important conclusions: Firstly, "image of God" does not mean a (as it were analytical) quality of a human being in itself; it is fragile and can be lost or damaged, yet actually is lost or damaged and had to be restored by Christ (who is the "real" human being, i.e., the human being that corresponds to God's will). Secondly, the term "in Christ" displays "image of God" as an eschatological category, and thus it designates a form of existence that combines an arising presence with a future that is still to come — "already and not yet." Or, in other words: "In Christ," a person is already awarded being "image of God," although apart from his or her relation to Christ he or she lacks the crucial characteristics of "image of God." Thus, to attribute "image of God" to someone, in some respect does not describe an "empirical reality"; it entails moments of "more than reality" and even "against visible reality."

The second point seems to show certain structural parallels to the concept of "person."[6] But unlike "person," the term "image of God" as it is used in the NT does not qualify the human species as such, and therefore it may be doubted whether it is suitable as an anthropological category anyway. In any case, there has to be given a dogmatic explanation of how the "new" human being "in Christo" refers to the "old" human being "extra Christum" with respect to the "image of God": If only the "new" human being (due to his or her communion with Christ) is "imago Dei," then is the "old" one not, or not any longer, or only potentially, or not perfectly, or only in a perverted form . . . ?

The crucial relevance of this question becomes evident if we transfer it to the concept of person: Are there human individuals who are not, or not any longer, or only potentially, or not perfectly, or only in a perverted form — persons?! As is well known, exactly this was the question that was heavily discussed in the debates on the utilitarian ethics of Peter Singer.[7] Singer declared that it makes only sense to ascribe personhood to an individual if this individual actually possesses certain characteristics and abilities. Consequently, according to him, human individuals who permanently lack these characteristics and abilities need not be addressed as and treated as persons, whereas nonhuman individuals that are endowed with these qualities (e.g., primates and dolphins) have to be considered as persons and should enjoy all the rights of protection

6. For a deeper philosophical examination of the concept of person, cf. the paper of Andreas Kemmerling in this volume. Cf. also my paper: "Umrisse der Persönlichkeit. Personalität beim jungen Schleiermacher — ein Beitrag zur gegenwärtigen ethischen Diskussion," in *Evangelische Theologie* 60 (2000): 9-24. For a "constructive Christian theology of the person" cf. the chapter by Philip Clayton in this volume.

7. Cf. P. Singer, *Practical Ethics* (Cambridge: Cambridge University Press, 1979, ²1993).

that follow from the dignity of a person. Against this position (with its immense impact on the euthanasia debate) it was argued that the category of person actually implies certain characteristics and abilities which, however, have to be attributed to the species in general and not necessarily to any individual of the species separately.[8] To use a phrase of Dietrich Bonhoeffer: Human (and therefore person!) is anyone who stems from a human mother.

Thus, if the concept "image of God" is supposed to be used within that context, a dilemma arises: If sin damages or even (as the Reformers put it) destroys the "imago Dei," then it seems that the concept is not suitable as a fundamental category of anthropology and does not provide a helpful argument in favor of the unalienable personal dignity of any human individual. If the term, conversely, serves as a common characterization of any human being, then it apparently loses its theological complexity.

The fact that Christian theology very early started to distinguish elements of the "imago Dei" that can and cannot be lost (*eikon* and *homoiosis*, or *imago* and *similitudo*) shows that from the beginning there was a feeling of the complexity of the concept. In the following, I will not give a full outline of the historical development of the concept, but will rather discuss historical positions only insofar as they help to define the systematical problems. My main focus will be put on the question: What characterizes the "image of God"? In this respect, I will differentiate between three types of definitions: quality, duty, and relation. Before doing that, however, I will insert some reflections on how the OT use of the term "image of God" is related to the prohibition of images and on the interpretation of "image of God" in the context of Genesis 1.

2. "In the Image of God Created He Him" — "Imago Dei" in the Biblical Narrative of Creation

Without doubt, Genesis 1 stresses the particular position of humankind in the created world by saying that God created the human species "in his own image, in the image of God" (Gen. 1:27). For the understanding of the passage it is important to consider that in the quoted phrase the Hebrew word for "image" is *zelem*, while in Genesis 1:26 the word *d'mut* is also used.[9] In the

---

8. Cf. R. Spaemann, *Personen. Versuche über den Unterschied zwischen "etwas" und "jemand"* (München: C. H. Beck, 1996).

9. "Let us make the human being as *(b')* our *zelem* and as *(k')* our *d'mut*" (Gen. 1:26). "Semantically, and because the change of prepositions in Gen. 5:1 (cf. 5:3), *b* and *k* here are

history of the reception of the text the above-mentioned distinction of two different aspects of "image of God" gained widespread acceptance. In the Hebrew, however, the use of two different words is primarily due to the literary style of parallelism and marks at the most a nuance of meaning, which some translations try to render, e.g., "in our image, after our likeness."[10] Yet *d'mut* does imply "neither a weakening nor a strengthening of the claim "image of God."[11] As to *zelem,* the basic meaning of the word is "statue" and refers to the sphere of artificial depiction, particularly to the ritual worship of the Godhead which is visibly present in the picture.[12] Therefore, the relation between the human being as "image" of God and the general prohibition of any "images" of God in the Old Testament has to be explained. Two points are particularly relevant: Firstly, it is God himself who creates the human being as his image; there is no idea of human beings who as it were compete with God by creating images of God (and exactly this is what the prohibition of images inveighed against). Secondly, worship or adoration is never spoken of with reference to the human being as "image of God." At best the special protection, which every human being enjoys as "image of God," might be a remote reflection of a particular "sacredness" of humankind, which nevertheless nowhere exceeds the sphere of creation.

That humankind is created as "image of God" thus does not imply a "deification." Indirectly, this is also displayed by the fact that the *priesterschrift* obviously does not judge the term "image of God" to contradict the "Jahwist" narrative of paradise, where "being like God" is the great temptation of the human beings.[13] We might be allowed to conclude from that the more the human being intends to "be like God," the less he or she is "image of God."

What is it, then, that constitutes the "image of God"? The text itself provides two options. Firstly, in Genesis 1:26 the decision to create humankind is supplemented by the claim that this human being has "dominion over the

---

practically interchangeable." Walter Groß, "Gottebenbildlichkeit, I. Altes Testament," in *Lexikon für Theologie und Kirche* 3, no. 4 (1995): col. 871-73, 871 (my translation).

10. *The Holy Bible,* Authorized King James Version, undated edition.

11. Groß, "Gottebenbildlichkeit, I. Altes Testament," col. 871 (my translation).

12. Cf., e.g., A. Schüle, "Die Würde des Bildes. Eine Re-Lektüre der priesterlichen Urgeschichte," *Evangelische Theologie* 66 (2006): 440-54, 445f.

13. Conversely, in the canonical shape of the Bible the statement "You shall be like God" gains its temptative power through its semantic proximity to the "image of God." Will the human destination of being "image of God" not be realized — the serpent suggests — exactly by eating from the forbidden tree? Cf. my paper "Der suggestive Trug der Sünde. Römer 7 bei Paulus und Luther," in *Sünde. Ein unverständlich gewordenes Thema,* ed. S. Brandt, M. H. Suchocki, and M. Welker (Neukirchen-Vluyn: Neukirchener Verlag, 1997), pp. 125-52.

fish of the sea, and over the fowl of the air, and over the cattle, and over all the earth, and over every creeping thing that creepeth upon the earth." According to Genesis 1:28, exactly this is part of the mandate that God gives to the human being: "Be fruitful, and multiply, and replenish the earth, and subdue it: and have dominion over the fish and over the fowl of the air, and over every living thing that moveth upon the earth." Secondly, the narrative of the creation of humankind is followed by the remark: "male and female created he them" (Gen. 1:27).

As to the mandate of *dominium terrae,* it is controversial whether it displays the meaning of "image of God" in itself or rather is only a consequence of being "image of God," of which the meaning, then, would have to be defined otherwise. That the meaning of "image of God," however, could be found in the polarity and the relational character of the two genders, is obviously supported by the syntactical structure of the respective passage in Genesis 1.[14] The text, nevertheless, gives no explicit explanation.[15] Anyway, the idea of identifying the gender relation as an analogy of the relational character of the triune God[16] is a Christian, particularly modernist interpretation, which has hardly any proof in the text (except, perhaps, a subtle reference to the mandate

---

14. Cf. Schüle, "Die Würde des Bildes," pp. 446f. For an interpretation of this passage with reference to modern gender theories cf. the chapter by Isolde Karle in this volume.

15. Schüle ("Die Würde des Bildes") bases his interpretation of "image of God" on the relational character of "male and female" in Genesis 1. He argues that human beings are images of God not as members of a species (unlike the animals, God did not create them "after their kind") but as individual persons who exist in concrete relations with other individual persons and have the capability to shape these relations in order to create a loving community. By doing *this,* they represent God on earth. He underlines his interpretation by the observation that the three references of "image of God" in the priestly *Urgeschichte* locate the concept within the sphere of social relations: Genesis 1:26-28 the relations of man and woman, Genesis 5:1-3 the relations of generations, and Genesis 9:4-6 the relations between individuals. He claims that the *priesterschrift* "characterizes human being as a being that is empowered to shape the nexus of relations *(die Beziehungsgeflechte)* among which he lives in an autonomous and free way . . . and thus appears similar to God" (p. 447; my translation). Following this interpretation, Schüle qualifies the relevance of the concept of "dominion on earth" for the understanding of "image of God." Although Schüle's "relecture" subtly displays nuances of the text, further exploration is needed into whether it legitimates his far-reaching systematical conclusions. Particularly, it may be doubted whether the meaning of "image of God" should be *exclusively* focused on social relations.

16. This was strongly emphasized by Karl Barth; cf. *Kirchliche Dogmatik* III/1 (Zürich, 1945), pp. 206-20; *Kirchliche Dogmatik* III/2 (Zürich, 1948), pp. 384-91. Barth developed from this an elaborated (albeit problematic) theory and ethics of gender that is based on the idea of the complementary character of male and female, cf. *KD* III/4 (Zürich, 1951), pp. 127-269.

of propagation), but quite obviously introduces the systematical interest of establishing a relational anthropology (or even ontology) in the text.

An interpretation that carefully stays close to the text at least allows us to say that being "image of God" has to do with special duties and capacities God has given humankind — particularly the duties of shaping the social relations on the one hand,[17] and the *dominium terrae,* the ruling over other creatures, on the other hand. Being "image of God," then, enables humankind to fulfill certain duties of creating and maintaining order in that part of creation which is accessible to it. Whether the mandate of propagation — which emphasizes the worldwide spreading ("Be fruitful, and multiply, and replenish the earth") — is supposed to mirror the universality of God's power over his creation, might be taken into consideration; if so, this mandate would have a strong link to the mandate of *dominium.* But in any case the human being, by shaping his social life as well as by "subduing the earth," represents God within (this part of) the world. This particular function distinguishes humankind from any other creatures.

The question of what qualifies humankind to that duty suggests itself, but the text gives no explicit answer; it dominates, however, the history of its interpretation. I should mention here the conspicuous fact that the NT use of the term "image of God" hardly reflects the perspective of anthropology and creation. That Christ is "image of God" is stated less with respect to the cosmological function of ruling the world but rather in the sense of authentic revelation and powerful fulfillment of God's saving will. Certainly, the concept of "image" also appears in the context of a "cosmic Christology" (cf. particularly Col. 1:15ff.), yet without explicit reference to a mandate of ruling, but rather with reference to Christ as mediator of creation and redeemer, as protological "firstborn of every creature" (1:15) and eschatological "firstborn from the dead" (1:18) and "head of the body, the church" (1:18).[18] This indicates quite clearly that the concept of "image of God" cannot be defined exclusively with reference to the use of the term in the *priesterschrift* narrative.[19] Nevertheless, the focus on Christology and soteriology does not exclude any reference to anthropology and creation. Christ is the "second Adam" who fulfills the destination of humankind according to the will of the Creator and therefore is the "image of God" by which God has created humankind. As we will soon see, in the his-

17. Here I follow Schüle, "Die Würde des Bildes."

18. Surely, the mediation of creation implies that also "thrones, or dominions, or principalities, or powers . . . were created by him, and for him" (Col. 1:16) and thus are subject to him. But it can hardly be said that in Colossians 1 particularly this aspect is crucial for being the "image of God."

19. Cf. Ebeling, *Dogmatik I,* pp. 404f.

tory of the interpretation of the text the insight, that being "image of God" is realized by corresponding to the will of the Creator, always had to be balanced out with the attempts to derive from the mandate of "ruling the earth" certain characteristics of humankind that constitute its being "image of God."

3. Different Types of Interpreting "Image of God"

Considering the history of Christian theology, we can basically distinguish three types of interpreting "image of God," focusing on a quality, or a duty, or a relation. This does not mean that these three types necessarily mutually exclude each other; rather, they are partly historically interrelated and conceptually overlapping.

3.1. Quality

To recognize "image of God" in a certain quality of the human species apparently suggests itself due to the fact that in the biblical narrative of creation being "image of God" distinguishes humankind from other creatures, vesting it with dominion over them. Not incidentally, therefore, already in the ancient church the theologoumenon "image of God" amalgamated with the fundamental anthropological definitions of ancient philosophy: If the human species is defined as *zoon logon echon,* animal rationale, then the *differentia specifica* that distinguishes it from other creatures is ratio, logos, reason, even (due to the multivalent meaning of the Greek term logos) language. The intertextual correlations to the basic claims of biblical anthropology are evident: Adam, giving names to the animals in Genesis 2 (which implies that he understands what they essentially are); the human mind, which is specifically related to the mind of God; the "Logos," which not only "was with God" and "was God," but also "was made flesh" (John 1). Augustine stated a very special correlation between "image of God" and the human mind: Looking for "traces of Trinity" *(vestigia trinitatis)* in creation, he found the threefold structure of the human mind, which operates in a strictly self-referential unity, but is at the same time differentiated in the three functions *memoria, intellectus,* and *voluntas,* of which every single one respectively represents the whole mind. Thus, being "image of God" means being "image of Trinity."[20]

20. *De trinitate,* IX-X. Cf. B. Oberdorfer, *Filioque* (Göttingen: Vandenhoeck & Ruprecht,

The procedure of recognizing "image of God" in crucial aspects of human nature, however, has not been limited to ancient church times. Insights of modern philosophical and biological anthropology as well could be theologically adapted: e.g., the "upright way of walking"[21] or the "open horizon" *(Horizontoffenheit)* that enables human beings to always transcend their respective state of being.[22]

Without doubt, the very strength of this approach lies in its ability to correlate the theological qualification of humankind with phenomenological descriptions of the human species. Certainly, it is a problem of this method that it tends to define human nature particularly with respect to what discriminates it from other species. Moreover, focusing "image of God" on a human capacity is in danger of depicting a merely individualistic and/or rationalist conception of human nature. But these consequences are not inevitable. On the contrary, this kind of anthropological description could actually stress the crucial relevance of the bodily character of human existence (contrasting, e.g., to the angels). It could also (following old traditions) supplement the formula of *animal rationale* by the formula of *animal sociale* in order to emphasize the fundamentally social character of human life.[23]

The theological problem of this type, however, lies in the fact that it (not only correlates but rather) identifies "image of God" with the basic qualities of human nature. That the "image of God" might be lost in a strict sense cannot

---

2001), pp. 119-25. For Augustine's concept of image of God see also the chapter by Eiichi Katayanagi in this volume.

21. It is evident that this physiological disposition, taken as such, cannot be the reason of a special distinction of humankind, because in this case (according to a surprisingly humorous word of Gerhard Ebeling) the penguin would also have to be called "image of God" (cf. *Dogmatik I*, p. 406). The upright way of walking rather is being referred to as a physiological prerequisite or indicator of the human capacity to look over the edge, i.e., to transcend the limited spheres of living.

22. This method of correlating theological and modern philosophical anthropology is classically represented by Wolfhart Pannenberg. Cf. his *Was ist der Mensch?* (Göttingen: Vandenhoeck & Ruprecht, 1964) and particularly his *Anthropologie in theologischer Perspektive* (Göttingen: Vandenhoeck & Ruprecht, 1983).

23. The formula of *animal sociale,* taken as such, however, does not distinguish humankind sharply enough from other species, of which many are social too. In this regard, the Greek equivalent *zoon politikon* is more precise, because, at least in the historical context of its origins, it meant exactly "polis-building animal," focusing on the capacity to shape autonomously the common life of free citizens; thus, it included freedom and rationality. This difference was particularly emphasized by Hannah Arendt, cf. *The Human Condition* (Chicago: University of Chicago Press, 1958). The prize of this increased precision was that it excluded all individuals who were not free and autonomous (slaves, women!) from full humanity.

be conceived then in a consistent way, because this would abolish any human existence at all. Confronted with this dilemma, the theological tradition began to differentiate aspects of "image of God" that can and cannot be lost: *imago* and *similitudo*. The imago consists in the mentioned basic qualities of human nature and therefore remains in a state of sin. The sinner, however, loses the similitudo, because his or her way of living does not correspond to the Creator's will and thus does not represent God. The reformers declined this model because they argued that it implied the fatal supposition of a sphere of human reality that is not contaminated by sin and therefore needs not be released. This contradicted their conviction that humankind is in need of salvation in a radical and universal sense. Nevertheless, also in Protestant theology the discussion on dimensions of permanence in the concept of "image of God" could never be suppressed. For that, the debate of Karl Barth and Emil Brunner about the need of an *Anknüpfungspunkt* (point of reference) for the gospel in the reality of creation (Brunner focused on language as being the necessary prerequisite to understand the word of God),[24] is only a particularly prominent example.

3.2. Duty

To define "image of God" with reference to a specific duty that humankind is assigned to, is strongly supported by the text of Genesis 1. Moreover, it evidently converges with some elements of the "Jahwist" narrative in Genesis 2. As already mentioned, the focus lies on the "mandate of dominion" to which the "mandate of propagation" is subordinated. Most interpreters understand the "mandate of dominion" in the sense of representation: Humankind is God's representative within the sphere "below heaven," as it were working as "housekeeper" of God's "economy." Being representative of the Creator within (a part of) creation is humankind's dignity, but also involves responsibility. Humankind has the duty to fulfill in its particular sphere God's will concerning this sphere. To use the words of Genesis 2: Humankind has been instructed "to dress and to keep" the earth (Gen. 2:15). By that, humankind is involved in God's work of shaping the world, not acting, however, as God's remote-controlled puppet but rather representing God's freedom, too. This presupposes that humankind knows God's will — and is able both to fulfill and not

---

24. Cf. E. Brunner, *Natur und Gnade* (Tübingen: Mohr, 1934), and K. Barth, *Nein! Antwort an Emil Brunner* (München: Kaiser, 1934).

fulfill it, to correspond to it and to objectify it. Not incidentally, in the "Jahwist"
narrative of paradise God's commandment plays a crucial role. To understand
"image of God" as a duty therefore implies constitutively an element of relation: In receiving and fulfilling or objectifying God's commandment, humankind stands opposite to God.

It may be argued that human beings are "images of God" in the world only
if and insofar as they correspond to God's will in their behavior. As soon as
they do not fulfill the duty they are engaged to, as soon as they could no longer
be called "image of God" (or only in the mode of failure), the only remaining
option would be to confront them with the commandment they have failed to
fulfill, and to demand them to return to a life that corresponds to God's will
and thus to take responsibility for their part of creation. Interestingly enough,
however, the *priesterschrift* calls humankind "image of God" without qualification even after the Fall, under the condition of human evil, and underlines
by that the physical inviolability of any human individual. Being "image of
God," then, apparently does not depend on the actual fulfillment of God's mandate. Human beings are "image of God" even when they contradict God's will.
Therefore — if we are not willing to eliminate from the concept of "image of
God" any reference to the "mandate of dominion" — it is necessary to supplement that concept with an element of attribution "against reality" (or instead,
of "lacking reality"): The reason of being "image of God" is not the actual
fulfillment of God's commandment but the fact that humankind is honored
with that mandate. In this respect, the "image of God" actually cannot be lost.

Interestingly, the approach from human qualities (cf. above in 3.1) might
lead to similar reflections if we focus on freedom as a human "quality." If the
"mandate of dominion" involves a free participation of humankind in God's
"governance of the world" and if freedom therefore is constitutive to the concept of the "image of God," then this includes the idea that this freedom is realized even in the renunciation of God's commandment. However, this evokes
a paradox that is hard to tolerate: the paradox that resistance against God must
be interpreted as an expression of being "image of God." The theological tradition tried to solve the problem by distinguishing formal and material aspects
of freedom: formally, freedom as part of the nature of humankind (which is
"image of God") is maintained even in the case that materially it is activated in
opposition to its original intention. The reformers objected to this distinction
because assuming formal continuity seemed to imply the claim of an incorrupt
and even indestructible substance or essence of humankind on which sin has
no impact. They did not doubt that in God's as it were "top-down" perspective,
humankind indestructibly remained "image of God." But on the level of the

empirically conceivable reality of human existence they declined any continuity; from a "bottom-up" perspective the "image of God" must be regarded as totally lost. Since Adam's Fall, as a famous Reformation hymn says, human nature has been "totally corrupted" *(ganz verderbt).* Thus, "image of God" does not consist in the attribution of a quality or of a mandate, but rather alone in God the Creator's loyalty to his own will. In other words: Humankind is "image of God" only because and insofar as God, without reference to any achievements, has elected and destined it to be his partner. With this idea, however, we have already crossed the line to a relational understanding of "image of God."

3.3. Relation

Relational understanding does not mean here the idea that interhuman community represents God within creation, be it in the problematic form of focusing on the matrimonial community ("and created them male and female"), or be it in the wider sense of a love-orientated community.[25] This would result in nothing more than a variant of the other types, because "image of God" would be defined with reference to a characteristic quality or activity of human beings. Relationality, rather, constitutes a different type of "image of God" if a human being is regarded as "image of God" because of his or her relation to God, his or her existence in the face of God, his or her turning to God. By faithfully answering to God and thus honoring God, a human being proves to be an authentic witness of God within the world. Thus, being "image of God" does not become a reality by activating a human quality or by fulfilling a duty but rather by faith. Certainly, faith also includes obedience against the will of God and implies consequences for human actions to shape the world; but its focus actually lies on the faithful turning to God, and by that it represents God within the world.

It is fairly clear that this understanding of "image of God" is based on the doctrine of justification. From this derive two conclusions that are difficult to coordinate: On the one hand, being "image of God" is strictly a gift, independent of any proven realization of qualities or fulfillment of duties; therefore, it would be as it were a categorical mistake to claim that it could be "lost" by human misbehavior. On the other hand, however, it is evident that a human being, if he or she does not believe in God, honor God, authentically witness to God, then he or she is actually not "image of God" within the world. The

---

25. Cf. Schüle, "Die Würde des Bildes."

conclusion seems inevitable that the nonbeliever or the sinner[26] is not an "image of God." Whether or not, then, one speaks of a "loss" of being "image of God," depends on whether the Adamite state *(status integritatis)* is regarded as a "historical" state of origin from which humankind could "fall" or whether the biblical narratives of creation are rather interpreted only as a mythical expression of the creational "destination of humankind."[27]

Anyway, it is clear that, if "image of God" is understood with reference to the doctrine of justification, the concept cannot simply work as a quality of the human species. From God's side, "image of God" is a gift of salvation for the "elected," and this election is based in itself, does not depend on any capacities or achievements that can be recognized by the individual itself or by others. From humankind's side, therefore, it cannot be objectified as a proven fact.

As far as I can see, this soteriological and relational type of understanding "image of God" is widely accepted in contemporary theology. There are good reasons for that. However, this seems to make impossible the anthropological use of the concept because apparently it implies universality only in a negative sense: There is no human being whose actual way of living would allow the identifying of him or her as an "image of God." On the positive side, we only seem to have the particularistic election by God.

4. Christological Focus and Eschatological Universality

First of all, it has to be emphasized that soteriology always has references to creation. Therefore, the theological tradition had good reasons when it started out from soteriology to regain anthropological universality. Both of the decisive arguments for that are Christological: First, Christ's work of salvation is not restricted to a limited group but rather aims at all people. Second, Christ as "real human being" *(vere homo)* is representative to all human beings by fulfilling the creational "destination of the human species" to be "image of God"

26. In some respect, the term "nonbeliever" seems to be more precise than the term "sinner" because the latter might suggest a moralistic misunderstanding. Sin, however, is basically noncorrespondence to the will of God, and can — but need not — articulate itself in moral misbehavior. In another respect, conversely, the term "sinner" seems to denote the *universality* of the phenomenon more clearly than the term "nonbeliever," which appears to designate only one of two subsets. The believer eliminates this separation by acknowledging the fragility of his or her own faith: "Lord, I believe; help my unbelief" (Mark 9:24).

27. Cf. W. Pannenberg, *Systematische Theologie,* vol. 2 (Göttingen: Vandenhoeck & Ruprecht, 1991), pp. 250-66.

on behalf of them. When the New Testament radically focuses the concept of "image of God" on Christology, this actually has a strong background of creation-based universality. "Overcoming the world" — as the Gospel puts it (John 16:33) — does not eliminate the fact that we are creatures but rather fulfills the destination that God gave to his creatures. Christ corresponds to God's will, which Adam had contradicted. The New Testament use of the concept of "image of God" therefore does not decline its Old Testament use but rather is based on it, comments on it, and gives it a soteriological and eschatological emphasis.

If, however, being "image of God" is mediated through Christ and becomes real by the gift of participation in Christ, community with Christ, and faith in Christ, the critique of the particularity of the Christian concept of "image of God" seems to be strengthened rather than invalidated because, as is evident, not everybody actually believes.

As to this, however, it helps to consider precisely the function the use of the term "image of God" has in anthropological and ethical contexts. Actually, it is supposed to attribute to any human individual a dignity that is not dependent on the real possession of capabilities and achievements and therefore cannot be limited or eliminated in the case of one's lacking it — a dignity that cannot be withdrawn and that an individual cannot even withdraw from him or herself. How can it be stated in this sense that all human beings are "image of God"?

Essentially, there are three arguments to be brought forward: First, the universality of Christ's work of salvation does not allow the exclusion of any individuals *a priori*. Of no one can it be claimed that he or she definitely will not participate in the community with Christ or definitely has lost it. Conversely, this universality of Christ's work of salvation commits Christians to treating non-Christians as people to which Christ's work is valid as well, although such persons do not (yet) know or (not yet or no longer) acknowledge it. Second, faith includes a knowledge of its own persistent fragility and of the continual need of redemption; this prevents any fixed discrimination of persons "in" and "out" of salvation. Third, the eschatological character of salvation implies a dynamic culture of expectation that recognizes the present status quo as transformable and as it were imagines amidst the present state its future fulfillment.

Thus, the fact that the concept of "image of God" is developed via Christology enables us to give it a more complex and more differentiated form and to remove it from the idea of a substantial state of being. Moreover, the alternative of either counter-real attribution or real possession of being "image of

God" proves to be inadequate. Actually, "image of God" is not an empirical quality, but nevertheless it realizes the creational destination of humankind. And as the vocation to be "image of God" is independent of any available capabilities and achievements, so too the promulgation of God's unqualified attribution of being "image of God" in the communication of faith motivates an inner-worldly evolutionary dynamics through which individuals help each other to "be made conformable" to Christ (cf. Phil. 3:10). Thus the unqualified attribution of being "image of God" does not simply constitute a trans-empirical reality that has no other empirical impact than the powerless "God loves you as you are." It rather motivates an individual as well as a social way of living that mirrors the ascribed dignity. Whenever this does not succeed, the dignity of being "image of God" may be obscured to the point of invisibility or contorted to caricature — but it cannot be lost or destroyed.

5. Conclusion

Far from leading to an exclusivist view, focusing on a Christological and so-teriological understanding of "imago Dei" rather provides good reasons for a Christian affirmation of the idea of human dignity and the universality of human rights. At first glance, this result might seem of little use for interdisciplinary studies. How does it help nontheologians and even non-Christians to see this, and how does it benefit Christian churches to adopt a secular concept they fought against for a long time and to reformulate it within the conceptual frame of their own theological traditions?[28] In my view, there are at least two arguments to be brought forward: First, as Christian traditions form a significant part of the cultural and intellectual sources of European history, and as the churches are still important and powerful agents in the cultural and intellectual life of modern societies, it is therefore of public interest how they define in their intrinsic (religious and theological) communication basic normative concepts of social life like "person," "human dignity," "human rights," or "civil rights."[29] Second, the Christian concept of "imago Dei" is more than just a copy of the idea of human dignity. This idea, anyway, as Stephan Kirste rightly put it,[30] is not a concept of which there is only one valid interpretation.

28. It is part of this "adoptation" that the churches rediscovered elements of their *own* traditions in this supposedly secular context.
29. This is emphasized by Jürgen Habermas in his recent publications. Cf. *Zwischen Naturalismus und Religion. Philosophische Aufsätze* (Frankfurt am Main: Suhrkamp, 2005).
30. Cf. his chapter in this volume.

Thus, although there is a need of a common understanding of human dignity, such a common understanding cannot simply be taken for granted but rather has to be elaborated in dialogue between the different traditions of interpretation — of which the Christian is an important one.

What can Christian theology, then, contribute to a complex concept of human dignity and personhood? First, the idea that "imago Dei" had to be and has been restored by Christ reminds us of the fact that human dignity is not as it were a natural quality that can be (and therefore has to be) realized by human beings' own efforts and activities. It is not an empirical reality. Nevertheless, second, the term "image of God" does not indicate an ideal that has nothing to do with "real life," but rather ascribes a "trans-empirical" dignity to real empirical individuals: You actually are "image of God" although your state of being and/or your behavior may not display that in a full sense, and thus you merit to be respected as being "image of God." Third, then, if the dignity of being "image of God" does not suggest itself but has to be ascribed, this ascription has to be communicated. Ascribing to someone being "image of God" is a performative act that, in some sense, only creates what it means. Likewise, the respect for human dignity requires a semantic culture of "human dignity." This culture of "human dignity" and "image of God," however, will only gain credibility if it is based on an ethos of "human dignity." Thus, fourth, the concept of "image of God" as well as the concept of "human dignity" implies consequences in ethics, morality, and law.

This goes for any part of social life. Particularly, yet, it means a challenge for the churches themselves. If they accept the idea of "human dignity" and "human rights," what follows from that for their own life and doctrine? Is the exclusion of women from the ordained ministry in some churches a gender-based discrimination? And what about the rejection of same-sex marriage? Does the adoption of the concept of "human dignity" require a change of attitude towards other religions or nonbelievers? Is the doctrine of eternal damnation ("hell") still plausible if "human dignity" has to be ascribed to every human being in an unqualified sense? Thus, the dynamics of this concept include the Christian churches themselves and will be on their agenda for a long time. The debates are only about to begin.

Human Dignity and the Concept of Person in Law

Stephan Kirste

1. Introduction

The idea of human dignity seems not to fit into the law. It is the most fundamental material principle in all constitutions that have acknowledged it. Apparently, the principle of human dignity has a meaning that is too broad and a form that is too strong to achieve a systematically satisfying position in legal argumentation.[1] Because of its fundamental content it serves either as the universal legal solution to any kind of infractions, such as a wrong spelling of names in public files. At the same time it serves as a trump that always wins the trick, because it is so closely linked to the human being as such. If this latter meaning is poured into the legal form of an individual right, it surmounts every other right in a legal order. Actually, modern constitutions like the German Basic Law or the Charter of Fundamental Rights of the European Union put further emphasis on the form, because human dignity cannot be balanced against any other right. But what to do with a collision of the human dignity of one with the human dignity of another?[2]

Apart from the form of law as a certain kind of norm, the concept of the

1. For a critical analysis of legal argumentation based on human dignity cf. U. Neumann, "Die Tyrannei der Würde. Argumentationstheoretische Erwägungen zum Menschenwürdeprinzip," *Archiv für Rechts und Sozialphilosophie* 84 (1998): 426ff.; E. Hilgendorf, "Die mißbrauchte Menschenwürde. Probleme des Menschenwürdetopos am Beispiel der Bioethischen Diskussion," *Jahrbuch für Recht und Ethik* 7 (1999): 137ff.

2. W. Brugger, "Würde gegen Würde," *Baden-Württembergische Verwaltungsblätter* (1995): 414, 446ff.

legal person is the fundamental legal institution. By being a legal person a man has a legal standing, can make use of his rights, have legal objects, and defend his or her interests. In law the institute of person has a technical value. It can be attributed to whatever entity should be legally capable of having rights and using them. Accordingly, a company may have the status of a juridical person. At the same time, in history often members of social groups were denied the status of a person in law, for instance the Slavs or Jews under the national-socialist regime in Germany.

Whereas the fundamental material principle of human dignity has a difficulty in finding its appropriate legal form, the institute of person has difficulties in gaining material criteria to decide who should receive the status of a person. In this chapter I will argue that both problems can be met, if human dignity is understood as a right to be acknowledged as a legal person. Before I come to this, let me investigate the principle of human dignity to some extent and later on the development of the concept of person in law.

2. Human Dignity

2.1. *Some Aspects of the History of the Concept of Human Dignity*

The roots of the history of the concept of human dignity go back to antiquity. Theologically as well as philosophically it is many-faceted. In clear contrast, the history of the legal institution is relatively short. It begins with a reference in Article 151 I of the German Weimar Constitution of 1919.[3] More explicit was the Irish Constitution of 1937, mentioning the "dignity and freedom of the individual" in its preamble. The Franco Constitution of Spain made inflationary use of the term — affirming "dignity of human life" (Art. I 1) and "personal dignity of the one who works" (Art. I 2) but also "dignity of the fatherland" (Art. I 3), with similar wording in Article 1, 25, of the Charter of the Spaniards (17 July 1945). After World War II the institute of human dignity began its unrivaled triumphal procession through the texts of international law, human rights declarations, and constitutions. For example, the Preamble of the UN Charter reaffirms "faith . . . in the dignity and worth of the human person." The preamble to the Universal Declaration of Human Rights (10 December 1948) states that "recognition of the inherent dignity and of the equal and

---

3. "Die Ordnung des Wirtschaftslebens muß den Grundsätzen der Gerechtigkeit mit dem Ziele der Gewährleistung eines menschenwürdigen Daseins für alle entsprechen."

inalienable rights of all members of the human family is the foundation of freedom, justice and peace," as well as affirming "faith in fundamental human rights, in the dignity and worth of the human person"; Article 1 of the same declaration states: "All human beings are born free and equal in dignity and rights. They are endowed with reason and conscience and should act towards one another in a spirit of brotherhood."[4] In the Federal Republic of Germany the concept of human dignity was first codified in several state constitutions and finally in the Basic Law of 1949. The latest station of its victorious march through twentieth- and twenty-first-century constitutions marks Article 1 of the Charter of Fundamental Rights of the European Union, which is about to become binding European law: "Human dignity is inviolable. It must be respected and protected."

The remarkably short legal history in contrast to the century-old philo-sophical and theological tradition of the concept may explain why the legal discourse about the institute of human dignity has not yet moved far away from the other discourses about this concept. The import of extra-legal ideas of human dignity into the law causes two problems, however: On the one hand these concepts that are developed from an ethical, political, or theological background have the above-mentioned broad content and implications that do not easily fit into a legal context. On the other hand the plurality of these concepts calls for a decision among them or an abstraction of certain common aspects between them. Choosing one of the concepts needs criteria for that choice. Where should that come from? And also the search for a common meaning in all of these concepts needs a focusing point. This again may lead to the danger of a vague general concept that is incapable of providing argu-mentative grounds for legitimated legal decisions.

The intensive jurisprudential discussion in part concerns the question of whether there should be a philosophical or theological foundation of the

4. Compare also the International Covenant on Civil and Political Rights of 16 December 1966, Preamble, Article 10, and Article 13. For regional conventions, see the African [Banjul] Charter on Human and Peoples' Rights, adopted 27 June 1981, Article 5; the Charter of the Or-ganization of American States, entered into force 13 December 1951, Article 45; the American Convention on Human Rights, entered into force 18 July 1978, Article 5, 2; Article 6, 2; and Article 11, 1; the American Declaration of the Rights and Duties of Man, adopted by the Ninth International Conference of American States (1948), Preamble; the European Convention for the Protection of Human Rights and Fundamental Freedoms, entered into force 3 September 1953, Article 3; the European Convention for the Prevention of Torture and Inhuman or De-grading Treatment or Punishment, entered into force 1 February 1989; the European Consti-tutional Treaty (2004), Article I-2 on the Union's values, as well as the preamble to Part II and Article II-61: "Human dignity is inviolable. It must be respected and protected."

legal concept of human dignity at all, and in case there is an agreement about this, which one should become the basis of the legal understanding of the term: Should the constitutional concept of human dignity be understood in a moral-theological Catholic way, in a Protestant way as "the community of God's children" ("Gotteskindschaft"), in a humanist way in the sense of Pico della Mirandola, or in an aesthetical sense in the way that Friedrich Schiller conceptualized it, according to the doctrine of the Enlightenment philosophers Christian Wolff and Samuel Pufendorf?[5] Should human dignity be understood in the light of Kant's, Fichte's, or Schelling's Idealism?[6] Or is it best seen in the light of Karl Marx's, Ferdinand Lassalle's, or Ernst Bloch's socialism?[7] Or should it be understood in an existentialist way like that of Jean-Paul Sartre or of Martin Heidegger; or on the basis of the discourse theory of Jürgen Habermas, or on the basis of the assumptions of the Theory of Social Systems of Niklas Luhmann, or in the theoretical framework of utilitarianism?[8]

The more these concepts are attached to natural law theories, the more difficult it is to receive them within the law. Even today some scholars claim that human dignity has an extra-legal foundation and the codification shows only the acceptance of this fact. Law is most severely dominated by natural law concepts of human dignity, when — following a tradition that goes back

5. For a Catholic view, see E. Schockenhoff, *Naturrecht und Menschenwürde* (Mainz, 1996). For a Protestant approach, see E. Biser, *Gotteskindschaft und Menschenwürde* (Limburg, 2005); Leiner in Gröschner/Kirste/Lembcke (2007). G. P. della Mirandola, *Über die Würde des Menschen/Oratio de hominis dignitate* (Hamburg, 1990). F. Schiller, *Über Anmut und Würde* (Stuttgart, 1994), pp. 69ff.

6. I. Kant, *Grundlegung zur Metaphysik der Sitten. Werke*, vol. 7, pp. 59ff.; I. Kant, *Die Metaphysik der Sitten*, pp. 568f.; I. Kant, *Grundlegung zur Metaphysik der Sitten. Tugendlehre*, A 77ff. *Kant-Werke* vol. 8, pp. 557ff. J. G. Fichte, *Über die Würde des Menschen, beim Schlusse seiner philosophischen Vorlesungen gesprochen von J. G. Fichte*. F. W. J. Schelling, "Neue Deduktion des Naturrechts," in Schelling, *Schriften von 1794-1798* (Stuttgart/Augsburg, 1857), pp. 125-61.

7. K. Marx and F. Engels, "Manifest der kommunistischen Partei," in *Marx-Engels-Werke*, vol. 4 (Berlin, 1980), pp. 464f. F. Lassalle, *Das Arbeiterprogramm. Ges. Reden und Schriften*, ed. E. Bernstein (²1919), pp. 173f. E. Bloch, introduction to *Naturrecht und menschliche Würde* (Frankfurt am Main, 1972), pp. 11ff., 14.

8. J.-P. Sartre, "Ist der Existenzialismus ein Humanismus?," in *Drei Essays* (Frankfurt am Main/Berlin, 1986), pp. 7-51, 10f. M. Heidegger, *Über den Humanismus* (Frankfurt am Main, 1981), pp. 12f., 37f., 43f. J. Habermas, *Die Zukunft der menschlichen Natur* (Frankfurt am Main, 2001), pp. 62ff. N. Luhmann, *Grundrechte als Institution* (Berlin, ⁴1999), pp. 53ff. N. Hoerster, *Ethik des Embryonenschutzes. Ein rechtsphilosophischer Essay* (Stuttgart, 2002), pp. 11ff.; Hoerster, *Abtreibung im säkularen Staat* (Frankfurt am Main, 1991), pp. 121ff.

to the church fathers (Origen)[9] — dignity is considered to mean that man is an image of God and law has to guarantee this as an individual right. All human beings have an individual right to the recognition of their dignity, which they obtain because of this character. According to this genesis of the right to dignity, it is absolute. Being absolute means that it cannot be balanced against any other right. The strategy behind this argument is to extend human dignity up to an infinitesimal point against which all other basic rights seem to be finite points of lower quality. This theologically inspired concept is being heavily criticized. The foundations of it are too strongly attached to a certain worldview. This is not suitable for a secular state with its neutrality towards religion. The absolute character of human dignity is not convincing, when it comes to a confrontation of dignity against dignity as in the case of using torture against a kidnapper to save the life of the victim if the hideout is unknown.[10] Also, the strong metaphysical assumptions about the beginning of human life are contested on the grounds of modern scientific findings and ethical criticism.

The mere fact that texts as contrary as the Code of the Canon Law, the Constitution of the Islamic Republic of Iran, or the Constitution of the People's Republic of China can refer to human dignity shows this uncertainty in developing an autonomous, legally coherent concept of human dignity in general.[11] The increasingly differentiated constitutional provisions about particular aspects of the violation of human dignity — namely the prohibition of torture, the protection against arbitrary arrest (habeas corpus), the protection of honor, the protection of the embryo, and other medically endangered values[12] — are

9. T. Kobusch, "Die Würde des Menschen — ein Erbe der christlichen Philosophie," in Gröschner/Kirste/Lembcke, *Des Menschen Würde — Wiederentdeckt und erfunden im Humanismus der italienischen Renaissance* (Tübingen, 2008).

10. W. Brugger, "Darf der Staat ausnahmsweise foltern?," *Der Staat* 35 (1996): 67-97. W. Brugger, "Vom unbedingten Verbot der Folter zum bedingten Recht auf Folter?," *Juristenzeitung* (2000): 165-73.

11. Code of the Canon Law (CIC 1983), Canon 208: "From their rebirth in Christ, there exists among all the Christian faithful a true equality regarding dignity and action by which they all cooperate in the building up of the Body of Christ according to each one's own condition and function"; cf. also Canons 212 and 768. The Constitution of the Islamic Republic of Iran, adopted on 24 October 1979, includes this language: the Preamble reads: "this Constitution . . . regards as its highest aim the freedom and dignity of the human race" (preamble) and "The dignity, life, property, rights, residence, and occupation of the individual are inviolate, except in cases sanctioned by law" (Art. 22). The Constitution of the People's Republic of China, adopted on 4 December 1982, says: "The personal dignity of citizens of the People's Republic of China is inviolable" (Art. 38).

12. Cf. Art. 119a of the Constitution of Switzerland, adopted on 18 December 1998: "Article 119a Transplantation Medicine (1) The Federation provides regulation for transplantation of

signs of the attempt of constitutional framers to gain clear distinctions, hereby giving the principle juridical manageability. The general concept of human dignity does not lose its significance by these developments. The question is, however, what remains as its proper legal function and how to determine it.

A lawyer would first think of the classical methods of interpretation of law to find out about the proper meaning of the principle of human dignity. I will show that this has limited success, however. If the principle is too broad in content and too strong in the form of a right, a reduction of either the meaning or the form could be a strategy to fit the principle into law. I come to this later.

2.2. Human Dignity as a Legal Term

Only in part does the interpretation of the term dignity follow the common paths of legal hermeneutics. Taking the range and vagueness into account, the wording does not tell very much. Neither can the historical interpretation present clear results — at least for the German Basic Law: The opinions of the framers were too heterogeneous and so is the history of the idea. Only the distinguished provisions of Article 1 of the German Basic Law provide some room for a systematic interpretation. Even this method has to take for granted the term itself.

The still not very technical understanding of the term, its generality as a value, and its short legal tradition facilitate the import of extra-legal convictions. It is not surprising then that especially in the early stages of the development of the interpretation of human dignity, many Christian theological estimations were made.[13] The more or less secular character of Western legal traditions resisted this approach, however. It seems that the integration of the term into a constitution produces a certain self-contained meaning. Disregarding the vagueness of the term, this establishes a filter against the reception of the rationalities of arguments from other social systems.

Seemingly, this filter lets philosophical conceptions pass through, permitting them as patterns for the interpretation of human dignity. Again considering the distinguished legal discourse on human dignity, it is not surprising that

---

organs, tissue, and cells. It thereby protects human dignity, personality, and health"; Art. 120 II: "it shall take into account the dignity of creation. . . ."

13. Böckenförde, "Zur Eröffnung," in *Menschenrechte und Menschenwürde. Historische Voraussetzungen — säkulare Gestalt — christliches Verständnis,* ed. R. Spaemann (Stuttgart, 1987), pp. 14f. Critically, N. Hoerster, "Zur Bedeutung des Menschenwürdeprinzips," *Juristische Schulung* (1983): 93ff.

initially, approaches dominated the field that relied on consent and enabled authors that were unsuspicious about totalitarian utilization. In part because of this, an interpretation that relied on Immanuel Kant dominated the field. Kant permitted a view that could give room for a Christian interpretation, without restricting the secular understanding of the constitution too much.[14]

Another method of the foundation of human dignity is the investigation of understandings of the word, the attitude or convictions of people in regard to human dignity.[15] Here too there will be an unclear consciousness of the violation of human dignity in the beginning. But starting with this "moral sentiment" (David Hume) via abstraction and refinement the positive principles can be elaborated.

From this background, it is not surprising that a historical interpretation in a broader sense is being introduced to understand the term human dignity. This method is supported by the fact that human dignity was often inserted into constitutions as a reaction to the experience of injustice committed by former dictatorial or totalitarian regimes. The German Basic Law did so as a reaction to the massive violation of human rights by the Nazi regime, especially by denying legal capacity to Jewish and other parts of the German population on the basis of race legislation. Other countries reacted with a ban on torture as a concrete violation of human dignity. Taken together, these approaches argue more juridically because they refer to the function of the constitution in securing the rule of law, thereby preventing regimes from arbitrarily disregarding human beings.

From these patterns a rather systematical conception emerged, holding that human dignity cannot be defined positively but only negatively, from possible violations of it.[16] The negative approach thereby replaces the question about what human dignity is by the question of when and under what conditions it is being violated. In Germany, Günther Dürig wrote: "There is an exact consensus on how the state and social order should look. . . . Naturally one should not claim to interpret the principle of human dignity as positively binding; one can only say what infringes it."[17] Degradation, denunciation, arbitrary persecution,

14. I. Kant, *Kritik der reinen Vernunft*, Werkausgabe, vol. 3, ed. W. Weischedel (Frankfurt am Main, 1988), p. 32.

15. M. S. Pritchard, "Human Dignity and Justice," in *Ethics* 82 (1972): 300f.

16. See P. Kunig, Art. 1, margin number 22, in Münch/Kunig, *Grundgesetz. Kommentar* (München, ⁵2000).

17. G. Dürig, "Zur Bedeutung und Tragweite des Art. 79 Abs. III des Grundgesetzes," in *Festgabe für Theodor Maunz zum 70. Geburtstag*, ed. H. Spanner (München, 1971), pp. 41ff. See also O. Schachter: "Human Dignity as a Normative Concept," *The American Journal of International Law 77* (1983): 849, who adds, however: "Without a reasonably clear general

and ostracism are violations of human dignity, as is torture, punishment of the body, the use of lie detectors, or the injection of truth serums. As convincing as they may be, however, these theories depend on three conditions: First, they presuppose respective experiences. This prevents them from being useful for new challenges to human dignity. Second, without a positive understanding of what human dignity means, they cannot tell what infringes it. By what criteria would this experience qualify as a violation of human dignity as such, if there is no idea of what it is? Finally, this concept lacks clear criteria for the distinction, if the feeling of injustice relates particularly to a violation of dignity or of another value: the negative approach provides no closed catalog of criteria for estimating what kind of disrespectful behavior infringes human dignity and what does not. This theory, however, argues with respect to constitutions containing the rule of law principle. It is the central task of the law to prevent infringements of rights. This is the positive aspect from which this theory can start and relative to which unjust action can be qualified as to be negated acts. It therefore is not necessarily attached to a nonlegal, philosophical, or theological foundation of human dignity, but to the law itself in its functioning, and it approaches the concept from the legal prevention of violations.

If on the one hand law has the task of deciding social problems, meaning that we expect the legal staff to give definitive answers, and if on the other hand there is a plurality of understandings of human dignity, it may be a good idea to start the definition of it from the infringements of rights — because positive rights stem from the discursively legitimated decisions of legislators and other law-creating procedures.

This tendency suggests that we look for a juridical foundation of human dignity. Before further elaborating this approach, I will present a short overview of the material concepts of human dignity. Here too we will focus on the question as to what extent extra-legal considerations have shaped the respective concept.

2.3. Formal Relativization of Human Dignity

In their attempt to make human dignity an operable legal concept, constitutional framers as well as juridical practitioners have tried to qualify the

---

idea of its meaning, we cannot easily reject a specious use of the concept, nor can we without understanding its meaning draw specific implications for relevant conduct," or compare the long catalog of infringements (852).

foundation of human dignity. It meant a first step in this direction to consider dignity not as an individual right, but as an objective principle or value.[18] As an objective legal principle, dignity places an obligation on the state but does not grant the individual a corresponding right to recognition and protection of his dignity, however.[19] Some modern constitutions have adopted this idea, when they mention dignity in the preamble or at another position in the text outside the part on basic rights, as does the Spanish Constitution (Art. 10).[20]

This tendency to weaken the legal form of dignity is even further pursued when authors deny it the character of applicable law altogether. In a classical formulation the German scholar for public law, Ernst Forsthoff, stated that human dignity is a "general concept" (ein "allgemeiner Begriff") under which "it is impossible to subsume."[21] Others speak of it as an axiom of the constitution with "appellative character," a constituting principle, a supreme goal of all law, a confession or a sentence with the obligatory force of a preamble.[22]

The advantage of this relativization of the form is the riskless import of strong conceptions of the content of human dignity. If no one can claim human dignity, it may be described as an image of God and may have an absolute status. As an objective principle the state has to take it into account, especially in interpretation, but no concrete legal consequences can be deduced from it. If dignity is not a normative sentence or at least not a subjective right, it also needs not to be balanced with other constitutional values or principles. As a principle it can be regarded more highly the smaller the deducible legal consequences are. Pathos and legal consequences fall apart. Because of the

---

18. Dürig held that human dignity was a value that was only recognized and confirmed by the constitution, but not an individual right; "Der Grundrechtssatz von der Menschenwürde," *Archiv des öffentlichen Rechts* 42 (1956): 119.

19. C. Enders, *Die Menschenwürde in der Verfassungsordnung. Zur Dogmatik des Art. 1 GG* (Tübingen, 1997), p. 118: "Der Absolutheit des Begriffs der Menschenwürde und der Unbestimmtheit ihres Schutzbereichs entspricht es demnach, wenn sich positivrechtlich aus Art. 1 I GG kein eigenständiges subjektives Recht ergibt, dieser vielmehr nur in einer objektiv-rechtlichen und auf alle Grundrechte bezogenen Funktion zum Tragen kommt."

20. I. G. Gutierrez, *Menschenwürde als europäischer Verfassungsbegriff — Rechtsvergleichender und verfassungsgeschichtlicher Beitrag zur Debatte um die Menschenwürde* (2006), p. 385.

21. E. Forsthoff in *Der Staat* 18 (1969): 524.

22. R. Gröschner, "Des Menschen Würde. Humanistische Tradition eines Verfassungsprinzips," in Gröschner/Kirste/Lembcke, *Des Menschen Würde — Wiederentdeckt und erfunden im Humanismus der italienischen Renaissance* (published 2008), manuscript p. 14. Entscheidungen des Bundesverfassungsgerichts 93, pp. 266ff. (293) — *Soldaten sind Mörder*; E 87, pp. 209ff. (228) — Tanz der Teufel. Entscheidungen des Bundesverfassungsgerichts 12, pp. 45ff. (51).

diminution of the form, the legal term dignity would be open equally to a Christian, a transcendental-philosophical, or an immanent understanding.

2.4. *The Relativization of the Content of Human Dignity*

Other theories try the opposite method: By reducing its meaning they strengthen the formal impact of human dignity as a right, especially as a basic right. The respective theories can be distinguished into two main groups with different subdistinctions. First of all, there are theories that aim at specifying the content of dignity on the basis of a qualitative change of its meaning. Secondly — and I will concentrate on these — there are theories that establish a quantitative threshold, below which a violation would be considered a mere pestering, but not a substantial infringement of human dignity.

In a systematic perspective the first kind of concepts takes the secular character of most Western constitutions into account. If the understanding of human dignity as man being an image of God would be adopted, this understanding would collide with the rights of religious freedom, the right to anti-discrimination because of religion, and the abolition of any state church. Other than with constitutions like the Irish that begin with a full *invocatio Dei,* thereby showing a way to integrate a theological perspective into the constitution in secular constitutions, a strongly religious concept of human dignity is an alien element. To give human dignity a meaning, interpreters often rely on Immanuel Kant. In his view, man's dignity is the result of his autonomy.[23] From this it follows that human dignity is oriented towards individual action. This again means that all human beings have the right to the recognition of these abilities. On the basis of Kant, human dignity can be constructed as a subjective right.

This theory, which is very prominent in Germany and is being adopted in the jurisdiction of the Federal Constitutional Court as the so-called "object formula,"[24] leaves open the problem that it is strongly committed to the idealist assumptions of Immanuel Kant. It also unites with strong metaphysical assumptions on the reasonable nature of man that can hardly be subscribed to by everyone — not even all philosophers. This obstacle helped search for

---

23. I. Kant, *Grundlegung zur Metaphysik der Sitten. Werke vol. 7,* ed. W. Weischedel, p. 69.

24. First elaborated by G. Dürig ("Der Grundrechtssatz von der Menschenwürde," pp. 117-57) and later received by the Court: Entscheidungen des Bundesverfassungsgerichts 9, 89ff. (95); 27, 1ff. (6); 28, 386ff. (391); 45, 187ff. (228); 50, 166ff. (175); 50, 205ff. (215); 57, 250ff. (275); 72, 105ff. (116); 87, 209ff. (228).

STEPHAN KIRSTE

theories that refuse a strong positioning of man as a *homo phaenomenon* or *homo noumenon*. For this, the universal renaissance scholar Pico della Mirandola is a promising candidate. He assumes that man as a second Adam has to give himself his own position in the world. He is — as many other renaissance authors thought — a being that resembles a chameleon, a being capable of constant change. This genial ability distinguishes him from all other creatures. Both the problem of a tension between the neutral Western democratic state and a strong concept of human dignity on the one hand and the problem of human dignity that is to be protected only in general on the other hand could be omitted when we rely on Pico. However, some questions remain. Almost no constitutional framer referred to Pico della Mirandola, Petrarch, Giannozzo Manetti, or other renaissance authors. And finally, it is not yet clear in which quality the specific human capability is being expressed.

Metaphysical assumptions can be avoided by conceptions that consider dignity not as a substance of a human being, but as an achievement. The sociologist Niklas Luhmann holds it that dignity is the result of the self-demonstration of the individual.[25] Human dignity then is a value attributed by communication. This view is supported by some human rights declarations like Article 45b of the Charter of the Organization of American States: "Work is a right and a social duty, it gives dignity to the one who performs it. . . ." But these formulations are rather exceptions than the rule. If dignity is relative to achievements, this right is unable to address a problem for the solution of which the concept was introduced, namely the dignity of those persons, who are, because of mental or other handicaps, incapable of acting or articulating themselves. It is also quite clear that this theory would altogether exclude unborn life from the protection of this principle. From Niklas Luhmann's sociological perspective it may be true that dignity is a result of ascription based upon communication. But as a concept of a legal right it is problematic, because it does not protect a human being in a state of his development, when help is needed the most: during its prenatal existence.

Other approaches emphasize the context-specificity of dignity.[26] One can subscribe to the Christian understanding of the human being as an image of God; one can agree to the assumption that man is distinguished by his reason or self-createdness; but still one has to make a difference between these aspects

25. *Grundrechte als Institution,* pp. 68ff.; for Luhmann's concept of human dignity cf. also A. Noll, *Die Begründung der Menschenrechte bei Luhmann — Vom Mangel an Würde zur Würde des Mangels* (Basel/Genf/München, 2006), pp. 369ff.

26. Cf. Habermas; H. Hofmann, "Die versprochene Menschenwürde," *Archiv des öffentlichen Rechts* 118 (1993): 353-77.

of human beings and the dignity of it. And it is important for the understanding of dignity to make sharp distinctions between dignity and the relevant subject. The dignity itself expresses the recognition or the claim for recognition. It is a normative principle. There is no necessary connection between any anthropology — be it scientifically oriented, Christian, or secular — and the claim for recognition. What dignity is, results from the context in which it is situated. The dignity of a Christian is as such different from the dignity as a partner in social communication. And within the systems of communication one can distinguish several dignities. Because of this context-specificity of dignity, a Christian obligation to recognize an elaborated dignity of man as an image of God is not excluded. But these religious obligations for the foundation of law cannot be equaled with legal duties in its application. The task is to grant man a legal dignity that is the equivalent of his ethical dignity as a moral person or his dignity as an "image of God" or a "child of God" in a Catholic or Lutheran context etc.

Again, other theories relativize human dignity by establishing certain quantitative thresholds.[27] Infractions under this level would not be accepted as violations of human dignity although they may relate to aspects of honor or social status. Their general aim is, not to make inflationary use of the term, thereby playing down its role in the end. This restriction of the principle, however, means a rather peripheral correction and also fails to present criteria for the threshold.

All attempts to specify the concept of human dignity try to fit this general, fundamental concept that is based on strong philosophical or theological presuppositions into the legal system. The formal attempts were driven by the intuition that such a demanding philosophical idea could only be received by law if its formal status was being reduced from a right to an objective principle or even to a non-normative "axiom." The other group of theories, which I call material theories, try to specify human dignity by excluding certain connotations from its content. Thereby they could keep up the strong formal status of human dignity as a right. Whereas the first group is in danger of making the application of human dignity irrelevant, because it does not show concrete legal consequences, the other group is in danger of eroding human dignity from inside, because it is a right, but does not protect it in situations when it is meant to help the individual. The task would be to avoid both problems and present a conception of human dignity that combines the formal relevance as a

---

27. E. Hilgendorf, "Die mißbrauchte Menschenwürde," *Jahrbuch für Recht und Ethik* 7 (1999): 137ff.; Hofmann, "Die versprochene Menschenwürde."

subjective right with the traditional content that human dignity is the highest value in moral philosophy.

2.5. Foundation and Relation of Dignity

A way to do so could be to pick up the idea of the context-sensitivity of dignity and ask what function human dignity has in the context of law. The idea that dignity is context-sensitive has a long tradition.

The Stoic philosopher Marcus Tullius Cicero spoke of "excellentia et dignitas," showing that dignity is a characteristic of a person, not its essence.[28] He made a distinction between dignity as a value and the bearer of it. Accordingly, dignity was not restricted to human beings. The state ("dignitas rei publicae") or the Roman people ("dignitas populi Romani") could also have a dignity. Founded on one's concrete social status, dignity was a comparative and relative value.[29]

Medieval philosophy considered dignity itself to be eternal. Accordingly, dignity is separated from the respective bearer as a mortal being. Dignity therefore is connected to hierarchical orders (God-men, pope-bishop, king-officers) within which a person may receive a dignity, but may also lose it again. The dignity of a human being as such surmounts these other dignities: The character of being an image of God cannot be taken away from any human being.

For Samuel Pufendorf and Christian Wolff — just to mention two Enlightenment philosophers — dignity referred to man as a moral person.[30] Not the whole of the human being obtained dignity, but only its better, its reasonable, moral part. Thomas Hobbes spoke of dignity as the "public value of man."[31] This hints at the idea that dignity expresses the validity of its bearer in a certain social or philosophical context. Even Immanuel Kant, who considered human

28. And this again was the basis for an unequal dignity. As Cicero put it: "Equality is unequal, if it does not know steps in dignity" (*De officio 1*, 30, 105f.).

29. Cicero, *De re publica I*, 27, 43.

30. M. Lipp, " 'Persona moralis,' 'Juristische Person' und 'Personenrecht' — Eine Studie zur Dogmengeschichte der 'Juristischen Person' im Naturrecht und frühen 19. Jahrhundert," *Quaderni Fiorentini per la storia del pensiero giuridico moderno* 11/12 (1982/83): 217-63; T. Kobusch, *Die Entdeckung der Person. Metaphysik der Freiheit und modernes Menschenbild* (Darmstadt, ²1997), pp. 67ff.

31. T. Hobbes, *Leviathan*, ed. P. Smith (Oxford, 1965), Part I, chap. 10, p. 68: "the publique worth of a man, which is the Value set on him by the Common-Wealth, is that which men commonly call Dignity."

dignity to be an "intrinsic," "absolute" value and not merely relative, referred to the substrate, the bearer of the dignity, as a reasonable human being. As such, man is absolute, not as an empirical subject.

This historical sketch may show that dignity always refers to a certain distinguishing aspect of man, not his entirety. The dignity of the office reflects its importance in the hierarchical order of the state. The dignity of man in Christian perspective refers to the order of all creatures, within which man obtains a special position because of being an image of God. Dignity in a philosophical sense may refer to participation in a moral order. This supports the idea that in determining the meaning of dignity we have to distinguish between its basis in a substrate (man, animal, office, etc.) and the respective framework. With respect to the latter, dignity is relative, whereas with respect to the former, the substrate, it may be absolute. Dignity has different relations if it concerns a Christian in his or her religious surrounding, asking for mercy regardless of one's deeds, or if a criminal, does the same to the head of the state. From this framework to which dignity relates, we have to distinguish its foundation in a certain substrate. In the case of human dignity this is a human being. This foundation can have a dominating position with respect to other substrates. To be a human being can have an uppermost importance. Dignity then is the expression of the systematic value of this substrate, of the human being.

If dignity refers to a value, acknowledged to a certain substrate with respect to a specific context, we may ask more precisely: Is there a way to respect the request of the framers to recognize human dignity as an uppermost value, or do we have to speak of it pathetically but give it no hard legal relevance? The answer is that this could be done by understanding human dignity as the right to be a legal person.

3. The Concept of Person in Law

In the concept of the legal person we have a technical term that has gradually developed from its philosophical roots. It refers to the position of a homogeneous substrate in law. In the form of the "natural person" it denotes the position of man in law. It is founded in his legal subjectivity, meaning the ability of being addressed by rights and duties.[32]

32. Kobusch, "Die Würde des Menschen"; S. Kirste, "Verlust und Wiederaneignung der Mitte — zur juristischen Konstruktion der Rechtsperson," *Evangelische Theologie* 60 (2000): 25-40; S. Kirste, "Dezentrierung, Überforderung und dialektische Konstruktion der Rechts-

The philosophical development of the term from an unspecified under-standing as a mask ("prosopon") at first brought aspects of a specific function of the term, when the theological problem of trinity was discussed by the church fathers. The well-known definition by Boethius (475-524) expressed this quite well: "Persona est rationalis naturae individua substantia" — "The person is the individual substance of a rational nature." Accordingly, the quality of being a person does not refer to the empirical nature, but to reason. However, this does not mean reason in general, but reason as it shows in an individual substance.[33] Bonaventura (1221-1274) developed a theory of moral action that understood all men as responsible "moral persons." Thomas Aquinas perceived "person" as the "most dignified," reasonable nature. It is characterized by a special way to exist, the "per se existere."[34] With respect to the form, he emphasized that the person holds a middle position between the species — like man — and an individual name — like Socrates.[35] Taken together, person is the name of a privatizing of the universal reason in a singular human being and seizing its higher essence. Wilhelm of Auxerre introduced the concept to law: "Persona est nomen iuris, id est potestatis et dignitatis."[36] The connection of person, law, power, and dignity are commonplace in the medieval.

Beginning in late Scholasticism and later in its most elaborated form in the Enlightenment philosophy of Samuel Pufendorf and Christian Wolff, "persona moralis" becomes a term for the nature of man as part of a moral world. From this second nature as a moral person man deduces his specific dignity. Man is divided into two persons, so to speak, a natural and a moral person. From this construction it is clear that person signifies a specific function with respect to the different ontological frameworks. Whereas Pufendorf consid-ered the status in the world of morals as a basis for the personality, Christian Wolff took norms as a starting point of his argumentation and considered

---

person," in *Verfassung — Philosophie — Kirche. Festschrift für Alexander Hollerbach zum 70. Geburtstag*, ed. J. Bohnert, C. Gramm, U. Kindhäuser, J. Lege, A. Rinken, and G. Robbers (Berlin, 2001), pp. 319-61.

33. E. Fuhrmann, "Person I. Von der Antike bis zum Mittelalter," in *Historisches Wörter-buch der Philosophie* VII (Basel, 1989), columns 269-83, especially 280; Kobusch, "Die Würde des Menschen," 28.

34. B. Kible, "Person II. Hoch- und Spätscholastik; Meister Eckhart; Luther," in *His-torisches Wörterbuch der Philosophie* VII (Basel, 1989), Column 283-300, especially 287f., 291; on the concept of dignity in Thomas Aquinas and its legal implications, see C. Enders, *Die Menschenwürde in der Verfassungsordnung. Zur Dogmatik des Art. 1 GG* (Tübingen, 1997), pp. 180-84.

35. *Kible* 1989 (note 319), column 292.

36. *Kible* 1989 (note 319), column 287.

personality to be the ability of ascription or imputation of norms. *Persona moralis* now is the status of having moral rights and duties.[37]

Immanuel Kant could finally separate the legal and the moral foundation of the person. Although he spoke of the duty to respect all other human beings as persons in his *Groundwork of the Metaphysics of Morals*,[38] he does not mention this duty in his legal theory, but only again in the foundation of ethics.[39] Accordingly, respect to others as legal persons is not a legal duty. The ability to be subject of imputation is the decisive criterion to distinguish person and object. This ability is — at least in principle — inherent in all human beings. Kant makes it clear that person is always relative to a certain system of norms. It follows from this that there can be moral persons and different from them, legal persons.

It is not surprising that the term "person" was now prepared for its reception in law. This reception led to a differentiation of the term that followed legal necessities. When Friedrich Carl von Savigny — head of the Historical School of Law — took up the term, he decidedly rejected the use of "persona moralis" but insisted on a distinguished legal meaning of the term "person."[40] For this specific legal understanding von Savigny concentrated on legal capacity. Legal capacity is a strictly legal term that can be attributed without any binding to other systems, including morals. The one who has legal capacity is a legal subject. The bond with morals is not cut, however. Von Savigny held that "[e]ach and every human being, and only the individual human being, is capable of holding rights and duties."[41] Whereas von Savigny constructed the

37. Wolfgang Schild, "Artikel: Person, IV. Recht-Rechtsperson; Rechtspersönlichkeit," in *Historisches Wörterbuch der Philosophie* VII (Basel, 1989), columns 322-35, especially 324; Martin Lipp, " 'Persona moralis,' 'Juristische Person' und 'Personenrecht' — Eine Studie zur Dogmengeschichte der 'Juristischen Person' im Naturrecht und frühen 19. Jahrhundert," *Quaderni Fiorentini per la storia del pensiero giuridico moderno* 11/12 (1982/83): 217-63, 238.

38. I. Kant, *Grundlegung zur Metaphysik der Sitten,* ed. W. Weischedel (Frankfurt am Main, 1974), pp. 7-102, 61: "Handle so, daß du die Menschheit sowohl in deiner Person, als in der Person eines jeden andern, jederzeit zugleich als Zweck, niemals bloß als Mittel brauchest."

39. I. Kant, *Die Metaphysik der Sitten* (1797-98), ed. W. Weischedel (Frankfurt am Main, 1977), AB 31, 600.

40. F. C. von Savigny, *System des heutigen römischen Rechts. Zweyter Band* (Berlin, 1840), pp. 240f.: "Früher war sehr gewöhnlich der Name der moralischen Person, den ich aus zwey Gründen verwerfe: erstens weil er überhaupt nicht das Wesen des Begriffs[der juristischen Person, K.] berührt, der mit sittlichen Verhältnissen keinen Zusammenhang hat: zweytens weil jener Ausdruck eher dazu geeignet ist, unter den einzelnen Menschen den Gegensatz gegen die unmoralischen zu bezeichnen, so daß durch jenen Namen der Gedanke auf ein ganz fremdartiges Gebiet hinüber geleitet wird."

41. Savigny, *System des heutigen römischen Rechts,* p. 2.

legal capacity from his notion of human beings, his student, Friedrich Puchta, turned the argument around: "This is the first step to the ascertainment that man as a being with a will is a legal subject, because the subjective right is a power of the will, and not: The subjective right is a power of the will, because it serves the realization of the human will."[42] Finally, Hans Kelsen brought the process of the legal differentiation of the person to an end, declaring it his concern to "bring physical and legal persons . . . on the common denominator, on the denominator of law."[43]

Person is a functional term. It has to be understood from the respective normative system as the focal point for the ascription or imputation of norms. Each normative system has different criteria for attributing the status of a person. These criteria are not dependent upon arguments from natural conditions or other normative systems. These persons are not created out of bones and flesh; their body consists of rights and duties. Accordingly, it is possible to treat a mentally disabled or even an unborn subject as a person in law, which may have certain rights even if it is incapable of acting. This also means that new knowledge from neuroscience[44] does not determine whether or not to acknowledge someone as a person in law. The term person gives human beings a standing in law, but one that is shaped according to the needs of men as well as of the legal system. This standing is the legal body of the natural person or other entities given the power to be addressed by rights and to act legally. It is, in medieval words, the "mystic" or the juridic body, that the person in law possesses.[45] The pure capacity is the basis for freedom and equality as well.[46] In this capacity all legal subjects are equal. Accordingly, Gustav Radbruch was right, stating that the concept of the legal person is a concept of equality.[47] At the same time, the legal person is the basis for legal liberty: To have rights means to have legal power independent of public or private influence.

---

42. U. John, "Einheit und Spaltung im Begriff der Rechtsperson," *Quaderni Fiorentini per la storia del pensiero giuridico moderno* 11/12 (1982/83): 947-71, 949.

43. H. Kelsen, *Allgemeine Staatslehre* (Berlin, 1925), p. 63.

44. Cf. the chapters by Warren S. Brown and by Philip Clayton in the present volume.

45. Cf. E. Hartwig Kantorowicz, *The King's Two Bodies*, p. 209.

46. H. Coing, *Europäisches Privatrecht. Band I. Älteres Gemeines Recht (1500 bis 1800)* (München, 1985), p. 171.

47. G. Radbruch, *Rechtsphilosophie*, ed. E. Wolf and H.-P. Schneider (Stuttgart, ⁸1973), p. 225; for Radbruch the fundament of equality is the idea of man being an end in himself, however. He considers it to be sufficient for collective legal persons to be an expression of the human beings behind them. Accordingly he summarizes: "Alle Personen, die physischen wie die juristischen, sind Geschöpfe der Rechtsordnung. Auch die physischen Personen sind im strengsten Sinne 'juristische Personen'" (p. 227).

From this it is clear that with the differentiation of law and morals in the nineteenth century, the legal person has inherited the position of the moral person in law. Together with our considerations on dignity we may conclude that the dignity of the person is a legal dignity that stems from its participation in the legal world, just as the dignity of the moral person corresponds to its status in a moral world.

4. The Respect for Human Dignity as the Right to Be Recognized as a Legal Person

There is a dispute among German scholars of constitutional law over how the first sentence of the Basic Law is to be understood: "The dignity of the human being is inviolable" ("Die Würde des Menschen ist unantastbar").[48] Is it a descriptive sentence, because norms necessarily contain an ought and this is formulated as an indicative? Whereas normative sentences contain counterfactual provisions, descriptive sentences can — in general — be proven as true or false. If it were a descriptive sentence, it would have been falsified, because obviously human dignity can be and has been violated. Accordingly, to make sense we have to understand the sentence as a normative sentence: the "is inviolable" has to be understood as "shall not be violated."[49]

I further suggest that it is to be understood as a legal sentence.[50] But it can have this form only if understood as containing a right. If it contained a principle only, this legal principle could be balanced against other legal principles. This again means that it could be infringed in some cases. To be subject of infringement, it would not be compatible with the apodictic formulation.

However, it can contain a right only if human dignity is understood as legal subjectivity. Being a legal subject is the highest dignity law provides. It

48. The same wording in Article 1 of the Charter of Fundamental Rights of the European Union.

49. Cf. H. Dreier, Art. 1 I GG, Rn. 42f., in H. Dreier, *Grundgesetz. Kommentar. Band 1, Präambel, Art. 1-19* (Tübingen, ²2004). M. Herdegen, Art. 1 Abs. 1, Rn. 17ff., in Maunz-Dürig-Herzog-Scholz, *Grundgesetz. Kommentar. Band I, Art. 1-5* (München, 49. Lieferung März, 2007); Christian Stark, Art. 1, Rn. 13 u. 23f., in Mangoldt-Klein-Starck, *Bonner Grundgesetz. Kommentar,* vol. 1 (München, ⁴1999); C. Enders, Art. 1 Rn. 47ff., in Friauf-Höfling, *Berliner Kommentar zum Grundgesetz,* vol. 1 (2005).

50. This is my major disagreement with Christoph Enders (*Art. 1 Rn. 47ff., 68f., in Friauf-Höfling, Berliner Kommentar zum Grundgesetz,* vol. 1 [2000]); C. Enders, *Die Menschenwürde in der Verfassungsordnung* (Tübingen, 1997), pp. 94ff., who denies the legal character of human dignity in Art. 1 I of the German Basic Law.

means the ability to make legal use of one's liberty. This ability is realized, if the subject is attributed certain rights. To have a right means the power to act legally. The right that human dignity provides is the claim to the recognition of the legal capacity of each human being. If then, legal capacity means to be a subject of rights, this claim is satisfied, as soon as a human being is subject to the attribution of rights and not a mere object of rights of others.

Now, if we understand human dignity as a right to be recognized as a legal subject and if being a legal subject means having rights and duties, then this right is legally proclaimed and fulfilled at the same time: In the form of an individual right it bestows all human beings with the claim to become a legal person; since being a legal person means being a subject of legal rights and duties, the right is fulfilled by proclaiming it. The right to human dignity is unique indeed. Whereas other claims are being fulfilled by further action, the right of being recognized as a person in law is fulfilled by its codification as a basic right. By its codification the human being gets a right that is necessary to be a legal subject. The content of the right of human dignity is the basic right to be recognized as a legal subject. This content is indeed elementary for the law. This claim is fulfilled by the form of a right. The indicative form of the sentence is appropriate, because once this right is acknowledged in the constitution, it cannot be violated.

Human dignity understood in this legally technical way provides an aspect that the concept of legal person did not contain. The mere concept of the legal person as I have sketched it before does not say anything of who should have the quality of a legal subject. With the separation of the legal person from the concept of "persona moralis," the law had to find its own criteria for the attribution of this quality. Whoever has legal rights and duties is a legal subject and a legal person. But who should that be? This is the question. Human dignity answers: All human beings have to be treated as legal subjects.

There is of course a key objection to this interpretation of human dignity as a legal concept: In its reduction of the content of human dignity to the right of being recognized as a legal subject, it changes and minimizes this concept to a formal and technical tool. In this emptied-out form the concept seems to be incapable of providing the protection to human beings they deserve. But on the one hand, reducing the content to the right of being recognized as a legal subject means strengthening it legally: The individual gets a right to be recognized that way. Such a right would have prevented Jews or gypsies from being denied the legal status as persons in the Third Reich. This right need not and cannot be balanced against other rights or values and is in this sense absolute. No one can more or less be a legal subject. Either he or she has rights and duties or does not. If he has a right, he is a legal subject; if he does not, he is not a legal subject.

One can further object that, if one right should be enough to fulfill the right to be recognized as a legal subject, then why not give the individual the right to be a slave? But this is no sweeping objection. Here the form of a right hollows out his position and does not grant him a right. Having the right to be a slave means having the right not to have rights or duties. Being a slave means not to have any rights or duties and to be a mere object in the hands of the master. When in 1824 Dred Scott returned from Illinois, where slavery was forbidden, to Missouri, where it was permitted, he or his wife were not asked to fulfill their duties; they were simply considered to be part of Sanford's mobile private property. They belonged to Sanford as objects and were not treated as subjects. If on the other hand a slave would be given the freedom he deserves as a human being not by an act of paternalism, but because the master acknowledged his right to be free, he was at the same time recognized as a legal subject. By the mere recognition of this right, he is respected as a person and loses the status of a slave. If we apply this rationale to our problem of giving a legal subject the right to be a slave, then we see that there can never be a right to slavery, because slavery means having no rights.

This is not the last constitutional word on human dignity, however. Especially, if a constitution not only states that human dignity is inviolable, but demands its respect and protection, it imposes an obligation on the state to grant the individual more rights. Remember that we saw the legal subject as having potential for the attribution of basic rights such as liberties and equality rights. Fulfilling the obligation of respect for and protection of human dignity means that the state grants the individual these rights. Just as man is a human being even without arms and legs, he is a legal subject if he has a right to be recognized as such, but no further rights. In such a state he would obviously miss important abilities. His self-determination would have a very small range. He is not only a person, but a personality also. As a personality he has the potential to act reasonably. Respecting him as such means granting him more rights to realize his potential. Modern constitutions take this into account by protecting the individual against torture, abolishing the death penalty, respecting a person's privacy, and protecting him or her against other "inhuman or degrading punishment or treatment" (Art. 15, 1 of the Spanish Constitution or Art. 5 III of the Brazilian Constitution).[51] Just as legal capacity does not

---

51. For a thorough investigation and comparison of human dignity in the German and Brazilian Constitutions cf. A. P. Barbosa, *Die Menschenwürde im deutschen Grundgesetz und*

mean the capacity to act legally, but is a prerequisite of it, human dignity is a right to be respected in the potential to have further rights and does not mean to actually have them. The other basic rights give persons the freedom to act unimpaired by public intervention. But, as Hans Carl Nipperdey has put it, human dignity is "the last root and fountain of all later formulated basic rights."[52] It guarantees the ability to have further rights.

This root is not necessarily bound to the individual life. The unborn may have dignity even as dignity does not necessarily end with death. It may go too far, as Baldus wrote: "The emperor in his person must die, but the Dignity itself . . . is immortal."[53] He conceived the person to have two bodies, one natural and one mystical — or in modern words: one empirical and one based on social expectations. The latter, he says, is the bearer of dignity. Baldus met the point that the dignity is dependent upon ascription and not bound to the natural matter. Law has kept Baldus's distinction but turned it upside down: Every human being has the right to a legal social recognition. That is his dignity. And the legal expression of this dignity is his juridical personhood. This right remains, even if the person — both the natural and the legal — has ceased to exist. From its dignity man has a right to the postmortal protection of his personality.

The proposed concept of human dignity as a right to be recognized as a legal subject avoids any further material theological or philosophical assumptions. The basic elements of it were once developed by theological and philosophical speculation, but they were transformed into legal arguments. Accordingly, it fits well into constitutions that have a neutral character towards religion and worldview. If, however, a constitution like the Irish contains a stronger, a religious or a philosophical concept of human dignity, it is not contradictory to the just-presented interpretation. The concept of dignity as a right to be recognized as a legal subject does not preclude that the number of rights that fulfill this claim could be greater, could include autonomy, creativity, self-determination, etc., if only the constitution indicates this. But this broader content of the term depends on respective constitutional indications and does not stem from the term "human dignity" itself. Human dignity as a legal concept demands the basis, the right to be able to have rights, and that means to

---

in der brasilianischen Verfassung von 1988. Ein Rechtsvergleich (Dissertation, Heidelberg 2007); also A. P. Barbosa, "A Legitimação Moral da Dignidade Humana e dos Princípios de Direitos Humanos," in *Legitimação dos Direitos Humanos,* ed. R. Lobo Torres (Rio de Janeiro/São Paulo/ Recife, ²2007), pp. 137-68, who applies the approach of Carlos Santiago Nino.

52. H. C. Nipperdey, *Die Grundrechte II,* pp. 1, 11f.

53. Kantorowicz, *The King's Two Bodies,* p. 398.

be acknowledged as a legal person. This concept is free of any extra-legal value, thereby omitting value conflicts in the interpretation of human dignity. But it is open to values. It contains the necessary decision about the value that every human being has the right to be recognized as a legal subject. What this legal subject "looks like," what further rights it should have, is up to the decision of the constituent power or the legislator, whose decision is legitimated by the respective procedure about them.

"The state exists for the human being; human beings do not exist for the state."[54] This goal, discussed among the frames of the German Basic Law, can be achieved by the state that obeys the rule of law only by means of the law. Because this state is for the individual, it achieves this aim by guaranteeing the individual rights. The state therefore transforms the pre-legal human being into a legal human being, and that means into a legal person. This is no abstract ideal with the practical relevance of a Sunday speech. On the contrary: The law is dependent on the fulfillment of this ideal. Without legal persons there would be no laws. Their capability of being subjects of imputation is the basis of all legal relationships.

The contrary is also true, however: without the law there would be no legal persons. Oriented towards the ideal, the framers and legislators understand it in different ways as they force it through the eye of the needle of the legal form. Just as the ethical perfection of man is the free personality as the basis of its dignity as a *persona moralis,* in law the legal personhood is the fundament for all further rights, including the rights he deserves as a reasonable personality. In morals, autonomy is the basis for dignity, as Kant said. In law, legal subjectivity is the basis for liberties. In these rights the legal subject expresses itself. But the legal person gets richer, receives more spheres of action, without public intervention. The transformation of dignity into the law turns foundation and result inside out: the dignity that follows autonomy in ethics is the basis for liberties in law, and the status as a person that is the expression of this liberty becomes the legal basis for the execution of his freedom in a legal form.

It seems to be part of the dialectic of human dignity as a legal principle that it loses legal importance the more it is burdened with extra-legal content and that it fulfills its function the more it is reduced to the subjective foundation of the legal system. The one who demands everything from the point of

---

54. Article 1 of the draft of the Herrenchiemseer Konvent: "(1) Der Staat ist um des Menschen willen da, nicht der Mensch um des Staates willen. (2) Die Würde der menschlichen Persönlichkeit ist unantastbar. Die öffentliche Gewalt ist in allen ihren Erscheinungsformen verpflichtet, die Menschenwürde zu achten und zu schützen."

view of morals or natural law is in danger of devaluating it as law altogether. Understood as a right to be acknowledged as a legal person, human dignity avoids these dangers.

As this is a strictly legal perspective on the dignity of the human being, it does not preclude philosophical criticism and philosophical alternatives to this concept. The legal question, however, would be, how can they be transformed into the law?

On the Relation of Personhood and Embodiment

Frank Vogelsang

1. Meaning of the Term "Person"

A pivotal meaning is accorded to the term "person." Human personhood is
not only a distinguishing characteristic vis-à-vis inanimate things and objects
of the world, but also vis-à-vis other nonhuman forms of life. Jurisprudence
identifies persons as the bearers of rights and duties. A human being has the
possibility of invoking his or her rights in a constitutional state as a person.

Throughout the centuries, the manner in which human beings have
been assigned personhood has varied, but the exclusivity of the distinction
has remained constant. Robert Spaemann has described this constituent
difference of personhood as the simple difference between "something" and
"someone."[1] The exclusivity of human personhood is vital to the very concept of personhood.

The current problem is that along with the waning cultural acceptance of
metaphysical foundations for personhood, doubt in the fundamental exclusivity of personhood itself is growing. This situation is brought on in large part
by findings in the natural sciences. Though there has always been a critique of
the anthropocentrism that certain critics see as an unwanted relic of ancient
times, today such sentiments are substantially more widespread. Three areas
feeding this doubt are sketched here:

Firstly, biological research shows that the difference between animals and

---

1. R. Spaemann, *Personen. Versuche über den Unterschied zwischen "etwas" und "jemand"*
(Stuttgart: Klett, 1996).

FRANK VOGELSANG

humans is not so easy to specify. Claims founded on, for example, linguistic capacity or brain complexity are difficult to defend in the face of recent findings. More precise analyses show that there are only gradual differences[2] and that though these differences may be enormous,[3] they are not of a fundamental nature. In the face of certain human diseases and the astounding abilities of various animals, a sharp distinction between person and nonperson becomes untenable. Instead, one can only speak of more or less "personal" beings. This "more or less," however, is fully incompatible with the concept of the person: no human can be less or more a person than anyone else. The distinction "person" is either given entirely or not at all. This fact is difficult to reconcile with the gradual differences of biology.

Next, the hopes of artificial intelligence research are geared toward the eventual creation of a being whose behavior and reactions could not be qualitatively differentiated from those of humans. Assuming that these computers of the future that react and communicate like humans can be built (which is still unproven), will they be granted the status of person? And if such status would be denied to them, how then could one define the opposition of personhood and artificial intelligence? With his Chinese room argument, John Searle objects to the claims of artificial intelligence research.[4]

Finally, recent progress in brain research has at least provisionally shed light on many processes that only decades ago were fully unobservable. Among these are mechanisms that put the breadth of humans' conscious self-control in question. But if our will is not free, doesn't this problematization of self-determination also put the very distinction of human personhood in question? How can a human be a person if his or her central organ is composed "solely" of complex neural excitation patterns with causal relations? These were the central questions of the famous debate around Benjamin Libet's investigations.[5]

These examples demonstrate how scientific and technical progress puts certain old, unproblematized assumptions into question, and forces them into debate. A complex understanding of the human being as person must be defended anew.

2. M. Jeeves, "Brains, Minds, Souls, and People: A Scientific Perspective on Complex Human Personhood" (in this volume).
3. W. Brown, "The Emergence of Human Distinctiveness" (in this volume).
4. J. Searle, *Mind: A Brief Introduction* (Oxford: Oxford University Press, 2004).
5. M. Pauen, *Illusion Freiheit? Mögliche und unmögliche Konsequenzen der Hirnforschung* (Frankfurt am Main: Fischer, 2006).

2. Traditional Responses to the Privileging of the Person

A short survey of traditional responses to the above questions reveals their inadequacy in the face of our contemporary knowledge of the world.

First in the list is the traditional idea of a substantive, immortal soul, only temporarily bound to a mortal body. In this view, human beings are distinguished from other life-forms by this immortal soul. Though the idea of the soul remains quite popular, it is constantly subjected to a variety of interpretations and critiques. Furthermore, linking a conception of the soul to the scientific image of humanity has proven more than difficult. It remains unclear how the concept of the soul can be integrated into our contemporary understanding of the human in such a way that it could represent more than a privileged term without connection to other insights, scientific or otherwise. A theological critique in this direction has been elaborated by Paul Tillich.[6]

Next is the Cartesian differentiation of the *res cogitans* and the *res extensa* — product of Descartes' methodological skepticism. In this view, human beings are distinguished from other life-forms by the *res cogitans*.[7] This substance is possessed solely by humans, making animals, according to Descartes, no more than complex machines. This idea of substantive duality is, as with the soul, no longer tenable. There is absolutely no indication in neuroscience how such a substance as the *res cogitans* might even be thinkable. In particular, the place where such a substance would come into contact with other substances and where the exchange of information would have to take place remains fully unclear. Eccles's related proposal to take the mechanisms of quantum physics into account provokes more questions than it is able to answer.[8]

Finally, the classical distinctive characteristic of humans is the allocation of reason. The definition in the scheme *genus proximum differentia specifica* reads: man is a rational animal — that is, an animal whose particularity lies in his or her intelligence. However, the idea of rationality as an isolatable, clearly determinable capacity (as insisted upon in the classical philosophy of someone like Kant) is today for various reasons untenable. Research such as Antonio Damasio's, for example, has shown that human reason is not so much a conceptual ability, but rather something embedded in the bodily existence of

6. P. Tillich, *Systematische Theologie*, vol. 3 (Berlin/New York: De Gruyter, 1966), 35.

7. R. Descartes, *Meditationes de prima philosophia*, *Philosophische Bibliothek Volume 250a* (Hamburg: Felix Meiner Verlag, 1992 [1641]), p. 50.

8. K. Popper and J. Eccles, *The Self and Its Brain — An Argument for Interactionism* (London: Routledge, 1984).

human beings.[9] And of course, philosophy itself has meanwhile radically put in question any kind of fixed and timeless conception of reason.

Apparently then, personhood no longer allows itself to be conceived as a substantial phenomenon as according to its classical definition. It is simply not possible to refer to a form of being or substance that can be accorded only to humans and from which personhood can then be deduced. Thus in the definition of the human, it is in a first step necessary to rely on biological research whose methods, in particular those of the neurosciences of the past decade, could stand for significant improvement.

3. Personhood and Natural Science

Man is necessarily a bodily entity. Therefore, human personhood cannot be determined without the consideration of biological constitution. Biological research indicates that even in the most precise analysis, no substance or aggregate beyond the material-biological is to be found. The results of such research also show no sign of any human attributes that fundamentally diverge from those of animals. In the factors that biological research takes into consideration, there are only relations of more or less, never of all or nothing. And yet for the denomination of personhood, precisely this is required: an attribute that is either total or not at all. As stated before, personness can in no way be gradually allotted. What this means is that though the human being as a biologically describable entity is a necessary precondition for the determination of personhood, this in itself is not sufficient.

And yet, the significance of biological findings on the determination of personhood cannot be understated. The importance of biological research comes to the fore in the face of controversial cases involving bioethics. In such cases, biological knowledge repeatedly plays a decisive role in offering conflicting parties arguments for or against a given dispute. It is thus impossible to pursue the question of personhood independent of biological research, though on the other hand, again, no stable, effectual criteria for personhood can be deduced from biological knowledge alone. Whatever the definition of a person may be, its significance is obviously much farther-reaching than a mere set of biological findings. A human being is on the one hand just another part of nature, but on the other hand is an agent of culture. The reduction of

9. A. Damasio, *The Feeling of What Happens: Body and Emotion in the Making of Consciousness* (Orlando, FL: Harcourt Brace, 2000).

the human to its natural aspect offers absolutely fundamental and necessary insights, but is not enough to embrace all aspects of the human. Especially in understanding a human being as a person, the naturalistic approach alone falls short.

4. Approaching Personhood via Recognition

According to our reflections so far, we are searching for an approach to personhood that goes beyond an exclusively biological approach, but that also does not rely on metaphysical assumptions. My proposal here is to adopt an understanding of personhood via recognition as suggested by Robert Spaemann. This understanding of personhood will be explored with the help of phenomenological analysis, especially the phenomenology of the body as elaborated by Maurice Merleau-Ponty. No one in his or her isolated being is a person; he or she can only be so in and through the recognition of others. The personness of a human being is thus substantially conditioned via the recognition of other humans. *"[Die Anerkennung] setzt ein passives Gegebensein voraus. Der Andere muss mir in der sinnlichen Erfahrung und als Lebewesen 'Mensch' gegeben sein, in der spezifischen Weise, wie uns Lebendiges gegeben ist. Sein Personsein ist aber wesentlich das nie Gegebene, sondern in freier Anerkennung Wahrgenommene."*[10]

This conception of personhood via recognition unites two different approaches: the biological, which identifies specific sorts of living entities, i.e., the passive givenness of the "human being," as well as the additional approach of unconstrained recognition. Both are necessary. Personhood can only be described in a twofold manner. Firstly, a person can be seen as a member of the species *homo sapiens,* a human being, which can be described biologically. But this is not enough. Additionally, a person must simultaneously be seen as something more. The decisive question is then how this second, additional aspect can be expounded, and thus why it is not possible to produce a definition based upon the first aspect alone.

---

10. Spaemann, *Personen,* p. 194: "[Recognition] postulates a passive givenness. The Other must be taken as a given both empirically and as the particular life form 'human being' in the same way that all living things can be taken as givens. The personness of the Other, however, is not intrinsically given, but is rather perceived in unconstrained recognition."

FRANK VOGELSANG

4.1. The Biological Aspect of Personhood

This first aspect corresponds to the scientific approach of biology. Spaemann's understanding of personhood takes scientific findings into consideration without constraining itself to them. Here it becomes clear that there is a determinate difference between a biological description of a human being and the question of personhood. No analysis of an organism or organ can generate criteria that in all cases could differentiate persons and nonpersons. Spaemann tackles this by declaring that "person" is not a term of "sort";[11] that is, the quality of personhood does not designate elements of a particular group differentiated from other groups by specific characteristics. A person is not a thing or life-form with some special individuating attribute. The difference between a person and any other life-form, between someone and something, is not determined by any measurable characteristic.

If, as Spaemann concedes, a person is not essentially a biological given, why is it at all necessary to refer to and rely upon humans' biological foundations? Why shouldn't one concentrate exclusively on our second, decisive aspect of personhood? The importance of the biological approach becomes obvious when one asks how illegitimate candidates for personhood might be screened out. Here, the biological approach can serve an important function.

The identification of something as a person can thus be questioned. The biological aspect of a given candidate for personhood offers us a framework for criticizing unsubstantiated applications of personhood — if, for example, one were to attempt to classify pets as persons. Pet owners often communicate with their pets as though these were persons. Humans have an inclination to assign human characteristics to entities in their surroundings. Psychological studies have shown that even geometrical forms like triangles, if moved in an appropriate way, are interpreted by observers as intentional beings. But such intuitions cannot be rationally substantiated. The biological reference point helps constrain possible candidates for personhood to the members of humankind.

Biological knowledge is also critical in a more complex aspect of the appropriate application of personhood: namely, when it must be decided whether or not a human being is alive. Here, the allocation of personhood requires not only a human being, but a living human being.[12] The many criteria for

11. Spaemann, *Personen,* p. 43.
12. G. Thomas, "Human Personhood at the Edges of Life" (in this volume).

defining the beginning and end of life are all fiercely disputed when it comes to bioethical discussions. Such criteria often very much depend on religious and value-oriented positions. But values alone cannot solve the problem. Biological knowledge is absolutely necessary in deciding whether or not a human being is alive.

Thus, a "passive givenness" is indeed required in the allocation of personhood. Recognition can take place only if a human being is the focus of interest. A human being is something that can be identified by biological analysis. A human being differs from a machine and from an animal. He or she belongs to the human species. Science fiction deals with cases in which it is doubtful whether or not a being is still human. The development of human body enhancements provokes similar questions. The relevance of such considerations to our current discussion, however, is questionable. Indeed, it seems unlikely that such cases could ever prove relevant, as they underestimate the complexity of human beings.

Although a biological reference point is necessary to an understanding of personhood, this science-related approach continues to remain inadequate, as personhood cannot be defined sufficiently by biological criteria alone. Although the literal quantity of living human beings and of persons might be identical, the notion of personhood comprises more than a biological definition. Personhood requires a broader approach. It connotes additional features that cannot be addressed in exclusively biological terms. Spaemann proposes discussing these additional features in terms of recognition.

4.2. The Recognitive Aspect of Personhood

Thus far we've argued for a definition of personhood via recognition. As such, however, the definition of personhood turns out to suggest some far-reaching philosophical questions. Biological findings are made from a third-person perspective. This implies a methodological approach to reality dominated by the assumption that the observer is unrelated to that which is observed. If a person acknowledges another human being as a person, however, it is no longer possible for the observer to treat the Other in an objective mode (the biological, third-person methodological approach), but must also take his or her own observation into account. Recognition is thus fundamentally different from objective observation.

But how then can this additional feature, recognition, be described? How can something transcend objective description without referring to metaphysical entities? What is the epistemological basis for an appropriate description of this approach? My answer is the phenomenology of the body as elaborated by Maurice Merleau-Ponty. This approach relies on several fundamental insights. First of all, that every human being has a bodily existence. This fact is not accidental. It determines the manner in which we relate to reality and to other human beings. We cannot view reality from the outside; we must explore it from the inside. We are not simply minds accidentally bound to a material substrate. Our involvement in our material surroundings is instead essential. Further, we cannot approach the Other as an unknown object, because as a living body we are always already dependent on other bodies. One of the most important conclusions to draw from our embodied situation is that a plurality of perspectives exist with which we can explore ourselves, others, and reality as a whole. The third-person perspective, the perspective of the detached observer, is one possible perspective but not the only one, and this perspective alone cannot refer to all aspects. There are other perspectives, in which the role of the observer is constituent. This will prove critical for an understanding of personhood defined via recognition. The investigation of recognition points not to some special feature of humans, not to any new, hidden quality, but instead to the fact that humans can only be understood if they are observed from a multitude of perspectives. Some of these perspectives are marked by the inevitable influence of the observer. I want to expand upon these arguments in two steps. First, I want to give a short introduction to the important insights of Merleau-Ponty concerning his understanding of the body (meaning in the first place the understanding of one's own body), and second, I want to refer to Merleau-Ponty's treatment of the Other, the encounter with another person.

5. Personhood and the Phenomenology of the Body

To understand the constitutive element of recognition in the definition of personhood, we first have to consider the mode of existence of a human being. If we reduce the human being to a given entity, which means relying solely on the third-person perspective, it is impossible to find anything apart from his or her biological features. To move beyond this, we must first seek out an appropriate description of bodily existence, and then, in a second step, we must take the interpersonal relationship into account.

5.1. *What the Body Is Not About*

Our point of departure, embodiment, must not be confused with certain (mis) understandings of the body. The very notion of "the body" is heavily loaded, as well as often misused and oversimplified. In such cases, it often stands for authenticity, for that which precedes all forms of alienation: for the mystification of immediacy and the originary. Even certain philosophers of embodiment seem to want to express this.[13] As such, the body is that which can be seen solely from an intimate perspective. Here we find a congruent but different error to that which we encountered before, again reducing the mode of perception to a single perspective — in this case: first-person instead of third. These misunderstood connotations are not so easily dismissed. If, however, the term is not to be misused as a simple contrast to allegedly abstract scienticity, it must be grasped dialectically, encompassing both the scientific and unreflectively experiential approaches. The term "integral body" takes into account the fact that the human relationship to the material body is at once one of identity and nonidentity. On the one hand, one is identical with one's material body. It is unimaginable that one would remain the same being if one's body were other. What could there be to account for continuity? And yet it is also the case that man *can* dissociate him or herself from his or her body. But then who or what is it that steps apart from the body? This phenomenon is known "eccentric positionality."[14]

5.2. *Toward an Understanding of the Integral Body*

Our primary question is how to achieve the fullest picture of personhood: how to relate biological findings concerning the human body with the necessity of recognition. Maurice Merleau-Ponty's theory of the body is specifically designed to avoid classical impasses of bodily understanding. He rejects both classical approaches to the body: both rational and empirical. In various ways, he attempts to steer between the main currents of European philosophy. His conception of the body does not posit the body as a given entity. In his late writings, he advocates a theory of the body that attempts to begin at a point where subject and object are not yet distinguished.

---

13. H. Schmitz, *Der Leib, der Raum und die Gefühle* (Bielefeld/Locarno: Aisthesis, 2007).

14. H. Plessner, *Die Stufen des Organischen und der Mensch* (Berlin/New York: De Gruyter, 1975).

Merleau-Ponty's approach offers a broad view of the reality of human beings no longer confined to an objective perspective. The phenomenological philosophy of the body points precisely to the human situation — that a human person as an embodied being is not a thing, that is, is not entirely conceivable from a third-person perspective. The body is not only an entity within reality, but is at the same time a mode of access to reality.[15] Acknowledging the embodied body gives us the opportunity to widen our range of perspectives. And yet, there is no single perspective from which a person could be viewed without mediation.

But how can we justify these different perspectives? One of Merleau-Ponty's central insights stems from the observation that the body can be simultaneously subject and object. This is best described in the well-known experiment of one person's two hands touching each other: the right hand explores the surface of the left hand and vice versa. This leads Merleau-Ponty to the conclusion that the absolute differentiation of subject and object is a misguided assumption. The Cartesian legacy's demand for unambiguous propositions has given priority to the extremes of *res cogitans* and *res extensa* over any understanding of their intermediation. This quest for certainty's price is the disappearance of embodied existence. It was precisely Descartes' methodological skepticism, with which all uncertainties were to be put aside, that led him to the strict division of *res cogitans* and *res extensa*.

And yet, even Merleau-Ponty's approach draws in part on this Cartesian division. His attempt at describing a middle way presupposes these extremes.[16] Merleau-Ponty does however invert the focus of the discussion. Instead of focusing on these extremes, which are supposedly recognizable as *clare et distincte,* he gives his attention to the manifold shades of intermediation between these extremes — to that which constitutes reality.

The body as exemplary facet of reality represents an alternative field situated between the extremes of dualistic approaches. With this insight, the key to a third way between the extremes unfolds: between subject and object, between an aloof consciousness and an untouched world. The determination of a sphere of the "Between" was the goal of Merleau-Ponty's late philosophy.[17] Merleau-Ponty's approach evades the opposition of monism and dualism. Reality is not

---

15. M. Merleau-Ponty, "Phänomenologie der Wahrnehmung," in *Phänomenologisch-psychologische Forschungen,* vol. 7, ed. C. F. Graumann and J. Linschoten (Berlin: De Gruyter, 1945), p. 103, first part, §4.

16. C. Bermes, *Maurice Merleau-Ponty zur Einführung* (Hamburg: Junius, 1998), p. 141; B. Waldenfels, *Phänomenologie in Frankreich* (Frankfurt am Main: Suhrkamp, 1998), p. 199.

17. Waldenfels, *Phänomenologie in Frankreich,* p. 199.

dualistic; there are not two spheres of being or substance. And yet, reality is also not simply flattened into a monism. Instead, reality exists in the zone of the "Between": the gap that makes multiple and divergent forms of knowledge plausible.

This prompts Merleau-Ponty to deploy a metaphor that appears more and more frequently in his late writings: the chiasm. The chiasm is a quasi-metaphysical construction that helps in establishing an understanding of the integral body. According to Merleau-Ponty, the body can best be understood as an entanglement, an intertwining, or, as he called it: a chiasm — derived from the Greek letter "Chi."[18] Two things are interlaced: "The seen world is not 'in' my body, and my body is not 'in' the visible world. . . . There is a reciprocal insertion and intertwining of the one in the other."[19] At this point it is critical to emphasize that this description is not meant objectively (that is, referring to the body of anyone), but refers exclusively to one's own body. We can only understand the metaphor of the mutually touching hands by relying on our own bodily experience, our own subjectivity. This initial restriction is important because it de-privileges the dominance of a perspective from the outside, a third-person perspective. To understand the integral body, we must begin with our own body and not the idea of an objectively given body. Reliance on objective, "outside" perspectives is dominant in our society, but these approaches are not able to offer an adequate systematic account of personhood.

5.3. Perspectives on the Body

If the body is a given thing, an object, and is at the same time a subject, a subjective way of exploring the world, then no one perspective can suffice to describe an integral body. The third way of Merleau-Ponty necessitates the use of fundamentally different perspectives. In discussions of the philosophy of mind, first-person perspective and third-person perspective are often contrasted.[20] The phenomenological philosophy of the body offers several reasons why these perspectives must both be considered, though even this might not suffice to deliver an overall consistent picture.

From the first-person perspective, we have access to the body such that we experience "inner" modes — thoughts and feelings. As argued above, this per-

18. M. Merleau-Ponty, *The Visible and the Invisible*, followed by working notes ed. C. Lefort, trans. A. Lingis (Evanston, IL: Northwestern University Press, 1968), p. 130.

19. Merleau-Ponty, *The Visible and the Invisible*, p. 138.

20. See T. Metzinger, ed., *Bewusstsein. Beiträge aus der Gegenwartsphilosophie* (Paderborn: Mentis, 2001).

spective should not be confused with simple intimate knowledge. Nevertheless, this perspective cannot be simply reduced to something describable from third-person perspective.[21] Instead, this perspective comprises all perspectives where the observer is fundamentally inseparable from the observed. We can feel our own bodies, we can experience our bodies in such a way that we know this body is essentially our own body. What the body experiences, we experience as well. The first-person perspective implies the constitutive participation of the subject. This includes not only all declarations of "I," but also all declarations of "you," for only a directly participatory subject can speak of a "you."

If one approaches the body from a third-person perspective, one observes the physical substance of the body as given and the passive parameters that one can apprehend with analytical methods. The body seen from third-person perspective is what we call the corporeal, objective body. The integral body, on the other hand, must be described with the involvement of both first- and third-person perspective. It is not so simple that the phenomenologically analyzed body refers solely to first-person perspective. In order to get an idea of what the integral body means, we must analyze it from different perspectives. The ultimate assertion of the integral body at its most extensive would be to refer to all different perspectives simultaneously. The integral body, a concept that regards the body as subject and object at once, can only be comprehended when one implements both first- and third-person perspectives together.

6. The Other

6.1. The Fundamental Social Relation

So far, our description of the integral body remains insufficient to serve as a basis for an understanding of the notion of personhood. According to Spaemann, recognition plays a crucial role in personhood and thus the role of a second human being must also be considered. Having discussed assumptions about the bodily existence of human beings, we can now turn to the relations between human beings.

Our analysis of embodied existence has thus far left out one fundamental fact: no one body becomes a body on its own. When we describe humans as embodied beings, we cannot ignore social surroundings. Social relations are

---

21. Against D. Dennett, *Sweet Dreams: Philosophical Obstacles to a Science of Consciousness* (Cambridge, MA: MIT Press, 2005).

inevitably connected to their material basis. The human body is joined at birth to other bodies. The body understood as an embodied body cannot simply be an isolated entity. Furthermore, social relations are heavily stamped by cultural influences and shared language. Our thoughts stem from intimate communication with other humans. Beginning in earliest childhood, our material body is inevitably connected to our parents' generation. Humans are fully social beings, and a description of a human being as an integral body would be necessarily incomplete, if it did not take into account this social interdependence.

How can the social world, the shared world of at least two human beings, be described? According to the philosophy of embodiment, the human body is never in a total isolation. Merleau-Ponty suggests the terms "intercorporeality"[22] and "intermundane spaces"[23] to indicate the basic relatedness of human beings. The philosophy of embodiment does not begin with an isolated human being, but instead with the intermediate sphere between different bodies. This distinguishes it, once again, from other philosophical traditions that rely on concepts of Descartes.

Merleau-Ponty describes the ambivalent place of the Other as not simply in front of me like other objects, but beside me.[24] This calls attention to another fundamental realization: if we want to understand other humans, we must take into account the fact that they have always been there. We have never been in a totally solipsistic situation. Whatever we are, we became ourselves only with the influence of others. We are always engaged in social relations; we can never explore them from the outside. Thus, the Other is never a totally unknown being, but he or she is part of my own social existence. It was George Herbert Mead who pointed to the fact that my own identity as a "Me" is always interconnected to the social relations within which "I" live. This leads to the conclusion that the Other, like my own body, is not describable from the third-person perspective alone.[25]

6.2. Perspectives on the Other

Merleau-Ponty does not refer to the notion of personhood explicitly, but nevertheless elaborates on this notion of the Other. Understanding the Other is

22. Merleau-Ponty, *The Visible and the Invisible*, p. 141.

23. Merleau-Ponty, *The Visible and the Invisible*, p. 84.

24. M. Merleau-Ponty, *Die Prosa der Welt,* ed. C. Lefort, trans. Regula Giuliani (München: Wilhelm Fink, 1969), p. 149.

25. G. H. Mead, *Mind, Self and Society* (Chicago: Chicago University Press, 1968).

dependent upon the phenomenological analysis of the body. It has been shown that the integral body cannot be described by one perspective alone. The same applies to describing the Other.[26]

Our description of the integral body can now serve as a basis for expanding our discussion of personhood. A human being is not "there" in the same way a stone is. With a stone, one can simply abstract subjective influences of the stone's observer and then observe the object as a pure opposite term. This would also be possible with a human being if one could abstract and reduce him to his bodily givenness. However, a human being is only recognizable as a person when in addition to his or her bodily presence the subjective coexistence of the observer (!) is taken into account.

A human being whom we encounter can be considered as a distinct entity within reality. At first, one might conclude that the Other comes into view, that is, suddenly occupies a place in front of us where he had not been before. But such a conclusion gives precedence to a single perspective: third-person perspective. In such a description, the Other is like a thing that can be placed in front of us and likewise removed. This is certainly not a comprehensive description! Different perspectives must be applied that accept and integrate the involvement of the observer, of myself, of the he or she who encounters the Other. If we accept that whoever thinks about the human situation is him or herself also a part of that very situation, then it seems obvious that we must take different perspectives into account (as with the exploration of our own body). This is what the phenomenological analysis of the body strives for.

But then, how can the Other be described? Our intuition tells us that the Other has a bodily existence similar to our own, which means that his objective body is not the whole but only a trace of the integral body.[27] There is something else that we cannot grasp from a third-person perspective. The Other is not an object, but someone, somewhere, between subject and object — like ourselves.[28] The Other is an object in front of me and at the same time a subject observing me.

Thus, he or she must be dealt with as we deal with our own body: both first- and third-person perspectives alike must be utilized. The philosophy of the body aims at broadening the range of perspectives by which one approaches a person. "For a philosophy that is installed in pure vision, in the aerial view of the panorama, there can be no encounter with another: for the

26. Merleau-Ponty, "Phänomenologie der Wahrnehmung," p. 403, second part, §46.
27. Merleau-Ponty, "Phänomenologie der Wahrnehmung," p. 400, second part, §45.
28. Merleau-Ponty, "Phänomenologie der Wahrnehmung," p. 401, second part, §45.

look dominates; it can dominate only things, and if it falls upon men it transforms them into puppets which move only by springs."[29]

The simultaneous application of first- and third-person perspectives is precisely what recognition demands. It seems obvious that the recognition of a person depends on human intervention. The observer him or herself must be taken into account. It would be impossible to expect a machine, even a computer with a brilliant detecting device, to recognize a person as a person, because recognition is by definition a mutual relationship between persons. Thus, recognition is something that can only be fulfilled by another person.

Access to personhood is only possible when a fragile and reciprocal balance between subject and object, observer and observed comes into being. The philosophy of embodiment shows us that though human beings cannot be reduced to their physical bodies, the physical body remains a necessary precondition of humanness. First-person perspective teaches us that the observer cannot ignore his or her own participation in the process of recognition. We can only qualify another being as person if we can in some way or another relate to him. This occurs in the form of recognition, which we've spoken of from the beginning and which is a keystone to understanding an individual's personhood.

The necessity of recognition points to the preeminence of social relationships. If one imagines a laboratory test situation in which one would assess how a subject enters a room and is or is not recognized as a person by observers, one's point of departure would be incorrect. As humans, we exist always already in relationships with each other. Human essence is always essence-in-relation. Embodied existence insists that humans are always bound into a network of reciprocal relationships that are unavoidable when it comes to the question of personhood.

Being a person is the recognition of a relationship to the extant. Because of this, any assessment made after the fact of recognition is artificial. In the case of any such retroactive assessment whereby an assessor assesses a being that his or her assessment has isolated, no decisive argument for recognition can be made, as the supporting structure upon which recognition is based is already destroyed.

29. Merleau-Ponty, *The Visible and the Invisible*, p. 77.

6.3. The Otherness of the Other

Until now, we have emphasized the relatedness, the intrinsic similarity of the observer and the observed, of myself and the Other. Merleau-Ponty suggests that the Other "is born *from my side,* by a sort of propagation by cutting or by subdivision, as the first other, says Genesis, was made from a part of Adam's body."[30] But this cannot serve as a complete description of the Other, because the opposite is also true. The Other is also completely different: she or he is not simply my extension within the world. The encounter with the Other is a real encounter, which means, it shows an even deeper alienation than the encounter with a material thing. In this central argument, the writings of Emmanuel Levinas and Merleau-Ponty make use of similar expressions.

"It is not from a point of space that the other's gaze emanates."[31] This means that I cannot become familiar with the Other in such a way that I know him or her fully. There is a similarity between us, but this similarity is totally different from a similarity of things seen from a third-person perspective. Although the Other is on my side, which means, he or she exists in intimate closeness; I have no idea how he or she exists. "There is no perception of the Other by me. . . . In appearance, this manner of introducing the Other as the unknown is the sole one that takes into account and accounts for his alterity."[32]

It would seem inappropriate to assume that the Other is a kind of equivalent to oneself, yet: "if the other is really the other, that is, a For Itself in the strong sense that I am for myself, *he must never appear so before my eyes. . . .*"[33] The Other is not a thing within my world; he or she is invisible. The Other is characterized by a certain absence.[34] It is an absence that I realize within my world and is observed from the third-person perspective.

It is thus highly instructive that Merleau-Ponty does not isolate this feature of the Other, but instead tries to reintegrate it into a broader philosophy of the body. In *The Phenomenology of Perception,* he argues that it is not only the Other who is essentially unknown to me, but that I myself am not totally transparent.[35] Thus both intransparencies are congruent with each other. Because I cannot know myself totally, it is possible to realize the Other as a similar being. The Otherness of the Other is never total, because this Otherness

30. Merleau-Ponty, *The Visible and the Invisible,* p. 59.
31. Merleau-Ponty, *The Visible and the Invisible,* p. 59.
32. Merleau-Ponty, *The Visible and the Invisible,* p. 78.
33. Merleau-Ponty, *The Visible and the Invisible,* p. 79.
34. Merleau-Ponty, *The Visible and the Invisible,* p. 82.
35. Merleau-Ponty, "Phänomenologie der Wahrnehmung," p. 404, second part, §46.

stems from the same source as my own intransparency. This source is located in the notion of personhood. This is why the intuitively simple assumption of human beings' dignity as persons is almost entirely irreconcilable with the problem of how exactly to define this dignity.

6.4. Neglecting Personhood

Personhood cannot be defined in the third-person perspective. This means that there is no objective quality, no feature, that can be measured to detect personhood. This peculiarity of personhood is also the source of a significant problem: there is always the possibility of withholding recognition. A compulsion to recognition is experienced only by someone who already recognizes another as a person.[36] Considering human history, it is more than obvious that such recognition can also be withheld. Those who do not articulate recognition experience no compulsion to do so. Whosoever recognizes another's personhood does so because he or she cannot do otherwise (though the confirmation of this recognition is in no way mandatory for others). Recognition is thus always also a fragile act that can be rejected from the outset. Recognition behaves in a sense like an argument in a debate: if one admits to the terms of the argument, any further true statement can take on a strength that requires confirmation, not arbitrarily, but for the sake of consistency. However, no one is required to agree to the terms of the argument; one can also try to solve differences of opinion with violence. And yet, even if one agrees to the basic terms of the argument in the case of personhood, different values and worldviews can still cause significant complications in the attribution of personhood. This is obvious in bioethical controversies: at the beginning or end of a human life, or in cases of serious illness, where consciousness is irretrievably lost. The discussion of the "zombie problem" in the philosophy of mind shows, for example, that even consciousness is not an unequivocally given and objective entity. And although the "zombie-problem" is not univocally agreed upon,[37] it nevertheless shows that consciousness is in constant contestation and remains in certain senses a hypothetical factor in social communication.

The personhood of the Other is not a given; rather it is something perceived in "unconstrained recognition."[38] Nevertheless, the act of recognition

---

36. S. Kirste, "Human Dignity and the Concept of Person in Law" (in this volume).
37. See Dennett, *Sweet Dreams: Philosophical Obstacles to a Science of Consciousness*.
38. Spaemann, *Personen*, p. 194.

is not arbitrary. The personhood of a human being does not rely upon a purely idiosyncratic or cultural consensus.

How can the philosophy of embodiment tackle this problem? First, the very assumption that objective criteria for personhood can be defined must be questioned. Such assumptions are necessarily speculative and simply reflect the worldview of the asserter. The philosophy of embodiment shows that all hopes for objective criteria are faulty.

Second, if one questions the arbitrary applicability of personhood, one should consider one's own situation. We are ourselves fragile, finite beings, who are not able to understand ourselves fully. These are the conditions of our bodily existence. We will never come to know ourselves entirely within such worldly terms. We will never know ourselves fully. We can only know ourselves from various perspectives and are unable to combine these into a total picture. "Now I know in part; then I shall know fully, even as I am fully known" (1 Corinthians 13).

Third, it is impossible to recognize a person as a person without one's own involvement. We can recognize others only because we ourselves are persons and able thus to address the Other likewise. Personhood can only be acknowledged if we are engaged in an encounter with the Other. This does not entirely dismiss a third-person perspective, but it does enrich it.

7. Personhood via Recognition

Human beings are persons because they mutually adjudge personhood. This is not an arbitrary cultural phenomenon, but a consequence derived from the bodily existence of human beings. The form of our existence bears within it an unsolvable secret. We are material beings and at the same time can abstract ourselves from our material condition. The concept of the integral body as elucidated by Merleau-Ponty accounts for this situation. The concept of the integral body serves as a philosophical basis for the understanding of human beings as persons. A person cannot be defined by any specific characteristics. There is no substrate of specific and/or accidental determinations. A person cannot be identified in the third-person perspective. At the same time, we can no longer refer to certain metaphysical constructions to assign and assure personhood. We can however realize our existential situation, which is determined by our bodily existence. Phenomenological analysis offers several useful arguments as to why and how humans are discernible only from a multitude of perspectives. This is not only true for individual bodily existence, but applies also for other humans. When we speak about persons, we are always already involved. There is no objective access to personhood. Personhood stems from human encounters and mutual recognition. We will never *know* what a person is as such — in him or herself alone — but we can encounter a human being and recognize him or her as a person. Doing so, we *realize* personhood.

Can Ethics Be Fully Naturalized?

Maria Antonaccio

1. The New Naturalism in Ethics

The humanities have often claimed to possess their own unique forms of discourse and interpretation distinct from those of the natural (and social) sciences. Recently, however, humanistic inquiry has been undergoing a marked turn to so-called naturalistic forms of explanation. In philosophy, religious studies, and even literature, there has been an increasing tendency to apply the methods and data of the natural sciences to phenomena that have often been seen as resistant or irreducible to such explanations. As a result, we now have fields such as neurophilosophy and neurotheology, books that purport to "break the spell" of religion by explaining it as a wholly naturalistic or adaptive phenomenon, and literary critics who contend that a scientific understanding of the mind can help us measure the delight we get from detecting patterns in works of fiction.[1]

The field of ethics has not escaped this trend. In fact, ethics is one of the primary sites of the naturalistic turn, as a spate of recent books on the subject

1. See, for example, the work of Patricia Smith Churchland and Paul Churchland on neurophilosophy, D. Dennett's book *Breaking the Spell: Religion as a Natural Phenomenon* (New York: Penguin, 2006); and B. Boyd, "The Art of Literature and the Science of Literature," *The American Scholar* 77, no. 2 (Spring 2008).

I wish to thank William Schweiker for helpful comments on earlier drafts of this essay, and the other contributors to this volume for their responses to my work as it progressed.

attests. To take just one example, in *Moral Minds: How Nature Designed Our Universal Sense of Right and Wrong,* Marc Hauser argues that human beings are born with a universal moral grammar that is hardwired into their neural circuits by evolution.[2] Other thinkers, such as Larry Arnhart and William Casebeer, have tried in different ways to show how Darwinian biology supports a neo-Aristotelian view of ethics rooted in human nature.[3] Further examples could be noted to make the point that the naturalistic agenda is now being pursued by a range of thinkers working at the intersection of ethics and fields such as evolutionary biology, empirical psychology, and cognitive science. As described by one proponent, their aim is to treat morality "as a natural phenomenon subject to constraints from, influenced, and [perhaps even] ultimately reduced to the sciences."[4]

What does the current effort to "naturalize" ethics imply for an interdisciplinary inquiry into the complex unity of the human person, and more specifically, for the human being as moral agent? Not surprisingly, many humanists recoil from the overt reductionism of some versions of naturalism. For those whom the philosopher Kwame Anthony Appiah refers to as the "no-science-please — we're-humanists" camp, the increasing power of science in human culture is a source of anxiety.[5] Ethicists and moral philosophers in this camp regard the trend towards naturalization as a potential threat to the autonomy of ethics as a field with its own distinctive methods and commitments. The idea that moral philosophy could be reduced to an empirical science, in their view, utterly misunderstands the nature of ethics as a normative enterprise, and fails to account for what it means for human beings to be moral agents.

On the other hand, many proponents of a naturalized ethics see themselves as forwarding a humanistic agenda of their own — one that they believe will enhance human life by making ethical theory more accountable to the facts of human psychology or human evolution, or by challenging religious forms of ethics whose appeal to authority or revelation they find oppressive

---

2. M. Hauser, *Moral Minds: How Nature Designed Our Universal Sense of Right and Wrong* (New York: Ecco, 2006). For a discussion of Hauser's work, see William Schweiker's contribution to this volume.

3. See L. Arnhart, *Darwinian Natural Right: The Biological Ethics of Human Nature* (Albany: State University of New York Press, 1998); and William Casebeer, *Natural Ethical Facts: Ethics, Connectionism, and Moral Cognition* (Cambridge, MA: MIT Press, 2003).

4. Casebeer, *Natural Ethical Facts,* p. 3.

5. Kwame Anthony Appiah, *Experiments in Ethics* (Cambridge, MA: Harvard University Press, 2009).

or outmoded.[6] For these thinkers, the success and ascendancy of the natural sciences is an opportunity to apply new insights and data to ethics, in the hopes (for example) of shedding new light on the cognitive processes involved in moral reasoning, or developing moral norms (e.g., ideals of good character or principles of social justice) appropriate to our ever-increasing knowledge of human nature. They believe that what we learn about human beings from the natural sciences should at the very least set constraints on what our ethical theories affirm, or (more radically) that ethics should be subsumed into science altogether.

The fact that both the proponents of a naturalized ethic and its critics can claim to be advancing a humanistic agenda suggests that the question of whether the project of naturalization advances or inhibits a complex account of the human person is not clear-cut. As a moral theorist, my concern in this chapter is to assess what the naturalization of ethics means for a complex account of human moral being and moral experience. Much depends, of course, on what one means by "complex" (as opposed to simple or reductionistic), as well as by "natural" (or "naturalized"), and "morality." Like the other contributors to this volume, my inquiry starts from the assumption that complexity is to be preferred to reductionism in an account of human being. The phenomenon requires a multiperspectival approach, rather than a reduction to one approach or discipline, or a focus on only one component or attribute of human being (e.g., body, soul, spirit, mind, brain, etc.). Second, I assume that any adequate anthropology must include an account of what makes human beings distinctive from other beings (if not necessarily "superior" to them; see Warren Brown's paper in this volume). I further assume that at least part of that distinctiveness has to do with the fact that human beings are not only natural or biological beings who are part of a causal system and subject to the laws therein; they are also self-conscious, meaning-seeking, and culturally creative beings with the ability to reflect on their own natures and on the reasons and motives for their actions. Finally, I use the term "morality" in this chapter to refer to the set of norms and values by which persons and communities understand and orient their lives, and "ethics" to refer to second-order critical reflection on morality.

Given these assumptions, I am joining the debate over the naturalization

6. Some would regard the naturalization of ethics as a continuation of the Enlightenment project of "ma[king] the study of man into a science," with the critical aim of rendering an accurate and realistic account of human beings to better the human condition. See Peter Gay, *The Enlightenment: An Interpretation,* vol. 2: *The Science of Freedom* (New York: W. W. Norton, 1996).

of ethics from a particular perspective and with an initial orientation. On the one hand, I share some sympathies with those who see any form of reductionism as a potential threat to a complex account of human being, and who may be wary of the encroachment of the natural sciences into humanistic inquiry. If, for example, the naturalization of ethics presupposes an exclusively scientific (and hence monoperspectival) conception of what counts as "natural" for human beings, or assumes that only empirically based arguments and evidence count as "real," then it would seem to inhibit the scope of an interdisciplinary inquiry like the one pursued in this volume. At the same time, I believe that humanistic scholars should not assume a defensive posture too quickly by dismissing all forms of naturalized ethics as "reductionistic." If, for example, the project of a naturalized ethics challenges those forms of ethics (whether secular or religious) that neglect the embodied and material conditions of human life, or that seek to escape or denigrate human finitude with respect to some otherworldly or supernatural realm, then the insights of a naturalized ethics could support and enrich a complex account of human being.

This chapter tries to give substance to a basic intuition: that neither the defensive rejection of naturalized ethics, nor an uncritical acceptance of it, is adequate to render a complex account of human being and the role of morality in human life. My argument will proceed as follows. In the next section, I present an overview of the traditional distinction in metaethics between naturalism and nonnaturalism and suggest that this distinction serve as an interpretive tool for understanding certain constitutive features of moral experience. In the third section, I outline a typology of positions in the current debate over naturalization, and argue that a nonreductive version of ethical naturalism is most conducive to a complex account of human moral being. Finally, in the fourth section, I attempt to lend structure and substance to these intuitions by formulating a methodological principle regarding the use of the empirical sciences in ethics, and specifying a set of criteria for what constitutes an adequate moral anthropology on this basis.

2. Options in Ethical Theory and the Nature of the Ethical Demand

In order to understand contemporary debates over the naturalization of ethics, we need first to understand the longstanding distinction between naturalism and nonnaturalism in moral theory. These positions differ over what is perhaps the most basic issue in metaethics: how the moral is related to the nonmoral (i.e., how the distinctive claims and concerns of morality are demarcated from what is considered morally irrelevant or indifferent). The key issue in this distinction is whether the proper domain and concerns of morality are defined in continuity with some notion of "the natural" (hence naturalism) or in distinction from it (hence nonnaturalism).

The naturalism/nonnaturalism distinction is important to my inquiry for two reasons. First, the very terms of the distinction indicate that a conception of "nature" or "the natural" has been central to how morality is understood and justified in ethical theory. One implication of this is that changes in our conception of what is meant by or included in "nature" — i.e., changes of the kind that we are currently seeing in many domains of scientific inquiry — might be expected to have some impact on how the claims of morality are understood and justified. The current debate over "naturalization" is an instance of this. Second and more importantly, the distinction between naturalism and nonnaturalism is important to my purposes in this chapter because it contains an implicit hermeneutic of human moral being. That is, it highlights the fact that human beings are the kind of beings who can experience morality either as a fulfillment of their natures or in tension with their natures. The fact that each of these options contains its own limitations and dilemmas suggests that there may be persistent irresolvable features of human moral experience.

Nonnaturalism (as the term implies) defines the justification and purpose of morality without recourse to an account of nature or of natural human needs or capacities. That is, it denies that moral values or norms can be derived from any determinate account of nonmoral nature. As Kant famously put this point, "The ground of obligation must not be sought in the nature of the human being or in the circumstances of the world in which he is placed, but a priori simply in concepts of pure reason."[7] Ethics, in this sense, is autonomous from nature and from the empirical facts of human psychology. A similar assumption underlies the discourse ethics of Jürgen Habermas, which attempts to explain the obligatory nature of morality by appealing to the structures of communicative rationality.[8]

The nonnaturalist view of the purpose and justification of morality is often thought to imply a particular understanding of the meaning of moral terms such as "goodness." Nonnaturalism holds that moral facts or properties have a unique mode of existence: they are nonnatural, and thus cannot be identified

7. I. Kant, *Groundwork of the Metaphysics of Morals,* ed. Mary Gregor (Cambridge: Cambridge University Press, 1997), p. 3.

8. See J. Habermas, *The Theory of Communicative Action,* vol. 1 (Boston: Beacon Press, 1985).

with or reduced to any natural property or state of affairs. G. E. Moore, for example, believed that the moral property called "goodness" could not simply be identified with a natural property like "happiness." Rather, he argued that "good" is a nonnatural or *sui generis* property that requires a special kind of moral knowledge (i.e., intuition) to be perceived. Divine command theory could also be considered an example of ethical nonnaturalism. The Christian theologian Karl Barth, for example, held that the command of God defines a revealed morality that may differ radically from what reason can discover. The domain of moral value, defined by a command or duty, is discontinuous with the realm of nonmoral "nature."

Naturalists, by contrast, deny that there are distinctive moral facts or properties over and above those that can be specified using nonmoral terminology, and that are known by intuition or God's command. On this view, goodness (or rightness) is not a nonnatural moral property; rather, moral facts or properties are considered reducible to or identical with natural facts and properties. Unlike nonnaturalists, therefore, naturalists emphasize the way in which morality is continuous or interwoven with human nature. The point on which versions of naturalism differ is in their accounts of "nature" and what kind of natural facts matter to ethics (e.g., psychological, biological, social, etc.). Aristotle, for example, believed that moral values can be derived from certain natural facts about human capacities and propensities and their proper end or *telos*. From these natural facts, he identified certain goods proper to human nature and certain virtues conducive to human flourishing. Many religious traditions can also be considered "naturalistic" in this sense. Thinkers like Thomas Aquinas, in Christian ethics, and Moses Maimonides, in Jewish ethics, held that moral terms like "good" or "right" can be predicated of actions and beliefs that conform to the principles of natural law. (As we will see, some of the more radical recent efforts to "naturalize" ethics presuppose a conception of natural facts that identifies the natural with the empirically testable or verifiable. Ethics is thereby rendered dependent on, or derivative from, the data of natural sciences such as psychology, evolutionary biology, etc.)

As I noted earlier, the distinction between naturalism and nonnaturalism is not simply a theoretical abstraction. Rather, it can be viewed as an interpretation, or hermeneutic, of human moral being. That is, the two theories represent different ways of construing human moral being and moral experience, and each captures certain dilemmas that arise within the moral life so construed. Nonnaturalism articulates the sense that there may something unique about moral claims and requirements that exceeds what can be described in exclusively natural or empirical terms. It captures the idea that there may be an important discontinuity between the demands of morality and natural human desires. This categorical nature of moral requirements — what Richard Joyce calls their practical clout or "oomph" factor — is what we experience when we feel a sense of duty that provokes us to override or interrupt the flow of our desires by some obligation.[9] The term "ought" refers in ethical theory to the overriding or categorical character of moral requirements, the sense that there is a distinctive character of moral claims that makes human life "fraught with ought."[10] Since morality on this view requires something more (or something other) than what human beings desire, ought claims are often experienced as coming from "somewhere out there" (i.e., somewhere apart from or beyond our desires and preferences).

The attraction of nonnaturalist positions is their ability to account for the experience of morality in this sense. They capture the overriding character of moral demands and highlight the dignity of a life that is committed or obedient to those demands. However, there are at least two potential problems associated with nonnaturalism. First, by defining morality in isolation from the descriptive features of human psychology, nonnaturalism risks inflating the demands of morality to such a degree that the moral life may become simply uninhabitable for human beings — a charge that is frequently brought against Kant's ethics. Casebeer, for example, contends that a Kantian approach "at root makes demands that are psychologically unrealistic" and therefore "has at best heuristic value."[11] A second danger of nonnaturalism is implicit in the first. Nonnaturalist positions may demean or denigrate the embodied or material conditions of human existence for the sake of promoting a heightened sense of the ethical demand. For example, in the resurgence of violent fundamentalist religious movements worldwide, we are witnessing certain forms of religious nonnaturalism that are willing to sacrifice innocent human life in obedience to an absolute moral demand.[12]

Naturalism, on the other hand, encompasses a different set of possibilities

9. See R. Joyce, *The Evolution of Morality* (Cambridge, MA: MIT Press, 2007).

10. The phrase is Wilfred Sellars's, quoted by Robert Pippen in his essay, "Natural and Normative," posted on the National Endowment for the Humanities website in connection with its colloquium "Autonomy, Singularity, Creativity" (http://asc.nhc.nc.us/news/?page_id=4).

11. See Casebeer, *Natural Ethical Facts*, p. 7.

12. This is the phenomenon Schweiker has called "moral madness," the view that morality requires supreme obedience "to an overriding obligation, even to the destruction of obvious natural goods [such as life itself] . . . in the hopes of reclaiming these goods as reward for obedience." See his *Theological Ethics and Global Dynamics: In the Time of Many Worlds* (Oxford: Blackwell, 2005), p. 164.

and dangers. It expresses the sense that morality is "natural" to human beings, i.e., that the capacity for morality is continuous with and responsive to other natural human capacities. The purpose of morality, on this view, is to help human beings achieve the good that is conducive to the kinds of beings they are, and to articulate values and virtues appropriate to their natures. Forms of virtue ethics, for example, treat moral excellence as broadly analogous with other forms of human skill or excellence that can be acquired by careful cultivation and habituation. Instead of interpreting the ethical demand as having the binding force of duty or obligation, the purpose of ethics is to direct natural impulses to their fitting end. Naturalist positions thus seem to avoid some of the dangers associated with nonnaturalist positions because they conceive morality as the fulfillment of natural propensities, rather than the restraining or ordering of those propensities by an "ought" claim.

However, naturalism has its own dangers, which are the mirror image of those associated with nonnaturalism. First, by attempting to accommodate the empirical facts of human nature in the formulation of its norms and ideals, naturalist positions run the risk of reducing the ethical demand by "tailoring our sense of what should be to fit the [empirical] account of what is."[13] Ethical naturalism may thereby promote a certain banality with respect to human aspiration. We might call this the danger of moral mediocrity or moral conventionalism. If morality is simply the fulfillment of natural human propensities, a critical stance towards those propensities seems to be ruled out from the beginning.[14] The second potential danger of ethical naturalism is the flip side of the first danger: rather than lowering the ethical demand to fit human capacities, ethical naturalism could be seen as exaggerating or overestimating what human beings are able to achieve, morally speaking. Some naturalist positions, for example, encourage a vision of human self-fulfillment in terms of an ethics of heroism or of the superhuman, without any sense of what would count as a proper limit or restraint on human fulfillment — even (as in Nietzsche's ethics) to the point of the self-overcoming of the human.[15]

---

13. J. Schloss, "Introduction" to *Evolution and Morality: Human Morality in Biological and Religious Perspective,* ed. P. Clayton and J. Schloss (Grand Rapids: Eerdmans, 2004), p. 15.

14. As Schloss puts this objection to some recent forms of naturalized ethics, "[I]nferring moral norms from biological desires has been criticized on the basis of the reduction of ethical demand this entails; in other words, if specific moral norms are ultimately justified by desire, how can specific desires be categorically assessed and justified by morality?" See Schloss, "Introduction" to *Evolution and Morality,* p. 16.

15. Claims about the self-overcoming of the human, whether for good or ill, are common tropes in the current literature on posthumanism and transhumanism. They are often implicit,

In sum, naturalism and nonnaturalism articulate the possibilities and dilemmas that attend different construals of morality and its demands. Together, they constitute a picture of human moral being. Nonnaturalism articulates our sense that there may be an important discontinuity between natural goods and the demands of morality. It suggests that the primary function of morality is to thwart or restrain human desire in order to promote justice or achieve right action. Accordingly, moral principles have a *sui generis,* nonempirical quality that sets them apart from the (merely) natural. Naturalism, on the other hand, resonates with an entirely different aspect of our moral experience. It expresses our sense that morality is a deeply human phenomenon that is continuous with and responsive to fundamental human needs and desires. The purpose of morality, on this view, is to help us achieve the good that is conducive to the kinds of beings we are.

The point of this overview of naturalism and nonnaturalism is not to suggest that we must choose one of these positions over the other. Rather, both may be needed to render the full complexity of moral experience. The very fact that certain persistent dilemmas arise within each suggests that the tension between naturalism and nonnaturalism may be a constitutive feature of human moral experience, a corollary of the complexity of human being itself. If that is the case, the question this chapter must address is the following: Are naturalized forms of ethics able to account for this complexity? Can an ethic that strives to be "fully naturalized" accommodate the insights of nonnaturalism? In short, what account of human moral being and of the demands of morality is implied in the naturalization of ethics? In the next section, I present a selective typology of contemporary forms of naturalized ethics with the aim of determining which of these approaches, if any, is most conducive to a complex account of human moral being.

3. Contemporary Forms of Naturalized Ethics

Whether naturalist or nonnaturalist forms of ethics are dominant at a particular moment in intellectual life depends on many factors, including trends within academic discourse, insights from other fields that affect the study of ethics (including, but not only, the sciences), and the practical problems (e.g., political, technological, environmental, economic, etc.) that emerge in social

---

as well, in the debate in bioethics regarding the permissibility of technological enhancements of human traits and capacities.

and cultural life at a given time. After many decades in which forms of non-naturalism (e.g., variants of Kantian rationalism) dominated ethical inquiry, the last decades of the twentieth century saw a marked return to the insights of ethical naturalism, particularly Aristotelian virtue theory. More recently, increasingly rapid advances in fields such as genetics, evolutionary biology and psychology, and neuroscience have intensified the turn to naturalistic forms of explanation across many fields of the humanities, leading in ethical inquiry to the recent calls for a "new naturalism" or the "naturalization of ethics."[16]

The central assumption of naturalism, when considered as a general philosophical worldview, is that "there is only the natural order" and hence "there are no objects or properties that can only be identified or comprehended by metaphysical theorizing or non-empirical understanding."[17] That is to say, there are no gods or God, no Platonic forms, Kantian noumena, "or any other agents, powers or entities that do not (in some broad sense) belong to nature."[18] Naturalists define human beings as fully included in nature; there is nothing about humans that places them above or beyond nature.[19] However, not all versions of naturalism agree on every point. As Nicholas Sturgeon has noted, "there are theorists who wish to identify their views and approaches as naturalistic without embracing reductionist physicalism. There are also some approaches that can plausibly be described as naturalistic that are quite self-consciously anti-scientistic."[20]

Much of the current debate over the naturalization of ethics, in fact, concerns how to understand "nature" and what sort of natural facts are relevant to morality, as well as "how open [naturalism] should be to the form and content of what is accepted as belonging to science."[21] What seems to

16. Some thinkers have proceeded to naturalize ethics by harnessing the insights of the natural sciences to correct or complete traditional accounts such as Aristotle's. Casebeer, for example, attempts to rescue Aristotelian functionalism by interpreting it through the lens of modern accounts of natural function supplied by Darwin. See also Arnhart, *Darwinian Natural Right*.

17. "Naturalism," by J. Jacobs. *The Internet Encyclopedia of Philosophy* (http://www.iep .utm.edu/).

18. Jacobs, "Naturalism."

19. For this reason, the agenda of naturalism is often associated with the rejection of religion, as in the so-called new atheism of thinkers like Richard Dawkins and Daniel Dennett. See R. Dawkins, *The God Delusion* (New York: Mariner Books, 2008), and Daniel Dennett, *Breaking the Spell: Religion as a Natural Phenomenon* (New York: Penguin, 2007).

20. Nicholas L. Sturgeon, "Ethical Naturalism," in the *Oxford Handbook of Ethical Theory*, ed. David Copp (New York: Oxford University Press, 2007), p. 7.

21. Sturgeon, "Ethical Naturalism," p. 13.

distinguish recent versions of naturalized ethics from traditional versions of ethical naturalism is the extent to which nature is now identified primarily or exclusively with "the order of things accessible to us through observation and the methods of the empirical sciences."[22] For the purposes of constructing a rough (and admittedly selective) typology of positions from a crowded field of options, contemporary forms of a naturalized ethics can be distinguished by how they answer the following question: "Can normative ethical questions be adequately and exhaustively answered by appealing to facts generated by a scientific or empirical account of human being?"[23] This question is, in effect, a new way of posing the standard metaethical question noted earlier of how the moral is related to the nonmoral (or natural). In the context of the new naturalism, however, nonmoral nature is now understood primarily as the object of scientific investigation.

Strict ethical naturalists — proponents of what is often referred to as a "fully naturalized ethics" — generally answer "yes" to this question. They argue that moral norms can be identified with or derived from a set of natural scientific facts. Thus they advance a frankly "reductive" account of the relation between the moral and the nonmoral. For this reason, strict naturalists often contend that ethics should be subsumed into science. As Casebeer puts it, "robust moral norms are part of the fabric of the world and can be constrained by and derived from the sciences."[24] As a strict naturalist, Casebeer's approach is to determine what constitutes the distinctively human function on the basis of evolutionary biology and cognitive science, and to articulate what a plausible "moral science" would look like on that basis. Other strict naturalists go even further: they "wish to 'unify' science and ethics by eliminating the purportedly illusory subject matter of ethics," as in E. O. Wilson's sociobiology.[25]

A second group of contemporary ethical naturalists, whom I will call "moderate ethical naturalists," conceives the relation between normative inquiry and the empirical sciences in less reductive terms. Thinkers in this group "allow the findings of the sciences to place limits on the demands that norms can legitimately place upon us, or to rule out some moral theories as inconsistent with our best natural knowledge."[26] However, moderate ethical naturalists

---

22. See Jacobs, "Naturalism."

23. For the slightly different version of this question, see the introduction to *Mind and Morals: Essays on Ethics and Cognitive Science,* ed. Larry May, Marilyn Friedman, and Andy Clark (Cambridge, MA: MIT Press, 1996), pp. 3-4.

24. Casebeer, *Natural Ethical Facts,* p. 34.

25. Casebeer, *Natural Ethical Facts,* p. 34.

26. Casebeer, *Natural Ethical Facts,* p. 34.

contend that the normative dimension of ethical theory is not wholly reducible to or exhausted by a mere description of the facts of human being. The empirical psychologist Owen Flanagan is an example of this position. Flanagan contends that "morals are radically underdetermined by the merely descriptive [or] the observational," and further, that "no important moral philosopher, naturalist or nonnaturalist, has ever thought that merely gathering together all relevant descriptive truths would yield a full normative ethical theory."[27] Nevertheless, Flanagan proposes that a moral theory's specification of the basic capacities and propensities of human being should be tested by the human sciences to determine their moral viability. To that end, Flanagan has formulated what he calls the "principle of minimal psychological realism" (PMPR), which is intended to keep morality "realistic" by holding it accountable to the empirical facts of human psychology.[28] The principle states: "Make sure when constructing a moral theory or projecting a moral ideal that the character, decision processing, and behavior prescribed are possible, or are perceived to be possible, for creatures like us."[29] To that extent, Flanagan's moderate ethical naturalism renders ethics dependent on the findings of empirical psychology.

A third group of contemporary ethical naturalists, whom I will call "nonreductive ethical naturalists," would agree with moderate naturalists that what a moral theory asserts about morality or moral agency should at the very least not contradict what is known about human beings from the empirical sciences. However, nonreductive naturalists insist that theories of morality or moral agency need not be constrained by empirical evidence as the final or decisive test of its viability. In this respect, nonreductive naturalists wish to guard the relative autonomy of ethics as a distinctive form of inquiry. They resist the attempts of strict naturalists to subsume ethics into science, or to reduce what counts as "natural" to the data of the empirical sciences. The theological ethicist James M. Gustafson can be considered a nonreductive naturalist in his view of the relation of theology to the natural sciences. Gustafson embraces the

27. O. Flanagan, "Ethics Naturalized: Ethics as Human Ecology," in *Mind and Morals: Essays on Ethics and Cognitive Science,* ed. L. Mary, M. Friedman, and A. Clark (Cambridge, MA: MIT Press, 1996), p. 21.

28. In addition to avoiding the danger of an unrealistic moral rigorism, Flanagan's principle of minimal psychological realism is also intended to address the potential of a naturalized ethics to promote moral mediocrity. It seeks to chart "a middle course between an ethics that is too realistic — socially parochial or leaving no room for ideals — and one that is too idealistic, giving no weight to our natures." See his *Varieties of Moral Personality: Ethics and Psychological Realism* (Cambridge, MA: Harvard University Press, 1991), p. 32.

29. Flanagan, *Varieties of Moral Personality,* p. 32.

view (a variant of Ernst Troeltsch's) that "the substantial content of theology, if it is not in perfect harmony with scientific knowledge, cannot be in sharp incongruity with it, and what we say about God must be congruent with what we know about human experience and its objects through the sciences."[30] However, this does not mean that "one draws theological inferences directly and immediately from what we know from sociobiology or physics."[31] Rather, Gustafson insists that "there is a measure of autonomy in religion; it makes sense only with the acknowledgment of piety."[32]

The ethics that flows from Gustafson's theological stance is similarly nonreductive. Beginning with a description of human beings as "valuing animals," Gustafson contends that "human choices and intentions" have a naturalistic origin or foundation; they are "'built' on desires and wants."[33] Moreover, he insists that "the continuities between the biological, social, and cultural aspects of what we are . . . must be taken into account" as data "not only for a description of moral and religious life but also for more 'normative' constructions of the ethical and religious aspects of human experience."[34] However, Gustafson stresses that human beings are also distinguished "by our capacities to examine critically various objects of our desires, ends of our motives, and objects of our valuations."[35] This capacity, while natural in origin, allows human beings to gain critical distance from their desires and to exercise choice and discernment regarding which of these to pursue.

For my purposes in this chapter, the feature of nonreductive naturalism that is most important in distinguishing it from strict naturalism is the following: it defines human beings not only in terms of their animal or biological natures, but also by the aspiration to exceed their animality. Or, put differently, it regards the scope of human aspiration as exceeding what strict naturalism defines as "natural." Much depends, in this instance as in others, on what is included in "nature" or "biology." Insofar as strict naturalists understand human beings as "fully part of or included in nature," they hold that both the

---

30. See J. M. Gustafson, *Ethics from a Theocentric Perspective,* vol. 1 (Chicago: University of Chicago Press, 1981), p. 252.

31. Gustafson, *Ethics from a Theocentric Perspective,* p. 252. Gustafson further explains: "[I]t is clear that one cannot draw scientific conclusions or hypotheses from theological statements. . . . Yet theology cannot make claims about God's relations with the world that are incongruous with well-established scientific data and theories." See pp. 257-58.

32. Gustafson, *Ethics from a Theocentric Perspective,* p. 257.

33. Gustafson, *Ethics from a Theocentric Perspective,* p. 286.

34. Gustafson, *Ethics from a Theocentric Perspective,* p. 286.

35. Gustafson, *Ethics from a Theocentric Perspective,* p. 286.

origin and the end of human aspiration are fully natural as well. This explains why some strict naturalists who acknowledge that humans are distinctive as a species because they have some degree of independence from their biology nevertheless regard this independence as itself a fact of biology.[36] In other words, although strict naturalists may acknowledge that human beings have certain aspirations (as expressed, for example, in their religious beliefs, moral ideals, and cultural forms), they regard these aspirations as fully natural, and capable of being explained in naturalistic terms.

In contrast, nonreductive naturalists challenge the seeming inability of some strict naturalists "to imagine a fact about [human beings] that is not a biological [or other scientific] fact."[37] They resist the reduction of what is considered "natural" to the empirical or biological. On their view, although the human aspiration to transcend the limits of biology may be natural or biological in origin, the end or destination of that aspiration exceeds the natural strictly speaking. As Susan Neiman writes, "Human beings are beings who are not restricted to the ends dictated to them by biology. Because they can think about futures, imagine things not as they are, but as they could and should be, they can posit ends of their own."[38] Nonreductive naturalists regard the tension in human experience between our biological or animal origins and the capacity to imagine ends that exceed those origins as endemic to human experience.

Of the forms of contemporary ethical naturalism presented here, nonreductive naturalism seems most conducive to a complex account of human moral being because it captures both sides of the hermeneutic of human moral being noted earlier. It embraces the naturalist insight that the domain of morality is not radically discontinuous from the natural. However, moral norms and values cannot be identified with or derived from a set of natural scientific facts. In this respect, nonreductive naturalism borrows an insight from non-naturalism; it holds that a higher-order principle of obligation is required to order the natural human goods and desires. Nonreductive naturalists have a variety of ways of making this point; I will note just two. Some, whom we

36. Casebeer expresses a variation of this point when he says, "Understanding nature doesn't transcend nature itself." See *Natural Ethical Facts*, p. 10. For a critique of this view, see Leon Wieseltier's review of Daniel Dennett's *Breaking the Spell*, in *New York Times Book Review*, February 19, 2006.

37. Wieseltier, *New York Times Book Review*. Appiah quotes a similar point made by Gilbert Ryle: "Physicists may one day have found the answer to all physical questions, but not all questions are physical questions" (Ryle, quoted in Appiah, p. 196).

38. S. Neiman, *Moral Clarity: A Guide for Grown-Up Idealists* (New York: Harcourt, 2008), p. 191.

might call "deliberative" naturalists, hold that, while the domain of morality includes natural goods, these goods must be ordered by a principle of choice or assessment that is not reducible to those goods.[39] Others, whom we might call "perceptual" naturalists, hold that, though morality has primarily to do with the quality and direction of natural desires and psychic energies, the latter must be ordered by a principle of right perception that is both internal to but also transcends consciousness.[40] In either case, principles of obligation are understood as necessary "to protect and promote some domain of goods, but their meaning and validity are not reducible to those goods."[41]

On the basis of this overview of contemporary naturalism, and with the advantages of a nonreductive version of naturalism in mind, I want to propose some criteria that will lend substance and structure to the question of what constitutes a moral anthropology adequate to a complex account of human being. These criteria are intended to make explicit the hermeneutic of moral being implied in the distinction between naturalism and nonnaturalism, as well as to provide some methodological guidance for the relation of ethical inquiry and the natural sciences.

4. Assessing Naturalized Ethics: Some Tentative Criteria

My proposal can be stated as a basic methodological principle: Ethical inquiry may be enriched by engagement with the natural or empirical sciences insofar as this engagement ensures that a moral theory makes meaningful contact with facts about human nature and experience relevant to morality. However, ethical inquiry may be impoverished by too close a relation to or dependence on the empirical sciences alone. This basic principle can be elaborated to identify certain conditions under which an impoverishment of ethics might occur, and thereby to provide some criteria for what would constitute a theory of ethics adequate to render a complex account of the human being as moral agent.[42]

First, a theory of ethics may be considered descriptively impoverished if

39. See for example W. Schweiker, *Responsibility and Christian Ethics* (Cambridge: Cambridge University Press, 1995).

40. See for example Iris Murdoch, *The Sovereignty of Good* (London: Routledge & Kegan Paul, 1970).

41. Schweiker, *Theological Ethics and Global Dynamics*, p. 163 (italics added).

42. Similar criteria would need to be developed with respect to how ethical theory could be *enriched* by engagement with the sciences. For a helpful outline of the issues involved in the interaction between normative ethics and scientific inquiry, see J. M. Gustafson, "The Relation-

it ignores the natural or empirical facts of human being in the formulation of its ideals and principles (as nonnaturalism tends to do), or, on the other hand, if it construes those natural facts too narrowly by identifying them primarily or exclusively with what can be investigated by the empirical methods of the natural sciences (as strict naturalism does). This criterion supports the naturalist insight that a moral theory must be "realistic" if it is to avoid the danger of an excessive rigorism. Both moderate and nonreductive naturalism seem to meet this criterion in their contention that what an ethical theory requires of us must at least not contradict what is known about human being from the natural sciences. At the same time, this descriptive criterion also assumes that an excessive dependence on empirical evidence, or an overly narrow construal of what constitutes a fact of nature or human nature, diminishes the complexity of an account of human being insofar as it neglects the insights and contributions of other (nonempirical or nonscientific) disciplines.

Second, a theory of ethics may be considered normatively impoverished if its account of morality merely reflects the existing values of a community, promotes a mediocre moral standard, or otherwise collapses the distinction between what is and what ought to be.[43] This criterion supports the nonnaturalist insight that morality often exerts a significant pressure on our natural or habituated desires, laying claim to conscience and holding us accountable to duties perceived as categorically binding and inescapable. The assumption behind this criterion is that an account of morality that fails to recognize that moral experience is often "fraught with ought" may also fail to recognize a constituent feature of human moral being: that morality requires us to distance ourselves from, redirect, and sometimes even to deny, our natural needs and desires for the sake of some higher-order principle of obligation. As we have seen, nonreductive naturalism preserves this insight in its acknowledgment that principles of obligation are necessary to direct and orient our pursuit of natural goods.

Finally, a theory of ethics may be considered theoretically impoverished if it collapses the normative and descriptive dimensions of ethical theory, and recognizes no distinctive function for ethical inquiry as such. This criterion assumes that a multiperspectival approach to the phenomenon of human being as moral agent is superior to an approach that attempts to reduce the insights

---

ship of Empirical Science to Moral Thought," in *Theology and Christian Ethics* (Philadelphia: Pilgrim Press, 1974), pp. 215-28.

43. Although I cannot pursue the point here, it is not clear that strict and even moderate ethical naturalism have the resources to avoid this danger.

of one disciplinary perspective to that of another. The more radical forms of fully naturalized ethics, which seek to subsume ethics into science, or to do away with ethics altogether, clearly fail to meet this criterion.

5. Conclusion

In this chapter, I have tried to render explicit certain intuitions about the nature of morality and of human moral being that are implicit in the longstanding distinction between naturalism and nonnaturalism, and I have tried to assess contemporary forms of naturalized ethics on that basis. The criteria I have proposed substantiate the basic intuition with which this chapter began, that neither the defensive rejection of a naturalized ethics, nor an uncritical acceptance of it, is adequate to render a complex account of human moral being. Moderate and nonreductive versions of ethical naturalism recognize that an adequate moral anthropology should be informed by well-established insights of the natural sciences, while insisting that the normative inquiry of ethics has its own aims and methods distinct from the sciences.

A description of "nature" or of "the facts of human nature" does not exhaust the depth of the human person as moral agent, nor do the natural sciences exhaust the data and methods needed to explore who and what human beings are. As the contributions to this volume demonstrate, some of the wiser practitioners of the sciences already know this truth; ethicists and theologians have good reasons to agree.

Beyond Distinct Gender Identities:
The Social Construction of the Human Body

Isolde Karle

Today it is common knowledge that there are a multitude of interdependencies between body, soul, and spirit. Nevertheless, when it comes to sexual identity it seems that the body continues to represent a solid and unshakable, objective point of reference while the soul and spirit only come into play secondarily. In any case, a healthy understanding of the human being seems to assume that there simply just are men and women and that both are mutually exclusive — *tertium non datur*. Gender difference appears to be biologically set, and even the creation narratives seem to confirm this idea from a biblical-religious perspective. Women might behave in unladylike ways, but they are still women. Men might feel effeminate, but that hardly means they can escape that masculine identity rooted in their bodies. The classification of persons into men and women seems to be distanced from all cultural interpretation and to be fixed, so to speak, "objectively" prior to all social constructs.

This paper aims to disturb these everyday assumptions and to show that, when it comes to gender identity, it is not only the body that is the basis for gender-associated cultural ascriptions, but rather that cultural norms and constraints also have an incredible impact both upon the body and upon how the body is experienced. Indeed, they can change and disfigure the body. Moreover, everything dealing with the human body can only ever be observed and described under very particular cultural conditions. Especially with respect to gender identity, it is not only religion and culture but also the apparently objective sciences of biology and medicine that are ideologically

---

Translated from the original German by Stephen Lakkis.

charged.[1] This exposes the mythical nature of the idea of an objective body or of the natural division of gender into a binary structure.

1. Gender as Habitus

When one examines gender identity, it becomes clear how closely body, mind, and soul are related to one another. Using his concept of habitus, the French sociologist Pierre Bourdieu has illustrated how, contrary to popular opinion, it is not the body that presents the objective, causal basis for the derivation of binary conceptions of gender, but it is rather the particular cultural conceptions and typologies that crystallize in the experience of corporeality. The binary differentiation of gender, which would not be possible without our familiar forms of culture and language, is so to speak "embodied." It is "in the embodied state — in the habitus of the agents, functioning as systems of schemes of perception, thought and action."[2] Consequently, with a habitus one is dealing with an unreflected process of internalization, with "embodied" habits, the incarnation of the schemes and structures of social praxis.

The asymmetry in bipolar gender relations is thus expressed first and foremost in posture and its corresponding scripts of perception. According to Bourdieu's thesis, this habitus exists primarily in two forms: one male, one female. Each gender-differentiated habitus exists in relation to the other. Accordingly, the habitus is created in the form of two opposing yet complementary postures (hexis) together with their respective principles of vision. While "habitus" refers to a deep structure that also encompasses the schemes of perception, Bourdieu uses the term "hexis" to refer to that external and perceivable ensemble of permanently acquired postures and physical movements. This ensemble of permanently acquired postures, which arise through the unconscious imitation of particular, gender-differentiated motor movements and behaviors, is a basic dimension of one's sense of social orientation. Consequently, the social aspect is efficiently embodied and naturalized via posture, primarily because posture and feeling correspond to one another. Thus gender

1. On the constructive character of anatomy, cf. T. Laqueur, *Auf den Leib geschrieben. Die Inszenierung der Geschlechter von der Antike bis Freud* (Frankfurt am Main/New York: Campus, 1992), pp. 188ff.

2. P. Bourdieu, *Male Domination* (Cambridge: Polity, 2001), p. 8. "The Habitus is the product as well as the producer of practices: repeated experiences condense in bodies as perceptive, cognitive and behavioural schemes and in this way remain actively present."

norms exist "in the way in which people move, in their gestures, indeed even in the ways in which they eat."[3]

The secret behind the successful production of these two genders lies in the fact that it occurs for the most part "automatically," without conscious direction or reflection. It is anchored in the routines of the division of labor and the routines of one's physical body. Each person (man or woman) is required (both implicitly and explicitly) constantly to emphasize those characteristics that correspond to the social definition of his or her gender identity and to carry out corresponding practices while suppressing inappropriate behaviors.[4] "Early upbringing tends to inculcate ways of bearing the body, or various parts of it . . . , ways of walking, holding the head or directing the gaze, directly in the eyes or at one's feet, etc., which are charged with an ethic, a politics and a cosmology."[5] Thus women learn to smile, look down, and accept interruptions. In a particular way, women are taught how to sit, occupy space, and adopt appropriate postures.

For example, among the emerging bourgeoisie of the eighteenth and nineteenth centuries, it was forbidden for a woman to play the cello since it would have required her to spread her legs.[6] When in 1845 a female cellist first performed publicly, it was not her musical skill that took center stage but rather "the shameful and obliquely-posed question whether this musician would dare to take the instrument between her legs."[7] In bourgeois society a female musician — in contrast to a female member of the aristocracy — was subject to strict regulations. Women in the eighteenth century in particular were "rigidly subjected" to a newly developed "mimetic ideal"[8] that forbade any overly emotional facial expressions. Yet not only was the choice of instrument regulated, but also the instrumental piece itself. In their performances, women were "not to overstep the boundaries of tender femininity."[9] The piece was to be limited to the higher, "feminine" register; a hearty virtuoso piece performed with the entire body would be regarded as improper.

This example shows the wide-reaching consequences that were drawn from a gender-adequate habitus, particularly in the nineteenth century —

3. J. Lorber, *Gender-Paradoxien* (Opladen: Leske + Budrich, 1999), p. 68.

4. Cf. Bourdieu, *Die männliche Herrschaft* (Frankfurt am Main: Suhrkamp, 2005), p. 48.

5. Bourdieu, *Male Domination*, pp. 27-28.

6. Cf. F. Hoffmann, *Instrument und Körper. Die musizierende Frau in der bürgerlichen Kultur* (Frankfurt am Main/Leipzig: Insel, 1991), pp. 196ff.

7. Hoffmann, *Instrument und Körper*, p. 197.

8. Hoffmann, *Instrument und Körper*, p. 51.

9. Hoffmann, *Instrument und Körper*, p. 206.

the period when that dichotomous gender metaphysic (with which we still struggle today) was developed. Today, moral importance is still attached to a woman's posture, and this is clearly differentiated from the male perception of the body. The image of a drunken woman in public — who can no longer control her own body — generally strikes us as much more negative than that of a drunken man. Furthermore, girls and women are only given limited freedom to move their bodies: a woman's clothing reduces her possibilities for movement. It "has the effect not only of masking the body but of continuously calling it to order . . . without ever needing to prescribe or proscribe anything explicitly . . . either because it constrains movement in various ways, like high heels or the bag which constantly encumbers the hands, and above all the skirt which prevents or hinders certain activities (running, various ways of sitting, etc)."[10] The collection of these mostly implicit "calls to order" then result in a particular posture that persists even when the clothes no longer demand it: young women in pants and flat shoes still often walk with quick, small steps. These continual, tacit orders lead most women to completely accept arbitrary gender norms and proscriptions as natural and self-evident, "proscriptions which, inscribed in the order of things, insensibly imprint themselves in the order of bodies."[11]

In this way, the social order leads to a significant transformation of the body and mind, "imposing a differentiated definition of the legitimate uses of the body . . . which tends to exclude from the universe of the feasible and thinkable everything that marks membership of the other gender . . . to produce the social artifact of the manly man or the womanly woman. The arbitrary nomos which institutes the two classes in objectivity takes on the appearance of a law of nature . . . only at the end of a somatization of the social relations of domination."[12]

2. The Opacity and Inertia of Corporeally Anchored Schemes

In Western society — unlike traditional societies — male domination works in a very subtle way. It is a symbolic, gentle, and invisible form of violence that reproduces the asymmetrical order of dual sexuality. It ensures that men and women develop a differing habitus and brings women to submit "voluntarily"

10. Bourdieu, *Male Domination,* p. 29.
11. Bourdieu, *Male Domination,* p. 56.
12. Bourdieu, *Male Domination,* p. 23.

to the gender norm, and to limit themselves when they become mothers, for example, within the home or within a private female world. "The effect of symbolic domination . . . is exerted . . . through the schemes of perception, appreciation and action that are constitutive of habitus. . . . Thus, the paradoxical logic of masculine domination and feminine submissiveness, which can, without contradiction, be described as both spontaneous and extorted, cannot be understood until one takes account of the durable effects that the social order exerts on women (and men)."[13]

Young girls and boys become familiar with the binary schemes of perception and appreciation through the experience of a gender-differentiated social order and through socialization and upbringing. Yet this remains inaccessible to consciousness. "Already at five years old children participate in what they perceive to be normal male or female activities."[14] Generally, this leads them to accept the social order as normal and natural just as it is. Thus most people anticipate their own fate, so to speak, both by rejecting those career opportunities that are not allowed for and by pursuing those options that "naturally" suggest themselves. Correspondingly, we find that the appropriate functions or occupations for women are an extension of their domestic function — such as caring, teaching, the raising of children, social networking, assisting, and advising. As Bourdieu points out: "The constancy of habitus that results from this is thus one of the most important factors in the relative constancy of the structure of the sexual division of labour."[15] Since these processes are beyond conscious control, this leads us to witness the often-observed discrepancy between formulated, emancipatory declarations on the one hand, and factual, relatively traditional, and gender-typical behavior on the other.

Last, but not least, the asymmetry in the experience of corporeality is evident in sexual practices and conceptions. Thus young men in particular describe a sexual relationship completely in the logic of conquest, while young women are socially prepared to experience sexuality as an emotionally, highly charged experience.[16]

The creation of gender-differentiated habitus takes place in an essentially unobservable and insidious way. It is carried by a form of power "that is exerted

13. Bourdieu, *Male Domination*, pp. 37-38.
14. H. Kotthof, "Geschlechtertypisierung in der kindlichen Kommunikationsentwicklung. Ein Bericht über ausgewählte Forschung," in *Jahrbuch für Pädagogik 1994. Geschlechterverhältnisse und die Pädagogik* (Frankfurt am Main: Peter Lang, 1994), p. 271.
15. Bourdieu, *Male Domination*, p. 95.
16. Cf. Bourdieu, *Male Domination*, p. 20.

on bodies, directly and as if by magic."[17] This symbolic violence is branded upon the deepest parts of the body in the form of dispositions that are deeply anchored in our bodies. When the body blushes, shivers, or acts reflexively, it does so withdrawn from the directives of consciousness. Thus women often tacitly accept the barriers laid upon them, which leads to the contemporary self-exclusion of women in place of those explicit exclusions that are today prohibited by law in Western society. The foundation of symbolic violence lies in the dispositions that lend their hypnotic power to social injunctions, suggestions, seduction, threats, and reproaches.[18] Emancipation certainly cannot be achieved merely through a "dawning of consciousness" or through enlightenment regarding this situation. Such an approach fails to appreciate the opacity and inertia that stem from the embedding of social structures in bodies.[19]

And of course, these observations are also valid for men. Men too are prisoners of dominant gender conceptions and must learn over the long-term what it means to be a man, and thus superior. "Being a man, in the sense of vir, implies an ought-to-be, a virtus, which imposes itself in the mode of self-evidence, the taken-for-granted."[20] In the male body too there is inscribed an ensemble of dispositions, "inscribed in the body in the form of a set of seemingly natural dispositions, often visible in a particular way of sitting and standing, a tilt of the head, a bearing, a gait, bound up with a way of thinking and acting, an ethos, a belief, etc."[21] In this way, a man also learns to accept behaviors as unavoidable and natural — behaviors that for women are hardly possible. Men lay their arms protectively and possessively across the shoulders of a woman — the reverse image is hardly thinkable.

The social became flesh, and works as an *amor fati*, a bodily inclination. Bourdieu compares the construction of manliness with the construction of the noble man. Both forms of identity — to be manly and to be noble — are products of a social practice of transferal, which ensures that this social identity becomes "natural," a habitus. As with the nobility, manliness must also be validated by other men and certified by recognized acceptance in the group of "real men." Many rites in school, the military, and police force contain such corresponding tests of manliness, which testify to the dependence of one's declaration of masculinity upon the judgment of the group.[22]

17. Bourdieu, *Male Domination*, p. 38.
18. Bourdieu, *Male Domination*, p. 42.
19. Cf. Bourdieu, *Male Domination*, p. 40.
20. Bourdieu, *Male Domination*, p. 49.
21. Bourdieu, *Male Domination*, p. 49.
22. Cf. Bourdieu, *Male Domination*, p. 52.

Manliness is extraordinarily vulnerable. Why else would so much energy in our society be invested in violent male games, above all in sport? Combat sports and the martial arts are particularly good at highlighting the visible signs of masculinity. It is for this reason that women find it particularly difficult to enter those sports.[23] And men must continually prove themselves in those most serious of competitive games: politics and economics. Competition among men, which with the nobility found its classic expression in the duel, therefore plays a central role. To this extent, "male privilege is also a trap, and it has its negative side in the permanent tension and contention, sometimes verging on the absurd, imposed on every man by the duty to assert his manliness in all circumstances."[24]

Manliness lives from the fear of the feminine. For this reason, particular forms of courage — as required above all in the military and police force — are finally nothing more than expressions of fear: "fear of losing the respect or admiration of the group . . . and being relegated to the typically female category of 'wimps.' . . . What is called 'courage' is thus often rooted in a kind of cowardice."[25] Dictatorships function in a similar way. They live off the fear of men — the fear of being ostracized from the world of "hard men," murderers and tormentors.

To summarize: It is not the biological body that produces, and is the basis of, gender identity but rather it is the gender order that leads to the feminization and masculinization of bodies, persons, behavioral codes, postures, corporeal experiences, schemes of perception, emotions, and sensations. Our culture directly imprints gender upon the body via a sexually differentiated habitus. In an even more extreme form, this can be observed in cultures that not only imprint upon the body but rather purposefully change or even mutilate it. In parts of Chinese society the feet of young girls were bound into tiny stumps. In some African regions, the clitoris of prepubescent girls is still excised today. These are particularly extreme and painful forms of the gender-differentiated imprinting of the body. Yet they display again the extent to which the human body is to be understood as thoroughly, socially imprinted.

---

23. While women participate in most forms of sport, sports *per se* are still very segregated and gender-biased. For more detail, see I. Hartmann-Tews et al., eds., *Soziale Konstruktion von Geschlecht im Sport* (Opladen: Leske + Budrich, 2003); and Isolde Karle, *"Da ist nicht mehr Mann noch Frau. . . ." Theologie jenseits der Geschlechterdifferenz* (Gütersloh: Gütersloher Verlagshaus, 2006), pp. 111ff.

24. Bourdieu, *Male Domination*, p. 50.

25. Bourdieu, *Male Domination*, p. 52.

3. The Complexity and Variety of Nature

One could object that nature does indeed produce clear, binary standards — standards that fail to be appreciated adequately if gender differentiation is simply reduced to differences in habitus. Such an objection requires a detailed response, one that would begin by explaining that the male or the female body does not exist — contrary to what many of the anatomical pictures in our schoolbooks suggest. Language does not simply express some intrinsic meaning found in nature. Language does not simply reflect reality but is rather a cultural system of signs and symbols that only then gives rise to meaning. This is not merely discourse-theoretical sophistry, rather it is evident whenever nature is not immediately pressed into that fixed Procrustean rule of the cultural, binary system of gender; in other words, whenever the attempt is made to perceive gender in a more differentiated, and thus more realistic, way.

Nature does not offer such a precise or far-reaching classification of gender as our binary language conventions would suggest. On the contrary, in nature we find fluid and fluctuating transitions, overlaps, and ambiguities with regard to gender. Culture — with its either-or system that is valid from birth and is thought of as absolutely constant and unchanging — extends radically beyond what nature itself offers. It is precisely such classificatory rigorism that exposes this as a social classification, "since 'the reality' of human appearances does not present itself as 'dimorphic' as 'social perception' believes; 'actually' there would be much more cause for ambiguity and 'androgenous doubt.'"[26]

Not least, the long-denied existence of those who are physically intersexual testifies to this issue today. That which we see externally does not always correspond to that which exists or is lacking internally: hormone levels, gonads, and the genome. The term "intersexuality" gathers together a wide variety of such physical "inconsistencies." Intersexual individuals exhibit a physical mixture of male and female characteristics. Thus some newborns possess internal testicles and a masculine genetic composition even though they appear externally to be female and are therefore classified as such — since as far as cultural classification is concerned, morphological gender is decisive. Thus so-called "XY women" have a male set of chromosomes yet appear externally as females. There are many other forms of intersexuality.[27] According to the bi-

---

26. H. Tyrell, "Geschlechtliche Differenzierung und Geschlechterklassifikation," in *Kölner Zeitschrift für Soziologie und Sozialpsychologie 38* (1986): 462.

27. Presentation is variously estimated at between 1:50 and 1:2000. According to Fausto-

ologist Anne Fausto-Sterling, many bodies evidently mix together anatomical components conventionally attributed to both males and females.[28] What this displays is that nature encompasses more than just two unambiguous genders. It moves back and forth between both poles with flexible boundaries and transitions. "Sex does not represent a fixed criterion but rather a flexible and variable template."[29] It is thanks to biology, with its exact scientific method, that we see the diversity in individual male and female appearances as well as just how fluid the transitions are from female to male.

The plurality of ethnophysiologies also points us in the same direction. Genders do not always refer to the same things in all places. There are cultures that distinguish between more than two genders and that even provide relatively easy options for gender changes — notably without the need for altering the insignia of physical gender. Moreover, many of the differences in bodily experience that are commonly attributed to natural physical dimorphism are more precisely the result (rather than the cause) of this binary gender differentiation — for example with respect to physical strength and hormone levels.[30] Indeed, when dealing with experiences of the body, gender beliefs function as self-fulfilling prophecies. Thus differences in the pitch of one's voice or in intonation cannot simply be attributed to anatomical differences but are significantly reinforced, if not actually produced, by cultural conventions. In contrast to Asian culture, in the West the pitch of women's voices has become noticeably deeper over the last decades, to the point where some voices (e.g. that of the American pop singer Tracy Chapman) are no longer immediately recognizable as female.

One of the main arguments constantly to be advanced for binary gender classification points to the fact that only women can become mothers. According to common sense, it is this fact that in principle distinguishes

---

Sterling's definition of intersexuality, 1.7 percent of human births are intersexual. The very different estimations depend on the definition of intersexuality (from any deviation of the usual phenotype to true hermaphroditism).

28. Cf. A. Fausto-Sterling, *Sexing the Body: Gender Politics and the Construction of Sexuality* (New York: Basic Books, 2000); and A. Fausto-Sterling, *Myths of Gender: Biological Theories about Women and Men* 2nd ed. (New York: Basic Books, 2000). See also S. Schröter, *FeMale. Über Grenzverläufe zwischen den Geschlechtern* (Frankfurt am Main: Fischer, 2002).

29. According to the biologist M. Maurer, "Sexualdimorphismus, Geschlechtskonstruktion und Hirnforschung," in *Wie natürlich ist Geschlecht? Gender und die Konstruktion von Natur und Technik,* ed. U. Pasero and A. Gottburgsen (Wiesbaden: Westdeutscher Verlag, 2002), p. 100.

30. Cf. I. Karle, *"Da ist nicht mehr Mann noch Frau. . . ."* pp. 100ff.; on physical strength cf. esp. the chapter on gender and sport, pp. 111ff.

women from men. In the West, especially since the nineteenth century, far-reaching assumptions were drawn from the concept of motherhood (particularly among the bourgeoisie), which not only associated pregnancy and birth with women but even the raising of children and housework, as well as representing warmth, security, and empathy as genuinely feminine virtues. In contrast, men had to prove themselves out in the hostile world, taking control of the public realm and thus the power centers of society. To this day we are still striving to dismantle this bourgeois gender metaphysics and its associated gender virtues.

Yet at this point, one should also note that neither motherhood nor menstruation, lactation, and pregnancy fundamentally distinguish women from men. Not all women will become pregnant or bear a child. The reasons here are not only socio-cultural. For those women who want to have children yet are unable to, the reasons are also often physiological. Statisticians estimate that of those women born after 1960 approximately one quarter will remain childless; for those born after 1965 this figure could rise to one third. Thus in this respect, motherhood cannot form a constitutive element of their gender classification. And even when women do become pregnant (or currently are), they only remain so for a limited time. "Menstruation, lactation and pregnancy are individual experiences of female existence but are not a determinant of the social categories 'female' or 'woman.'"[31] The bearing of children as well as "menstruation, which is understood as a sign of a woman's childbearing ability are valid neither for all 'women' nor at all times for any one woman. It is not its realization but rather the attribution of the possibility which is then linked with gender."[32]

In this respect, focusing only on the "biological" fact of motherhood is not enough to distinguish in principle between women and men. It is even far less useful for the interpretation and mythologization of motherhood. From a historical and intercultural perspective, the appointment of women to motherly duties and their specialization upon these tasks (as is typical in Western middle-class families), has been the exception rather than the rule.[33] Many societies have judged the role of motherhood as one of only secondary

31. Lorber, *Gender-Paradoxien*, p. 87.
32. C. Hagemann-White, "Wir werden nicht zweigeschlechtlich geboren . . . ," in *Frauen-MännerBilder. Männer und Männlichkeit in der feministischen Diskussion*, ed. C. Hagemann-White and M. R. Rerrich (Bielefeld: AJZ-Verlag, 1988), p. 229.
33. Cf. H. Tyrell, "Überlegungen zur Universalität geschlechtlicher Differenzierung," in *Aufgaben, Rollen und Räume von Frau und Mann*, ed. J. Martin and R. Zoepffel (Freiburg/München: Alber, 1989), p. 60.

importance and have managed without a corresponding differentiation based on such a division of labor.[34]

To summarize: The physiological facts do not organize themselves into a system of two genders; they do not by themselves inevitably push us on toward a binary classification. This relativization of the obvious difference between men and women does not at all mean the underestimation of corporeality. It is not that the anatomical differences of the human body should be denied. There is a natural body, but as soon as we picture and describe it, it stops being a natural body. A strict, binary, dichotomous view then takes hold — a view through which modern culture perceives the body, loading it with meaning and then, if necessary, even surgically transforming it so that it finally "fits" within the social classification.[35] If gender is externally unclear at the time of birth, this is generally made more clear by the use of surgical intervention. In medical terminology, one speaks of a surgical clarification, a procedure that has been practiced in Western culture since the middle of the twentieth century. Parents are advised to choose the child's future gender according to what is surgically easiest to achieve. Only since the 1990s has this procedure come under increasing critique. Gender ambivalence is obviously unacceptable for our culture. Even intersexual persons, whose "anomalies" only become apparent in later life, must often submit themselves to painful and completely unnecessary operations.[36]

34. Cf. Tyrell, "Überlegungen zur Universalität geschlechtlicher Differenzierung," p. 61. Despite the social changes of the last decades, in Western culture the socio-emotional primacy of the mother-child relationship still remains normatively valid. This is due in no small part to the influence of popularized developmental psychology, which attributes high priority to motherly care for small children ("good enough mothering"). Hartmann Tyrell notes: "The modern female dilemma between family and profession visibly has its roots in the fact that the role of the mother has been culturally accepted and accentuated as such a demanding role." H. Tyrell, "Soziologische Überlegungen zur Struktur des bürgerlichen Typus der Mutter-Kind-Beziehung," in *Lebenswelt und soziale Probleme. Verhandlungen des 20. Deutschen Soziologentages zu Bremen 1980*, ed. J. Matthes (Frankfurt am Main/New York: Campus, 1981), p. 424. German mothers often only see themselves as good mothers when they are able to ensure their continual physical presence twenty-four hours a day. Vinken speaks here of the "fetish of the presence of the maternal body"; B. Vinken, *Die deutsche Mutter. Der lange Schatten eines Mythos* (München: Piper, 2001), p. 154.

35. T. Laqueur gives an impressive overview here with respect to biology and its ideological forms of perception in past and more recent history. Cf. Laqueur, *Auf den Leib geschrieben*.

36. Thus, for example, the testicles of one XY woman were removed, which led to the subsequent presentation of significant physical and psychological problems. Cf. Karle, *"Da ist nicht mehr Mann noch Frau,"* pp. 98f.

4. Complementary Gender Difference in Theology

Twentieth-century Christian theology and social ethics largely reflected this nineteenth-century, bourgeois gender metaphysics, though certainly without recognizing its socio-cultural limitations. In the twentieth century, Karl Barth was particularly vocal on this topic, referring to the creation narratives in an attempt to establish "the natural supremacy" of the man (and thus the nonreciprocity of the man-woman relationship). "She is I as his Thou. She is [a person] as the completion of his humanity."[37] These sentences from the *Church Dogmatics* are typical of the modern idea of complementarity, which Christian social ethics has largely identified (or confused) with biblical patterns of thought. This quote clearly exposes the way that the "complementary theory" of equality in difference is always thought of asymmetrically, even to this day: the motherly woman is related to the man as an attentive carer; she is not herself a subject but is rather created for the completion of his humanity, whereas the man, as an autonomous subject, makes his way out into the hostile world and attempts to prove himself there in games of competition. In the background we find the idea of opposing male and female spheres of thought, emotion, and action.

This ideology was expressed once again quite clearly several years ago in the doctrinal document "On the Collaboration of Men and Women in the Church," released by the Catholic Church's Congregation for the Doctrine of the Faith.[38] According to the church jargon of the statement, the creation narrative confirms the permanent difference between men and women. The woman is essentially bride and companion and devotes herself to the well-being of others. These attributes are not cultural but rather arise from the incontrovertible will of the creator God: "From the first moment of their creation, man and woman are distinct, and will remain so for all eternity."[39] It belongs to the "genius of women" to be there for the family. Motherhood is her nature. Thus neither are women allowed to compete with men. The decisive exemplar for all women is Mary: her willingness to suffer, her natural self-withdrawal, her posture of humility and faithfulness. The precariousness of such a "revaluation" of femininity can be seen in the consequences to which it

37. K. Barth, *Church Dogmatics,* III/1 (London: T. & T. Clark/Continuum, 2004), p. 309.

38. Congregation for the Doctrine of the Faith, Letter to the bishops of the Catholic Church on the collaboration of men and women in the church and in the world (May 31, 2004. Published online at www.vatican.va/roman_curia/congregations/cfaith/documents/rc_con _cfaith_doc_20040731_collaboration_en.html).

39. Ibid. p. 12.

leads: Due to the essential difference between men and women, only men are permitted to become priests. Even the maleness of Jesus is no accident but is rather claimed as an ontological necessity.

Even in the liberal tradition, which otherwise sees itself as the champion of personal individuality, there is no real break from this complementary gender construction. While contemporary liberal social ethicists do generally recognize that female virtues and behaviors are historically informed, they still stress that differences between men and women are to be recognized. The social ethicist Dieter Korsch even goes so far as to claim that in the relationship between men and women there are still nonreducible, biologically determined, fundamentally opposed differences that aim at an asymmetrical relationship.[40]

Thus while current social ethicists provide different accents, nowhere do we find any problematization of the idea that a person can only ever be either completely male (and thus finally hegemonic) or completely female (and thus motherly and caring). Instead, it is just seen as divinely willed and as a given fact of nature. The modern construct of the duality of genders is fundamentalized. And thus social ethics unreflectively follows typical modern stereotypes that (empirically) increasingly prove themselves to be precisely that: stereotypes and clichés. Today, reality increasingly shows us that there are caring fathers and female politicians conscious of their own power; there are emotionally uncontrolled men and cool-thinking, taciturn women; that mathematics and technology is not a male privilege, and that languages and welfare activities are not a female one.

Furthermore, social ethics still continues to associate the naturalness of binary genders with the imperative to procreation, thus generally unifying marriage and the family. In response, on the one hand one must say that from a Protestant perspective sexuality is not immediately related to procreation. Sexuality is a divine gift that can greatly enrich and intensify the relationship between two persons. On the other hand, today the married lifestyle can no longer be described in a unified way. It has differentiated itself into many varying models. Thus there are currently many marriages that remain childless by choice, not only due to an underlying inability to bear children. In this respect, marriage cannot automatically be equated with a family.

As such, it is high time that Christian social ethics takes into account

---

40. Cf. D. Korsch, *Dogmatik in Grundriss. Eine Einführung in die christliche Deutung menschlichen Lebens mit Gott* (Tübingen: Mohr Siebeck 2000), pp. 97f. According to Korsch, the distinction between men and women is in principle the most extreme case of difference, to be understood as a community of "elementary opposites" that relate to each other in a complementary way (p. 99).

this reality as well as the great variety of "gender migrants," and stops seeing the plurality of individuals as a threat to the institution of marriage but rather as a liberation from the cultural chains of a historically contingent gender order that oppresses and excludes so many intersexuals, homosexuals, transgenders, "unmanly" men, and "unwomanly" women. Yet in doing so, can it possibly appeal to the Judeo-Christian tradition and Christianity's own self-understandings?

5. Creation and New Creation: Life in the Spirit of Freedom

To this day, it is primarily the creation narratives, especially Genesis 1:27, which are repeatedly called upon to provide a biblical basis not only for heterosexual preference and the institution (or "created order") of marriage but also the conception of two completely different, gendered beings. Even in feminist theology, repeated reference has been made to this passage (with the best intentions yet with paradoxical effects) in order to claim both the equality of women and their essential difference from men. Thus binary gender becomes the linchpin of the imago Dei. But in doing so we essentially miss the meaning of this passage.

The concept of the imago Dei is based on ancient Near Eastern royal ideology. In Egypt, the pharaoh was the image of God, and he would commission others to produce statues of himself. Though cultic images were forbidden in ancient Israel, this certainly did not mean an end to the concept of the image of God.[41] Thus in Genesis 1:27 we see the concept arise in a modified way: the image of God here shall not be statues but rather living human beings, an audacious concept in a cultural environment that only saw God represented through concrete images. Yet even more audacious is the associated idea that it is not only the king or pharaoh who is the image of God but rather all human beings. All persons, women as well as men, are to represent God in the created world, shaping it in accordance with his will. As such, to be an image of God did not mean corresponding to God in appearance or form but rather in function: that is, representing divine power in the world. Therefore in Genesis 1:27 the stress does not lie on the distinction between man and woman but upon a dignity and duty imparted and assigned to all human

41. Cf. here and for some following points: A. Schüle, "Made in the 'Image of God': The Concepts of Divine Images in Gen 1–3," in *Zeitschrift für die Alttestamentliche Wissenschaft* 117, no. 1 (2005): 1-20.

beings. The creation narrative aims at the participation of a totality, not at establishing the bipolarity of a dual gender system, let alone marriage. The stress in Genesis 1:27 falls upon a tendency to equality and inclusiveness, not upon the heterosexual pair.[42]

Even if one does not share this "relecture" — and the biblical traditions are undoubtedly shaped by patriarchal forms of thought and androcentric perspectives — one cannot ignore that Jesus (with his inclusive table fellowship) and the early Christian movement (with their shocking and by no means conflict-free eucharistic praxis) radically transcended the boundaries of race, ethnicity, social position, and gender.[43] Some exegetes[44] even suggest that it was precisely this boundary-crossing praxis that distinguished the early church movement from its social and religious environment and enabled it to develop into a new religion. Here the baptismal formula in Galatians 3:28 provides a significant proof: "There is neither Jew nor Greek, there is neither bond nor free, there is neither male nor female: for ye are all one in Christ Jesus."[45]

Let me come directly to the point and stave off any misunderstandings: Paul should not be instrumentalized here for a constructivist gender theology. Paul had no interest in feminist theology and often lingered quite far behind the standard that is expressed in Galatians 3:28. Nor should one deny his homophobic tendencies. Yet nevertheless we see in the baptismal formula that through faith in Christ the early Christian community enjoyed and practiced an incredible freedom with regard to cultural attributions and constraints. In baptism, Christians enter into the domain and jurisdiction of the new creation. Modern New Testament scholarship unanimously suggests that the resulting new social order was an empirically experienced reality and not merely a utopia. The field of women's studies has already shown comprehensively that women were apostles and were in leadership positions within the community. By being in Christ, former differences fell away. Here we encounter the existence of a new togetherness of human beings. These communities were

42. For greater detail, cf. Karle, *"Da ist nicht mehr Mann noch Frau,"* pp. 217-27, and on the paradise narrative in Genesis 2–3 (pp. 201-17).

43. Cf. here the exegetical papers in M. Ebner, ed., *Herrenmahl und Gruppenidentität* (Freiburg: Herder, 2007); and G. Theißen and A. Merz, *Der historische Jesus. Ein Lehrbuch* (Göttingen: Vandenhoeck & Ruprecht, 1996); as well as Jürgen Roloff, *Die Kirche im Neuen Testament* (Göttingen: Vandenhoeck & Ruprecht, 1993).

44. Cf. M. Ebner, "Von den Anfängen bis zur Mitte des 2. Jahrhunderts," in *Ökumenische Kirchengeschichte. Von den Anfängen bis zum Mittelalter,* Bd 1, ed. Th. Kaufmann, R. Kottje, B. Moeller, and H. Wolf (Darmstadt: Wissenschaftliche Buchgesellschaft, 2006), pp. 15-57.

45. Cf. Karle, *"Da ist nicht mehr Mann noch Frau,"* pp. 227ff.

spaces marked by the actual revolutionary reorganization of interpersonal relationships.[46]

In Christ, the attributes of this world are no longer valid — there is no more the criteria of race and class, "no more male and female" and, extending the sentence's line of argument, also "no more heterosexual or homosexual." Through baptism, in the new creation in Christ, we see the destruction of all boundaries between men and women, heterosexuals and homosexuals, rich and poor, black and white. New social behavior is made possible, behavior that is no longer oriented to the cultural customs of classification. In this way, the social order of binary genders is deeply relativized and transformed. What we are dealing with is the liberating release of individual experiences and talents beyond those culturally imposed restraints that impair persons, oppressing and disfiguring them, and compelling them constantly to conform themselves and their bodies to their assigned maleness or femaleness.

That Galatians 3:28 should be understood in this revolutionary way can be displayed in the direct and obvious reference to the "old creation" in Genesis 1. The Septuagint version of Genesis 1:27 is adopted word for word in Galatians 3:28c — and it is presented as its antithesis: "God created them male and female" (Gen. 1:27) becomes a direct negation: "no male and female" (Gal. 3:28c).[47] "Eschatologically, an extremely fundamental transcendence of gender is emphasized here."[48] By "'putting on Christ' in a type of eschatological travesty (1 Cor. 15:53f.; 2 Cor. 5:2-4), [the believers] are incorporated with their entire existence into Christ's salvific sphere."[49] A radical change of identity occurs. Their gender identity is "subversively dissolved";[50] from a bodily, spiritual, and cognitive perspective they have been freed from repressive gender norms. The old creation is transcended, the order of the old world is exalted and subsumed through the new creation in Christ.

To carry each other's burden (Gal. 6:2) and to live in the freedom of the

46. Cf. J. Roloff, *Die Kirche im Neuen Testament* (Göttingen: Vandenhoeck & Ruprecht, 1993), p. 94.

47. Cf. H. Thyen, "'. . . nicht mehr männlich und weiblich. . . .' Eine Studie zu Galater 3,28," in *Als Mann und Frau geschaffen. Exegetische Studien zur Rolle der Frau* ed. H. Thyen and F. Crüsemann (Gelnhausen: Burckhardthaus, 1978), p. 109.

48. R. Heß, "'Es ist noch nicht erschienen, was wir sein werden.' Biblisch (de)konstruktivistische Anstöße zu einer entdualisierten Eschatologie der Geschlechterdifferenz," in *Alles in allem. Eschatologische Anstöße*, FS JC Janowski, ed. R. Heß and M. Leiner (Neukirchen-Vluyn: Neukirchener Verlag, 2005), p. 310. Thus the new figuration of gender in baptism also has a thoroughly bodily dimension.

49. Heß, "'Es ist noch nicht erschienen, was wir sein werden,'" p. 311.

50. Heß and Leiner, eds., *Alles in allem.*

Spirit, which no longer allows any slavery and body-soul justifications of any kind (Gal. 5:11ff.), these are signs of the new creation. This leads to the creation of a free space that allows people to live together in a "de-dualized" and anti-hierarchical way. For in Christ the new creation is at hand, the old has passed away, the new is emerging (2 Cor. 5:17). While the early church community practiced this approach at least partly, they also realistically pointed out that even our most elementary self-perceptions still require transformation in a way that is hardly imaginable to us: "We are now children of God, yet what we will be has not yet been made known" (1 John 3:2). This present, fragmentarily experienced corporeality and identity will only be unpacked properly in the eschaton. Yet at the same time, faith in Christ is already breaking apart disastrous and dichotomizing attributions and models of expectation in the present, setting free new experiences both of body, soul, and spirit.

6. Body, Soul, and Spirit: From Difference to Creative Plurality

However one wishes to evaluate the precarious "physical foundation" of gender identity, it is clear that social and cultural norms are superimposed on the body and have a far-reaching influence on both soul and spirit. And however optimistically or pessimistically one might judge the transformative and liberating power of the biblical traditions in this context, they expressly prohibit their use in grounding a naïve insistence upon a natural gender differentiation, to forcefully integrate women (and men) unwillingly into bourgeois gender clichés, and to oppress, disparage, disfigure, and damage intersexuals, homosexuals, and gender migrants of all forms.

Theology and the church must develop more sensitivity to the ways in which they have contributed to a gender system that still continues to oppress and disfigure souls and bodies. To this extent, a sociological as well as theological (self-)enlightenment about the diverse interdependencies of body, soul, and spirit with respect to gender identity is required if theology and the church no longer wish to participate in the cultural ideologization of bodies and identities. If the Spirit does not distribute its gifts along cultural lines of difference but rather provocatively crosses boundaries, then the name of Jesus Christ can no longer be used to label and assign people to antiquated gender types.

This then challenges both theology and particularly the church to stop uncritically supporting modern gender metaphysics, and instead to promote a creative body-soul variety that distances itself from a culturally demanded dichotomization and its potential for repression. The church should encourage people in all their variety to develop their God-given gifts, abilities, and talents. Yet this also means that the quality of relationships (and not of already-determined normative roles) becomes the criterion of responsible Christian relationships and community. From this perspective, the church can only welcome it when Christian same-sex couples wishing to live long-term together come and ask for God's blessing on their shared journey, just as with traditional weddings.[51] In the end, it is not an orientation to the anatomical details of a body, but rather a life in the spirit of Christ, a spirit of love, trust, and freedom, that is the characteristic mark of the church of Christ.

51. For greater detail on the consequences for church politics, cf. Karle, *"Da ist nicht mehr Mann noch Frau,"* pp. 237-70.

Moral Inwardness Reconsidered

William Schweiker

1. Introduction

In what follows, I want to consider a basic question in philosophical and Christian ethics. The question is two-sided. On the one side is a normative concern: What is the relation between our sense of inwardness — the ongoing stream of thoughts, desires, beliefs, sensibilities, and valuations in and through which we cobble together our identities — and a conception of moral goodness related but not reducible to the ambiguous sense of inward life? This way of formulating the question is related to wider debates in theology and philosophy about the moral sources of identity and whether those sources do or do not entail beliefs about the meaning and value of being itself.[1] The other side of the question is in terms of a conception of human "nature," namely, given advances in scientific research does it make sense to speak of "inwardness" and, further, can "morality" itself be found to be wired into the physical makeup of human beings? Insofar as most Western ethics had linked morality to our sense and conception of action and agency — the idea that we are intentional acting beings in the world — then the two sides of the question are deeply linked. If morality is rooted in the invariant features of our physical makeup, then previous conceptions of "subjectivity" are clearly mistaken, but so too might inherited ideas about moral agency. My intention is to enter this debate

---

1. For a brief summary of the discussion see "Commitments in a Post-Foundationalist World: Exploring the Possibilities of 'Weak Ontology,'" *The Hedgehog Review* 7, no. 2 (2005, special issue).

about moral subjectivity on both sides of the question and thereby probe the depth of the human person.

Of course, many contemporary theologians are suspicious of the idea of human inwardness. They are driven by a worry about religious subjectivism and the reduction of theological claims to psychological ones. I will note these problems below. Nevertheless, my sense is not that the acids of criticism have left us conceptually poor and lacking complex images and metaphors with which to examine the depth of human life. The ancient and enduring injunction to "know thyself" is hard to meet when the very idea of the "self" seems vapid. In response to this situation I intend briefly to explore metaphoric schemes that dominated much classical Western thought and which, I think, need to be reengaged in our time. They are about the dignity but also the struggle, even warfare, of the "soul" with itself. This essay is an exercise in hermeneutical reclamation and conceptual revision in order to help sort out viable resources for thinking theologically and ethically about human existence in our global times.

2. Setting the Question

If one looks at currents within contemporary Western culture, it would seem that the task of being a self, the struggle rightly to integrate the bits and pieces of one's existence for oneself and with others, is believed either to be a rather easy thing or an unimportant thing. Easy, because being a self is supposedly no more than forming an identity through cultural resources with respect to one's preferences. Within the context of "liquid modernity," as Zygmunt Bauman has called it, identities have themselves become consumable realities, made and discarded with ease. There is, apparently, nothing internal to the "self" that resists formation, no insurmountable limit to self-fashioning.[2] Conversely, being a self is unimportant, we are told, because what really matters are social and cultural forces, the claim of the other, or natural features of the human species. Finally, it is also obvious that we are living in a time in the West when the cultural resources of this civilization seem, for many people, powerless to address real challenges because of their complicity with colonialism, inequality, sexism, and mass-death. These resources — rightly peppered by criticisms over the last several centuries — seem to lack vitality and resonance. This is

---

2. See Z. Bauman, *Does Ethics Have a Chance in a World of Consumers?* (Cambridge, MA: Harvard University Press, 2008).

especially true of classical ideas about the human self that are indebted to specific social, racial, ideological, and gendered conditions. From all sides, then, the question of how we can and ought to conceive of ourselves as "selves" falls upon deaf ears. Or so it would seem. But is the human self really such a flimsy and unimportant thing? Is it the case that there are no resources — maybe even obvious ones — in our cultural heritages that can aid in thinking about the human adventure?

These are real and pressing questions in the current global situation. If anything characterizes our situation it is the manifold endangerments to life ranging from the ecological crisis to the ongoing and flagrant abuse of human rights. If we are to meet the challenge of this age, then we need a viable account of the "human" as a moral creature sturdy enough to back human rights discourse and yet also robust enough to clarify the capacities for responsibility needed to meet global challenges. Of course, showing the validity of human rights or even the conditions and scope of moral responsibility will not answer every moral and political challenge! Human life is situated in complex social systems, even subsystems, as well as within natural processes that have specific demands, entail specific limits and possibilities, and therefore must be considered in their complex interactions if we are to address global problems. Even the meaning of basic moral concepts (say, freedom; responsibility; duty; good; etc.) shifts when they are used in different spheres. All of this is obvious. Nevertheless, one task is to gain some measure of clarity about human beings as moral creatures even if the demands of moral, political, and religious reflection do not end with that clarity. In order to have a purchase on what we mean by saying that human beings are moral creatures requires that one clarify the connection between our sense of inwardness as beings who can act in the world and the claims of goodness on our lives and the rightness of actions and relations. At the heart of current challenges to life is found the ancient and yet very pressing question, "What is man?"[3]

To be sure, there are forms of ethics for which this question about "man," or moral inwardness as I am calling it, is not much of an issue. In (say) divine command ethics, the justification and purpose of moral goodness and what is morally right are not defined in relation to human nature, however conceived. If what is good and right have their origin and purpose in God's command, then obedience to that command is morally required irrespective of the "nature" of human beings and how that nature might back ideas of goodness and

3. See, for example, D. Janicaud, *On the Human Condition,* trans. E. Brennan, with intro. S. Critchley (New York: Routledge, 2005).

rightness. Similarly, certain forms of liberal ethics along the lines developed by John Rawls and, somewhat differently, by Jürgen Habermas, seek to justify moral norms in rational, social procedures (e.g., communicative action) wherein any conception of "human nature" and the good(s) needed to sustain human flourishing are deemed unimportant to the domain of moral rightness and justice.

Further, moral intuitionism and some forms of rationalism require no reference to human needs, capacities, or goods in order to sustain their conception of what is right and just. For all these various forms of ethics, what theorists call nonnaturalist ethics, my inquiry is ethically uninteresting, and, in fact, seemingly detracts from establishing norms of justice. Put more technically, for nonnaturalist ethics the question of the "right," and so obligations and principles binding on moral agents, is separable from the "good," namely, ends of human flourishing. If that is so, the "right" remains no matter what account one gives of human "nature" with its goods, needs, capacities, and fallibilities.[4]

It is also the case that for other kinds of Western religious and philosophical ethics what is morally good and right is related in some manner to a conception of human being and also human well-being. In terms of moral theory, these positions contend that any principle of right, any binding obligation, is related to and must further the attaining of the "good," however defined. These are versions of ethical naturalism. Most of these kinds of ethics are, additionally, deeply concerned with our experience of being moral creatures insofar as they insist that human beings can and must aim at attaining certain goods, specific ends. Theologically considered, the question then becomes the relation between the human goods and aims and the living God and whether a distinction between natural goods and religious goods is appropriate and necessary.[5]

Kinds of ethical naturalism can be specified in terms of the ideas of body or soul or spirit. From ancient materialists and hedonists to contemporary sociobiology and the attempts to isolate the origin of morality in brain functions, there have been those who seek the origin and purpose of morality in the "body." Conversely, ancient thinkers from Plato through medieval theologians like Thomas Aquinas thought that human good, the *summum bonum,*

---

4. One should note that in more recent work Habermas has realized the threats now posed to human "nature" and how that demands some revision in his formalist ethics. See J. Habermas, *The Future of Human Nature* (Cambridge: Polity, 2003).

5. At issue here is what moral theorists variously call basic goods and their relations to distinctly moral goods. For an account of some of this debate and also my own position, which charts four interlocking kinds of goods, see W. Schweiker, *Responsibility and Christian Ethics* (Cambridge: Cambridge University Press, 1995).

was rightly predicated of the "soul," no matter how much they differed in their conceptions of the soul. And the idea that human beings have some capacity of freedom and self-transcendence, are endowed with "spirit," likewise has a long heritage in Western ethics, reaching a high point in the modern world among Idealists and Existentialists. In each of these cases, body or soul or spirit was conceived in various ways as what endows human beings with moral dignity and in relation to which any viable conception of the good must be developed and principles of right justified. Again, this naturalistic impulse is true whether the ethics is religious or not, theologically articulate or not. While Aquinas designated the highest good as the *beatific vision,* how that Good was conceived was intimately related to a conception of the soul and its perfection. The same could be said of nontheological versions of the other options for parsing "body" and "spirit" as ideas for the basic mode of human moral being.

One task of current ethics is to escape the conceptual reductions that have dogged reflection when just "body" or "soul" or "spirit" is taken to articulate *in toto* the complexity of human being. Extreme versions of these classic options lead to odd conclusions, as when (for example) Descartes has to relate the *cogito,* the "I think," to the body through a gland, or when ardent materialists, ancient and modern, have to struggle to reduce consciousness to brute matter, or, when Hegel conceived Spirit as coming to itself in and through nature and history. Any robust account of the human existence will have to make sense of the phenomena designated by these terms (body-soul-spirit) and yet avoid a reduction that makes it impossible to articulate their relations and distinctions as in, say, body-soul is just spirit, or soul and body are at war, or soul-spirit is only body.

Stated otherwise, it is crucial that one adopt, methodologically speaking, a pluralist and multiperspectival approach in which knowledge of any phenomenon, like moral inwardness, is defined and grasped through interlocking but irreducible questions that drive inquiry.[6] There is, in other words, no "theory of everything" or one foundational perspective. Knowledge is a complex circuitry constituted by the connections among questions. As the philosopher Mary Midgley has put it:

> We exist, in fact, as interdependent parts of a complex network, not as isolated items that must be supported in a void. As for our knowledge, it too is a network involving all kinds of lateral links, a system in which the most

---

6. W. Schweiker, "On the Future of Religious Ethics: Keeping Religious Ethics, Religious and Ethical," in *The Journal of the American Academy of Religion* 74, no. 1 (March 2006): 135-51.

varied kinds of connection may be relevant for helping us to meet various kinds of questions.[7]

How might we best picture or construe or interpret moral inwardness, the sense of being moral creatures? What is the most basic mode of moral being if we must think beyond the old triad of body or soul or spirit? What is moral inwardness? I venture further into this topic with the trenchant warning of Jean-Jacques Rousseau. In *A Discourse on Inequality*, he notes that "every author produces under the pompous name of the study of man nothing more than the study of men of his own country."[8] That question of human "nature" must now be answered with full awareness of cultural, moral, political, and religious diversity as well as modern scientific advances.

3. Is There Moral Inwardness?

Obviously just one research project, let alone one scholarly essay, will not answer these massive questions! How then to proceed? With some sense of the situation of the question before this inquiry, I now turn to the next step of reflection and to current debates about the connection between science and morality. Two recent proposals for how to connect morality to our existence as creatures advance naturalistic accounts of morality. One proposal explores a universal moral grammar wired into human nature about matters of right and wrong. The other examines the character of moral freedom with respect to the complexity and conflict of human desires and motivations. In this way, one position focuses on questions of right while the other gives an account of the human good, the good of freedom. That discussion will be followed by the hermeneutical detour through classical images of human inwardness. We will see, ironically, that the ancients anticipated many of the contemporary insights of the two recent proposals, even if there are problems in the classic accounts as well. What the ancients grasped, and the moderns forego, is that the "self" also has an essential relation to the divine bound to its innermost vulnerability. Why that is the case and the theological problems and possibilities it entails will concern us later. My strategy is to attempt to think within the intersections and tensions between these accounts on the way to what I hope is a robust account of moral inwardness.

7. M. Midgely, *The Myths We Live By* (New York: Routledge, 2003).
8. J.-J. Rousseau, *A Discourse on Inequality*, trans. M. Cranston (New York: Penguin, 1984), p. 159.

3.1. A Universal Moral Grammar

Recently Marc Hauser, professor of psychology, organismic and evolutionary biology, and biological anthropology at Harvard University, has published a book that has received considerable scholarly and popular attention. In his *Moral Minds: How Nature Designed Our Universal Sense of Right and Wrong,* Hauser argues that we are born with abstract rules and principles that are given guidance by nurture in particular moral systems.[9] Those rules and principles are the result of evolutionary processes and also aid the development of the human species. In terms of the history of ethics, the argument here is for "innate moral ideas," that is, human beings have hardwired into their existence knowledge of moral principles. This claim has been challenged in many ways in modern Western thought through attention to the force of history and society and the formation of human moral capacities. Indeed, it is difficult to find among theologians and philosophers any remaining advocates of innate moral knowledge. In this light, it is extremely interesting to see science reclaim and defend ancient ideas against modern critics!

Hauser's argument, in brief, is that there is an area of mind, variously called by him a moral organ or moral faculty, which, somewhat like Noam Chomsky about language, supplies a universal moral grammar from which specific moral belief systems are built. Drawing on experimental work, Hauser notes that very young children can differentiate acts and intentions that are wrong or good and even, he contends, distinguish between bad actions if the intention of the agent *seems* to be good. The difference between social convention and a moral rule is the seriousness of infractions. A moral rule, in other words, entails both a prescriptive set of beliefs about what one ought or ought not to do and also emotions that attend such actions. In fact, "rather than a learned capacity . . . our ability to detect cheaters who violate social norms is one of nature's gifts." Designed by nature, morality is fundamentally rooted in human social nature, and so, in some ways, in kin relations. It is the crucial deep grammar for distinctive and culturally specific forms of social life, including religious ones. This means, like so many thinkers, one must decisively divorce morality and religion. "I will argue," Hauser notes, "that this marriage between morality and religion is not only forced but unnecessary, crying out for divorce."[10] As noted below, Christians and Jews who believe in natural law

9. M. D. Hauser, *Moral Minds: How Nature Designed Our Universal Sense of Right and Wrong* (New York: Ecco/HarperCollins, 2005).

10. Hauser, *Moral Minds,* p. xx.

or the Noahide covenant can only respond to Hauser's intention to divorce religion and morality by noting that it is neither needed nor possible. It is not needed, because human beings do in fact have a natural moral knowledge even if they do not have religious convictions; it is not possible because the natural moral knowledge is also and always some dim awareness, no matter how distorted, to the divine.

According to Hauser, morality is grounded in biology, and, given this fact, "inquiry into our moral nature will no longer be the property of the human-ities and social sciences, but a shared journey with the natural sciences." As Richard Rorty — no friend to the natural backing of morality or anything else — has noted in his spirited response to this book, the relation of "grounding," according to Hauser, is not that of axioms to theorems or that what is right or wrong can be simply inferred from neurons. The way morality is "grounded" in biology is "more like the relation between your computer's hardware and the programs you run on it. If your hardware were of the wrong sort, or if it got damaged, you could not run some of the programs."[11] In other words, there is a universal moral "grammar" or program behind all of the various moral systems found among the world's people. This universal sense of right and wrong provides scientific backing to the "moral faculty" but also, presumably, some means to test specific moral systems in terms of more general moral principles. Arguments like Hauser's raise the hackles of thinkers (say, Rorty) who insist that morality is a cultural construction all the way down. It is the old debate between moral realists (Hauser) and anti-realists (Rorty) as well as between naturalists in ethics (Hauser) and their anti-naturalist critics (Rorty). More will be said on this point below.

Hauser's argument is obviously important for any kind of ethical natu-ralism insofar as it provides scientific backing to the claim that morality has some connection to natural capacities, needs, and aspirations of human beings. Without recognition of that backing, either too grand or too simple ideas of morality and human moral capacities might be assumed. Recognizing the biological connections to morality also rightly places the theological question where it belongs, namely, in how the divine relates to the totality of human existence and the world. Likewise, Hauser, unlike some within the sciences (Dawkins) and philosophy (Dennett) is not a simple reducer. He insists on collaboration between the sciences, the humanities, and the social sciences in order to grasp the similarities and differences among people's moral outlooks.

The conclusion that can be can drawn from Hauser's work is that it makes

11. R. Rorty, "Born to Be Good," in *New York Times Book Review,* August 27, 2006.

sense to avoid a reduction in either the direction of subjectivity, and so a kind of dualism (body or soul), or objectivity, and thus a wooden form of physicalism. This conclusion brings us to another, but different, proposal for thinking about the connection between morality and our biological makeup.

3.2. Freedom and the Conflict of Motives

A long contributor to debates about philosophy and science, the British philosopher Mary Midgley formulates the ground of morality in terms of struggle for wholeness that characterized human freedom and our sense of self. Human freedom is the capacity to order or organize conflicting desires by the whole of the self for the sake of the whole of one's life. "Coherence within our lives," she argues, "is not just something convenient. It is necessary for making any meaningful choice at all."[12] Rejecting dualistic views of human beings (bodies with souls stuck in them) but also overly reductionistic pictures, Midgley's point is that a human being is a complex creature within the realm of natural life who has the distinctive capacity to bring from its whole being some coherence in life. "Human morality," she writes, "is not a brute anomaly in the world. Our freedom is not something biologically bizarre."[13] This means, however, that human beings are not the only "moral creatures"; there are other forms of natural social life. And she continues, that "human moral capacities are just what we could expect to evolve when a highly social creature becomes intelligent enough to become aware of profound conflicts among its motives."[14]

The distinctiveness of human beings is the degree of reflection people have about the conflict in their motives and the extent to which on occasions we can abstract from specific motives in order to order life. The proper meaning of freedom is found in this capacity for distance and the power to order and resolve conflicts of motives coming from the whole self and acting on the whole self. The distinctive work of being a moral creature, and so the depth of the human person, is this labor of freely overcoming conflicts within our lives. But this work is not something that disconnects us from other forms of life; it is simply the human way of being a natural, moral creature. Importantly,

---

12. M. Midgley, *The Ethical Primate: Humans, Freedom and Morality* (New York: Routledge, 1998), p. 151.

13. Midgley, *The Ethical Primate*, p. 3.

14. Midgley, *The Ethical Primate*, p. 3.

Midgley can endorse the naturalistic and evolutionary impulse in the work of people like Hauser. Yet she provides the means to speak about moral inwardness and freedom with respect not just to social relations, as Hauser does, but in terms of the demand for the integrity of life with respect to conflicts of motives and impulses, the stream of desires and inclinations that saturate moral consciousness.

Midgley's argument is a cogent one for a naturalistic account of moral subjectivity and freedom. That being said, it seems to leave out or neglect an extremely important insight because her account formulates the issue of moral inwardness primarily in terms of a conception of freedom. By taking a hermeneutical detour through classical conceptions of the "self," I want to show that something else comes to reflection missed in Hauser's and Midgley's accounts. This has to do not with freedom (Midgley) or some supposed deep moral grammar (Hauser), but, rather, a unique form of human vulnerability that characterizes our lives as moral and religious beings. This vulnerability is difficult to grasp, let alone explain, solely in terms of freedom or the physical background to pervasive moral sensibilities. Making this point requires a brief engagement with classical images of the human "soul."

4. Metaphors of Inwardness

Two metaphors for the inner-life were widely used in the ancient world and have had an extremely profound history of effects on modern outlooks even while they have analogies in the traditions of other civilizations. We might call these the legacies of Plato and Paul. I imagine that we need a contemporary rapprochement between their insights, at once different and yet related to previous synthetic outlooks in Christian thought.[15] At issue is the connection between perfection and freedom in moral inwardness, a connection missed in Midgley's work and also in scientific analyses like Hauser's on the biological roots of morality. So, in this step of my argument the tactic, methodologically speaking, is to see how highly symbolic and metaphorical discourse provokes reflection aimed at truth about moral subjectivity. The metaphoric scheme examines under imaginative form actual structures of lived experience. By

15. We are, in fact, in the midst of a renaissance of interest in Plato and Paul, usually one pitted against the other. For an example of the "new Paul" see A. Badiou, *Saint Paul: The Foundation of Universalism,* trans. R. Brassier (Stanford, CA: Stanford University Press, 2003). The most creative recent retrieval of Plato for ethics is the work of I. Murdoch. See, for example, I. Murdoch, *Metaphysics as a Guide to Morals* (New York: Penguin, 1992).

exploring these schemes we are then seeking to bring to articulation those structures of life in order better to understand and orient existence.[16]

4.1. Horses That Buck

One dominant metaphor for moral inwardness is found in the Platonic texts and it has exerted immense influence on the history of Western thought, even until modern Freudian psychotherapy and other forms of thought. Plato argues in the *Phaedo* and *Republic X,* in the famous myth of Er, that the soul is immortal. His claim in the *Republic IV* is more germane: the human soul is composed of three capacities or parts: reason, the spirited part *(thumos)* that has the "power to reflect about good and evil," and unreasoning appetite (cf. 439bff.). There is justice in the soul when "reason" properly orders *thumos* and appetites. The soul's nature and justice are conveyed through the metaphor of a charioteer (reason) seeking to guide two unruly horses (spirit; appetite) all too ready and able to buck their driver. The struggle of the moral life is the proper, rational ordering of the soul, as Midgley might argue.

This metaphoric scheme of the soul pictures the inward struggle of the self as the quest for order, peace, and self-sufficiency. The peace of the self and polis, which St. Augustine and later theologians would also champion as the *summum bonum,* is defined by Plato as the soul's relation to itself in itself as an eternally existent substance (an idea that Augustine and all Christians have to reject). In other words, the justice of the soul for ancient Platonists and others was inseparable from a metaphysical claim about its immortality. In the course of Western history, this metaphysical claim has been rejected even by recent advocates of *askesis,* a topic I cannot explore in this essay.

It is not difficult to grasp how this account of the "soul" has some intuitive plausibility; it resonates with a lot of common experience. Human beings are creatures of desire, we want and value many things, and yet our desiring must be rightly ordered if there is to be some measure of tranquility in our lives. The crass hedonist or libertine disregards this demand of order usually to the destruction of life; greed and the lust for power disorder the social order and also the lives driven by them. Additionally, the "Platonic" account, as I

16. Call this an exercise in "hermeneutical realism": the detour of interpretation through imaginative forms has the intent of grasping real dynamics in human moral existence. See W. Schweiker, *Power, Value and Conviction: Theological Ethics in the Postmodern Age* (Cleveland: Pilgrim Press, 1998).

am calling it, insists that whatever order is to be attained must be rational insofar as a genuine good of the self has to be knowable. Finally, this account articulates a deep insight that was readily picked up by Stoics and Christian thinkers throughout the ages. Insofar as "justice" is an attribute of the "inward man," as Socrates says, then in a profound sense only the self can do injustice to itself. The rectitude of the self cannot be taken from oneself against one's own will since it is predicated of the self's own ordering. This is what is meant, morally speaking, by self-sufficiency; it is a claim about the meaning of moral vulnerability. Contemporary interest in personal "authenticity" and identity has some of its roots in this conception of the soul, shorn of Platonic and Christian overlays.

This classic account, despite some recent retrievals of it, suffers from various problems. Advances in psychology and biology, as we have seen, challenge its descriptive adequacy insofar as the "reason" orders but also transcends the "natural" parts of the soul; there is, in a word, a kind of dualism in the Platonic account, as usually interpreted. Existentially the picture of the soul seems to lack the means to articulate the individuality of moral experience (the virtuous all start to look a lot like Socrates!). Further, the position risks being circular in its normative dimension, that is, it assumes what it is meant to demonstrate (i.e., the rationality of virtue). There is also a theological problem, at least from a biblical and Christian point of view. The soul is imagined as a kind of interior *sacred space* which is simultaneously immortal, and so divine, and yet seeking divinity, its unification with the Good. The distinction, as far as I can see, is that while the soul is preexistent and immortal, it is also changeable; to be God-like requires immortality and unchangeability, something attained through virtue.[17] So imagined, the self configures the theological difference, that is, its specifics include the distinction of "God" and other beings, and yet it also effaces that difference in its aspiration to be God-like. This is the insight missed by recent positions, like Midgley's, that are nevertheless formally similar to Plato's account. As many Protestant theologians have noted, especially twentieth-century ones, this conceptual framework seems decidedly unbiblical and risks an apotheosis of the self that collapses the theological difference. The problem returns, namely, how to think theologically about the character of human being body-soul-spirit.

These problems (descriptive; existential; normative; theological) illuminate why the "Platonic" picture of the human is alien to contemporary patterns

17. Even St. Augustine, in *Civitas Dei*, continues this line of thought, noting that human beings are created good but changeable, whereas God is eternal and unchanging.

of thought, and yet, oddly enough, how it retains some power of resonance with ordinary experience of having to order desires. It is not surprising that contemporary thinkers, like Midgley, who rightly seek a robust understanding of the human self as backing for claims about human dignity, have sought to retrieve some of these insights while overcoming enduring problems in the account.[18] I happen to be unconvinced by these various ethical and theological proposals for reasons that will have to be enumerated later. Granting the saliency of these worries for the moment, they provoke one to reflect on a different metaphoric framework for thinking theologically about our moral being.

4.2. *The Sting of Conscience*

On some accounts, conscience, which first appears in the Bible in Paul's Corinthian letters in his conflict with the Gnostics and yet is used at least twenty times in others contexts, continues the older Hebraic idea of the "heart" as the core of individual human being.[19] These ideas (heart/conscience), especially when later joined to certain Stoic ideas, span out into a complex metaphoric scheme about the human self. In 1 Corinthians, the issue comes to focus for Paul on the "weak" whose conscience was offended by the idea of eating meat sacrificed to idols. These individuals felt the "sting" or "pang" of conscience when engaging in what they judged to be immoral action. The Gnostics, contrariwise, saw conscience as the "spirit-self" that had to be educated in order to be saved, even when this education meant violating one's sense of right and wrong. Paul grasps the fact that to violate conscience, even if it is empirically wrong in a specific judgment (Paul knows the theological insignificance of pa-

---

18. Besides Midgley, thinkers like Martha Nussbaum, Alasdair MacIntyre, Tzvetan Todorov, and Leon Kass have tried to redress these issues by developing a theory of capabilities (Nussbaum) or tradition-constituted rationality (MacIntyre) or claims about the finality of the other person (Todorov) or ideas of human powers and vulnerabilities (Kass). These proposals cannot be explored in this essay.

19. The literature of "conscience" and its history is of course mountainous. For this essay I have just drawn on standard reference works in biblical studies, like R. Jewett's article "Conscience" in the *Interpreter's Dictionary of the Bible*, Supplementary Volume (Nashville: Abingdon, 1976), pp. 173-74 and W. Schrag's essay "Ethics in the N.T.," in the same volume, pp. 281-89. One can also see standard works in the history of ethics, e.g., K. Kirk, *Conscience and Its Problems: An Introduction to Casuistry* (Louisville: Westminster John Knox Press, 1999); A. R. Jonsen and S. Toulmin, *The Abuse of Casuistry: A History of Moral Reasoning* (Los Angeles: University of California Press, 1990); and J. Mahoney, *The Making of Moral Theology* (Oxford: Clarendon, 1987).

gan practice), is to violate the integrity of the self. He counsels that the "strong" should respect the needs of the "weak," thereby to guard the tranquility of the self and peace in the community.

From this conception of conscience flowed two ideas crucial to Western and Christian ethics, namely, the inviolability of conscience (i.e., the fact that conscience ought to be obeyed even if it could be mistaken, as Roman Catholic moralists have long insisted), and, further, that moral integrity and sensibility are profoundly social even if they ought not be coerced. The question then becomes whether or not conscience is an autonomous *source* of moral norms or if it is, rather, a *medium* for apprehending the moral law. This would also seem to be Hauser's point: any particular person or even culture is merely the *medium* through which the universal moral "grammar" is perceived. There is, thereby, an objectivity to morality not reducible to specific cultures or persons. In order to avoid the possibility of subjectivism when conscience is thought to be a source of norms, there developed historically forms of casuistic reasoning but also various practices of educating conscience as kinds of *askesis*. Yet the larger point is that descriptively the idea of "conscience" is meant to articulate the experience of the integrity of the self with respect to judgments about right and wrong actions in relation to others. And existentially it enables one to clarify human inwardness, our sense that who we are as persons is accentuated and not obliterated in right action, without thereby denying the fact that moral sensibilities are socially formed. The idea of freedom of conscience stems from this insight. Importantly, this idea arose first in terms of freedom of religion, that is, faith cannot be coerced and remain faith. One can imagine that contemporary "rights" talk finds one of its origins in these ideas.

The Pauline account of conscience, and other ones as well, also address specifically normative questions. In Romans 2:14-15 we read the following (cf. Rom. 9:1):

> When the Gentiles, who do not possess the law, do instinctively what the law requires, these, though not having the law, are a law to themselves. They show that what the law requires is written on their hearts, to which their own conscience also bears witness. . . .

Conscience bears witness to, or is a medium of, the moral law "written on the heart." This law has been variously conceived as the Noahide covenant among some Jewish thinkers, the so-called "Golden Rule," and the Natural Law so basic to much Western theological and philosophical ethics. The claim in these various forms, despite their obvious differences, is that self-knowledge is always a co-knowing, a *con-scientia (syn-eidesis),* of self with the moral law.[20] The expectation, then, is that human beings have a moral sensibility for the most primitive demands of justice. Here ancient religious texts and philosophical reflection have anticipated by many centuries claims made by contemporary thinkers like Hauser. The moral law is not a product of social convention, personal preference, or political utility; the moral law has a claim to reality, and has ontological depth, mediated through conscience.

Beyond descriptive, existential, and normative aspects of the metaphoric scheme of conscience, a scheme marked by ideas about the "call" of conscience, its "sting," weakness and strength, and freedom, there has always been a distinctly theological aspect. Especially in Protestant ethics the idea of "voice" is often linked to a conception of the inner-self as a *sacred space* constituted like a courtroom in which the self stands before God. The terrified and free conscience, as Luther would put it, is defined by the futility of self-righteousness (terrified conscience) and the bounty of divine grace (free conscience). Paul Tillich, the twentieth-century theologian, took this imagery to its ontological level and thereby spoke of the divine as the "depth" of the conscience, the reality of the transmoral conscience.[21] Yet the verbalization of conscience as a "voice" or "call," found also in some of the Pauline texts, is just one theological construal. Other thinkers, like the Stoics, spoke of the "spark" of conscience as manifestation in the mind of the divine *logos.* Still, others, say in the letter to the Hebrews and elsewhere, use the language of the "pure" and "defiled" conscience, often in relation to baptism (cf. Heb. 9:14) in order to articulate its theological meaning. In each of these cases the idea is that the inner-self knows itself along with knowing the voice or spark or freedom of God and God's law.

Analogous theological problems arise with the idea of conscience and its metaphoric reach as those found in the image of the soul aspiring to unity with God. The difficulty is how to retain the distinction between God and conscience, and thereby to avoid, as Paul already knew, Gnosticism. Nevertheless, this discourse of "conscience" seems to resonate with common experience of human inviolability and thereby opens the possibility for theological and ethical reclamation.

20. These matters became even more complex with the introduction by St. Jerome of a distinction between *synderesis* (a basic grasp of first moral principles not effaced by the sin of Adam, the "spark" of conscience) and *syneidesis* (the act of reasoning to a practical judgment), which has bedeviled the history of especially Roman Catholic moral theology. I need not explore these matters in this essay.

21. See P. Tillich, *Morality and Beyond,* foreword by W. Schweiker (Louisville: Westminster John Knox Press, 1995).

5. Conclusions

I have attempted to show the complexity of the issues within ethics in speaking about moral inwardness and to explore briefly two ancient and paradigmatic metaphoric schemes used to articulate conceptions of the self. Additionally, I have tried to clarify how the question of moral inwardness forges connections between ethics and other modes or forms of inquiry at descriptive, existential, normative, and theological levels of reflection. One can easily imagine, for instance, how developments in biology like the work of Marc Hauser have impact on descriptions of moral inwardness; it is also obvious that advances in psychology and debates in theology would likewise impinge on this inquiry. By the same token, I have shown through a hermeneutic detour how ancient religious and philosophical texts anticipate many debates and ideas found among thinkers like Hauser and also Midgley. Indeed, it should be obvious that many of Midgley's concerns for the whole of the self organizing the self where anticipated by Plato even if she helps us avoid the possible "dualism" found in Plato's account. Similarly, St. Paul could speak of a universal moral grammar, the "law written in the heart," in ways that foreshadow claims by Hauser and others even while contemporary science can provide a more adequate natural explanation of that capacity. Yet what the ancients saw, and moderns like Midgley and Hauser do not, is the fact that the moral struggle and capacities of the self are theologically rich with meaning. The question of "moral inwardness," as I have called it, becomes a prism through which to interrelate various trends in thought across a host of disciplines in order to provide a robust and complex picture of the human as body-soul-spirit. It opens anew theological reflection in the midst of this intersection of forms of thought.

The work of this essay has been decidedly hermeneutical in nature. I have attempted to explore the complexity of moral inwardness by using cultural and religious resources that admittedly seem spent or impotent to many contemporary people. Importantly, around the metaphoric schemes we have examined swirl related images and concepts: the bucking of horses and travail of the charioteer; the voice and also sting of conscience as an "inner-chamber." One needs to understand the self within the semantic density of these ideas and their interconnections. In one scheme human existence is pictured as endless striving for unchangeable perfection; in the other the "soul" is a co-knowing of self and the divine law of freedom. I briefly noted the legacy of these pictures in current thought in ways that relieve the tension within the self, and so make the problem of being a self an easy one, or in ways that collapse the difference of self and other into authenticity of the self, a move that has led some thinkers to reject the importance of the self in favor of the ethical claim of the other.

Theologically construed, these discourses of "soul" picture the inner-life of the human self as a *sacred space,* but one within which the crucial difference between the divine and the self is too easily transgressed or it is reduced to the abstractions creator/creature or inauthentic/authentic self. More profoundly, the "soul" can be a space of divinization and/or profanization. Those conclusions mean, I think, a dangerous apotheosis of human power and aspiration or the loss of human dignity and worth. Each of the classic schemes, then, captures something intuitively right about human experience and relations to the divine. Where positions differ is in how the relation between aspiration and law, unity with the good and purity of conscience, perfection and freedom, are conceived. They also differ on how to retain the theological difference, as I have called it. This "difference" is important in order to avoid the reduction of God to self, the worry of any proper theological ethics.

Where then does this leave us? Two insights seem worthy of note. First, we have isolated in the so-called "Platonic" account of the soul the deeper questions of how to avoid an invidious dualism while also retaining a robust sense of the vitality and passion of life against eradication or divinization. We have also seen how the discourse of conscience can be used to articulate the right to have rights on behalf of the human being as a bulwark against forces that efface moral recognition. A picture of the soul as the labor of conscience integrating the dynamics of life also designates the right to have rights (recall St. Paul's claim about the weak against the strong). It does not specify the *content* of particular human rights, but, rather, why human beings have a right to rights at all. To be a human being is to be the work of conscience; that is the mode of our moral being. Actions and policies that violate "conscience" attack the very right of human beings to bear other rights and duties and responsibilities. They demean and destroy the possibility of people's struggle for the integrity of life with respect to felt "qualia" of experience, namely, the felt claim to inviolability and moral recognition in conscience and the erotic struggle rightly to integrate passional existence. Most importantly, it is crucial to avoid reducing one metaphoric scheme to the other, as if conscience is just a kind of passion or the passions can and ought to be self-integrating and the obvious ground of the right to have rights. Part of the trick, it seems, is to keep the semantic and hermeneutical density of these alternate metaphoric schemes in play. It is to weave a third way through cultural resources, neither just Greek nor only biblical.[22]

22. On this, see D. E. Klemm and W. Schweiker, *Religion and the Human Future: An Essay in Theological Humanism* (Oxford: Wiley-Blackwell, 2008).

This brings us to a second insight. Interestingly, each of the ancient ac-counts, unlike Hauser or Midgley, turns on how the "soul," the integrity of self, can be lost, forsaken. In an age in which global media and market forces move unceasingly to forge our desires and perceptions, and so our inner-selves, and in which social and political forces compete for loyalty and thereby challenge claims to the dignity of human beings as such, might we not learn something about the vulnerability of the self to internal disorder and also the inviolability of human life manifest, as St. Paul saw, in the sting of conscience? Insofar as these different schemes show the vulnerability of selves to the chaos of desire and the violation of the self in misplaced loyalty and authority, they provide hermeneutical tools needed in order to counter forces at work on the global scene. From within the criticism of inherited intellectual, cultural, and religious legacies one thereby reclaims resources to meet present-day problems. Is it not the case that the "soul" is now mightily endangered by manipulation of desire and tyrannous political and religious forces? In order to resist the denigra-tion of human beings from within their own vulnerability and to counter the violation of human dignity through forced conformity and domination, we need a rich and robust idea of what makes human beings valuable creatures with the right to have rights. I have tried to outline such an account by tracing the inner connection of reflection through biological (Hauser), philosophical (Midgley), and imaginative, symbolic forms (Plato/Paul).

Much current thought, it seems to me, tries to ignore the complex legacy of the interaction of the resources charted in this essay. By exploring symbolic forms of thought emblematically associated with Plato and Paul, one can insist that if we are to overcome the loss of cultural resources we must think within tensions that drive the heritage of this civilization. This is a kind of third-way thinking, neither Greek nor biblical but arising at their intersection. It is to think of the self within the move to self-overcoming and in response to the solicitude of conscience and thereby to counter the forces of decadence and degeneration working in our cultures as well as to counter the authoritarian-ism that is too present in social and religious existence. I have sought to think together these paradigms precisely in terms of the theological difference.

Some of the most basic facts of our time are the endangerment to human and nonhuman life around this planet, the fanatic religious hatred of finite life and moral reasonableness, and also the endless profaning of life in all forms. The terrifying possibility of human freedom is that the lust for more and more power will rid this world of life. The call of consciences must be heard anew — a call to respect and enhance the integrity of life and not just heroically endorse one's own authenticity. Further, the tragic freedom of human love, the chaos that demands some order in our lives, motivates too many religious people in various traditions to unflinching devotion and attachment to a God that leads to the hatred of all that is ungodly. The claim of conscience must be brought against religious distortion with resolute gratitude for life. Finally, the cynical reduction of human life to its most profane level must be resisted by unfolding the aspiration of the soul and also the call of conscience that combats forces of profanation. These possibilities of the human domination of life, the religious hatred of finite imperfection, and the endless cultural spreading of the profane are betrayals of goodness. Against these horrible possibilities we need a picture of humanity that is open to a sense of the divine but endorses the transcendent reach and dignity of finite life in and through the inwardness of our own being. In that light, I have outlined in these pages a theological and also humanistic vision of the soul.

Human Personhood at the Edges of Life: Medical Anthropology and Theology in Dialogue

Günter Thomas

1. Introductory Remarks

Human beings live across a vast span of time. This "lifetime" extends from periods of high dependence, marked by processes of development and maturation, through strong phases in the midst of life, and eventually into periods of various forms of deterioration with increased experiences of transience. A theological and phenomenologically realistic discussion of the person and of human dignity must touch upon these "edges of life." Any sound concept of the person must deal with those crises connected with the "edges of life."[1]

The general thesis of this paper is that, when explicating and unpacking what it means to be a person, such "edges of life" are, hermeneutically, highly significant. For this reason the paper argues against conceptions of "personhood" that exclude these "edges of life" from their descriptions, thus denying personhood to those at the "edges of life."

In this paper, I would like to concentrate on those particular challenges connected with intensive experiences of finiteness encountered in the later phase of life: particularly, experiences of severe illness in old age. In view of the demographic development of Western societies, the scope of these challenges can hardly be ignored. Increasingly, they belong to those challenges that must

---

1. For an overview of the current discussion see D. Thomasma, D. Weisstub, and C. Hervé, eds., *Personhood and Health Care,* International Library of Ethics, Law and the New Medicine (Dordrecht: Kluwer Academic, 2001).

be addressed by our collective symbolic and interpretive praxis, including our religious symbolic inventory, i.e., theology.

2. The Human Person at the Edges of Life

Human beings are finite. Even after years of "healthy aging," intensified experiences of this finitude are unavoidable. The increasingly longer phase of stable and healthy forms of aging, between the age of sixty and eighty, has its cost: Researchers on Aging describe it as a "compression of morbidity" in the last years of life. The various experiences of irreversible decline and the limitations of life in old age can be understood as representing four crises.[2] Not all four crises occur, nor, if they occur, must they occur at the same time. And yet, they can overlap and even mutually enforce one another. In all four fields of the experience of finitude there is a significant shift from limitation as a mark of finitude to loss as a key feature of intensified finitude (also with limits on compensation). Even if refined mechanisms of selection, optimization, and compensation take place, this shift from limits to losses is finally unavoidable.[3]

2.1. The Crisis of Self-Determination

The relationship between self-determined actions and experiences determined by others is certainly asymmetrical in many of life's instances. Even for the most active life, total self-determination and autonomy are an operational

2. For an elaborate psychological account of these processes, but with a focus on the final phase of life, see A. Kruse, "Das letzte Lebensjahr. Zur Körperlichen, Psychischen und sozialen Situation des alten Menschen am Ende Seines Lebens," in *Grundriss Gerontologie* 1st ed., Bd. 21 Urban-Taschenbücher (Stuttgart: Kohlhammer, 2007); see also M. M. Baltes, *The Many Faces of Dependency in Old Age* (Cambridge/New York: Cambridge University Press, 1996); and P. B. Baltes and J. Smith, "New Frontiers in the Future of Aging: From Successful Aging of the Young Old to the Dilemmas of the Fourth Age," *Gerontology* 49, no. 2 (2003): 123-35.

3. P. B. Baltes, U. M. Staudinger, and U. Lindenberger, "Lifespan Psychology: Theory and Application to Intellectual Functioning," *Annual Review of Psychology* 50 (1999); G. Weaver, "Embodied Spirituality: Experiences of Identity and Spiritual Suffering among Persons with Alzheimer's Dementia," in *From Cells to Souls, and Beyond: Changing Portraits of Human Nature,* ed. M. A. Jeeves (Grand Rapids: Eerdmans, 2004), pp. 77-101; C. Thomas and G. Thomas, "Autonomie und Endlichkeit im Alterungsprozess. Gerontologische und systematisch-theologische Beobachtungen," in *Aging — Anti-Aging — Pro-Aging: Altersdiskurse in theologischer Deutung,* ed. M. Kumlehn and T. Klie (Stuttgart: W. Kohlhammer, 2009), pp. 128-43.

fiction. However, with increased experiences of finitude, one finds a substantial reduction of the possibilities for self-determination and self-determined behavior. In many instances, even primary forms of self-determination (e.g., regarding one's place of residence) are no longer a given. The current debate surrounding the so-called "living will" marks, on the one hand, a new culture of preparation for death and a new form of *ars moriendi,* while on the other hand it is highlighting the increased fear within the public consciousness of a loss of self-determination.[4] In this respect, living wills testify to a collective cultural problem. Instead of heroic preparations for death, we have arrangements filled with fear and the anticipation of the loss of self-determination. In a striking way, living wills display the difficulty of attempts to practice self-determination in the light of its foreseeable loss — in other words, they represent an attempt to "stock up" on self-determination in the face of life's complexity.[5] At least in times of foresight, what most people are most afraid of is the increasing, gradual, or more discontinuous loss of this "autonomy."

2.2. *The Crisis of Temporally Extended Identity*

Alzheimer's disease provides a dramatic insight into the paradoxical structure of our experiences of finitude. Progressively limited horizons of possibility lead to a heightened experience of the past — memories of that life once lived become increasingly more important for one's current experiences. At the same time, the gradual loss of orientation and memory (at first recent and then long-term memories) erode this supporting pillar of identity. If "being a person" is only determined by one's own grasp of a temporally extended identity, then these processes of deterioration which are accompanied by a loss of memory can lead to the disintegration of the person. Even if autobiographical memory is not a slowly emptying container but an ongoing re/construction through narratives and conversations, the Alzheimer patient experiences a fundamental change in the ability to access/construct their own past.[6] Insights into the temporal nature of a narrative identity based on memory intensify this crisis.

4. D. Godkin, *Living Will, Living Well: Reflections on Preparing an Advance Directive* (Edmonton: University of Alberta Press, 2008).

5. On the legal notion of "prospective autonomy" see N. L. Cantor, *Advance Directives and the Pursuit of Death with Dignity,* Medical Ethics Series (Bloomington: Indiana University Press, 1993), pp. 23-32.

6. For such a concept of narrative identity based on G. H. Mead and P. Ricoeur, see D. Ezzy, "Theorizing Narrative Identity," *Sociological Quarterly* 39, no. 2 (1998): 239-52. In a

2.3. *The Crisis of Corporeality*

Many strands of twentieth-century philosophy, cultural theory, and theology document an insight that is not at all self-evident (at least against the background of Greek philosophy, a strong Augustinian heritage, and an equally strong Cartesian tradition), namely, that there exists a constitutive unity between body, soul, and mind, between reason, emotion, and biological bodily existence.[7] This unity makes it impossible to contemplate human identity without human corporeality. The human mind is an embodied mind, and this body is not a prison.[8] Nonetheless, human persons can relate to their own body as part of their self-referential activities. Such practices of intense self-observation range from sport to meditation and biofeedback practices.

As justified as the anti-Gnostic and anti-Idealistic impulses are, one should not ignore the fact that placing oneself in an active relation to one's own "bodily state" — which, in cases of massive physical limitation, includes aspects of dissociation — is a peculiarly human trait. In cases of illness and bodily deterioration, the human being can (and is indeed sometimes forced to) relate to his or her own body in ways that are critically distanced. In contrast to the situation with Alzheimer's disease, many age-related limitations compel people to distance themselves from their own physical deficiencies by maintaining, among other things, a "strong spirit." If human identity and "being a person"

---

similar vein, Gergen and Gergen develop a narrative self-concept in which individuals are able to shape their own ongoing and emerging self-conception. This is based on a central "self-narrative" that consists of "the individual's account of the relationships among self-relevant events across time. In developing a self-narrative the individual attempts to establish coherent connections among life events." K. J. Gergen and M. M. Gergen, "Narratives of the Self," in *Memory, Identity, Community: The Idea of Narrative in the Human Sciences,* ed. L. P. Hinchman and S. Hinchman (Albany: State University of New York Press, 1997), p. 162. In both conceptions, identity is the result of a productivity, without adequate consideration for its fragility and dependency on external attributions that both precede and outlast one's own productivity.

7. Shifting from phenomenological considerations to gender theory, Saskia Wendel, "Der Körper der Autonomie. Anthropologie und 'Gender,' " in *Endliche Autonomie: Interdisziplinäre Perspektiven auf ein Theologisch-Ethisches Programm,* ed. A. Autiero, S. Goertz, M. Striet (Münster: LIT, 2004), pp. 103-22; in the context of theology and medical ethics, J. J. Shuman and B. Volck, *Reclaiming the Body: Christians and the Faithful Use of Modern Medicine* (Grand Rapids: Brazos, 2006), pp. 41-62; reclaiming the link between the concept of the person and the body, G. Meilaender, *Body, Soul, and Bioethics* (Notre Dame: University of Notre Dame Press, 1995), pp. 37-59.

8. On the enduring and powerful tradition of this metaphor, see P. Courcelle, "Gefängnis (Der Seele)," in *Reallexikon für Antike und Christentum,* ed. T. Klauser et al. (Stuttgart: Hiersemann, 1976), col. 294-318.

are based to a very high degree on a physical integrity that must continuously be appropriated, then the deterioration of physical vitality must be interpreted as the decay of that person's integrity. In this situation, the crisis of corporeality consists of an increasing inability to adjust one's identity to those significant changes of one's body that come along with old age or severe illness.[9]

2.4. The Crisis of Relationality

Severe illness has the power to transform one's own social networks. In the late-modern period, significantly longer life-spans and the processes of age-related illness lead to experiences of loss within the structure of social relationships based on interactions. While many changes that occur in old age can be understood as reorganizations and transformations of social relationships, this should not distract from the fact that real losses do occur. For the great majority of people, the reduction in one's social "sphere of resonance" is both an unavoidable and bitter experience that cannot be completely compensated for by occasional intensifications of other relationships or by the buildup of new relations. A noticeable shift of attention in newspaper-reading habits (from a focus on news to the obituary notices) may mark a shift into this phase of life. That which can be described philosophically as "interpersonality in mutual acceptance and appreciation" can no longer be realized in as many lived social relations as the individual may desire.[10] Even necessary socio-cultural change, in terms of new forms of housing and cohabitation (apartment-sharing communities), may only partially compensate for these dramatic changes. The emphasis on human relationality as an essential dimension of human life not only leads to the discovery of life's richness, but also its vulnerability: the inevitable diminishment or even breakdown of relationships that occurs in old age and in periods of intense and enduring illness.

When comparing these edges of life, we must take into account an important differentiation.

Philosophically speaking, it is different notions of "possibility" that differentiate between the beginning of life and phases of harsh limitation and loss in old age. The deficits of old age can no longer be mitigated by a process

9. It is a telling psychological finding that the older people become, the wider the perceived gap between their actual age and how old they feel mentally. The "truly old" are always others.

10. For attempts to link a basic notion of relationality to personhood, as manifested in kinship, see R. Spaemann, *Personen. Versuche über den Unterschied zwischen "Etwas" und "Jemand"* (Stuttgart: Klett-Cotta, 1996, 1998), p. 255.

of "modalization" directed toward the future: those events at the "early edges of life" that were understood as potentialities (as real possibilities) waiting to be realized in the future, can then only be understood as "past opportunities" when they are later encountered among the intensified experiences of one's own transience and fragility. While both the early and later phases of life give rise to moments of intensified finitude and dependency, they fundamentally differ in terms of their type of potentiality.[11]

3. The Edges of Life in Current Debates on "Personhood"

Why are these crises, so characteristic of the second "edge of life," relevant to the issue of human personhood? The reason is clear: In one way or another, they play a significant role in current bioethical debates about the person and the moral status of personhood. The four crises discussed above are at the center of the search for criteria that could guide bioethical decision making.[12] They are "trouble spots," focal points in the discussion regarding the attribution of personhood. In the lively debate on the concept of "person," the way in which these crises are dealt with provides us with a differentiating criterion. In short, in an aging society with limited resources, we must remember that there is more at stake in attempts to conceptualize the "person" than theoretical definitions alone. Even a short, and admittedly broad, look at these debates will make the reasons for this clear.

In medical ethics, the various positions on the status and nature of the human person can be divided (very roughly) into two polarized groups.[13] We might call the first group "metaphysical-conservative," and the second "empirical-liberal."[14] Surprisingly, they do not differ significantly on the content of person-

11. This difference plays a significant role in ethical debates about the moral status of embryos or of very young infants. At the least, they have the potential to become a self-conscious moral agent.

12. This is quite evident in the contributions to Thomasma, Weisstub, and Hervé, eds., *Personhood and Health Care.*

13. For an overview of the philosophical debate, including a historical dimension, cf. D. Sturma, ed., *Person: Philosophiegeschichte — Theoretische Philosophie — Praktische Philosophie* (Paderborn: Mentis, 2001).

14. In the first group we could place Eva F. Kittay, Robert Spaemann, Theo Kobusch, Ulrich Eibach, Ludger Honnefelder, Allen Verhey, Gilbert Meilaender, and in a specific sense, Theda Rehbock. The second group would include Jeff McMahan, Norbert Hoerster, Michael Tooley, John Harris, the early H. Tristram Engelhardt, Peter Singer, and possibly Dieter Birnbacher. For an attempt to distinguish two streams in the philosophical traditions, see Ludwig Siep,

hood (the intension of the concept) nor on the respective descriptive and normative implications of the term, namely a rational, self-conscious, autonomous, and self-determining being who has certain rights and deserves legal recognition and social acceptance.[15] The central point of contention in this heated debate is the extension of the concept and its far-reaching normative implications. Are all human beings persons, with a justified claim for the recognition of one's dignity and elementary rights, or only those human beings who can show and practice certain properties, specific capabilities, and dispositions?[16] Especially with regard to problems at the beginning and end of life, the crucial question seems to be: Are all human beings at every moment of their lives really persons, or is personhood something that can be lost close to the final edge of life?[17] Both

"Der Begriff der Person als Grundlage der biomedizinischen Ethik," in *Person: Philosophiegeschichte — Theoretische Philosophie — Praktische Philosophie,* ed. Dieter Sturma (Paderborn, Mentis, 2001).

15. For a similar observation see S. K. Hellsten, "Towards an Alternative Approach to Personhood in the End of Life Questions," *Theoretical Medicine and Bioethics: Philosophy of Medical Research and Practice* 21, no. 6 (2000): 515-36, 520f.

16. For example, the philosopher McMahan would limit personhood to beings who can have "prudential unity relations"; J. McMahan, *The Ethics of Killing: Problems at the Margins of Life,* Oxford Ethics Series (New York: Oxford University Press, 2003), p. 68. See the critique of McMahan by E. Kittay, "At the Margins of Moral Personhood," *Ethics* 116 (2005): 105: "Strong prudential unity relations and the psychological capacities that enable them also coincide with the definition of personhood, that is, the complex, sophisticated psychological capacities that include self-consciousness, rationality, and autonomy. 'We,' then, are persons. Conversely, weak prudential unity relations arising from psychological functioning that falls short of these complex and sophisticated psychological capacities belong to those who are not persons." Peter Singer's separation of "human being" and "person" leads to a differentiation of varying degrees of self-consciousness and rationality that might be connected to the moral value of a person. See P. Singer, *Practical Ethics* (Cambridge/New York: Cambridge University Press, 1979), pp. 125f. Personhood is attributed to the highest state of self-consciousness and rationality. In the same line of thought, the bioethicist Tristram Engelhardt draws a distinction between human personal and human biological life. Consequently, "not only are some humans not persons, there is no reason to hold that all persons are humans." As a consequence, he distinguishes persons in the "strict sense" being "self-conscious, rational agents" and human beings who are persons only in a social sense. The latter concept is invoked "when certain instances of human biological life are treated as if they were persons strictly, even though they are not" (H. Tristram Engelhardt Jr., "Medicine and the Concept of Person" in *Contemporary Issues in Bioethics,* ed. T. L. Beauchamp and L. Walters [Belmont, CA: Wadsworth, 1982], p. 97). See also H. Tristram Engelhardt, *The Foundations of Bioethics,* 2nd ed. (New York: Oxford University Press, 1996), pp. 149f., where he distinguishes four social senses, and summarizes: "There is unavoidably a major distinction to be drawn between persons who are moral agents and persons to whom the rights of moral agents are imputed."

17. P. Singer, *Writings on an Ethical Life,* 1st ed. (New York: Ecco Press, 2000), pp. 76f.

groups consider this question decisive for establishing a normative foundation for decision-making processes in medical ethics — even if not all in the empiricist group would necessarily draw the same moral conclusions.[18]

That which sets both groups apart is a basic conceptual strategy: While the proponents of the "metaphysical-conservative" position would like to explicate and ground the specific position of the human being in the world, and its elementary dignity and worth, the other group is searching for criteria that would distinguish between persons and nonpersons. Based on the empirical observation that some human beings during some phases of life lack certain capacities, the concept of person thus serves to filter out individuals into human beings and nonhuman beings. For the "metaphysical-conservative" group — which I would rather call essentialist — the set of human beings is coterminous with the set of persons, and personhood is a form of existence: The act of drawing a distinction takes place elsewhere, namely between *Homo sapiens* and non-*Homo sapiens*. Yet overall, both groups appear to be marked by certain deficiencies in their conceptualizations of the "person." Instead of taking sides in this debate I would like to question their shared assumption regarding the place of finitude, vulnerability, and dependency in developing the content (intension) of the concept of "person."

4. Three Intermediate Considerations

Given the ethical debate sketched out thus far, how should theological ethics deal with the apparent frailty and fragility of human beings? Even if critical remarks can be addressed to both sides of the debate, three intermediate considerations seem necessary at this point:

4.1. Why Not Abandon "Person"? "Person" as Network-Term

Should we keep the concept "person" or drop it from our theoretical vocabulary? Several philosophers, as well as other participants in the bioethical

18. Admittedly there are significant exceptions and variations with regard to consequences. The philosopher Martin Seel emphasizes that only moral subjects are persons. However, moral respect is present among persons and addressed to persons and nonpersons. For Seel, human beings can lose the status of personhood, but not their right to be respected and accepted. See M. Seel, *Versuch über die Form des Glücks. Studien zur Ethik,* 1st ed. (Frankfurt am Main: Suhrkamp, 1995).

debate, have noted a thorough vagueness in this concept.[19] The diverse histories and etymologies — ranging back to Greek thinking, as well as to early Christian reflections and even Enlightenment transformations — will never lead us to a clear and precise concept. Christian theology, legal thought, and bioethical reflections seem to use rather different concepts of the "person." As a consequence, several participants in the debate suggest abandoning the concept altogether, at least in its connection with normative claims.[20] While I do not question the diagnosis, I would reject the suggested cure since it confuses the problem with the solution. Attempts to abandon the concept altogether are based on a thorough misunderstanding of orientational discourses in modern, highly differentiated societies. Upon closer inspection, we find hardly any key concept with the same intension and extension in any of the multiple systemic self-descriptions modern societies have developed for their social subsystems, be it in law, religion, healthcare, science, arts, etc. This philosophical complaint about vagueness can only be grounded in a naïvely misconceived understanding of unity across differentiated realms of discourse.[21] What seems to be a problem is at least part of a solution to the problem of trans-discursive resonance in late-modern societies: "Person" is a "network-term" that bridges those discursive gaps that are unavoidable in and characteristic of late-modern societies.[22] Network-terms represent one possibility of creating constructive resonance between diverse fields of reflection, such as religion, law, medicine, etc. For this reason, theology, as a normative self-description of organized re-

19. See e.g. A. Kemmerling, "Was macht den Begriff der Person so besonders schwierig?" in *Gegenwart des Lebendigen Christus*, ed. G. Thomas and A. Schüle (Leipzig: Evangelische Verlagsanstalt, 2007), pp. 541-65. See also T. L. Beauchamp, "The Failure of Theories of Personhood," in *Personhood and Health Care*, ed. D. Thomasma, D. Weisstub, and C. Hervé (Dordrecht: Kluwer Academic, 2001), pp. 59-69, who claims that the notion of moral personhood does not require a metaphysical concept of personhood.

20. D. Birnbacher, "Das Dilemma des Personenbegriffs," in *Personsein aus Bioethischer Sicht. Tagung der Österreichischen Sektion der IVR in Graz, 29. und 30. November 1996*, ed. P. Strasser and E. Starz, Archiv für Rechts- und Sozialphilosophie. Beiheft (Stuttgart: Steiner, 1997), pp. 9-25; Beauchamp, "The Failure of Theories of Personhood," pp. 59-70.

21. For a similar observation, see A. O. Rorty, *Mind in Action: Essays in the Philosophy of Mind* (Boston: Beacon Press, 1988), p. 7: "Some of the apparently intractable debates about persons occur when the concerns of one context are imported to another, in the premature interest of constructing a unified theory, or as a rhetorical move in a political polemic."

22. That which is diagnosed as a problem by E. Erde, "Paradigms and Personhood: A Deepening of Dilemmas in Ethics and Medical Ethics," *Theoretical Medicine and Bioethics* 20 (1999): 141-60, 142, is in some respects a solution. The concept of "person" is used quite differently in a variety of language-games, and yet it connects these discourses in a loosely structured way.

ligion, must nourish its own understanding of the "person" while at the same time searching for interfaces to those understandings developed in other fields (in this case: medicine). If the apparent vagueness can be transformed into a productive tension and stimulating resonance, then constructive critique can emerge.

4.2. Person — The Unity of a Distinction

Before moving into the hermeneutics of finitude I would like to suggest a kind of framework, within which we can locate the individual aspects of that which is implied when we speak of "being a person," implications that reach back to the ancient understanding of "person" as derived from an actor's mask. At the same time, the following rather formal conception helps to detect the similarities as well as the differences between the multiple systemic discourses on being a person. It may help us to discover a field of consensus between the various approaches.

The mask as a physical object draws a distinction between that which is behind and that which is in front of the mask. In this position, the mask both reveals and represents while hiding and "decoupling." Yet when wearing the mask, the actor (behind the mask) willingly becomes the carrier of that which can be publicly observed. Picking up this ancient tradition, I want to suggest that the person is a dynamic, highly fragile, and embodied unity of a distinction between internal self-reference and complex, one-sided as well as mutual relations with outside entities. In contrast to the concept of human being, personhood implies an internally shaped and responsibly formed unity of a multiplicity of relations — a unity, which can take the form of various types of "self" or "selves" with varying degrees of heterogeneity.

The finding that the concept of person is closely linked to moral rights and obligations is grounded in the fact that the unity of this difference is not arbitrary but rather responsibly shaped, and places the "individual" in a dynamic social space. This fragile and constantly negotiated unity cannot be captured by the vague, yet nevertheless frequently used, term "relationality." Even the ideas of address and response as key features of a relational identity and of personhood operate with far too elevated presuppositions, insofar as that social space may initially be shaped by mutual perceptions and forms of passivity. Moreover, the notion of relationality does not address the co-presence of "closure" and "openness" in the unity of a distinction.

The ancient conception of the mask offers a further hint: Being a person is not a substantial, ontological property, but a situational and contextual attribution or ascription. Only on stage and during the play is the "person" perceived as a person and treated as such. This observation can be interpreted within both a sociological and theological framework. First, to be a person is a social and cultural attribution or ascription that covers the whole of finite life in all its stages and conditions; and we assume that every human being is a person. Vis-à-vis this sociological interpretation it becomes evident that for Christians, being a person is an attribution that has its reality within the framework (or: on the stage) of God's care for the world. Yet empirical observations of features of "being a person" are not themselves criteria for the ascription of personhood, but rather explorations of a space of possibilities opened up by these ascriptions. Hence the empirical observation of the unity of a distinction might for some time vanish, be less complex and less dynamic; it may be hoped for and expected, but also be remembered. In considering the unity of distinctions amid the four challenges of old age, we must keep in mind that, due to the double-sidedness of the mask, the unity of the distinction can be reconstructed both from inside and from outside. Even if we seem to observe only very reduced forms of internally formed unities — such as with those who are asleep, with very young children, people with severe dementia, or with other cognitive disabilities — we can still uphold our externally constructed view of the internally formed unity. Thus personhood is communicated in the very act of invested attention, communication, and care. Persons are persons in the very act of being treated as persons.

From a Christian perspective, this attribution is rooted in a complex divine attribution of personhood and dignity, a process that needs to be differentiated into the work of God the Creator, of Christ, and of the Spirit. Furthermore, the areas close to the edges of life serve as a hermeneutical key for exploring a realistic notion of the human "person."

4.3. Intensified Finitude and the Hermeneutics of Personhood at or Distanced from the "Edges of Life"

In their explorations of what it means to be a person, both sides of the debate take as their paradigm case the figure of an ideal, rational agent in midlife, perhaps a paradigmatic male around the age of thirty. For example, both Spaemann and McMahan take an average person of the human species as their paradigm case for personhood, a human being with fully developed mental and social capacities.[23] While there may arguably be some intuitive support for privileging young adults, it is by no means altogether convincing.[24]

In the end, two approaches can be taken in the search for key aspects of human personhood: One can look (a) for that which is shared by all, or (b) for that which is not necessarily experientially shared by anyone but which reveals essential aspects in its very particularity. At that point, it is not convincing to exclude those phases related to life's fragile "edges" from the relevant "context of discovery." Birth, early childhood, and death are shared by all human beings — illness and old age only count as very likely experiences. As Eva Feder Kittay states: "We are all — equally — some mother's child."[25] Therefore I argue for the inclusion of the edges of life into the search for that which is typical and essential for a person. Otherwise, this search suffers from a methodological short-circuit typical of empirical-philosophical approaches to personhood: That which is excluded at the beginning will certainly be excluded at the end.[26]

Over against this widespread privileging of the assumed center of life, I would like to take seriously an insight from information sciences: that the edges of a surface contain the most information. In any process, it is the cracks and ruptures that are most telling. Discontinuities and transitions shed most light on the processes in between. For this reason I would like to suggest a hermeneutics of personhood that extends its field of discovery to the edges

23. Even though for Spaemann the properties of personhood are not empirical, he is forced to find some way of determining what is typical of a person. At this point he suggests looking at healthy adults. Crucial here is not whether a distinct human person carries these properties but rather his or her "Zugehörigkeit zu einer Art, deren typische Exemplare über diese Merkmale verfügen" (Spaemann, *Personen. Versuche über den Unterschied zwischen "Etwas" und "Jemand,"* p. 11).

24. If it is not the thirty-year-old male that is taken as the ideal of the naturalist conception (as presented by Singer and McMahan), then we often find naturalism slipping into a Platonic ideal of personhood: "individual human beings are then mere imperfect copies of the ideal form, and the further they get from the ideal form of Mind or Reason, the less human they become and the less value they have" (Hellsten, "Towards an Alternative Approach to Personhood in the End of Life Questions," p. 525).

25. E. Feder Kittay, *Love's Labor: Essays on Women, Equality, and Dependency, Thinking Gender* (New York: Routledge, 1999), p. 25, emphasizes that "a conception of society viewed as an association of equals masks inequitable dependencies, those of infancy and childhood, old age, illness and disability" (p. xi). Likewise A. C. MacIntyre, *Dependent Rational Animals: Why Human Beings Need the Virtues* (Chicago: Open Court, 1999), p. 5, argues that "dependency, rationality and animality have to be understood in relationship to each other."

26. For a striking exception, see R. M. Zaner, *The Context of Self: A Phenomenological Inquiry Using Medicine as a Clue,* Series in Continental Thought 1 (Athens, OH: Ohio University Press, 1981).

of life, that even takes these edges to be an essential "context of discovery."
That which has to date been excluded in the debates by privileging the figure
of the healthy young (male) person, needs now to be re-included. The crises
that result from events of intensified finitude are events that are full of such
ruptures and challenges.

However, this hermeneutical turn to the "edges" as a paradigmatic field
of experience must not be understood as an attempt to idealize these experiences. In addition, a concentration on these edges does not aim at excluding
or rejecting that which can be found "at life's center."[27] And yet, a rich understanding of the person requires this shift of attention. Vis-à-vis the current
debate in medical ethics, I would argue that we need to question that which
both groups in the debate have commonly assumed with respect to personhood. In other words, we need to break up the consensus on the intension of
the term "person" ("What is it to be a person?") in order to deal with the issue
of the extension of the concept ("Who is a person?").

5. Personhood at the Edges of Life: Constructive Proposals for the Conversation between Theology and Anthropology

5.1. Person and the Bridges to Biblical Theology: Redemption of Creation, Christ and the Life of the Spirit

The term "person" is not a biblical one, although it was used very early in
Christian theology. In addition, it is not a term that can be connected to one
or two corresponding concepts in the writings of the biblical theologians. Metaphorically speaking, it touches larger areas on the map of Christian theology.
In the theological tradition, personhood was primarily linked to the concept
of the imago Dei found in the book of Genesis.[28] In bioethical debates, most
Christian writers in the essentialist group follow this track and bind together

---

27. This was repeatedly emphasized by Dietrich Bonhoeffer, who criticized the religious
exploitation of these "edges of life" as situations of human weakness. See D. Bonhoeffer, *Wid-
erstand und Ergebung. Briefe und Aufzeichnungen aus der Haft*, ed. C. Gremmels, 14th ed.;
D. Bonhoeffer, *Werke (Dbw), Bd. 8* (Gütersloh: Gütersloher Verlagshaus/Kaiser, 1998), pp. 407f.
(letter of April 30th, 1944): "Ich möchte Gott nicht an den Grenzen, sondern in der Mitte, nicht
in den Schwächen, sondern in der Kraft, nicht also bei Tod und Schuld, sondern in Leben und
im Guten des Menschen sprechen."

28. For further elaborations of this point see the contribution by Bernd Oberdorfer in
this volume.

a philosophical/theological concept of nature with a notion of the imago Dei that stems from creation theology. As theologically valuable as the imago Dei is, it is also at least partially responsible for the past development of reductionistic conceptions of the person, especially when such concepts failed to take into account the important Trinitarian aspects of the Christian doctrine of God. As Hans Reinders notes in precisely this context: "After all, Christians do not simply believe in God; they believe in God the Father, and the Son, and the Holy Spirit."[29] For a canonical view, as well as a Trinitarian perspective of the issue of imago Dei, this concentration on the Genesis account of the imago Dei is in itself not only deficient and misleading but conceptually dangerous. Protestant theology in particular must explore further possible "interfaces" — and Christology should be the first on the list. As Jürgen Moltmann has shown, the concept of the imago Dei located in the theology of creation and in theological anthropology must be correlated to its Christological transformation and eschatological horizon in the imago Christi.[30]

This shift from creation to Christ is a far-reaching reshaping of metaphorical fields and a reorganization of theological resources: for theological reflection and imagination, what it means to be a person becomes related to the life of Christ. For a Christian ethos centered on the life of Jesus, compassionate relationships to weak and fragile life turn out to be of crucial importance. Compared to the association of the imago Dei with power and dominion (Genesis 1) — regardless of how mercifully this dominion is exercised — in the context of the Christ event power is connected with weakness. Three arguments can be put forward in support of this move to a more Christological approach to personhood. First, the dignity and worth of every human person (which is so closely related to personhood) is attributed and divinely ascribed to every human creature based on the totally inclusive event of salvation and atonement. Seen in this light as an external ascription, the universality of human personhood can be maintained without resorting to some intrinsic

---

29. Reinders, "Human Dignity in the Absence of Agency," pp. 121-39, 123.

30. J. Moltmann, *Gott in der Schöpfung. Ökologische Schöpfungslehre*, 3rd ed., Eng. 1987 ed. (München: Chr. Kaiser, 1985), pp. 223-35. For the exegetical bases, see J. Jervell, *Imago Dei. Gen 1,26 F. im Spätjudentum, in der Gnosis und in den Paulinischen Briefen, Forschungen zur Religion und Literatur des Alten und Neuen Testaments, N.F. 58. Heft. Der Ganzen Reihe 76. Heft* (Göttingen: Vandenhoeck & Ruprecht, 1960). On Christ as the "image of God" in Paul see 2 Corinthians 4:4; Colossians 1:15; Philippians 2:6. The corollary, viz. the conformation of human beings into the image of Christ, is spelled out in Romans 8:29; 1 Corinthians 15:49; 2 Corinthians 3:18. Without this Christological dynamization of the creation account, the imago Dei itself can become a false abstraction away from the divine purposes.

human property. Second, in this way theological ethics can overcome the problem of the distortion of the imago Dei through sin — a crucial issue for Protestant theology. Third, if the dignity and worth of every person is based on a divine attribution, human beings are called to participate in the communicative attribution of this worth and dignity and also to respond to it.[31] In light of this Christologically based attribution, we find that while being a person encompasses being a natural, biological, cultural, and social being, it is not a natural property of this biological, cultural, and social being.

5.2. Sociality in Dependency Relations as a Key Feature

One essential feature of most conceptual accounts of personhood (both by essentialists and empiricists) is the rather atomistic or individualistic understanding of the key "properties" of a person. Free moral recognition and voluntary acceptance of the other, that is, "moral subjectivity," is often at the center of most conceptions.[32] However, in principle this does not exclude the dimension of a social life, as is presupposed in a concept of "mutual recognition."[33] And yet, such relations to other persons are construed as intrinsically one-sided or as social relations that are not constitutive for one's own personhood: acceptance by others is based on the assumption that the others exist in my social sphere. If those others did not exist, there would be no relationship that required mutual recognition. The contingent existence of the other in my social sphere creates the challenge of accepting him or her, as well as that of being accepted. These two problems could hardly arise if the other did not first exist. Hence even those understandings of personhood that emphasize a factual "mutuality" at their core presuppose a self-sufficiency as their starting point. In the context of "mutual recognition," dependency is not a central feature of personhood, and the other is first and foremost a problem to be managed.

31. It should be noted that in Christian theology the incarnation of Jesus Christ and the work of the Holy Spirit exemplify the divine willingness to embrace creaturely life in order to communicate salvation and atonement to the whole human and nonhuman world. Accordingly, human beings and particularly the church participate in the active attribution of such a type of personhood through communication in word and deed.

32. See for instance Seel, *Versuch über die Form des Glücks. Studien zur Ethik*, pp. 259ff.

33. On the structure of forms of social recognition, see A. Honneth, *Kampf um Anerkennung. Zur moralischen Grammatik sozialer Konflikte*, 1st ed. (Frankfurt am Main: Suhrkamp, 1992), chapters 4-6.

Yet even if we consider theological anthropologies, which regularly call attention to the essential and inescapable social dimension of human personhood, relations of dependency are often not part of the picture. The "conceptual temptation" in emphasizing relationality, community, and mutuality is to assume that most relationships are somehow symmetrical. Yet empirically speaking, this is certainly not the case: Moral agency, as with all human action, reproduces complex networks of asymmetrical relationships in which asymmetries of "inevitable dependencies" may change, and where multiple types of relations might coexist and form nets of "interdependencies."[34] These dependencies cover a broad range of forms and cannot simply be seen as I-Thou relations, especially as they often include relations to nonnatural persons.[35] Surprisingly, in theological anthropology such dynamic interdependencies are either generalized and simplified in order to assimilate them into the framework of such I-Thou relationships, or they are completely neglected.[36]

What is systematically neglected in such a conceptual framework, but becomes prominent at the edges of life, is that no human being could exist without the (natural and nonnatural) other, so that being dependent and encountering dependency become crucial, noncontingent aspects of human moral existence.[37] "Our dependency, then, is not only an exceptional circumstance."[38] Regardless of whether it is via a parent, a family, a social institution, or a whole set of complex cultural inventions in late-modern, functionally differentiated societies, the act of receiving and practicing care is the living

34. E. F. Kittay, B. Jennings, and A. A. Wasunna, "Dependency, Difference and the Global Ethic of Longterm Care," *Journal of Political Philosophy* 13, no. 4 (2005): 443-69, 444.

35. At that point many philosophical debates seem to be sociologically näive. An increasing number of dependency relations exist between natural persons and nonnatural persons and social systems such as institutions. In the case of older patients, these include nursing homes, insurance companies, pharmaceutical products, and hospitals, to name just a few. Modern societies are marked by heightened and strong dependencies upon nonnatural persons. Late-modern, functionally differentiated societies tend to generalize not only (functional) dependency relations but also the process of "acting on behalf of others."

36. Even though, e.g., John Macmurray conceives of the mother-child relationship to be constitutive, he considers it to be "a personal mutuality, as a 'You and I' with a common life" (J. Macmurray, *Persons in Relation*, Gifford Lectures, 1954 [London: Faber & Faber, 1961], p. 60).

37. For a subtle philosophical conception of "existence" that takes into account this elementary social aspect, see T. Rentsch, *Die Konstitution der Moralität. Transzendentale Anthropologie und praktische Philosophie*, 1st ed. (Frankfurt am Main: Suhrkamp, 1990), who considers several "inter-existentials."

38. Kittay, *Love's Labor: Essays on Women, Equality, and Dependency*, p. 29. Kittay's book offers a lucid and forceful critique of the exclusion of dependency relationships from philosophical anthropology. See in particular chapters 1-3.

GÜNTER THOMAS

context in which any act of "autonomy" of a bodily existence is embedded.[39] Under close inspection, we find that relationships of dependency touch on levels of biological life and identity, on cognitive capacities and potentials, as well as on one's social and cultural life.

And yet, we have to challenge even those understandings of "person" that consider the social and communal dimension to be constitutive, but still emphasize the mutuality of relationships.[40] The conceptual temptation to emphasize relationality, koinonia, and mutuality is based on an assumption that most relationships are symmetrical — if not at all times, then at least in sum "over the long run." However, this is empirically unsupportable and conceptually misconceived.[41] Asymmetrical relations of dependency are, as a matter of fact, the "default mode" of human relations, a fact that is often overlooked. A remarkable exception to this general error can be found in Karl Barth's anthropology. While most of his considerations are caught up in a model of personalism, he does demonstrate a surprising phenomenological sensitivity when he describes the key features of human personhood. After pointing out the way in which all personhood is grounded in the Word of Grace, he searches for structures and constants that specify "being in encounter" in realistic forms of co-humanity. While his recourse to seeing, speaking, and hearing are deeply wedded with ideas of symmetry, mutuality, and I-Thou encounters, his third marker of the human person is "the fact that we render mutual assistance."[42]

39. For a similar critique, see MacIntyre, *Dependent Rational Animals: Why Human Beings Need the Virtues,* p. 4: "habits of mind that express an attitude of denial towards the facts of disability and dependence presuppose either a failure or a refusal to acknowledge adequately the bodily dimension of our existence."

40. This is the main thrust of the contributions in C. Schwöbel and C. E. Gunton, eds., *Persons, Divine and Human: King's College Essays in Theological Anthropology* (Edinburgh: T. & T. Clark, 1991). See e.g. Macmurray, *Persons in Relation,* p. 69 on the importance of the constitutive reference to the other. Also on theological grounds, cf. the emphasis that J. Zizioulas, *Being as Communion: Studies in Personhood and the Church, Contemporary Greek Theologians* (Crestwood, NY: St. Vladimir's Seminary Press, 1985), places on the ekstatic existence of the person. Both positions are evaluated by A. J. Torrance, "What Is a Person?" in *From Cells to Souls, and Beyond: Changing Portraits of Human Nature,* ed. M. A. Jeeves (Grand Rapids: Eerdmans, 2004), pp. 199-222.

41. For this reason, one must distinguish between relations based on the exchange of gifts — which may at least assume temporalized symmetry — and relations that can be characterized as a form of sacrifice — without any realistic expectation of "adequate" return.

42. K. Barth, *Church Dogmatics* III/2, trans. G. W. Bromiley (Edinburgh: T. & T Clark, 1961), p. 260. "My action is human when the outstretched hand of the other does not grope in the void but finds in mine the support which is asked. . . . We are not guilty of idealisation when we say of man that he is created and ordained to receive help from his fellow-man and

So for Barth, a life spent in asymmetrical relations of assistance is not an assault on human personhood but rather a mode of flourishing, creaturely life.

However, pointing out the embeddedness of "autonomy" should not distract us from acknowledging the existence of destructive as well as manipulative dependencies. If the nourishing, shaping, and regulation of relations of dependency are so crucial for being a living human being, they are characteristic of being a moral person. Without being cared for, no human being could become what some call a "moral subject."

5.3. Moving beyond Intellectualism and Moral Self-Determination

Another aspect of autonomy and self-determination as distinctive features of being a "person" is pointed out by the philosopher of law Margaret Somerville: "This concept of autonomy is value-laden in at least two . . . respects. First, greater autonomy is regarded as a 'higher state of being.' Second, it postulates a particular kind of person as being most autonomous — namely, self-aware, reflective, and insightful. Those who are impulsive, act on instinct, or are emotionally influenced (and as a result, impetuous) are likely to be regarded as less autonomous. In other words, people whose cognitive functioning clearly dominates their emotional functioning are likely to be regarded as more autonomous."[43] Both the emotion and compassion that people practice in those fields close to the edges of life, as well as the routines for providing and receiving biological, social, and psychological care disappear from sight if the cognitive practice of autonomous decisions are taken to be the determining marker of personhood. Without doubt, the moral, legal, and political achievements tied to these traditions emphasizing autonomy, self-consciousness, and individual

---

to give help to his fellow-man. We are speaking of real man. And we are speaking of him realistically, whereas all the descriptions of man in which the presupposition is normative of an empty subject isolated from the fellow-man can only be called idealistic in the wrong sense. For in them, in more or less consistent approximation to Zarathustra, the reference is to a man who does not and cannot exist, but can only be the vision of a maniac" (*CD* III/2, p. 264). It is the framework of his personalism that does not allow Barth to see the multiple variations of "acting on behalf of the other" that characterize nontrivial forms of "assistance." For a rather sympathetic reconstruction of this anthropology see D. J. Price, *Karl Barth's Anthropology in Light of Modern Thought* (Grand Rapids: Eerdmans, 2002), pp. 97-164.

43. M. A. Somerville, *Death Talk: The Case Against Euthanasia and Physician-Assisted Suicide* (Montreal/Ithaca, NY: McGill-Queen's University Press, 2001), p. 313. Here we clearly see the dualistic Cartesian as well as rationalistic Platonic background to the concept of the autonomous, rational, and self-conscious person.

freedom must not be played down. And yet, Somerville rightly points out a dangerous and truly problematic aspect. However, it should be noted that theology has its own share in this problematic tradition — ranging from Augustine to Thomas Aquinas — not to speak of the more openly Neoplatonic traditions.[44] Contrary to positions endorsing the more or less hidden cognitivism of this "homo faber" of rational and self-conscious self-governance, emotions appear to be the basis of an elementary sense of the self in the self's relations to its own body.[45] The cultivation of passions and the nourishing of one's emotional life become essential aspects in living life as a person. An ability to be affected effectively (by music, art, but also by the pain of others, by care, and eventually by death) and to allow for the evocation of compassion in others is not a weakness but a life-enhancing capacity of passivity, and a key feature of personhood. The complex unity of cognitive, emotional, and biological bodily existence need not be destroyed by false abstractions.

5.4. The Social Narration of the Person

One aspect of dependency can be found in the relation between narrative identity and narrative dependency. Paul Ricoeur introduced the idea of "narrative identity" into the debate about the self and human identity.[46] This concept addresses a whole set of problems ranging from changes over time to the role of language in identity formation. According to Ricoeur, every narrative essentially combines two dimensions in varying proportions. The first is the chronological or episodic dimension; this characterizes the story as being made out of events. In contrast, the second is a rather nonchronological,

44. When quoting John of Damascus, Thomas Aquinas states: "being after God's image signifies his capacity for understanding, and for making free decisions and his mastery of himself" (Thomas Aquinas, *Summa Theologiae*, 1a, 93.5). The long philosophical and religious tradition emphasizing self-sufficiency, self-determination, and cognitive self-reference is lucidly described by C. Taylor, *Sources of the Self: The Making of the Modern Identity* (Cambridge, MA: Harvard University Press, 1989).

45. According to Antonio Damasio's neurophysiological theory of consciousness, the elementary sense of the self is connected to an emotional background perception of the body. Only on this basis do more developed forms of self-consciousness arise. See Antonio R. Damasio, *Ich fühle, also bin ich. Die Entschlüsselung des Bewusstseins,* 2nd ed. (München: List, 2000), p. 344. For a review of recent developments, see Martin Hartmann, "Die Repsychologisierung des Geistes. Neuere Literatur über Emotionen," *Philosophische Rundschau* 49 (2002): 195-223.

46. For an overview see P. Welsen, "Personale Identität als narrative Identität," *Phänomenologische Forschungen* 6 (2001): 25-40.

configurational dimension, in which significant wholes are configured out of scattered events.[47] Yet lacking in Ricoeur's convincing account of narrative identity is a sense of the narrative's narrator: Who is narrating this narrative of a person's life? Upon closer inspection we find that persons actually negotiate their own narratives, as well as the narratives of those about them, and the wider narratives of their culture. The unity of the public person and the intimate private person is also a narrative unity. This way of expanding Ricoeur's insight sheds light on a very particular type of dependency: at the edges of life the narratives of one's own life are increasingly narrated in and through the narratives of other persons — without personal "control" of this narration. For example, in cases of advanced phases of Alzheimer's disease one's own capacity to narrate is dissolving.[48] To acknowledge the fact that one's own life is narrated by a multitude of voices is to point to the richness of one's identity as well as its deep vulnerability.

Acknowledging the element of the social nature of narrative identity does not imply basing moral personhood on the narration of the community. In light of the crisis of relationality sketched out above, and in light of the fact that people suffer abandonment from their communities as well as isolation and loneliness, human communities cannot be the essential basis of moral personhood. Otherwise, there would be "uncertainty on the moral status of those with whom we have no social contacts (such as for instance some homeless, poor and other socially isolated people)."[49] The plea for a more empirical understanding of the person (in terms of the intension of the concept) is not aimed at basing the attribution of personhood on the social environment (the extension of the concept) — as seems to be the case in some strands of communitarian bioethics.[50]

47. For a lucid critique and critical reconstruction of this concept, pointing out the tension between the complexity of multiple narratives and the still-dominant search for a unified self, see J. Christman, "Narrative Unity as a Condition of Personhood," *Metaphilosophy* 35, no. 5 (2004): 695-713.

48. See J. Perry and D. O'Connor, "Preserving Personhood: (Re)Membering the Spouse with Dementia," *Family Relations* 51, no. 1 (2002): 55-62, esp. 56f.

49. Hellsten, "Towards an Alternative Approach to Personhood in the End of Life Questions," p. 526.

50. See e.g. Mark G. Kuczewski, *Fragmentation and Consensus: Communitarian and Casuist Bioethics* (Washington, DC: Georgetown University Press, 1997), pp. 27-48; M. G. Kuczewski, "Whose Will Is It Anyway? A Discussion of Advance Directives, Personal Identity, and Consensus in Medical Ethics," *Bioethics* 8, no. 1 (1993): 125-37. Even in G. Meilaender, *Body, Soul, and Bioethics* (Notre Dame: University of Notre Dame Press, 1995), pp. 37-59, the relation between the social dimension of narrative and the theological dimension is not always clear. As even

In the end, each person must hand over the narration of one's life to others and to God's transforming "knowledge" of one's life. The story of our personhood is eventually told by others — and in the end it can only be told by means of God's transforming remembrance.[51] Any empirical social narrative of remembrance and commemoration is only (a) responding to, (b) witnessing to, and (c) acting on behalf of the divine attribution of personhood. The community of care is always fallible and contingent in its relations of dependency, and yet it is still called to offer this form of co-humanity.

5.5. Dependency, Power, and the Life of the Spirit

In section 4.3, we saw that the concept of the person can be understood as the unity of a distinction. Furthermore, this understanding can be framed in different, yet specific, ways — for example, in Christian theology it can be understood within the frame of God's dramatic care for the world. Moreover, in 5.1 I suggested that theological anthropology must expand references to the imago Dei with an understanding of Christ as the image of God.

What then are the implications of this reorientation in the field of theological anthropology and, in particular, in the area of human personhood at the edges of life? I would like to suggest that, for the Christian community and for all human beings living the life of the Spirit, the issue of personhood at the edges of life must be seen through the lens of the living "Jesus Christ," or in other words: from the perspective of the incarnation, the life and cross of Jesus, and finally his resurrection from the dead.[52]

---

he summarizes: "Caught as we are within the midst of our own life stories, and unable as we are to grasp anyone else's story as a single whole, we have to admit that only God can see us as the person we are — can catch the self and hold it still" (p. 59).

51. On the issue of God's transformative and creative type of remembering, see B. Janowski, "Schöpferische Erinnerung. Zum 'Gedenken Gottes' in der biblischen Fluterzählung," in *Die Macht der Erinnerung,* ed. Martin Ebner (Neukirchen-Vluyn: Neukirchener Verlag, 2008), pp. 63-89.

52. This orientation resonates with Dietrich Bonhoeffer's insight that, theologically, the world must be seen as disclosed in the light of this Christological movement. Cf. D. Bonhoeffer, *Ethics,* ed. E. Bethge and N. H. Smith (New York: Macmillan, 1965). Based on an interpretation of the Lord's Supper, Michael Welker in a similar vein differentiates "God's sustaining, rescuing, and ennobling Creativity as a basis for a nonreductive anthropology" (M. Welker, "Theological Anthropology Versus Anthropological Reductionism," in *God and Human Dignity,* ed. R. Kendall Soulen and L. Woodhead (Grand Rapids: Eerdmans, 2006), pp. 317-30, 325.

(a) Incarnation

When caring for vulnerable and dependent life, people reflect God's faithfulness to creation, which itself was manifested in the incarnation of the Word of God. In their personal as well as institutional and systemic work for those who are vulnerable, fragile, and in need, in their provision of life-sustaining assistance for their fellow human beings, those involved in care communicate God's own caring attention for creation. Over against never-ending Gnostic temptations, Christians should rather embrace and affirm the goodness, worth, and intrinsic dignity of life, aspects affirmed in the very act of incarnation. Every Christmas Christians commemorate God's willingness and dedication to embrace vulnerable life, to take on life that is endangered not only biologically but also politically, culturally, and socially. The incarnation affirms God's honoring of the edges of life, the positive affirmation of a finite creation.

In late-modern societies a realistic and nonreductionistic account of "creation" encompassing "nature" and "culture" must not only entail person-to-person encounters but all cultural and technological inventions of care and medicine. In the life of the Spirit, the communal aspects of life, the web of life-sustaining interdependencies (personal as well as systemic) are recognized and valued. Care takes place in complex cultural and systemic settings requiring financial and legal frameworks.

(b) Life and Death of Christ

The life and death of Christ lend this view of creation a greater depth of focus. Christians respond to the love of Christ not only in terms of his will, but also in terms of his aversion to life-destroying forces in the natural, moral, social, and cultural worlds. The gospel witnesses to the increasing conflicts surrounding Jesus demonstrate the extent to which Jesus' love implies an opposition to and resistance against that which opposes God's will. Beyond mere co-suffering and cosmic companionship, Christ is the manifestation of God's saving intention and practice. Christians participate in Christ's passion by participating in his forceful resistance against such powers, which we see manifest at least partially in his healing practices.

This increased "depth of focus" also applies to the issue of anthropology: On the one hand, life in the Spirit increases our perception of the endangerment and vulnerability of life in its need for support, community, and care. In this respect, the life of the Spirit encourages people to see the world differently, to recognize responsibilities, and to perceive self-endangerment and self-destruction in nature as the "groaning of creation." In a network of asymmetrical relationships, marked not only by care and responsibility for others but also by being the recipient of care and by being entrusted to others, we see the emergence of an open moral space. Dependency-relations in times of old age, severe illness, and painful disability remind us of a Christ who addressed the ruptures and brokenness of creation. Even though life can flourish in networks of interdependencies, not every dependency is in itself affirmed by Christ.[53] Consequently, Christian care for those at the edges of life is also a fight against that natural evil that would stand against God's good intentions with this creation.[54]

And yet what needs to be emphasized vis-à-vis highly loaded moral markets and discourses — and what is also revealed in the life of Christ — is the converse side of this situation: namely, that that which makes autonomy so desirable and the experience of fragility and dependency so difficult is a distinct feature of asymmetrical relations. Such relations are relations in which the exercise of power can easily be destructive. In this respect, any dimension of vulnerability is potentially dangerous and should not be idealized. Moreover, the often subtle and manipulative use of vulnerability by "victims" also exemplifies the deep complexity of such power-relations. In this respect Christians create and inhabit a moral space knowing that moral codes can be misused by both the weak and the strong, by both the poor and the rich, and even with the best intentions. They know that even vulnerability can become a weapon and well-intended care can be counterproductive — yet they still risk responding to the manifest need for care evident in the most vulnerable of people.[55] In the life of the Spirit they risk the deformation of moral spaces and the misuse of moral claims in order to communicate God's attention and care.

53. Interestingly, in none of the Synoptic Gospels did Jesus affirm the status of an ill or sick person as something that should be accepted or that would confer some special status.

54. Admittedly, it is very difficult to draw a line between processes and conditions representing human finitude and processes and conditions in which natural evil is manifested. See e.g. the discussion in W. B. Drees, ed., *Is Nature Ever Evil? Religion, Science, and Value* (London/New York: Routledge, 2003). Glenn Weaver suggests that we might focus on those aspects that threaten the relationship with God: "disease processes that threaten our experiences of self-identity in relationship with God may be understood as manifestations of natural evil" (Weaver, "Embodied Spirituality: Experiences of Identity and Spiritual Suffering among Persons with Alzheimer's Dementia," p. 99).

55. Against moral discourses in which "good victims" and "evil victimizers" are neatly separated persons, the Gospels help us to identify situations of self-destruction as well as self-victimization.

(c) The Life of the Spirit as a Life in the Presence of the Risen Christ

The Christian life is not only shaped by the cross, but by the reality of the resurrection. Christians know about God's repudiation of the powers of victimization at work in the cross. At the same time they live by God's affirmation of the giving of life, love, and solidarity manifest in the life and death of Jesus. "The powers of love, the powers of forgiveness, the powers of healing, the powers of special attention to children, to the weak, to the rejected, to the sick, and to the suffering are communicated by the presence of the risen Christ. Important struggles with the so-called 'principalities and powers' — for example, with political and religious powers in the search for justice and in the search for truth — also take shape in the presence of the risen Christ. The person and life of Jesus Christ thus make available a multiplicity of powers for transformation and renewal."[56] In actions for the excluded and marginalized, in asymmetrical relations of care, support, and assistance for a life in dignity, the entire life of Jesus becomes alive again. In the life of the Spirit, in the actualization of Christ's life, asymmetrical relations (in which vulnerable and fragile life is perceived and taken care of, and in which personhood is facilitated, remembered, and bestowed) are not used for the enhancement of one's own life or for the rise of strong life over weak life.[57] Those who give can risk giving in a nonreciprocal manner, who can risk giving life to the weak and the fragile, can allow others to take care of them. In this shared and communal life of the Spirit, power and trust are renegotiated in ways that resemble the life of Christ. Christians are not only stewards of the creation; in their many forms of witnessing, "the powers of love, justice, mercy, and truth permeate the creation mediated through the body of Christ and through the members of this body, which are physically embodied human persons."[58] Through the Spirit the reality of the resurrection begins to emanate into the life of the dependent as well as into the life of carers.

56. M. Welker, "Who Is Jesus Christ for Us Today?" *Harvard Theological Review* 95, no. 2 (2002): 129-46, 144.

57. See Weaver, "Embodied Spirituality," p. 94. "These human experiences of upholding one another's personhood can encourage faith in the Christian confession that our finite identities as persons will finally be upheld by a merciful, loving God" (p. 99).

58. M. Welker, "The Addressee of Divine Sustenance, Rescue, and Elevation: Toward a Nonreductive Understanding of Human Personhood," in *From Cells to Souls, and Beyond: Changing Portraits of Human Nature,* ed. M. A. Jeeves (Grand Rapids: Eerdmans, 2004), p. 231.

5.6. Person and Eschatology

Whatever emergent processes are stimulated by the reality of the resurrection, they will be met by God's final consummation of a new creation. In the light of the resurrection the Christian hope envisages a completion that brings every human life to its fulfillment. Any participation in the resurrection through the "spirit that dwells in" the life of Christians (Rom. 8:11), which draws them into the realized life of Christ, will remain only a partial anticipation and finally only a fragment waiting to be taken up into God's coming, final reign.

The divine attribution of personhood is embedded in the "history" of the triune God. To link being a person merely to one's status as a created creature is insufficient, yet always a temptation to theological anthropologies based on mere theism. Instead, as human beings and persons we participate in the dynamic interaction of the triune God with God's own world.[59]

On the basis of this observation we can hope that decay, frailty, and death are no longer the last reality that human beings will face; instead we can look toward God's transforming future. For this reason, a theological recognition of dependency does not lead to a religious glorification of weakness and passivity, even though life may flourish in such relations. God's intentions as well as God's care (manifest in the resurrection through the power of the Spirit [Rom. 1:4]) do not come to an end with death. This care for all formations and deformations of human life creatively embraces this finite life. It is this dimension of hope that opens up the space for lament when, at the edges of life, life itself becomes an unbearable burden. In the confrontation with the painful edges of life, lament and hope allow us to endorse a realism that avoids both stoic forms of resignation and cynical affirmations of the strong life, either in personal behavior or in systemic formations. This hope confirms the insight that arose from the Greek context, namely that when the person is seen in terms of a mask, then being a person always entails an open horizon of imagined possibilities.[60]

---

59. For a similar inclusion of eschatology and consummation into anthropological consideration, see Reinders, who rightly refers back to Karl Barth's insights regarding the covenant between God and humanity as the inner ground of creation.

60. T. Fuchs, "Der Begriff der Person in der Psychiatrie," in *Nervenarzt* 73 (2002): 239-46, 241.

Contributors

MARIA ANTONACCIO, Dr. phil., is professor of Religious Ethics at Bucknell University, Lewisburg, PA.

WARREN S. BROWN, Dr. phil., is professor of Psychology at the Fuller Graduate School of Psychology in Pasadena, CA, where he is Director of the Lee Travis Research Institute.

PHILIP CLAYTON, Dr. phil., is professor of Philosophy of Religion and Theology at Claremont Graduate University. He is dean and interim Vice-President for Academic Affairs.

VOLKER HENNING DRECOLL, Dr. theol., is professor of Patristics in the department of Church History at Tübingen University.

MARKUS HÖFNER, Dr. theol., is research and teaching assistant in the department of Systematic Theology at Bochum University.

ORIGEN V. JATHANNA, Dr. theol., is professor of Theology at United Theological College, Bangalore.

MALCOLM JEEVES, Dr. phil., is professor emeritus of Psychology at St. Andrews University. He is a neuropsychologist and a past president of the Royal Society of Edinburgh.

ISOLDE KARLE, Dr. theol., is professor of Practical Theology and dean of the Faculty for Theology at Bochum University.

EIICHI KATAYANAGI, Dr. phil., is professor emeritus of Anthropology in the Faculty of Letters at Kyoto University.

ANDREAS KEMMERLING, Dr. phil., is professor of Philosophy in the Institute of Philosophy at Heidelberg University.

STEPHAN KIRSTE, Dr. phil., is professor of Law in the Institute of Law at Heidelberg University.

BERND OBERDORFER, Dr. theol., is professor and chair of Systematic Theology in the department of Philosophy and Sociology at Augsburg University.

JOHN CHARLTON POLKINGHORNE, Dr. phil., Dr. rer. nat., Drs. h.c. mult., KBE, FRS, is professor emeritus of Theoretical Physics at Cambridge University.

JEFFREY P. SCHLOSS, Dr. rer. nat., is professor of Biology at Westmont College in Santa Barbara, CA and Director of Biological Programs for the Christian Environmental Association.

ANDREAS SCHÜLE, Dr. theol., is Aubrey Lee Brooks Professor of Biblical Theology at Union-PSCE, Richmond, VA.

WILLIAM SCHWEIKER, Dr. phil., is professor of Theological Ethics and director of the Martin Marty Center in the Divinity School at Chicago University.

GERD THEISSEN, Dr. theol., Dr. h.c. mult., is professor emeritus of New Testament at Heidelberg University.

GÜNTER THOMAS, Dr. theol, Dr. rer. soc., is professor of Systematic Theology at Bochum University.

FRANK VOGELSANG, Dr. theol., is director of the Ev. Akademie im Rheinland.

MICHAEL WELKER, Dr. theol, Dr. phil., Dr. h.c., is professor and chair of Systematic Theology and executive director of the Research Center for International and Interdisciplinary Theology (FIIT) at Heidelberg University.